# Hinduism and Divorce

**From Dharamaśāstras to Statutory Law**

# Hinduism and Divorce

## From Dharmaśāstras to Statutory Law

### — A Critical Study —

**Hari Dev Kohli**

**Volume 1**

**Śāstric Law for Divorce and Global Perspective**

**Decent Books**

New Delhi

*Published and printed by:*
**Decent Books**
D-36/A-1, Mohan Garden
Najafgarh Road
New Delhi - 110 059

*Distributed by:*
**D.K. Printworld (P) Ltd.**
*Regd. office* : '*Sri Kunj*', F-52, Bali Nagar
New Delhi - 110 015
*Phones* : (011) 545-3975, 546-6019; *Fax* : (011) 546-5926
*E-mail*: dkprint@4mis.com

**ISBN**
**81-86921-09-5 ( set )**
**81-86921-10-9 (Vol. 1)**
**81-86921-11-7 (Vol. 2)**

First Published in India in 2000

# Preface

When I was a student of law, I was astonished to find that statutory Hindu Law was being taught without much reference to the Śāstric law, I found a similar disregard to the Śāstric Law in the legal profession where total emphasis was on the statutory law and the Śāstric Law was as if non-existed.

However, I got a penetrating feeling that for a study of Modern Hindu Law and its proper understanding, a thorough knowledge of Śāstric Law is essential because the modern law has merely amended and codified the Hindu Law which was hitherto embodied in the Sanskrit textbooks and not repealed it. This is in spite of a provision in the statutory Hindu Law 'overriding effect of Act', by which any text, rule or interpretation of Hindu Law or any custom or usage as part of that law shall cease to have effect with respect to any matter for which provision is made in this Act and any provision inconsistent with the provision contained in this Act shall cease to have effect.

As I actively involved myself as a social worker in the field of free legal counselling to settle matrimonial disputes outside the Court, I was greatly amazed to find that Śāstric Law played a large role in settling the matrimonial disputes amicably as Hindus still have awe and respect for Śāstric Law.

The most common but complex matrimonial dispute noticed was regarding the concept of equality which created disharmony in the matrimonial home leading to breaking-up of marriage. There I found that I could settle the disputes using more of Śāstic Law than statutory law and thus I thought of taking up the topic of 'divorce' for my thesis for the degree of Doctor of Philosophy in Law with a clear mind that I would endeavour to explain Hindu Law from a Hindu point of view.

I made an earnest attempt to have a harmonious reading of the Śāstric Law and modern Hindu Law on divorce wherein I laid stress on the status of Hindu woman as a daughter, wife and mother, the sanctity of Hindu marriage and customary and statutory divorce. To have a broader view I incorporated the evolution of divorce in other countries as well.

In this book, I have given the original Sanskrit texts wherever required so that the modern law is better understood. Attempt is made to give the English translation as far as possible so that there may not be any inconvenience for the reader who is not well-versed in Sanskrit.

To illustrate the point further, I have cited leading cases wherever needed. I have also made objective comments which are more soul-searching with a view to explaining the Hindu perspective more vividly.

I have kept in view the law students, the advocates, the legislature and the judiciary and conveyed to them the concern of the society. My role is very modest and I hope that this research work shall be well received by all.

6-20-7/11 **Hari Dev Kohli**
East Point Colony
VISAKHAPATNAM 530 017
Andhra Pradesh

# Contents

## Volume 1
## Śāstric Law for Divorce and Global Perspective



## Volume 2
## Statutory Divorce Under Hindu Law

**Alas ! O' Woman**
**I hear your cries**
**milk in your breast**
**but tears in eyes.**

# Acknowledgements

It is my firm conviction that, but for the parental guidance, given by respected Prof. **R. Jagan Mohan Rao**, this research would have been like a rudderless ship sailing asunder in a vast sea of uncertainty. He trimmed the shapeless pieces of material into elegance for which I am greatly indebted to him.

I am grateful to Prof. M.V.A. Naidu, Principal Dr. B.R. Ambedkar College of Law, Visakhapatnam, who provided me every facility needed for the completion of my thesis.

My respectful thanks to Profs. **A. Lakshmi Nath**, **R. Venkata Rao**, & **C. Rama Rao**, who willingly, without any inhibition, gave me advice whenever sought for and their contribution in this venture is praiseworthy.

I am thankful to all the other honourable members of teaching staff of Dr. B.R. Ambedkar College of Law who spontaneously and profusely gave me their full support in the accomplishment of my this research.

I pay my respects to Mr. A.T. Naidu and his daughter Rajani, Advocates who gave useful piece of advice at every point of time when needed.

Last, but not the least, I am really grateful to the librarian Sri **Sanyasi Rao**, who took pains to provide me with material without my searching the racks and was ever ready to help me.

**Hari Dev Kohli**

# To Remember

*No nation founded upon injustice can stand. From the sand enshrouded Egypt, from the marble wilderness of Athens and from every fallen crumbling stone of the once mighty Rome, comes a wail as it were the cry that no nation founded upon injustice can permanently stand.*

**— Robert G. Ingersoll**

# Abbreviations

| | |
|---|---|
| AC | Appeal Cases |
| AIR | All India Reporter |
| *AitBrā* | *Aitareya-Brāhmaṇa* |
| All | Allahabad |
| ALJ | Allahabad Law Journal |
| AllER | All England Reporter |
| ALT | Andhra Law Times |
| AP | Andhra Pradesh |
| *ĀpasDS* | *Āpastamba Dharma-sūtra* |
| Assm | Assam |
| *AV* | *Atharvaveda* |
| *ĀśvaGS* | *Āśvalāyana Gṛhya-sūtra* |
| *BaudhDS* | *Baudhāyana Dharma-sūtra* |
| BHCR | Bombay High Court Reports |
| Bom | Bombay |
| BLR | Bombay Law Reporter |
| Bṛh | Bṛhaspati |
| CA | Court of Appeal |
| Cal | Calcutta |
| CLR | Calcutta Law Reporter |
| CrLJ | Criminal Law Journal |

| | |
|---|---|
| CrLT | Criminal Law Times |
| Cut | Cuttack |
| CWN | Calcutta Weekly News |
| Del | Delhi |
| DMC | Divorce & Marriage Cases |
| EP | East Punjab |
| Fam | Family |
| FB | Full Bench |
| FC | Federal Court |
| FLC | Family Law Cases |
| Gau | Gauhati |
| *GauDS* | *Gautama Dharma-sūtra* |
| Guj | Gujarat |
| HLR | Hindu Law Reporter |
| HP | Himachal Pradesh |
| IA | English Law Reports, Indian Appeals |
| ICLQ | Islamic and Comparative Law Quarterly |
| ILR | Indian Law Reporter |
| JFamL | Journal of Family Law |
| JILI | Journal of the Indian Law Institute |
| J&K | Jammu & Kashmir |
| *KauṭArth* | *Kauṭilya Arthaśāstra* |
| Ker | Kerala |
| KLT | Kerala Law Times |
| Kant | Karnataka |
| Lah | Lahore |
| LQR | Law Quarterly Review |

| | |
|---|---|
| M | Madras Series of Indian Law Reports |
| Mad | Madras |
| Mani | Manipur |
| *Manu* | *Manu-smṛti* |
| MarrLJ | Marriage Law Journal |
| MatLR | Matrimonial Law Reporter |
| MB | Madhya Bharat |
| MIA | Moore's Indian Appeals |
| *Mit* | *Mitākṣarā* |
| MLJ | Madras Law Journal |
| MP | Madhya Pradesh |
| Mys | Mysore |
| Nag | Nagpur |
| *Nār* | *Nārada-smṛti* |
| Ori | Orissa |
| P | English Law Reports, Probate Division |
| *ParāGS* | *Parāśara Gṛhya-sūtra* |
| *ParāS* | *Parāśara Saṁhitā* |
| Pat | Patna |
| PC | Privy Council |
| P&D | English Law Reports, Probate and Divorce Division |
| Pesh | Peshawar |
| P&H | Punjab & Haryana |
| PR | Punjab Record |
| *ṚV* | *Ṛgveda* |
| Raj | Rajasthan |
| Ran | Rangoon |

| | |
|---|---|
| *ŚatBrā* | *Śatapatha Brāhmaṇa* |
| Sau | Saurashtra |
| *SBE* | *Sacred Books of the East* |
| SC | Supreme Court |
| SCC | Supreme Court Cases |
| SCJ | Supreme Court Journal |
| SCLR | Supreme Court Law Reporter |
| *TaiS* | *Taittirīya Saṁhitā* |
| Trav & Co | Travancore & Cochin |
| TLL | Tagore Law Lectures of Calcutta University |
| TLR | Tulane Law Review |
| *VaikhāDS* | *Vaikhānasa Dharma-sūtra* |
| *Vas* | *Vasiṣṭha-smṛti* |
| *Vis* | *Viṣṇu-Smṛti* |
| *Vyāsa* | *Vedavyāsa-smṛti* |
| WLR | Weekly Law Reporter |
| WN | Weekly News |
| WR | Weekly Reporter |
| *Yāj* | *Yājñavalkya-smṛti* |
| *YV* | *Yajurveda* |

# Transliteration Chart

| a | ā | i | ī | u | ū | e | ai | o | au |
|---|---|---|---|---|---|---|---|---|---|
| अ | आ | इ | ई | उ | ऊ | ए | ऐ | ओ | औ |

| ṁ | ḥ | ṛ |
|---|---|---|
| अं | अः | ऋ |

| k | kh | g | gh | ṅ |
|---|---|---|---|---|
| क् | ख् | ग् | घ् | ङ् |
| c | ch | j | jh | ñ |
| च् | छ् | ज् | झ् | ञ् |
| ṭ | ṭh | ḍ | ḍh | ṇ |
| ट् | ठ् | ड् | ढ् | ण् |
| t | th | d | dh | n |
| त् | थ् | द् | ध् | न् |
| p | ph | b | bh | m |
| प् | फ् | ब् | भ् | म् |

| y | r | l | v |
|---|---|---|---|
| य् | र् | ल् | व् |
| ś | ṣ | s | h |
| श् | ष् | स् | ह् |

| kṣ | tr | jñ |
|---|---|---|
| क्ष् | त्र् | ज्ञ् |

# Introduction

SOME say that man is a social animal but Hinduism regards man as divine. In the *Bhagvad Gītā*, in Chapter Daivāsura Sampad Vibhāga tells us the divine qualities in us and how an assiduous cultivation of those qualities leads us to a happy life here and hereafter and these qualities and their cultivation has been differently ordained in the Vedas that an Aryan is born burdened with three debts. "He owes the study of the Veda to the *ṛṣis*. Sacrifices to the Gods and a Son to the Manes"[1] and these three debts are highlighted by *Manu*[2] when he says:

> When he has paid the three debts, let him apply his mind to (the attainment of) final liberation, he who seeks it without having paid (his debts) sinks downward.
>
> Having studied the Vedas in accordance with the rule, having begot sons according to the sacred law and having offered sacrifices according to his ability, he may direct his mind to (the attainment of) final liberation.

Thus, to attain these laudable aims the concept of four *āśrama*s based on the supposition of the span of life to be hundred years, was introduced.

The *āśrama*s or the stages of life are concerned with a person's individual aspect and these four stages are:

(i) *brahmacarya* or the period of learning,

(ii) *gṛhsthāśrama* or the period of work for the world as a householder,

---

1. Mayne's *Hindu Law & Usage*, 13th edn., p. 94.
2. G. Bühler, *The Laws of Manu*, VI.35, 36, See *Taittirīya Saṁhitā*, VI.3, 10, 5 cited in *Vas*, XI.48.

(iii) *vānaprasthāśrama* or the period of retreat for the loosening of the social bonds, and

(iv) *saṁnyāsa* or the period of renunciation and expectant awaiting of *mokṣa*.

*Brahmacaryāśrama* is the period of learning. Basically it is the period of development of all round knowledge to develop capability to enter the *gr̥hasthāśrama*. (A student) who has studied the three Vedas, or two, or even one only, without breaking the (rules of) studentship, shall enter the order of householder.[3]

So family is the starting unit of Vedic sociology. It forms a link between the individual and the society and this *āśrama* is full of duties as it is the foundation of society. So without the married householder, continuity of society is unsustainable. The house holder's life begins with marriage. From the very commencement of the R̥gvedic age, marriage was a well established institution and the Aryan ideal of marriage was very high, wherein the spouses were tied to each other through *kāma*, *artha* and *dharma*. Man is not a tyrant nor woman a slave but both are servants of a highter ideal to which their individual inclinations are to be subordinated. Sensual love is sublimated into self-forgetful devotion. So *kāma* is the passionate desire to have an *aurasa* son because by marrying and begetting sons, he continues the line of the ancestors and is deemed to have discharged the debt which he owes to the manes. The desire for procreation finds its reflection in *Manu-smr̥ti* and *Yājñavalkya-smr̥ti* thus:

> Through a son he conquers the worlds, through a son's son he obtains immortality, but through his son's grandson he gains the world of Sun. — *Manu*, IX.137

> Because a son delivers his father from the hell called *pūta*, he was therefore called *putra* (a deliverer from *pūṭa*) by the self-existent (*svayambhu*) himself. — *Manu*, IX.138

So also Yājñavalkya says:

> Because continuity of the family in this world and the

3. G. Bühler, *Laws of Manu*, III.2.

> attainment of heaven in the next are through sons, son's sons and son's grandsons, therefore, women should be loved and protected. — *Yāj*, I.78

So the marriage has been idealised by the Hindus and considered as a sacramental union and it continued to be so in the entire Hindu period. According to *Ṛgveda*, the wife has been given a very exalted position.

> Be thou the mother of heroic children, devoted to the gods, be thou queen in the father-in-law's household. May all Gods unite the hearts of us two into one. — *ṚV*, X.85

Manu also highlighted the status of wife when he said that —

> The husband receives his wife from the Gods (he does not wed her) according to his own will; doing what is agreeable to the Gods, he must always support her (while she is) faithful. — *Manu*, IX.95

> Where women are honoured, there the gods are pleased. — *Manu*, III.56

But simultaneously, with the idealised picture of wife, the husband is "the lord and master of his wife", he must be adored and obeyed even if devoid of all virtues. Manu says:

> Though destitute of virute or seeking pleasure (elsewhere), or devoid of good qualities, (yet) a husband must be constantly worshipped as a god by a faithful wife. — *Manu*, V.154

Thus, Hindus conceived of marriage as a sacramental union, as a holy union and wife as the source of *dharma*, *kāma* and *artha* and the marriage as a union is primarily meant for the performance of religious and spiritual duties. It also connotes that it is a permanent union, i.e., it is a tie once tied cannot be untied. It also strongly indicates that it is an eternal union. This is why Manu says:

> A virtuous wife who after the death of her husband constantly remains chaste, reaches heaven, though she have no son just like those chaste men. — *Manu*, V.160

Inspite of such ideal picture depicted, we find some scattered passages in Smṛtis here and there by way of exception, do indicate fissures in marriage. Nārada and Parāśara mention five cases in which a woman can abandon her husband and can take another:

> (i) when the husband is missing, (ii) when he is impotent, (iii) when he has become an ascetic, (iv) when he is dead, and (v) when he is an out-caste.
>
> — *Nārada*, XII.18; *Parāśara*, X.26-35

Manu[4] has also spoken about men abandoning the wife in certain situations like:

> She who drinks spirituous liquor, is of bad conduct, diseased, michievous or wasteful, may at any time be superseded (by another wife). — *Manu*, IX.80

> A barren wife may be superseded in the eighth year, she whose children (all) die in the tenth, she who bears only daughters in the eleventh, but she who is quarrelsome without delay. — *Ibid.*, IX.81

So Hindu marriage is sacrament but there was an element of abandonment in exceptional cases but it was never considered as a contract except a reference in *Vyavasthā Candrikā*[5] wherein it is said that the marriage also partook in the nature of a contract. The absence of consent, the person to be married being minor or even of unsound mind, did not invalidate the marriage if it is duly solemnised.

But with the passing of Hindu Marriage Act, 1955, in particular, sections 5, 11, 12 and 13 raised a pertinent question as to whether Hindu marriage became a contract or still remained a sacrament. The tendency appears to be that the opinion is veering round the fact that the element of contract has crept in the marriage which was hitherto a purely sacramental in character. By the introduction of the concept that Hindu marriage is a civil contract then logically the outcome is also the dissolution of the union. So the marriage is

4. See also *BaudhS*, II.4, 6; *Yāj*, I.73.
5. *Vyavasthā Candrikā*, vol.II, p. 432.

a dissoluble union. So, it being a social institution, such concept is bound to evaporate with the incorporation of various provisions in the Hindu Marriage Act, 1955. Various questions of pertinent significance have agitated the mind. Whether there was any necessity to bring unheard of changes in the Hindu Law? Whether divorce was the need of the time to save the institution of marriage or it amounted to disintegrate Hindu joint family and in turn the society? Whether all such changes are due to the thinking that these are the steps to save the woman from inequality and cruelty and to bring in gender justice? and finally whether social problem can be solved by the enactment of law though the society is not prepared for it? So many such attendant questions have arisen, which need adequate answer and also whether such legal provisions have saved the institution of marriage and saved the weaker section from the injustice and thus the crucial question stares us glaringly on the face that whether it is gender equality which is the need or the gender harmony that is required.

## Objects of the study

When any transformation is carried through the legislative change, it gets reflected not only in the social institutions but also in the judicial system and process and in the name of amendment and codification of Hindu Law, a change in Matrimonial Law, which was hitherto conclusively and exclusively a personal law, with some changes here and there, brought out by the Britishers due to peculiar judicial pronouncements, made marriage dissoluble and stability of marriage came under severe attack. Later, after Independence, Indian socio-legal reformers borrowed Western concept of marriage and family and successfully destroyed Dhārmic Law. (See for details Derrett's *Death of a Marriage Law.*)

Marriage is a very significant and vital social institution in any society but for Hindus it is also a religious institution. Any legal attack on this institution under the garb of liberalism and secularisation and in the disguise of a plea that the women are the victims of the cruelty at the hands of the male chauvinism; is bound to be seen with distasteful touch, particularly when such law is bound to shatter the institution on which the society is itself standing and its decay is bound to bring decay in the society. The purpose of this study is to trace the reasons for bringing in the provision of divorce in the Hindu Law which was hitherto unknown to Hindu Law except customary divorce and whether the reasons given are sufficient enough to warrant the incorporation of the provision of divorce in Hindu Law. Whether it is to aim to aid the society in its changing outlook to keep pace, harmoniously, and as such whether it was needed or it was brought in, due to contemplation that since Matrimonial Law all over the world is undergoing change so there must also be a change in Hindu Matrimonial Law, immaterial whether it suits or not. Whether it is beneficial or suicidal.

After the departure of the Britishers, being influenced by the Western culture, our political reformers, ignorant of the social ethos of Hindu society, started imitating the loud cry of the Western jurists that women are a far inferior commodity as compared to men and they should be elevated and this got boost by the agitations of liberation of women movement and demand of rights became the clarion call and law took notice of it and brought in many enactments to remedy the instances of inequality and also measures to save women from the perpetration of cruelty on them. This is understandable. But to bring in law as a measure of relief, but in reality a measure of infliction of cruelty in another form, could not be understood. In order to make the institution of marriage to survive and its sacramental character remains intact, something like positive legal measures should have been taken but instead law resorted to negative approach. Various provisions in the Constitution were brought like Articles 14, 15, 15(3), 16(1), 16(2), under Fundamental Rights and Articles 39(*a*), 39(*d*), 39(*e*) and Article 42 under Directive Principles of State Policy and Article 51A(*e*) under Fundamental Duties, which are praiseworthy. Various legislative enactments like Dowry Prohibition Act, 1961, The Immoral Traffic (Prohibition) Act, 1986, Indecent Representation of Women (Prohibition) Act, 1986, The Commission of Sati (Prohibition) Act, 1987 and many social legislations were brought in which were in tune with the requirements so that the womanhood and motherhood is protected from all types of onslaughts. But legislation to prick the Matrimonial Law prevalent from time immemorial is casting doubts on its usefulness. So the whole gamut of Matrimonial Law touching marriage and consequently divorce flowing out of it became the subject-matter to analyse the present concept in relation to time tested stabilised notion and the corrective step, which, in fact, is needed so that the institution of marriage is saved and stabilised.

## Recent developments

If we look into the distant past, we find that there was no divorce. Even in England it appeared in 1857 through the Matrimonial Causes Act, 1857, ground being matrimonial misconduct. Later on, various other grounds were added, matrimonial misconduct and other grounds of *fait-accompli* or grounds of frustration. Then the seeds of irretrievable breakdown of marriage and divorce by mutual consent, were sown and in India Hindus faced this catastrophe in the year 1955 in the shape of Hindu Marriage Act and further changes in 1976 and still the matter is in the evolutionary stage and all efforts are being made to pay concerted attention not on the stability of marriage but on the development of the concept of divorce in Hindu Law which is needed to be stopped.

## Objective of research

The objective is to identify the problem and provide the solution. The problem is clearly manifest that divorce in Hindu Law is an evil. It is not in consonance with the social ethos. It has caused more harm than serving any useful purpose. It is a breaking of marriage creating deserted homes, neglected wives, and embattled innnocent children left to their own fate. How to meet this evil to eradicate it and if not possible, how to shackle it in helplessness condition so that the likely affected spouses could get sigh of relief and feel pleasure in their harmonious home.

## Hypothesis of the study

The prerequisite of research has always some problem which is baffling or some question which is agitating in our minds and the purpose of research is to find an answer to such problem through investigative process. The problem that being faced is the status of women in the changing social scenario and consequently the nature of marriage as a stabilised social and religious institution which is under shattering blows from those who are to preserve its sanctity.

So five main questions have arisen for consideration.

1. To what extent monogamy has accelerated the incorporation of divorce as a statutory provision?
2. Whether secularisation of marriage is in tune with the social scenario and how far it contributed to divorce?
3. How far the Western culture is responsible for social upheaval in Hindu society?
4. Whether divorce is the solution to solve the social evils created due to showing disregard to women?
5. Whether Law of Divorce needs a fresh look in view of its disastrous results and what look it should be?

## Research methodology

This research is not based on empirical approach but wherever required statistics have been provided. It is founded on the study of Śāstric Law leading to the codification of that law by bringing in confusion creating nerve centres. Thus, the methodology adopted for this research work is doctrinaire; analysing various views on the subjects and suggesting a remedial solution.

## Material surveyed

The research material has been collected both from the original and secondary sources. Special emphasis has been laid on the juridical literature of ancient texts like Vedas, Saṁhitās, Upaniṣadas, Dharma-sūtras and Smṛtis, coupled with it the juridical literary works like Mayne's *Hindu Law and Usage*, Mulla's *Hindu Law*, various books written on Hindu Law by Dr. Paras Diwan, and other erudite works of writers and scholars such as G.D. Banerjee (1896), P.V. Kane (1941), M.A. Indira (1955), A.S. Altekar (1956), Nilakshi Sen Gupta (1965), K.M. Kapadia (1966), Rajkumari Agrawal (1974), Rajbali Pandey (1976), Usha M. Apte (1977), C.K. Chatterjee (1978), *India of Dharam-sūtras* by Dr. Ved Mitra (1965). *Women in the Sacred Laws* (1959) by Shakuntla Rao

Sastri, many foreign scholars especially numerous works of JDM Derret pertaining to Hindu Law, in particular *The Death of a Marriage Law* (1978), coupled with it various articles written by indomitable intellectuals, native and foreign, on Hindu Law and divorce and divorce in global perspective, with much stress on Hindus Marriage Act, 1955.

## Scheme of chapterisation

This thesis is divided into 6 chapters. Chapter 1 deals with the status of women under Śāstric Law. She was given an exalted position both in family and the society and explanation that woman was considered a slave or inferior to man is a mere fiction or an imagination to degrade the womanhood and motherhood of India as Śāstric Law manifests and any constraints imposed upon a woman, were out of necessity of the time to safeguard and protect her from any undesirable onslaughts and to preserve the dignity of the family.

Chapter 2 deals with Hindu Marriage, its concept and nature that Hindu marriage was a sacrament and is a sacrament in practice even after the enactment of Hindu Marriage Act, 1955. Even in other religions, marriage is considered as a sacred institution though efforts are being made to bring in an element of contract and thus stress on its dissolubility has increased.

Chapter 3 deals with divorce, its concept and evolution in general and especially divorce and Śāstric Law. It was unknown to Hindu Law though there was customary divorce and later on it was recognised statutorily under Hindu Marriage Act, 1955 which is an act of imitation.

Chapter 4 deals with divorce, a global perspective wherein the evolution of divorce in Europe, in particular under English Law, Muslim Law, Judaism and other countries directly or indirectly but culturally connected with England to have a glance and how it was copied and is being copied in Hinduism.

Chapter 5 deals with statutory divorce in Hindu Law in detail as to grounds for divorce, its statutory evolution, keeping in view the developments of global perspective.

Chapter 6 deals with the critical analysis and the remedial dispositions, recommending abolition of divorce as it is a disaster for the Hindu nation and is a great evil and if at all it is necessary evil, then it must be like a tightly bridled horse, always under control.

*Be thou mother of heroic children, devoted to the gods, be thou queen in the father-in-law's household. May all gods unite the hearts of us two into one.* — ***Ṛ*****V, IX.85**

*Where women are honoured, there the gods are pleased, but where they are not honoured, no sacred rite yields rewards.* — ***Manu*****, III.56**

# 1

# Status of Women

FOUR enactments on Hindu Law were brought on the statute book with an object to codify and amend Hindu Law. Though state is constitutionally prohibited to intervene into the religious affairs as state has no mandate to stand between man and god but believing in the legal truthfulness of the escape route, when and where it suits, the state took shelter under some specific provisions, firstly under Article 15(3) and Article 39(*a*) of the Constitution of India and later on under Article 51A(*e*) of the Constitution of India and brought these enactments manifesting a desire to save the women from the indignities perpetrated on them on the touchstone of equality. But the true state of affairs seems to be otherwise. The so-called liberals, the enlightened few and pseudo-secularists basically influenced by the Macaulay-Maine doctrine of creating a white collar community overshadowed by the Western civilisation, wherein individuality and not family a basic unit of the society, tread the path strewn with confused notions. Sir Henry Maine studied empirically the historical background of legal systems and social behaviour in regard to three main societies of the world — The Anglo-Saxon, Indian and Germo-Roman. He pronounced a fundamental thesis that every society passes into two stages — the static and progressive. According to him the movement of progressive society has hitherto been a movement from status to contract. In the first stage of development in progressive society, the rights and obligations were determined on the basis of status of an individual in the society.[1]

---

1. Referred in Dr. Y.K. Tiwari's *Status of Hindu Women and Efficacy of Protective Legislation*, p. 21.

Without being swayed by any coloured vision, we should look to all shades of opinion throwing light on the status of women in general and in particular the status of women under Hindu System of Law and by way of comparison women in Islam and Christianity.

Dr. Shamsuddin Shams[2] states like this —

> Women like men, are both born and made still in almost all societies of the world, we find scathing attack against them.

The wise men of China have offered free advice for the benefit of husbands in these words:

> Listen to the counsel of your wife but act against it.

The Oldmen of Russia have said:

> There is only one soul among ten women.

The Spaniards say:

> We shall save ourselves from wicked women, and should never be captivated by any that have good looks.

The Italians go a step further and pronounce:

> As a horse, whether good or bad requires spurs, a woman whether good or bad requires thrashing.

In Japan the people said:

> In olden times, women were not allowed to pray or take part in religious exercises.

Even in Jewish society then, where Prophet Moses spoke of excellence in men-women relation, women were treated as the property of men and women were allowed no rights worth the name. Sermons of the Prophet Moses were forgotton. It is said that men in women saw a 'Scorpion' ever ready to sting.[3] According to the Mosaic Law, to betroth a wife to oneself meant simply to acquire

---

2. Dr. Shamsuddin Shams in his preface to the book *Women, Law and Social Change*, p. ix.
3. Dr. Tahir Mahmood, *Womanhood in Islam*.

possession of her by payment of the purchase money. The girl's consent was unnecessary. The woman being man's property, his right to divorce her, followed as a matter of course. Divorce was a privilege of the husband only.[4] But, however, the commands of Moses and finally by the Rabbinical Ordinance, the unbridled right of the husband to divorce his wife was put under legal shackles.[5]

The Christian society also then did not lag behind. For them Eve was the initiator of man's downfall. The women were kept under subjudication, in a state of complete servitude. The sermons of Jesus of Love and Compassion did not move the hearts of men to show respect to women folk.[6] Christianity seems to have been influenced by the Mosaic Law. Woman was described by the early church fathers (like St. Benard, St. Anthony, St. Banaventure, St. Cyprian, St. Jerome and St. Demaocene) as the 'gateway to hell', 'the origin of devil', 'the mother of all evils', 'a scorpion ever ready to sting', 'lance of the demon', 'daughters of falsehood', 'sentiment of hell', and 'the enemy of peace'. They enjoined her to live in continual penance on account of the curses she has brought to the world.[7] The worst remarks on women is that of Tertullian.[8] He says:

> Do you know that you are each an eve? The sentence of God on this sex of your lives in this age. You are the devil's gateway. You are the unsealer of the (forbidden) tree; you are the first deserter of the Divine Law; you are she who persuades him whom the devil was not valiant enough to attach. You destroyed so easily God's image, man.

Under the Roman Law wife was:

> A babe, a minor, a ward, a person incapable of doing or acting anything according to her own individual taste, a

---

4. Dr. Shamsuddin Shams, *Socio-Legal Rights and Privileges of Women in Islam*, p. 6. See also III *Encyclopaedia Biblica*, 2924-47 (1902).
5. George Horowitz, *The Spirit of Jewish Law*.
6. Dr. Tahir Mahmood, *Womanhood in Islam*.
7. See A.R.I. Doi, *Women in Sharia*, Zaria, 1983.
8. David and Verma Mace, quoting Tertullian: *Decultic Feminarium in Marriage — East and West*, p. 69.

person continually under the tutelage and guardianship of her husband.[9]

It is further said that in Roman Law a woman was even in historic times completely dependent . . . if married she and her property passed into the power of her husband . . . the wife was the purchased property of her husband and like a slave acquired only for his benefit. A woman could not exercise any civil or public office . . . could not be a witness, surety tutor or curator, she could not adopt or be adopted, or make will or contract.[10]

In Pre-Islamic Arabia the condition of women was the worst. It is said that here women were called, 'Devil's whip' and those among the new born girls who could escape the barbarous custom of female infanticide had to face throughout their lives all kinds of social indignities.[11] Among the pagan Arabs a woman was considered to be mere chattel. She formed an integral part of the ensure of her husband or her father and the widow of a man descended on his sons, by right of inheritance, as any other portion of his patrimons.[12] On the death of an Arab his possessions devolved on his male heirs capable of bearing arms, daughters, wives, sisters and mothers did not inherit at all.[13] Women had no legal rights whatsoever in the social and political life of the country.[14] Some ancient Arabic proverbs which illustrate the idea of Pre-Islamic areas as to the position of women are:[15]

"A man can bear anything but the mention of his wife",

---

9. Allen, E.A., *History of Civilisation*, II, p. 444.
10. XXVIII *Encyclopaedia-Britannica*, 782.
11. Dr. Tahir Mahmood, *Womanhood in Islam*.
12. Ameer Ali-II, *Mohammadan Law* (13-14) Lahore, 1950.
13. Abdur Rahim, *Muhammadan Jurisprudence*, 9-10, pp. 15-16, Madras, 1911.
14. A.R.I. Doi, *Woman in Sharia,* p. 16, Zaria, 1983.
15. Hughes, *Dictionary of Islam,* p. 677, Lahore, 1964.

> "Women are the whips of *satan*", "our mother forbids us to err and runs into error", "obedience to a woman will have to be repented of", "trust neither a king, a horse, nor a woman", "what has a woman to do with the council of a nation"?

The above-stated views or the state of affairs as depicted clearly show the deplorable position of women. This world speaks of four civilisations, i.e., (i) Roman, (ii) Egyptian, (iii) Greek, and (iv) Indian. Except Indian civilisation, all other civilisations disappeared from the Globe. The patriot poet Sir Mohd. Iqbal spoke about it thus:

> The Greek, Egyptian and Roman civilisations all disappeared from the globe, but our civilisation still survives. There is something basic and inherent for its survival and existence in spite of the assault of centuries by the enemies to distort and deform it.

And this basic and inherent trait of its survival even today lies on the fact that this civilisation is founded on *dharma*, the righteous conduct. It is not based on religion. There is an utter confusion between the thinkers who think that *dharma* and religion are synonymous. Indian civilisation and its cultural heritage was neither primitive in nature nor static in character. It is always dynamic and evolutionary keeping pace with the changing social scenario, but never divorcing from its foundation of *dharma*.

And *dharma* is one of those Sanskrit words which defy an exact rendering into English. While 'religion' is rather a loose English equivalent of *dharma*, 'duty' fails to convey all the senses in which the word has been used in ancient Indian literature. The best definition of *dharma* appears to have been given by Jaimini in the words:

*codanalakṣaṇo'rtho dharma*[16]

that is to say *dharma* consists in beneficial directions.

These directions, however, are manifold, they direct us in our lives as individuals and also as members of the society. They teach us

---

16. *Pūrva-mīmāṁsa-sūtra*, I.1-2.

how to conduct ourselves in matters both religious and secular.[17]

In the *Ṛgveda* the word is used in three different senses:

1. Upholder, supporter or sustainer when the word is used in masculine.
2. Religious ordinance or rites when in masculine or neuter.
3. Fixed principles or rules of conduct in some contexts.

In the *Atharvaveda*, the word means:

1. Merit acquired by the performance of religious rites.
2. A whole body of religious duties.

In the *Chāndogya Upaniṣad*, it means the peculiar duties of the *āśramas*.

In the *Taittirīya Upaniṣad*, the *Gītā*, the *Manu-smṛti*, the *Yājñavalkya-smṛti*, and all later Smṛti works all the above meanings are brought together and the word means:

> The privileges, duties and obligations of a man, his standard of conduct as a member of the Aryan community, as a member of one of the castes, as a person in a paricular stage of life.[18]

So in short Manu has said:

> In this (work) the sacred law has been fully stated as well as the good and bad qualities of (human) actions and the immemorial rule of conduct (to be followed) by all the four castes (*varṇa*). — *Manu*, I.107

> The rule of conduct is transcendent Law, whether it be taught in the revealed texts or in the sacred traditions, hence a twice born man who possess regard for himself should be always careful to (follow) it.[19] — *Ibid.*, I.108

17. S.C. Banerji, *Dharmasūtras, A Study of their Origin and Development*.
18. P.V. Kane, *Vedic Basis of Hindu Law*, as cited by R.S. Betai in his thesis for doctorate "A Reconstruction of the Original Interpretations of the Manu-smṛti".
19. G. Bühler, *The Laws of Manu*.

The conversation between Padmavasna and Nārada is significant:[20]

> *mṛtam śarīram utsṛjya kaṣṭhaloṣṭasamam kṣito, vimukhā bāndhava yanti dharmastam anugacchati* ।
> *dharmena hi sahāyena tamastarati dustaram* ॥
>
> Friends turn back leaving behind the dead body like a piece of stone or wood: *dharma* alone followeth him. By the help of *dharma* one crosses the terrible darkness of death.

So the status of women under Hindu Law is also based on the foundation of *dharma* and *dharma* means to follow the prescribed acts and avoid the forbidden acts. It is worthwhile to refer to the various *śloka*s of Yājñavalkya throwing light on the concept of *dharma* which in essence means duty.

> In what country there is black antelope. *Dharma*s must be known (performed) there. — *Yāj*, Bk. I, ch. I.2

*Mitākṣarā* commented this way that the country in which the black, the spotted antelope freely roams, in that country the *dharmas* which will be described hereinafter, are to be practised. The sense being that they should not be practised anywhere else.

> A reference be made to a verse in *Manu-smṛti* which says —
>
> that land where the black antelope naturally roams, one must know to be fit for the performance of sacrifices, (the tract) different from that (is) the country of the *mlecchas* (barbarians).[21]

Then Yājñavalkya spoke that,

> The Purāṇas, the Nyāya, the Mīmāṁsā, the Dharmśāstra, together with the Aṅgas and the Vedas are the fourteen seats or sources of sciences and of *dharma*.
>
> — *Yāj*, Bk. I, ch. I.3

Then Yājñavalkya spoke about the subjective causes of *dharma* when he says:

---

20. Shakuntala Rao Shastri, *Women in the Sacred Laws.*
21. See *Vas*, I.13-15, *BaudhDS*, I.2, 12-15.

> Whatever thing is fully given in (proper) country, at (proper) time, with (proper) means, accompanied by faith, to (proper) persons, that all is the cause of *dharma*.
>
> — *Yāj*, Bk. I, ch. I.6

Here *dharma* has been explained in two senses:

1. the agent performing the acts which produce *dharma*, the *kāraka hetu* — the subjective side of *dharma*.

2. the expositional or declaratory side of *dharma* — the books that declare what acts are productive of *dharma* — the *jñāpaka hetu*.[22]

Then Yājñavalkya speaks about *jñāpaka hetu* thus:

> The Śruti, the Smṛti, the conduct of good men what appears pleasant to one's own self and the desire which springs from a good resolution, are said to be the roots of *dharma*.
>
> — *Yaj*, Bk.I, ch. I.7

Then Yājñavalkya further says that

> of all works (consisting of) sacrifices, or rituals or control of conduct or harmlessness or liberality or the study of the Vedas, this alone is the highest *dharma* (duty) that one should see the self by Yoga.

So in nutshell, *dharma* is what we find the acts ordained to be done, the acts ordained not to be done or forbidden, the conduct of good men, the desire flows out of good resolve and not opposed to scriptures and in totality, the duty to do good for self in general and for all in particular and this concept of *dharma* is evolutionary, flexible and always based on goodness of the individual and the society.

So, now we have to see the status of women through the eyes of the Śruti, the Smṛti and the conduct of good men under the yardstick that the degree in which personal immunity and proprietary capacity of women are recognised in a particular state or community is a test of the degree of the advance of its civilisation.[23] It is,

22. S.C. Vidyarnava, *Yājñavalkya-smṛti*, Book -I, *The Ācāra Adhyāya*.
23. Sir Henry Maine, *Earlier History of Institutions*, p. 389.

therefore, clear that estimate in which woman is held, the status occupied by her in society and the treatment meted out to her are regarded as index to the degree of civilisation and culture attained in a country.

E.S. Shivaswami Iyer stated that the ideals of the society as to womanhood includes not merely the relations of husband and wife or mother and children or the other intimate relationship of family life but also the notions we find about her capacity, her character, her claim to equality, independence and freedom for developing, her rights to personal ownership and control of property, to the choice of her vocation and other rights as well as duties as a member of the society.[24]

Majority of the scholars of Hinduism are having near unanimity of views that Vedic era was the golden era so far as equality of status and personal freedom of women is concerned. During the period women enjoyed a fair amount of freedom and equality with men. Women studied with men in *gurukulas* and there are instances of many *brahmavādīnīs* like Ghoṣā, Gārgī, Maitreyī and many others who were well versed in Vedas and actively participated in intellectual and philosophical discussions and discourses. A wife was regarded as indisputable member of husband's family and a centre of domestic world. She was regarded as equal partner, friend and equal sharer in joys and sufferings of her husband's life, enjoying a status and prestige in society.[25]

Ramaswami J. in *Thota Shesharathamma* v. *Thota Manikyamma*,[26] speaking about the status of women said that in Vedic society women enjoyed equal status economically, socially and culturally with men and referred to the writings of Altekar.[27]

However, many hold the view that during the Sūtra and Smṛti period, the status of women took a nosedive. The many verses that

---

24. E.S. Shivaswami Iyer, *Revolution of Hindu Women*, 1935 edn., p. 64, as cited in *Thota Sesharathamma* v. *Thota Manikyamma* [1991] 3 SCJ 543.

25. Dr. Y.K. Tiwari, *Status of Hindu Women and Efficacy of Protective Legislation.*

26. [1991] 3 SCJ 543.

27. Altekar, A.S., *The position of Women in Hindu Civilisation,* pp. 335, 339, 409.

appear in the Sūtras and Smṛtis appear to be inconsistent and self-contradictory, perhaps due to the fact that European Jurists studied these verses in isloation and out of context and Indian scholars imitated them without real application of mind.

So it becomes necessary, firstly to refer to the rules laid down by the *sūtrakāras* and *smṛtikāras* in their factual form without any comments and then their study in conjunction with the state of society then prevailed coupled with other attendant situations that warranted such conflicting verses if at all they are.

Gautama is the earliest law giver and has been assigned to the Sāmavedic school. He has been assigned the period of seventh century BC and hence it is contemporaneous to the close of Brāhmaṇic period and also contemporaneous to the various developments that took place in other parts of the globe.

According to Gautama:

> A wife is not independent with respect to the fulfilment of the sacred law. — *GauDS*, XVIII.1
>
> "Let her not violate her duty towards her husband" and "let her restrain her tongue, eyes and actions".
> — *Ibid.*, XVIII.2,3
>
> In case the husband renounced the world, she had, then to lead a life of strict discipline and self-restraint.
> — *Ibid.*, XVIII.16
>
> When the husband had disappeared, the wife had to wait for him for six years before she could marry again and if at the end of six years the husband returned, she had to go back to him. — *Ibid.*, XVIII.15
>
> A father had to give his daughter in marriage as soon as she attained marriageable age and any negligence on the part of the father was considered a sin.
> — *Ibid.*, XVIII.22
>
> A father who had no male issue may appoint his daughter.
> — *Ibid.*, XXVIII.18

> *Sapiṇḍa*s, *sagotra*s those connected by descent from the same *ṛṣi* (*vaidika gotra*) and the wife shall share (the estate) of a person deceased without (male) issue (or an appointed daughter).
> — *GauDS*, XXVIII.21

But women could have separate property of their own which came to be designated in later Smṛti digests as *strīdhana* and such property was inherited by the unmarried daughters if there were any, at the time of her death and in the absence of any such, it went to the poor married daughters.[28]

The next law-giver of considerable importance and antiquity is Baudhāyana who belonged to the *Black Yajurveda* School.

Baudhāyana says that

> women do not possess any independence and they are protected in all stages of their lives. A woman is never fit for independence. Referring to Vedas it is said that women are considered to be destitute of strength and of a portion.[29]
> — *BaudhDS*, II.2, 3, 44-6

> Women who strive to do what is agreeable to their husbands are assured of the bliss of the heaven and any violation of this duty to be atoned for by a penance.
> — *Ibid.*, II.2, 3, 47

> Let him abandon a barren wife in the tenth year, one who bears daughters (only) in the twelfth year, one whose children all die in the fifteenth, but her who is quarrelsome without delay.
> — *Ibid.*, II.2, 4, 6

> Let him first feed his guests, next the pregnant women, then the infants and the aged.[30] — *Ibid.*, II.7, 135

Pregnant women were honoured. This injunction is only in Baudhāyana that a man should honour such women and it

28. Shakuntala Rao Shastri, *Women in the Sacred Laws*, p. 19.
29. Refer *TaitS*, VI.5.82 — *tasmāt striyo, nirindriya adayada apipapat puinsah upasthitaram*.
30. Refer *VasDS*, XI.6-8 & *Manu Saṁitā*, III.114-15.

is said that perhaps these are not the views of Baudhāyana but added later on or by his successors who compiled this book.[31]

Wives of men of all castes must be guarded more carefully than wealth. —*BaudhDS*, II.2, 4, 2

Beauty provoketh thieves sooner than gold.[32]

Any wrong done to women is severely punishable.
—*Ibid.*, II.22, 13 & 14

Daughters could inherit only the ornaments of their mother, presented according to the custom or anything else.
—*Ibid.*, II.2, 3, 43

Next in importance and antiquity to Baudhāyana in the Black Yajurvedic School is Āpastamba. Āpastamba's date has been considered to be not later than the third century BC.

It was a sin to look at a woman and sacred texts not be uttered when a śūdra woman looked a brāhmaṇa.
—*ĀpDS*, I.3, 9, 11, 12

If he has a wife who is willing and able to perform her share of the religious duties and who bears sons, he shall not take a second. If a wife is deficient in one of these two qualities, he shall take another, but before he kindles the fires of *agnihotra*. For a wife who assists at the kindling of the fires becomes connected with those religious rites of which that fire kindling forms a part.
—*Ibid.*, II.5, 11, 12-14

Married women must be saluted according to the respective ages of their husbands. —*Ibid.*, I, 4, 14, 21

If the marriage bow is transgressed both husband and wife certainly go to hell. —*Ibid.*, II.10, 27, 6

31. Winternitz, *Die Frau in den Indichen Religionen*, p. 17.

32. Shakespeare, *As You Like It*.

If adulteresses have performed the prescribed penance, they are to be treated as before their fault. For the connection of husband and wife takes place through the law. —*ĀpDS*, II.10, 27, 1

He who has unjustly forsaken his wife shall put on an ass's skin, with the hair turned outside and beg in seven houses, saying "Give alms to him who forsook his wife" that shall be his livelihood for six months. —*Ibid.*, I.28, 20

If a wife forsakes her husband she shall perform the twelve night *kṛccā* penance for as long a time.
—*Ibid.*, I.10, 28, 20

Regarding inheritance

A daughter can only inherit the property of her father on failure of sons, *sapiṇḍa*s, the spiritual teacher or his pupil who could succeed to the property in the above order on the failure of the heir, who took precedence.
—*Ibid.*, II.6, 14, 2, 3 & 4

Āpastamba, perhaps is the first who sounded the ascetic and conservative rules which found echo in *Manu Saṁhitā*. His rules were to presume the chastity of women and to confine them to household chores. It is worth noting that he lived in an age when Buddhism was at its zenith and all such laws which were found to be not good for the existing Hindu society were discarded to save the society from the demoralising effect caused by the reformatory movement of Buddhism.

Vasiṣtha belongs to Ṛgvedic School and is considered to be later than Gautama and Baudhāyana. He begins with a description of general rules for society and then he proceeds to the general laws that are applicable for all

His various verses connected with women are as follows:

A woman is not independent; the males are her masters.
— *VasDS*, V.1

To support it he refers to Vedas:

> The fathers protect them in childhood, their husbands protect them in youth, and their sons protect them in old age, a woman is never fit to be independent.
>
> — *VasDS*, V.2

Vasiṣṭha speaks about the appointed daughter and then refers to the Vedas and says that

> A maiden who has no brothers comes back to the male ancestors of her own family, returning she becomes their son.

This is further corroborated with the verse:

> I shall give thee a brotherless damsel, decked with ornaments; the son who she may bear shall be my son.

Vasiṣṭha speaks of remarriage thus:

> She is called remarried (*punarbhu*) who leaving the husband in her youth and, having lived with others, re-enters his family. And she is called remarried who leaving an impotent, outcast, or mad husband, or after the death of her husband, takes another lord. — *Ibid.*, XVII.19, 20

Vasiṣṭha allows a widow to remarry after an interval of six months during which time she has to lead an ascetic life.

> Young women, if they were not given in marriage by their guardians at the proper time, could choose for themselves and marry. — *Ibid.*, XVII.67, 68

> If she stays in the house after her marriageable age, sin falls on the father. — *Ibid.*, XVII.70

> The sin incumbent on the failure of marrying the daughter at the proper time is "equivalent to the slaying of an embryo; that is the rule of the sacred law".
>
> — *Ibid.*, XVII.71

> If a damsel has been abducted by force, and not been wedded with sacred texts, she may be lawfully given to another man; she is even like a maiden — *Ibid.*, XVII.73

The wife of an emigrant could marry after a lapse of five years. If she were unwilling to do so, she had to live like a widow. Five years each to a brāhmaṇa and kṣatriya wife, four years to a vaiśya and three years to a śūdra after which the abandoned wives could marry again.

— *VasDS*, XVII.75-8

Vasiṣṭha exempts from taxes widows who return to their former family, unmarried maidens, and the wives of the servants. — *Ibid.*, XIX.24

In prescribing penances for women the mental unfaithfulness of a wife has to be explained by a penance, which consists mainly of a frugal meal and sleeping on bare ground. — *Ibid.*, XXI.6

The three great crimes for which women can be outcast are "the murder of their husband, slaying a learned brāhmaṇa and the destruction of the fruit of womb".

— *Ibid.*, XXVIII.7

A wife could never be abandoned by a man on any account, though tainted by sin, whether she be quarrelsome, or has left the house, or has suffered criminal force or has fallen into the hands of thieves, a wife must not be abandoned for, to forsake her is not prescribed by the sacred law.

— *Ibid.*, XXVIII.2-3

Shakuntla Rao Shashtri commented, reading in conjunction these writings of the law-givers that Gautama being the earliest law-giver agrees more with the customs prevalent in Vedic times. Baudhāyana, Vasiṣṭha who is almost contemporary to Baudhāyana or next to him, is in substantial agreement with Baudhāyana in many of his laws for women, but in some respects he displays a more ascetic tendency. In Āpastamba this ascetic tendency finds its fullest expression among the earliest law-givers. He plays the part of a reformer, discarding the old order as being unfit for the new.[33]

---

33. Shakuntala Rao Shastri, *Women in the Sacred Laws*, pp. 48-9.

Now we should go further into the period of Kauṭilya and Vātsyāyana, without entering into the controversy about the specificness of the period and taking into consideration that Kauṭilya's *Arthaśāstra* is contemporaneous to the earlier set of law-givers.

Book III, ch. 2 of *Kauṭilya Arthaśāstra* deals with marriage and subjects relating to women and starts with "(All) transactions begin with marriage" and then he speaks about eight types of marriages. The first four are lawful with the sanction of father and the remaining with the sanction of father and the mother and then he speaks:

> In the case of all (forms of marriage) giving pleasure (to the bride by means of gifts) is not forbidden.
>
> — *KauṭArth*, III.2, 13

> Maintenance and ornaments constitutes woman's property. Maintenance is an endowment of a maximum of two thousand (*paṇa*s); as to ornaments, there is no limit.
>
> — *Ibid.*, III.2, 26-7

> A (widow) without sons, remaining faithful to her husband's bed, shall use her woman's property in the proximity of elders, till the end of her life. For, a woman's property is meant for calamities. After (her death) it shall go to heirs.
>
> — *Ibid.*, III.2, 33-5

> The (husband) shall wait for eight years if the wife does not bear offsprings or does not bear son or is barren, for ten if she bears dead offsprings, for twelve if she bears daughters only. After that he may marry a second wife with the object of getting a son. In case of transgression of that (rule) he shall hand over the dowry, the woman's property and half (that) as compensation for supersession and (pay) a fine of twenty-four *paṇa*s maximum.
>
> — *Ibid.*, III.2, 38-40

> A husband, who has become degraded or gone to a foreign land or has committed an offence against the king or is dangerous to her life or has become an outcast or even an

impotent one may be abandoned.

— *KauṭArth*, III.2, 48

Here Kauṭilya has used the word *tyajyaḥ*. Jayaswal (*Manu* and *Yāj*, p. 230) says that *tyaja* denotes separation from conjugal life, as opposed to *mokṣa*, the technical divorce.

> A disaffected wife is not to be granted divorce from the husband who is unwilling, nor the husband from the wife. By mutual disaffection (alone), a divorce (shall be granted) or, if the husband seeks divorce because of the wife's offence, he shall give to her whatever he may have taken. Or if the wife seeks divorce because of the husband's offence, he shall not give her whatever may have been received. There is no divorce in pious marriages. —*Ibid.*, III.3, 15-19

So Kauṭilya in Bk. III, chs. 2, 3, 4, speaks about the law of marriage, rules concerning woman's property, about supersession (of a wife) by a second marriage, about maintenance of wife, marital duties, cruelty, disaffection misconduct, leaving home, long absence from home, etc., and even penalties thereof for transgression of the rule.[34]

Kauṭilya has framed laws according to his times. Thus, he portrays the position of women in society in northern India in the fourth century BC. In Kauṭilya we meet with greater details in certain matters as the marriage of women, elopement and divorce. Bearing of son is still the dominant factor and desire. His rules are rather difficult for remarriage. He is more favourable towards women. He appears to be substantially in agreement with those of Baudhāyana and Vasiṣṭha. The influence of asceticism, set in by Buddhism, is clearly manifest in his laws, but his rules are not divorced from the Vedic concepts. Daughters are not excluded from inheritance and freedom is not denied to women but positively freedom has been ruled within the decent ambit of chastity.

Let us now enter the field where the sway of the *smṛtikār*s is undisputable but simultaneously speaking different tones, but never isolated from the Vedic concept of *dharma*, laying impregnable stress on the *dharma* of a woman as she being the mother of civilisation, the protector of the race and preservation and creator

34. R.P. Kangle, *These rules have been taken from The Kauṭilya Arthaśāstra.*

of the qualitative continuity of generations. *Manu-smṛti* is considered as a supreme law. It is said that the fountain source of all teaching in regard to matters beyond the reach of the ordinary human intellect is the Veda as Jaimini says:

> When the Veda fails us, then alone we have to look up to the other sources of law, such as Smṛti and custom or tradition. But if there is conflict between the Smṛtis, then *Manu-smṛti* shall prevail.[35]

Even in Vedas, the pre-eminence of Manu is declared in these terms: "whatever Manu says is medicine".[36] The code of Manu has been treated as of paramount authority.[37] So the various *śloka*s of Manu have been interpreted differently by the modern interpreters on the touchstone of present changing social scenario and let us have some of the *śloka*s of Manu for consideration here.

About the position and treatment of a daughter at home Manu says:

> One's slaves as one's shadow, one's daughter as the highest object of tenderness; hence if one is offended by (any one of) these, one must bear it without resentment.
>
> — *Manu*, IV.185

Speaking about the legal position of daughter he says:

> A son is even (as) oneself, (such) a daughter is equal to a son; how can another (heir) take the estate, while such (an appointed daughter who is even) oneself lives?
>
> — *Ibid.*, IX.130
>
> But whatever may be the separate property of the mother, that is the share of the unmarried daughter alone; and the son of an (appointed daughter shall take the whole estate

35. *Smṛticandrikā and Vīramitrodya* cited in Jha's Hindu Law in its sources, I.17, 43, 44.
36. P.V. Kane, *History of Dharmaśāstras*, pp. 136-7.
37. Per Lord Holihouse in *Sri Balusu's* case [1889] 26 IA 113, See *Amarendra's* Case [1933] 60 IA 242, *Ramalaxmi* v *Sivanantha* [1872] 14 MIA 570.

of (this maternal grandfather) who leaves no son.
—*Manu*, IX.131

Simultaneously Manu also says:

> But a prudent man should not marry (a maiden) who has no brother, nor one whose father is not known, through fear lest (in the former case she be made) an appointed daughter (and in the latter) lest (he should commit) sin.
> —*Ibid.*, III.11

Manu, then altering the position, says:

> He who has no son may make his daughter in the following manner an appointed daughter (*putrika*, saying to her husband). The (male) child, born of her, shall perform her funeral rights. —*Ibid.*, IX.127

He further speaks about the daughter and marriage as follows:

> To a distinguished, handsome suitor (of) equal (caste) should (a father) give his daughter in accordance with the prescribed rule, though she have not attained (the proper age). —*Ibid.*, IX.88

> (But) the maiden, though marriageable, should rather stop in (the father's) house until death, than that he should ever give to a man destitute of good qualities. —*Ibid.*, IX.89

Manu further says:

> Three years let a damsel wait, though she be marriageable, but after that time let her choose for herself a bridegroom (of) equal (caste and rank). If, being not given in marriage, she herself seeks a husband, she incurs no guilt, nor (does) he whom she weds. —*Ibid.*, IX.90-1

Coming next to the position of a woman in home and society, Manu is adhering to the Vedic order and says:

> Her father protects (her) in childhood, her husband protects

(her) in youth, and her sons protect (her) in old age; a woman is never fit for independence.[38] — *Manu*, IX.3

To be mothers were women created, and to fathers men; religious rites, therefore, are ordained in the Veda to be performed (by the husband) together with the wife.
— *Ibid.*, IX.96

Manu has said the same thing in fifth Book:

By a girl, by a young woman, or even by an aged one, nothing must be done independently, even in her own house. — *Ibid.*, V.147

In childhood she must be subject to her father, in youth to her husband, when her lord is dead to her sons; a woman must never be independent. — *Ibid.*, V.148

Simultaneously Manu also says:

Women must be honoured and adorned by their fathers, brothers, husbands and brothers-in-law, who desire (their own) welfare. — *Ibid.*, III.55

Where women are honoured, there the gods are pleased; but where they are not honoured, no sacred rite yields reward. — *Ibid.*, III.56

Where the female relations live in grief, the family soon wholly perishes; but that family where they are not unhappy ever prospers. — *Ibid.*, III.57

The houses on which female relations, not being duly honoured, pronounce a curse, perish completely, as if destroyed by magic. — *Ibid.*, III.58

But a woman who has been pregnant two months or more, an ascetic, a hermit in the forest, and brāhmaṇas who are students of the Veda, shall not be made to pay toll at a

38. See also *BaudhDS*, II.2, 3, 45.

ferry. —*Ibid.*, VIII.407

A wife, a son, and a slave, these three are declared to have no property, the wealth which they earn is (acquired) for him to whom they belong. —*Manu*, VIII.416

About widows Manu says thus:

At her pleasure let her emaciate her body by (living on) pure flowers, roots and fruit; but she must never even mention the name of another man after her husband had died. —*Ibid.*, V.157

Until death let her be patient (of hardships), self-controlled, and chaste, and strive (to fulfil) that most excellent duty which (is prescribed) for wives who have one husband only. —*Ibid.*, V.158

A virtuous wife who after the death of her husband constantly remains chaste, reaches heaven, though she have no son, just like those chaste men.

—*Ibid.*, V.160

But a woman who from a desire to have offspring violates her duty towards her (deceased) husband brings on herself disgrace in this world and loses her place with her husband (in heaven). —*Ibid.*, V.161

According to Kauṭilya remarriage of women was allowed after a certain period. Manu also made laws to that effect but the length of time she was to wait is lengthened. Verses 76 to 82 of Book IX are worth mentioning covering both husband and wife:

If the husband went abroad for some sacred duty (she) must wait for him eight years, if (he went) to (acquire) learning for six (years), if (he went) for pleasure three years.

—*Ibid.*, IX.76

For one year let a husband bear with a wife who hates him; but after (the lapse of) a year let him deprive her of her property and cease to cohabit with her.

—*Ibid.*, IX.77

> She who shows disrespect to (a husband) who is addicted to (some evil) passion, is a drunkard, or diseased, shall be deserted for three months (and be) deprived of her ornaments and furniture. —*Manu*, IX.78

> But she who shows aversion towards a man, outcast (husband), a eunuch, one destitute of manly strength, or one afflicted with such diseases as punish crimes, shall neither be cast off nor be deprived of her property. —*Ibid.*, IX.79

> She who drinks spirituous liquor, is of bad conduct, rebellious, diseased, mischievous or wasteful may at any time be superseded (by another wife).[39]

> But a sick wife who is kind (to her husband) and virtuous in her conduct, may be superseded (only) with her own consent and must never be disgraced. —*Ibid.*, IX.82

There are many other verses in *Manu-smṛti* which speak about wife and husband and their interaction:

> He only is prefect man who consists (of three persons united), his wife, himself and his offspring, thus (says the Veda) and (learned), *Brāhamaṇa*s propound this (maxim) like wise. The husband is one with the wife.[40] —*Ibid.*, IX.45

> Neither by sale nor by repudiation is a wife released from her husband; such we know the law to be, which the lord of creative (Prajāpati) made of old. —*Ibid.*, IX.46

> Once is the partition (of the inheritance) made, (once is) a maiden given in marriage (and) once does (a man) say, 'I will give', each of those three (acts is done) once only. —*Ibid.*, IX.47

About women, their nature, Manu has said:

---

39. See *Yāj*, I.73 & *BaudhDS*, II.4, 6.

40. See also *Vājasaneyi Brāhmaṇa*, *ĀpaDS*, II.14, 16.

> Through their passion for men, through their mutable temper, through their natural heartlessness, they become disloyal towards their husbands, how carefully they may be guarded in this world. — *Manu*, IX.15
>
> Knowing their disposition, which the Lord of Creature laid in them at the creation, to be such, (every) man should most strenuously exert himself to guard them.
>
> — *Ibid.*, X.16
>
> (When creating them) Manu alloted to women (a love of their) bed, (of their) seat and (of) ornament, impure desires, wrath, dishonesty, malice and bad conduct.
>
> — *Ibid.*, IX.17
>
> For women no (sacramental) rite (is performed) with sacred texts, thus the law is settled, women (who are) destitute of strength and destitute of (the knowledge of) Vedic texts (are as impure as) falsehood (itself) that is a fixed rule.[41]

Laws laid down by Manu are supreme and all subsequent work was mere recapitulation of his laws. However, if some changes here and there occur, it may be due to the pressing needs of the time. The most important of the latter law-givers are Yājñavalkya and Parāśara. Parāśara confines himself to two aspects of Hindu Law, i.e., *ācāra* and *prāyaścitta*. His account of household life is meagre. So we should have some glimpses of *Yājñavalkya-smṛti* on the matter in hand along with other law-givers of considerable importance like Viṣṇu, Bṛhaspati and Nārada.

Like any other *smṛtikāra*, Yājñavalkya laid great stress on the concept of family, the base of which is woman. *Yājñavalkya-smṛti* is divided into three *adhyāyas* or books namely *Ācāra, Vyavahāra,* and *Prayāścitta*. The first book *The Ācāra* speaks among others about marriage and *gṛhastha* and the 2nd book about the Civil Law.

---

41. *Manu*, II.66 says: "This whole series (of ceremonies) must be performed for females (also), in order to sanctify the body, at the proper time and in the proper order, but without (the recitation of) sacred texts."

    *Yāj*, I.13 says also: "These ceremonies, in case of women are (to be) performed in silence, but however, their marriage is (with the recitation of) *mantras*.

Yājñavalkya says:

> Without breaking (the rules) of studentship, let him marry a woman with auspicious characteristics who has not belonged to another man, who is lovely, who is not a *sapiṇḍa* and who is younger (than himself). —*Yāj.*, I.52

Yājñavalkya further says:

> She should be of a great family of *śrotriya*s, whose ten ancestors are renowned, but not of a family, though prosperous, that has any hereditary disease or taint.
> —*Yāj.*, I.54

Similarly, Yājñavalkya says that:

> The bridegroom too should possess these qualifications (and free from the same defects) and be of the same class (or of a highter), be a *śrotriya* (himself), young, wise, beloved of all, and one whose virile power has been examined.
> —*Yāj.*, I.55

In these verse Yājñavalkya has spoken about the qualities which the bride and the bridegroom should possess. These are the prerequisites ordained for tie-up in the wedlock to have eternal love between the couple for the smooth running of the family life and mutual love is the foundation of the family life wherein the bride and bridegroom need to be on the same wave-length.

Yājñavalkya has simply echoed what the other scriptures speak.[42] Manu to this effect speaks that

> Let him wed a female free from bodily defects, who has an agreeable name, the (graceful) gait of a *haṁsa* or of an elephant, a moderate (quality of hair on the body and on the head, small teeth and soft limbs).[43]

Other scriptures also speak about the qualities of a bridegroom such as Nārada says:

---

42. *GautDS*, IV.1, *Viṣṇu*, XXIV.9, *Vas*, VIII.1.
43. *Manu*, III.10.

> If his collarbone, his knee and his bones (in general) are strongly made, if his shoulders and hairs are (also) strongly made, if the nape of his neck is stout and his thigh and his skin delicate; if his gait and his voice is vigorous.[44]

Kātyāyana speaks about those bridegrooms who should be avoided:

> Those who lived in far off countries, who are illiterate, who follow the path of emancipation, who are heroes (soldiers), who are without *vrata*s or who are addicted to *vrata*s, to such, a girl should not be given by the wise.[45]

To quote Manu further:

> (But) the maiden, though marrigeable should rather stop in (the father's) house until death, than that he should ever give her to a man destitute of good qualities.[46]

The above verses of Yājñavalkya are the reflections of what the other law-givers have stated and also reflect that how the daughters were cared that they should be married to a distinguished, handsome suitor clad with excellences.

Yājñavalkya speaks thus about the duties of a wife:

> Wives should act according to the word (directions) of their husbands, this is the highest duty of wives. But if the husband be guilty of a heinous sin, she should wait till he be again purified.[47]

The other law-givers also lay stress on the duties of a wife as it is her character role which can idealise the home to be called heaven and Manu has spoken thus:

> I will now propound the eternal laws for a husband and his wife who keep to the path of duty, whether they be united or separated.[48]

---

44. *Nārada*, XII.10.
45. See also *Manu*, III.6, 9.
46. *Manu*, IX.89.
47. *Yāj*, I.77.
48. *Manu*, IX.1.

Manu in ch. IX after prescribing duties to be followed by the wife and the husband finally says:

> Let mutual fidelity continue until death, this may be considered as the summary of the highest law for husband and wife.
>
> Let man and woman, united in marriage constantly exert themselves that (they may not be) disunited (and) may not violate their mutual fidelity.[49]

Vasiṣṭha says:

> Faithful wives who are constatly pure and truthful (reside after death) in the same abodes with their husbands, those who are unfaithful are born as jackals.[50]

Devala says:

> Dependence, attendance on her, aid in his religious ceremonies, respectful behaviour to those who are entitled to veneration from him, hatred to those who bear enemity to him, no ill-will towards him, constant complacency, attention to his business, are the duties of women.

Viṣṇu says:

> Accompanying of her husband, reverence to his father, of spiritual parents, of deities and guests, great cleanliness in regard to the domestic furniture and care of the household vessels; avoiding the use of philters and charms attention to auspicious customs, austerities after the death of her hasband, no frequenting of strange houses, no standing at the door or window, dependence in all affairs, subjection to her father, husband and son, in childhood, youth and age, such are the duties of a woman.[51]

Gautama says:

> A wife is not independent with respect to (the fulfilment

49. *Manu*, IX.101-2.
50. *Vas*, XXI.14.
51. Colebrooke's *Digest* Bk.III, Ch.2, Sec. I-XCII.

> of) the sacred law. Let her not violate her duty towards her husband. Let her restrain her tongue, eyes and (organs of) action.[52]

Manu says that,

> a virtuous wife who after the death of her husband constantly remains chaste, reaches heaven though she has no son, just like those chaste men.[53]

The sayings of the above law-givers stress on two points, i.e., obedience and chastity for the simple reason that a wife is the radiance of the house. The wife is the home, a man should not consider his home a habitation ungraced by a wife, therefore, is she another home. Her chastity will enlighten the eternal love between them for which both have taken an oath before Agni.

Yājñavalkya, where he casts duties on the wife, there he also adorns the wife, when he says that,

> Because continuity (of family) in this world and getting of heaven in the next are through sons, grandsons and great grandsons, therefore women ought to be attended to and should be guarded carefully.[54]

Āpastamba puts it in a different way:

> He should go to his wife and not another woman, for the sake of religious and progeny.[55]

This law-giver has said:

> If he has a wife who (is willing and able) to perform (her share of) the religious duties and who bears sons, he shall not take a second.[56]

---

52. *GautDS*, XVIII.1-3.
53. *Manu*, V.160.
54. *Yāj*, I.78.
55. *ApasDS*, II.5, 11-12.
56. *SBE*, Vol. II, p. 125.

Yājñavalkya further says:

> Woman is to be respected by her husband, father, kindred (*jñāti*), mother-in-law, father-in-law, husband's younger brother, and the *bandhus*, with ornaments, clothes and food.[57]

As Yājñavalkya laid great stress on the smooth functioning of the family life, the touchstone of cultural heritage, the continuity of the race, preservation of the sanctity of *dharma*, he speaks of general duties of a woman.

> When a maiden, her father; when married, her husband, and when old, her sons should protect her. In their absence, the kinsmen (should take care of her). The women are never independent.[58]

Yājñavalkya has repeated what other law-givers have said:

> Viṣṇu says:
>
> Not to act by herself in any matter, to remain subject in her infancy, to her father, in her youth, to her husband, and in her oldage, to her sons.[59]

Manu to this effect —

> In childhood a female must be subject to her father, in youth to her husband, when her lord is dead to her sons; a woman must never be independent.[60]
>
> Her father protects (her) in childhood, her husband protects (her) in youth, and her sons protect (her) in oldage, a woman is never fit for independence.[61]

So finally Yājñavalkya says that —

> Devoted to the pleasure and to the good of her husband, of good conduct, with subdued passions (such a wife) obtains

---

57. *Yāj*, I.82.
58. *Ibid.*, I.85.
59. *Viṣṇu*, XXV.12, 13.
60. *Manu*, V.148.
61. *Ibid.*, IX.3.

> renown in this world, and after death attains the best end.[62]

> She who does not go to another, whether her husband be alive or dead obtains glory here and becomes happy with Umā.[63]

Yājñavalkya also speaks about wife who is found lacking in qualities ordained or shows disinclination to her *dharma* which is expected to be discharged and various *śloka*s are worth mentioning in this regard.

> The unchaste wife should be deprived of authority, should be unadorned, allowed food barely sufficient to sustain her body, rebuked, and let sleep on low bed and thus allowed to dwell.[64]

Nārada says:

> When a married woman commits adultery, her hair shall be shaved, she shall have to lie on a low couch, receive bad food, and bad clothing and the removal of sweepings shall be assigned to her as her occupation.[65]

But the same Yājñavalkya says:

> The purification from unchastity is at the season; in case of conception her abandonment is ordained so also in case of causing absorption or killing a husband or committing a heinous crime, and the rest.[66]

In this regard Vasiṣṭha says that:

> The wives of brāhmaṇas, kṣatriyas and vaiśyas who commit adultery with a śūdra may be purified by a penance in case no conception has taken place (from their adulterous intercourse) not otherwise.[67]

---

62. *Yāj*, 87.
63. *Ibid.*, I.75.
64. *Ibid.*, I.70.
65. *Nārada*, XII.91.
66. *Yāj*, I.72.
67. *Vasiṣṭha Smṛti*, XXI.12.

Manu also says:

> An exceedingly corrupt wife let her husband confine to one apartment, and compel her to perform the penance which is prescribed for males in cases of adultery.[68]

Viṣṇu says that,

> A woman who has committed adultery once must perform that penance which has been prescribed for an adulterer.[69]

According to Madhva on Parāśara:

> Where a woman commits adultery only once and then repents, such penance is prescribed.[70]

Then Yājñavalkya speaks of the situations when the husband can take the second wife:

> The liquor-drinker, the diseased, the cunning, the barren, the hitter of wealth, the unpleasant spoken, who bears female children should be superseded, so also (one) who hates people.[71]

Vasiṣṭha says that,

> Half the body of the husband falls if his wife drinks spirituous drinks.[72]

In this regard Manu has spoken very elaborately:

> For one year let a busband bear with a wife who hates him; but after (the lapse of) a year let him deprive her of her property and cease to cohabit with her. She who shows disrespect to (a husband) who is addicted to (some evil) passion, is a drunkard, or diseased, shall be deserted for three months (and be) deprived of her ornaments and furniture. But she who shows aversion towards a mad or

---

68. *Manu*, XI.177.
69. *Viṣṇu*, LIII.1, 2 & 8.
70. Madhva on Parāśara — Prāyaścitta Kāṇḍa II, Adhyāya X, Verse 28.
71. *Yāj*, I.73.
72. *Vasiṣṭha*, XXI.15.

> outcast (husband), a eunuch, one destitute of manly strength or one afflicted with such diseases as punish crimes, shall neither be cast off nor be deprived of her property. She who drinks spirituous liquor, is of bad conduct, rebellious, diseased, mischievous or wasteful, may at any time be superseded (by another wife). A barren wife may be superseded in the eighth year, she whose children (all) die in the tenth, she who only bears daughters in the eleventh, but she who is quarrelsome without delay.[73]

Yājñavalkya speaks the other side picture too:

> The superseded should be maintained, otherwise great sin is caused. When the husband and wife live in harmony, the three *varga*s prosper there. He who abandons an obedient and skilful, son-bearing and pleasant speaking wife should be made to give one-third of his property to her. If he has no property, he should maintain her.[74]

Nārada says that,

> If a man leaves a wife who is obedient, pleasant spoken, skilful, virtuous, and the mother of (male) issue, the king shall make him mindful of his duty by (inflicting) severe punishment (on him).[75]

To the same effect Devala ays:

> A person who leaves a blameless wife, should be punished as a thief.[76]

Manu says that —

> But a sick wife, who is kind (to her husband) and virtuous in her conduct, may be superseded (only) with her own consent and must never be disgraced.[77]

---

73. *Manu*, IX.77-81.
74. *Yāj*, I.74, 76.
75. *Nārada*, XII.95.
76. *Bālambhaṭṭa's Gloss.*
77. *Manu*, IX.82.

Yājñavalkya also speaks about the duties of a widow:

> Deprived of her husband, she should not reside apart from the father, mother, son or brother, from her mother-in-law or father-in-law, or from her old maternal uncles, otherwise she becomes infamous.[78]

This verse needs to be read with what is ordained that woman is never fit to be independent. She must be protected at every stage of her life. But *Viṣṇu-smṛti* speaks in the light of chastity and says that:

> After the death of her husband (the widow should adopt one of these two courses), either to preserve her chastity (*brahmacarya*) or to ascend the pile after him.[79]

Vyāsa says:

> Devoted to her husband, she entered the raging fire and thereafter she obtained her (dead) lord who was adorned with a variegated bracelet. Then afterwards the bird went in company with his wife to heaven and enjoyed it with her being honoured with all acts (of service).[80]
>
> Learn the power of the widow, who hearing that her husband is deseased, and been burned in another region, casts herself into fire.[81]

Manu says:

> At her pleasure let her emaciate her body by (living on) pure flowers, roots and fruits, but she must never even mention the name of another man after her husband has died.[82]

---

78. *Yāj*, I.86.
79. *Viṣṇu*, XXV.14.
80. *Vedavyāsa-smṛti,* Ananda Asrama edn., p. 362.
81. *Vyāsa*, CXXV-1.
82. *Manu*, V.157. Also read *Manu*, V.158-62.

Bṛhaspati says:

> A wife is considered as half the body of her husband, equally sharing the fruit of pure and impure acts, whether she ascend the pile after him or survive for the benefit of her husband, she is a faithful wife.[83]

Viṣṇu says:

> After the death of her husband, to preserve chastity, or to ascend the pile after him.[84]
>
> That woman, who on the death of her husband ascends the same burning pile with him, is exalted to heaven as equal in virtue to Arundhatī.[85]
>
> No other way is known for a virtuous woman after the death of her husband; the separate cremation of her husband would be lost, to all religious intents. If her lord dies in another country, let the faithful wife place his sandals on her breast, and pure, enter the fire. The faithful widow is pronounced no suicide by the recited text of *Ṛgveda*; when three days of mourning are passed, she obtains legal obsequies.[86]

Hārīta CXXXVII also speaks of two alternatives, i.e.,

1. when the person keeping sacred fire dies, or
2. if a person not keeping the sacred fire dies.

In the first case the widow is spoken to have performed the sacrifice called the ***strī-savana***. In the latter case, chastity and utmost self-control is ordained and she is asked to perform the ceremony in the *laukika* fire.

It has always been said that women were, as a rule, excluded from inheritance in the earliest times, perhaps taking clue from Manu where he aid that:

83. *Bṛhaspati*, CXXXII.
84. *Viṣṇu*, XXV.14.
85. Aṅgirāsa CXXIII.1, see *Dakṣa-smṛti*, p. 80, Ananda Asrama edn.
86. *Brahma Purāṇa*, CXXVI.1.3.

> In childhood, a female must be subject to her father, in youth to her husband, when her lord is dead to her sons; a woman must never be independent.[87]

or

> A wife, a son, and a slave, these three are declared to have no property; the wealth which they earn is (acquired) for him to who they belong.[88]

or

> when a maiden, her father, when married, her husband, and when old, her sons, should protect her. In their absence, the kinsmen (should take care of her). The women are never independent.[89]

This does not seem to be consistent with what has been stated in the various scriptures and that has been clarified by the commentators that a woman as daughter, wife, widow and mother was entitled to property.

About daughter Manu has said that:

> A son is even (as) oneself, (such) a daughter is equal to a son; how can another (heir) take the estate, while such (an appointed daughter who is even) oneself, lives?[90]

> But to the maiden (sisters) the brothers shall severally give (portions) out of their shares, each of his share one-fourth part; those who refuse to give (it) will become outcasts.[91]

Bṛhaspati says:

> A daughter like son, springs from each member of man; how then should any other mortal inherit the father's property while she lives.[92]

---

87. *Manu*, V.148.
88. *Ibid.*, VIII.416.
89. *Yāj*, I.85.
90. *Manu*, IX.130, see also *Manu*, IX.127, 128.
91. *Ibid.*, IX.118.
92. *Bṛhaspati*, XXV.56.

Aparārka says that:

> In the case of daughters, ownership in the father's wealth arises by birth itself as in the case of sons.[93]

*Mitākṣarā* citing the texts of Kātyāyana and Bṛhaspati declares that:

> The daughters inherit in the absence of wife.[94]

Kauṭilya says:

> To (brothers) who are not established (in life) they shall give an amount for their marriage, equal to that of those already settled, and to daughters an amount for bestowal in marriage.[95]

Yājñavalkya says:[96]

> पत्नी दुहितरश्चैव पितरौ भ्रातरस्तथा ।
> तत्सुता गोत्रजा बन्धुशिष्यसब्रह्मचारिणः ।। १३५ ।।

Regarding right of mother, Manu has said:

> A mother shall obtain the inheritance of a son (who dies) without leaving issue, and, if the mother be dead, the paternal grandmother shall take the estate.[97]

Yājñavalkya says:[98]

> एषामभावे पूर्वस्य धनभागुत्तरोत्तरः ।
> स्वर्यातस्य ह्यपुत्रस्य सर्ववर्णेष्वयं विधिः ।। १३६ ।।

So he places both parents after the daughter:

> According to Nārada,
>
> her right to a share is there on partition by the sons after

93. Cited in Commentary.
94. *Mit*, II, ii.2.
95. *KauṭArth*, 3, 5, 21.
96. *Yāj*, II.135.
97. *Manu*, IX.217.
98. *Yāj*, II.136.

the death of their father but does not refer to her as an heir.[99]

Gautama, Baudhāyana, Āpastamba or Vasiṣṭha do not speak about mother as an heir but Bṛhaspati and Kātyāyana state about the claim to property by the mother.[100]

Right of a widow is recognised by Manu, Yājñavalkya, Viṣṇu, Bṛhaspati, Kātyāyana, Devala and others. She is entitled to succeed to her husband.

Manu says:

> Always to that (relative within three degrees) who is nearest to the (deceased) *sapiṇḍa*, the estate shall belong, afterwards a *sakulya* shall be (the heir, then) the spiritual teacher or pupil.[101]

Kullūka, commenting on it says that:

> To the nearest among the *sapiṇḍa*s (male or female) the estate shall belong. Raghunandana agrees with it in substance but more fully he agrees with Yājñavalkya, II. 135-6.[102]

Bṛhaspati is most emphatic in her favour and says that she is in fact the first heir to the property of a man who dies without male issues:

> The widow of childless man, keeping unsullied her husband's bed, and preserving religious ceremonies, shall present his funeral oblations and obtain his entire share.[103]

Privy Council in *Katama Natchair* v. *Raja of Sivaganga* said that the interest of a Hindu widow so succeeding to her husband's estate is similar to that of a tenant in tail by the English Law, as representing the inheritance.

---

99. *Nārada*, XIII.12.

100. *Bṛhaspati*, XXV.63, Jagannath's *Digest*, tr. by M. Colebrook, II.550-2.

101. *Manu*, IX.187.

102. G. Bühler, *The Laws of Manu*, p. 367.

103. *Bṛhaspti*, XXV, 46, 47, 55. See also *GautDS*, XXVIII.21.

However, Āpastamba, Vasiṣṭha and Nārada do not apparently recognise right of the widow as heir.

Regarding wife: Sanskrit books speak very elaborately about *strīdhana*, woman's separate property. According to Kane, there is a mention of *strīdhana* in the Vedas.[105] We find its mention in *Gautama's Dharama-sutra*.[106] Āpastamba says that the share of the wife consists of her ornaments and the wealth which she may have received from her relations.[107]

Manu explains *strīdhana* as:

> What (was given) before the (nuptial) fire, what (was given) on the bridal procession, what was given in token of love, and what was received from her brother, mother, or father, that is called the six-fold property of a woman.
>
> (such property), as well as a gift subsequent and what was given (to her) by her affectionate husband, shall go to her offspring (even) if she dies in the lifetime of her husband.[108]

Yājñavalkya also speaks about *strīdhana* as follows:[109]

> पितृमातृपतिभ्रातृदत्तमध्यग्न्युपागतम्।
> आधिवेदनिकाद्यं च स्त्रीधनं परिकीर्तितम् ।। १४३ ।।
> अतीतायामप्रजसि बान्धवास्तदवाप्नुयुः ।। १४४ ।।

> What was given to a woman by the father, mother, her husband or brother, or received by her at the nuptial fire or presented on her supersession and the like is denominated woman's property. That which is given (to the bride) by her *bandhus*, *śulka*, *anvadheyaka*, these her kinsmen (*bāndhavas*) take if she dies without issues.

---

104. [1863] MIA 539.

105. Kane, 4; One such passage is *Ṛgveda*, I.109.2; see Dr. Ganganath Jha, *Hindu Law in its Sources*, II.526.

106. Dr. Jolly's *Tagore Law Lectures on Hindu Law*, 1883, p. 228. See also *GauDS*, XXVIII.24-26.

107. *ĀpasDS*, II.6, 14, 9.

108. *Manu*, IX.194-5.

109. *Yāj*, II.143-4.

The commentators, have further expanded the meaning of *strīdhana* like Vijñeśvara who explained the word *ādi* used by Yājñavalkya as property which she may have acquired by inheritance, purchase, partition, seizure and finding.

Kātyāyana says:

> Whatever is given to women at the time of their marriage before the nuptial fire, which is the witness of nuptials, is denominated by sages *adhyagnika strīdhana*.[110]

A text of Devala says:

> Her subsistence (*vṛtti*), ornaments, fee or *śulka*, or her gains are the separate property of a woman.[111]

Scholars have found difficulty in assessing the status of women in the ancient legal perspective either due to confused sound which our old records yield or due to deformed interpretation brought forth clad with Western materialistic culture which is still not capable of appreciating the Indian cultural heritage where woman has been considered as mother. Svāmī Vivekānanda has said:

> In the West, the woman is wife. The idea of womanhood is concentrated there as the wife. To the ordinary man in India, the whole force of womanhood is concentrated in motherhood. In the Western home, the wife rules. In an Indian home the mother rules.

So let us look to woman from the various angles keeping in view that India still holds on to spiritualism. The various angles are:

1. Concept of Aryan home.
2. Inheritance.
3. Woman as a widow.
4. Subjugation of women.

---

110. Cited in the *Smṛticandrikā*, IX.1.2.

111. *Ibid.*, IX.2, 15 & *Vīramitrodaya*, V.1, 7.

**Concept of Aryan home**

The concept is basically religious in character wherein the stress is laid on ancestor worship as stimulated by the Aryan race. According to Hearn:[112]

> the theory upon which it rested was the paramount and continuous obligation of ancestor worship. The practical object at which it aimed at was the regular and proper performance of the *sacra* — that is of the worship peculiar to the household. The machinery by which the *sacra* were maintained was the corporate character of the household and the perpetual succession of the housefather.

For Hindus the concept of *pater familias* developed as a result of religious directions unlike the Romans who developed the same in the legal direction.[113]

Manu has explained this concept in two of his *ślokas*:

> Offsprings (the due performance of) religious rites, faithful service, highest conjugal happiness and heavenly bliss for the ancestors and oneself, depends on one's wife alone.[114]

> He only is perfect man who consists (of these persons united), his wife, himself and his offspring, thus (says the Veda), and (learned) brāhmaṇas propound this (maxim) likewise, the husband is declared one with the wife.[115]

If we go back to the Vedic period, we find the same glimpses, an address to the bride while departing after marriage from the house of her father —

> Go to the house, that thou mayst be the lady of the house. A mistress of the house thou shall direct the sacrificial rites.[116]

---

112. Hearn, *The Aryan Household*, p. 63.
113. Lee, *Historical Jurisprudence*, 189.
114. *Manu*, IX.28.
115. *Ibid.*, IX.45.
116. ṚV, X.85, 25-6 on *Vivāh Sūkta*. See Usha M. Apte, *The Sacrament of Marriage in Hindu Society*.

And as she enters her future home the bridegroom welcomes her with the following *mantra*:

> May thy joy increase here through progeny. Be thou ever awake here in this house for thy duty as householder with me, thy husband, do thou unite thy body and as thou advancest in age thou shall teach the sacrificial law.[117]

The Vedic ideal of married life well appears from the following text cited by Śabara Svāmī in his commentary on *Jaimini Sūtras*:[118]

> Let the wife unite with the husband in sharing fruits of sacrifice. Let both the husband and wife join in bearing the burden of performing the sacrifice. Let them knowingly abandon the enemies. Let them commence the brilliant and imperishable life in Heaven.

Dr. Dwarka Nath Mitter in his thesis on *Position of Women in Hindu Law* has pointedly drawn attention to certain portions of the aphorisms of the Sage Jaimini and Colebrooke has said that:

> The logic of the Mīmāṁsā is the logic of the law, the rule of interpretation of civil and religious ordinances and the value of the light which Jaimini throws upon the legal institutions of long forgotten past cannot be gainsaid.[119]

This eminent sage in the third *adhikaraṇa* of his sixth book says that the use of a noun in the masculine gender in a Śruti text does not exclude the feminine, and men and women have equal right to perform sacrifices. Jaimini has entirely repudiated that "men alone have the capacity to possess wealth", "that women are the objects of sale and purchase and on the same footing as goods and chattels and", "that the wealth which they may earn is the wealth of the man to whom they belong".

It is well settled that no Smṛti text can prevail against the Śruti and the latter explicitly recognises that not only does a woman

---

117. *ṚV*, X.85-27.

118. *Pūrva-Mīmāṁsa*, VI.1, 3, 21.

119. *Miscellaneous Essays*, Vol. I, p. 317.

possess the desire for obtaining the fruits of action, but she is also entitled to earn those fruits.

It is said:[120]

फलोत्साहाविशेषात्तु।
अर्थेन च समवेतत्वात्।

No distinction can be made between men and women in respect of their earnestness to perform sacrifices with the object of reaping the fruit and women too are possessed of wealth. Upon these aphorisms. Śabara Svāmī has commented:

> According to the Śruti whoever has the desire of obtaining the reward of performing sacrifices can perform them. Therefore, women having the desire for the fruits of the act of performing sacrifices must, on the strength of the Śruti and in entire disregard of the Smṛtis, be held capable of possessing wealth and performing sacrifices. At the time of marriage when the bride is presented to the bridegroom, (the father of the bride) is required to utter the words:
>
> She (the bride) should not be prevented (by the bridegroom) from acquiring wealth and from fulfilling her (legal) desires.
>
> Therefore, although the Smṛtis speak of the incapacity of the wife to possess wealth, that is very unjust because that is opposed to the Śruti. The theory of their want of independence can only be supported to the extent necessary to restrict them in their dealings with society (as member thereof).[121]

To go back to Vedas, it is not to be forgotten that the culture attained by the women in the Vedic age is illustrated by the hymns composed by Viśvavarā and Lopāmudrā which still form part of *Ṛgveda*.[122] The gracious presence of women like Maitreyī and Gārgī and their intellectualism and philosophic supermacy is like a shining diamond in the ornament.

---

120. *Pūrva-Mīmāṁsa*, VI.1, 3, 13-14.

121. Cited in Dwarka Nath Mitter, *Position of Women*, pp. 76-8.

122. *ṚV*, V.5.28.

Sages like Yama and Hārīta categorically state that in those olden days all the four orders of life were open to both the sexes and maidens underwent initiation and tied the sacre cord preparatory to a study of Vedas and women even recited the most sacred of prayers.

पुराकल्पे कुमारीणां मोञ्जीबन्धनमिष्यते ।
अध्यायणं च वेदानां सावित्रीवदनं तथा ।।

To quote once again Dwarka Nath Mitter:

> The sacrifices must be performed in company with the wife because the wealth belongs jointly to the husband and wife. The wife is entitled to the wealth earned by the husband and vice versa. Hence, a sacrifice must be performed by both jointly for if one of them is unwilling to perform it, the gift cannot be valid. Therefore, a gift of money, even though earned by the husband, is invalid if the wife's consent be not obtained. In case there happen to be two wives, the gift cannot be valid unless the consent of the second wife be also obtained.[123]

It is again said:

> The wife is entitled to the wealth given at the time of marriage and whatever is aquired by the husband is permitted to belong to her. Women are made to perform sacrifices on account of their wealth. Wealth alone is their strength. By virtue of walth which they possess they are entitled to govern (their husband's) household.

Dr. Satish Chander Banerji says that:

> The Vedic conception of the perfect man is a family of three and it is interesting to compare with this the Egyptian theory that without the child and family did not attain its normal form. The ancient Egyptians arranged even their gods in triads of father, mother and son.[125]

123. Dwarka Nath Mitter, *Position of Women*, pp. 86-7.

124. *Ibid.*, 79.

125. Dr. S.C. Bannerji, *The Women in Hindu Law*, a lecture delivered at Cawnpur. *ALJ*, Vol. XI.

So Hindus scriptures looked a woman from the angle of family and an immortal and purest constituent of Aryan family and as such a Hindu joint family system will throw some more light on the Aryan household which was considered a foundation of the then vibrant society which is disintegrating now.

The ancient Indian thinkers not only realised the importance of the family but also laid down elaborate rules for maintaining the purity and continuity of it. In *Ṛgveda* it is said:

> *dhartavrata āditya isira are matkarta rehasurivagaḥ* |[126]
>
> O, Ādityas, keep away me from sin as a woman giving birth to a child (removes it).

It is the family through which all aspirations of mankind are possible to be realised and as such Hindu scriptures gave it the highest place and Aryan household was considered the nerve centre of every pulsating activity of human life that all the other *āśrama*s were drawing their inherent energy from this *gṛhasthāśrama* and that is why the institution of family was compared with Air.

Manu says:

> As all living creatures subsist by receiving support from air, even so (the members of) all orders subsist by receiving support from the householder.
>
> Because men of the three (other) orders are daily supported by the householder with (gifts of) sacred knowledge and food, therefore, (the order of) householders is the most excellent order.[127]

Manu further says:

> Let him worship, according to the rule, the sages by the private recitation of the Veda, the gods by burnt oblations, the manes by funeral offerings (*śrāddha*), men by (gifts of) food and the *bhūta*s by the *bali* offering.[128]

---

126. *ṚV*, II.29.1.
127. *Manu*, III.77-8. See also *Vas*, VIII.14-16, *Viṣṇu*, LIX.27-8.
128. *Ibid.*, III.81, See *Yāj*, I.104.

Since the word 'family' connotes the idea of jointness so the word used 'Him' in the verse *Manu*, III.81 connotes both masculine and feminine. So the Hindu joint family is a socio-legal institution and is the result of socio-spiritual philosophy. Derrett has said:

> I believe that it is the most characteristic and fundamental part of the life of Hindus as honour to the law. So much so that even marriage must be considered subordinate to it in some degree.[129]

In these two *śloka*s, the family (the household) has been said to be:

> *gṛhastho brahmacārī ca vānaprasthotha bhikṣukaḥ* ।
> *catvāra āśrmaḥ prottaḥ gārhasthyam ulakaḥ* ।
> — *Mbh, Aiva.*, 45.13

> *āśrmanstulaya sarvan dhṛtana hurmaniṣinaḥ* ।
> *ekaśca tṛya rājen gṛhasthāśrama ekataḥ* ।
> *samikṣya tulya parthā kāmam svargam bharta* ।
> — *Śānti*, XII.12, 13

So the whole concept of Hindu household is cabined in the four walls of the sacred concept of *ṛṇa*s (debt), and these debts one owes to the *devas*, *ṛṣi*s and *pitṛ*s which can be discharged only through the institution of family. Manu in this regard says:

> When he has paid the three debts, let him apply his mind to (the attainment of) final liberation; he who seeks it without having paid (his debts) sinks downward.[130]

The emphasis on the secular and social aspect of family in the light of these debts which ultimately intended for the society and humanity, is laid in the *Bṛhadāraṇyaka Upaniṣad* which says:

> *atha traya vava luka mānuṣya lokaḥ*
> *pitṛloka devaloka iti soyammanuśloka*
> *putrenaiva jayye nanyena karmana karmana*
> *pitṛloko vidyaya devalokaḥ* ।। — *BṛUp*, 15.16

129. J.D.M. Derrett, *A Critique of Modern Hindu Law*, p. 52 , 1970.

130. *Manu*, VI.35.

So the Aryan household is a socio-legal entity within the ambit of socio-religious functions which the wife along with the husband discharges. The household is the testing ground of the application of the knowledge obtained by the individual in the first *āśrama* and transmit the same to the next generation to ensure the augmentation and preservation of social heritage and the importance of the social aspect finds its expression in religious ceremonies, social customs and legal ordinances so that this lowest unit of the society should always remain cohesive and rigid, never intending to disintegrate. This is why Manu prescribed five daily duties or obligations for the householder which have social spiritual and legal significance.

Dr. S.D. Sharma speaking on the obligation says that:

> The obligations to perform certain duties by a householder is an evidence of the fact that the Hindu Jurists acknowledge the obligation of all beings higher and lower, for their contribution in their well-being.[131]

Manu speaks of the five duties thus:

> In order to successively expiate (the offences committed by means) of all these (five) the great sages have prescribed for householders the daily (performance of the five) great sacrifices.[132]

So the five duties are

1. *Brahman-yajña*: The most exalted doctrine of the modern age is 'all men are equal'. This principle was put into practice by the Hindus in the family through the *Brahman-yajña*. In Upaniṣad it is said:

> *sarvam hyetad brahmayamātmā brahman so amātmā* ।
>
> All this is surely, *Brahman*, this *ātman* is *Brahman*, this *ātman*, such as it is the possessed of four quarters.[133]

---

131. Dr. S.D. Sharma, *The Hindu Joint Family and its Socio-Legal Implications*.

132. *Manu*, III.69 —*yasam kṛmeṇa sarvasam niṣkṛtārtha maharsidhiḥ pañca kalaspta irhamedhinam* ।

133. *Māṇḍūkyopaniṣad*, I.2.

This concept is taught in *brahmacarya āśrama* and practised as a duty in *gṛahasthāśrama*. This concept of *Brahma-yajña* is not only of spiritual significance but also it manifests to a great deal its social and legal connotations.

Yājñavalkya says:

> The *bali-karma*, the *śrāddha*, the *homa*, the study of Vedas and honouring the guests are the great sacrifices to the *bhūtas*, the *pitṛs*, the gods the *Brahman* and men.[134]

In *Mitākṣarā* this *śloka* is explained as follows:

> *Bali-karma* (animal sacrifice) is *bhūta-yajña* (sacrifice to the ghosts). The *śrāddha* (giving of food after pronouncing the word *svadhā*) is *pitṛ-yajña* (sacrifice of food to fire) is *deva-yajña* (sacrifice to gods), *svādhyāya* (study of the Vedas) is *Brahma-yajña*, the honouring the guest is *mānuṣya-yajña*, these five great *yajña*s should be daily performed, because they are permanent duties.

Thus, *Brahma-yajña* is the study of Vedas, i.e., the study of knowledge by its application in *gṛhasthāśrama* and its true application is manifacet as Vedas have taught every type of knowledge of the universe and every aspect of human life, i.e., *ātmā* and *ātman* which includes spiritual, religious, moral, social, economic, legal and humanitarian way of life to be lead which should be rewardful for himself and for the society.

The second daily duty is *pitṛ-yajña*.

*Pitṛ-yajña* is giving of food after pronouncing the word *svadhā*. Firstly, it has a moral significance. It is a token of gratitude to the ancestors who lived and worked for us. From this moral concept, also follows the socio-legal bearing. Offering of food should be looked purely from a social angle, i.e., to think of others who belong to the society in which we live. Legally speaking, the Hindu Law of inheritance is based on the principle of ancestor worship. Āpastamba says:

---

134. *Yaj*, I.102.

*putrabhāve yaḥ pratyasannas sapiṇḍaḥ* ।[135]

Under the Hindu Law when there is no son, the nearest *sapiṇḍa* was to inherit the property who also used it for the spiritual welfare of the deceased:

> *yo dhanamadita sa tasmai śrāddham kuryāt*
> *piṇḍam ca tripuruṣamdodyat* ।।[136]

Even the Judicial Committee of the Privy Council remarked, under the Mitākṣarā Law the right of inheritance arises from blood relationship or propenquity among the *gotrajas* the test to be applied to discover the preferential heir is the capacity to offer oblation.[137]

Manu speaks about it in this way:

> To three (ancestors) water must be offered, to three the funeral cake is given, the fourth (descendant is) the giver of these (oblations). The fifth has no connection (with them).
>
> Always to that (relative within three degrees) who is nearest to the (deceased) *sapiṇḍa* the estate shall belong; afterwards a *sakulya* shall be (the heir, then) the spiritual teacher or the pupil.[138]
>
> But the *sapiṇḍa* relationship ceases with the seventh person (in the ascending and descending lines) the *samanodaka* relationship when the (common) origin and the (existence of a common family) name are no (longer) known.[139]

Then comes the third duty of a householder to perform *deva-yajña*; (sacrifice to gods). It is *deva-yajña* which reminds the householder of the higher life, i.e., the divine life which can be achieved by the householder by inculcating honest means to perpetuate *artha* which means the material happiness earned by adopting avocations and

---

135. *ApaDS*, II.6.14.2.
136. Quoted by Aparārka, p. 746.
137. *Budha Singh* v. *Laltu Singh* 42 IA 208.
138. *Manu*, IX.186-7.
139. *Ibid.*, V.60.

then with that honestly earned wealth, to perform *deva-yajña*, is a divine act, comes out of divine actions.

Manu says:

> Let him without tiring, always offer sacrifices and perform works of charity with faith; for offerings and charitable works made with faith and with lawfully earned money, (procure) endless rewards.[140]
>
> Let him avoid (the acquisition of) wealth and (the gratification of his) desires, if they are opposed to the sacred law and even lawful acts which may cause pain in the future or offensive to men.[141]

Actually speaking *deva-yajña* speaks of *artha* which impliedly speaks of *dharma* even while seeking material happiness. The essence is spiritualness even in materialism and that is *deva-yajña*.

The fourth duty of *gṛhastha* is to perform *bhūta-yajña* (sacrifice to the ghosts). This obligation reminds the Hindu that all creatures are related to us in one way or the other. Soul is immortal and migratory. As man changes his dirty clothes and wears clean clothes, so soul changes the perished body and assumes a new body. But Śāstras say that sometimes the soul does not assume new body and remains wandering due to various reasons believed by the Hindus. Even these wandering souls have been kept in view.

Manu has put it in a different way when he says:

> Let him gently place on the ground (some food) for dogs, outcasts, *cāṇḍāla*s (*śvapāk*), those afflicted with disease that are punishments of former sins, crows and insects.[142]

Yājñavalkya says:

> From the remainder of the food to the gods, let him offer the *bhūta-bali*. Let him throw on the ground for dogs, *cāṇḍāla*s and the crows.[143]

---

140. *Manu*, IV.226.

141. *Ibid.*, IV.176.

142. *Ibid.*, III.92.

143. *Yāj*, I.103.

The specific words used by Manu are:

> Those aflicted with disease that are punishments of former sins is significant. It clearly means that even the sufferers of their past sins should also not be ignored. So this means universal humanism for all creations. Motvani observes that the fourth duty is to nature's element. The *bhūta*s are those invisible agencies that help lower form of life to grow.[144]

This invisible agency is a migratory soul still not assumed new body.

The last duty is *mānuṣya-yajña*.

Manu says:

> Having performed this *bali* offerings, he shall first feed his guest and, according to the rule, give alms to an ascetic (and) to a student.[145]

Yājñavalkya says:

> (In the event) of the guests of all classes (coming together, they all) ought to be given according to ability and precedence. A guest is not refused even in the evening. With speech, room, grass and water (hospitality is to be shown).[146]

Manu further says:

> But let him offer, in accordance with the rule, to a guest who has come (of his own accord) a seat and water, as well as food, garnished (with seasoning) according to his ability.
>
> Grass, room (for resting), water and fourthly a kind word; these (things) never fail in the houses of good men.[147]

It depicts the concept of humanity in general without any

---

144. Dr. S.D. Sharma, *The Hindu Joint Family — Its Socio-Legal Implications*.
145. *Manu*, III.94.
146. *Yāj*, I.107.
147. *Manu*, III.99-101.

distinction. *Atithi devo bhava* is the ideal of Hindu view of life. It depicts that Hindu scriptures ordained that one should live not only for his own sake but for the sake of humanity also. It is said:

> *bhañjate tetvagham pāpa ye pacantyalma-karanat* ।[148]

Annie Besant has thus said:

> The householder may be said to play the part of each caste in his household; for as a priest of the household, he is a brāhmaṇa; as protector of the household, he is a kṣatriya, as provider of the household he is a vaiśya, as servant of the household he is a śūdra. Everywhere in noble human we see service and the householder incarnates service.[149]

So it is the Hindu family where, through the ordinances envisaged in scriptures, we learn the first lesson in social welfare philosophy, social justice and an urge to also live for others. But the moot question that arises is as to why such duties were imposed on the *gṛhasthāśrama* and not on the other three other *āśramas*. The answer is simple. *Gṛhasthāśrama* is the feeder of the other *āśramas*. It is the blancing power of the society which should always remain in soothing postures. It is the real preserver of the cultural heritage and a source for advancement of civilised notions which we always cherish.

This five-fold duty is well discharged because a man is not alone. It is a unit where the wife is a equal sharer and participator, taking numerous responsibilities, social and religious. This is why she is called verily the half of the husband. Such is the case only due to the wife for which scriptures spoke of ideals for wife and gave her special status.

A mythological story illustrates the status of a woman in the family. There is a pilgrimage centre in Rajasthan called Puṣkar, where there is a temple of Lord Brahmā. The story goes that Lord Brahmā was to perform a *yajña*. The time was fixed. Goddess Sarasvatī, his consort, was also to participate as without her

---

148. *Bhagavad Gītā*, III.13.

149. Annie Besant, *Hindu Ideals* (Annual Convention Lectures Theosophical Society 1901).

presence, the *yajña* cannot be performed. *Muhūrtam* to perform *yajña* was fast approaching but Goddess Sarasvatī was not traceable. The exact time fixed approached. In order to perform the *yajña*, Lord Brahmā with his *māyā* produced another Sarasvatī just for the sake of performing *yajña*. While the *yajña* was in progress, she appeared. Being enraged, she cursed Lord Brahmā that nobody will worship you. Lord Brahmā related the whole episode by which goddess Sarasvatī calmed down and said that I cannot take back my words but give a relaxation that you will be worshipped only in this place and no where else. So Puṣkar is the only place where Lord Brahmā's temple is there and he is worshipped.

Though the story is mythological but still it clearly speaks of the status of a woman. Let us once again remember that if there is any difference between two Smṛtis, *Manu-smṛti* shall prevail and if there is difference between Smṛti and Śruti, Śruti shall prevail. Modern interpreters of the Śāstras tried to interpret the status of women then from the coloured vision of today, greatly influenced by the Western culture. She was holding the status as a sacred symbol of motherhood.

Now we turn to women and property or inheritance.

The impression is given that women are unfit to inherit. This impression is drawn from Baudhāyana and it gained some currency during the Sūtra period. Baudhāyana says:

> Women do not possess any independence and they are protected in all stages of their life.

A woman is never fit for independence. The Vedas declare

> Therefore, women are considered to be destitute of strength and of a portion.[150]

The Vedic text is:

निरिन्द्रियाह्यदायादाः स्त्रियोऽणृतन्,

There is a passage in *Taittirīya Saṁhitā*:

150. *BaudhDS*, II.2, 3, 44-6.

*tasmāt strīyo, nirindriya adayada api*
*papat puinsaḥ upasthitaram* ।[151]

Manu says:

> For women no (sacramental) rite (is performed) with sacred texts, thus the law is settled, women (who are) destitute of strength and destitute of (the knowledge of) Vedic texts (are as impure as) falsehood (itself), that is a fixed rule.

The above cited passages seem to be derogatory to women and have been generally taken to spell the inferiour status of women.[152]

If we critically look to these passages, we find they have no bearing on women's right to succession. Dr. Jolly has commented that this does not take into consideration numerous laudatory references to women found in the Smṛtis themselves, pointing out that they are partners in life with their husbands, that without them the life of a *gṛhastha* is incomplete and that they should be treated with the utmost kindness and affection.[153]

Professor George Bühler, in his translation of the word अदायादा: (*adāyādāḥ*) called it 'destitute of a portion'. Madhva explains the Vedic dictum as meaning only that the wife does not get a share of the *soma* beverage.[154] The *Vīramitrodaya* states, however, as the better opinion that the text refers only to those women whose right to inherit has not been expressly declared.[155] *Vidyāraṇya* commenting upon the institutes of Parāśara gives the following explanation:

> The term अदायादा: (*adāyādāḥ*) indicates that the wife is not entitled to a share in case of her retirement to a forest; the term अनिन्द्रिया: (*anindriyāḥ*) embodies the reason for the same. For it appears from the text that it refers to *soma* juice.[156]

Madhva's interpretation of it has been accepted as correct by

151. *TaitSam*, VI.5.82.
152. See *Manu*, V.148, IX.3, *Yāj*, I.85, *Nār*, XIII.31, *Visṇu*, XV.12.
153. Dr. Jolly's *Tagore Law Lectures on Hindu law,* 1883, pp.192-3.
154. *Mādhavīya*, 44.
155. *Vīramitrodaya*, Setlur's edn., pp. 406, 423, *Dāyabhāga*, XI, vi, 8, 11.
156. *Vīramitrodaya*, G.C. Sarkar's tr., p. 175.

Varadarāja, as well as M/s. West and Bühler, Dr. Jolly, Mr. Kane and by the Bombay High Court.[157]

Yājñavalkya says:

> The wife, the daughters also, the parents, brothers likewise and their sons, *gotrajas*, *bandhus*, the disciples and the fellow students; of these, on failure of the first, the next in order is the heir to the estate of one who departed for heaven leaving no issue. This rule extends to all classes.[158]

Dr. Umesh Chandra Pandey has translated it into Hindī as follows:[159]

> भाषा – जिसके पूर्वोक्त बारह प्रकार के पुत्रों में से किसी भी प्रकार का पुत्र न होवे उस पुत्रहीन के मर जाने पर पत्नी, पुत्रियां, माता-पिता, भाई, भाईयों के पुत्र, गोत्र में उत्पन्न व्यक्ति, बन्धु, शिष्य और ब्रह्मचारी में पहले-पहले के न होने पर उसके बाद वाले धन के अधिकारी होते हैं। यह विधि सभी वर्णों के लिये है।। १३५-१३६।।

Vijñeśvara's view was in favour of the general competency of women to inherit.[160] *Mitākṣarā*, the *Vyavahāra Mayūkha* and the *Vivād Cintāmaṇi* accept Vidyāraṇya's interpretation of अदायादा: and they do not refer to it at all. Aparārka treats the text as an अर्थवाद and not a विधि. The balance of authority, therefore, is not in favour of what is believed to be Baudhāyana's theory and it seems that there was a cloud cast over a woman's right to inherit property in the Sūtra period, it was but a passing cloud.[161]

So to have clear picture we should look to the commentary of Aparārka who has dealt it with reference to various other Smṛti authorities.

Bṛhaspati says:

> In the revealed texts (of the Vedas), in the traditional law (of the Smṛtis), and in popular usage, the wife is declared

---

157. Jolly, *Law and Custom*, p. 186, *Lallubhai* v. *Manku Varbai* [1878] 2 Bombay 388, 428. See *Maine's Hindu Law and Usage,* 1991, para 521.
158. *Yāj*, II.135, 136.
159. Tr. by Dr. Umesh Chander Pandey, *Yājñavalkya-smṛti*, p. 297.
160. *Mit*, II.S 1 and 5.
161. Dr. Satish Chander Bannerji, *The Woman in Hindu Law, ALJ*, Vol.XI.

> to be half the body (of her husband), equally sharing the outcome of good and evil acts of him whose wife is not dead, half his body survives. How should any one else take the property, while half his body lives?

Although kinsmen (*sakulyas*), such as parents, brothers, uterine (or otherwise) be living, the wife of him who dies without leaving male issue shall succeed to his share. A wife deceased before (her husband) takes away his consecrated fire (*agnihotra*), but if the husband dies before the wife, she takes his property, if she has been faithful to him. This is an eternal law.

After having received all the movable and immovable property, gold, silver, grain, liquids, wearing apparel, she shall cause his monthly, six monthly and annual *śrāddhas* to be performed.

Let her propitiate with funeral oblations and pious liberality her husband's paternal uncles, *gurus*, daughters, sisters and maternal uncles of the husband, also aged and helpless persons, guests and women (belonging to the family), should agnates (*sapiṇḍas*) or cognates (*bāndhavas*) or enemies injure the property, let the king inflict on them the punishment destined for thief.[162]

Bṛhaspati says:

> Where a man dies leaving no issue, nor wife, nor brother nor father, nor mother, all his *sapiṇḍas* shall divide the property in due shares.[163]
>
> To a father, the funeral ball (*piṇḍa*) and water oblation shall be offered by his son; in default of a son, the widow (succeeds), in her default, a uterine brother.[164]
>
> To men a daughter, like a son, springs from every limb of the body; how then any other mortal inherit the father's property while she lives?
>
> Equal (in caste to her father) and married to a man of the

---

162. *SBE*, Vol. 33 pp. 377, 378, *Bṛhaspati* ch. 25, 46-52.

163. *Ibid.*, pp. 379, *Ibid.*, *śloka*, 60.

164. *Ibid.*, p. 380, *Ibid.*, *śloka*, 65.

> same caste as her own, virtuous, habitually submissive, she shall inherit her father's property whether she may have been (expressly) appointed or not.[165]
>
> When a man dies without leaving either wife or male issue, the mother has to be considered as her son's heiress or a brother (may succeed) if she consents to it.[166]
>
> Should a kṣatriya, vaiśya or śūdra die without leaving male issue or wife or brother, their property shall be taken (as escheat) by the king, for he is the Lord of all.[167]

Let us now look to Viṣṇu what he says:

> The wealth of a man who dies without male issues goes to his wife, on failure to his daughter, to his father, to his mother, to his brother's son, to the *bandhus*, to *sakulyas*, to a fellow student, on failure of him it goes to the king with the exception of a brāhmaṇa's property.[168]

Devala gives another order of inheritance:

> Then the uterine brothers shall divide the wealth of the person dying sonless or daughters of the same caste, or the father who is living, or the brothers of the same caste or the mother or the wife, in order.

Nārada also speaks about the order of inheritance thus:

> If among several brothers one childless should die or become a religious ascetic, the others shall divide his property, excepting the *strīdhana*. They shall make provision for his women till they die in case they remain faithful to the bed of their husband. Should the women not (remain chaste) they must be cut off that allowance.[169]
>
> Unless it should be the property of a brāhmaṇa a king

165. *SBE*, Vol. 33, p. 378, *Bṛhaspati*, ch. 25 *śloka*, 56-7.

166. *Ibid.*, p. 379, *Ibid.*, *śloka*, 63.

167. *Ibid.*, p. 380, *Ibid.*, *śloka*, 67.

168. *Ibid.*, Vol. 7, p. 68, *Viṣṇu*, ch. 17, *śloka*, 4-13.

169. *Ibid.*, Vol. 33, pp. 195, 196, *Nārada*, ch. 13, *śloka*, 25, 26.

> devoted to duty must allot a maintenance to his women. Thus has the law of inheritance been declared.[170]

> On failure of a son, the daughter (succeeds) because she continues the lineage just like (a son); both a son and a daughter continue the lineage of their father.[171]

> On failure of daughters, the *sakulyas* (are to succeed) and (after them) the *bāndhavas*; next a member of the same caste. In default of all that (wealth) goes to the king, unless it should be the property of brāhmaṇa.[172]

By the texts of Āpastamba beginning with 'by marriage arises companionship' it is laid down that marriage itself creates the ownership of the wife in the husband's wealth. It should be understood in the case of daughters, ownership in the father's wealth arises by birth itself as in the case of a son.[173]

Aparārka has commented on Kātyāyana thus:

> On failure of a son, the father shall take the wealth of a divided (coparcener); or the brother or the mother or his father's mother in order.

Thus, the term 'on failure of a son' is for the purpose of illustration. By that it is to be understood that it is on failure of wife and daughter. The mother should be known as the inheritor of the wealth or the brother with her permission. On failure of all these the deceased's grandmother, after the daughter and daughter's son.[174]

About the order of inheritance, Manu speaks thus:

> To three (ancestors) water must be offered, to three the funeral cake is given, the fourth (descendant is) the giver of these (oblations), the fifth has no connection (with them).

170. *SBE*, Vol. 33, p. 203, *Nārada*, ch. 13, *śloka*, 52.

171. *Ibid.*, p. 201, *Ibid.*, *śloka*, 50.

172. *Ibid.*, p. 202, *Ibid.*, *śloka*, 51.

173. *Madras Law Journal*, Vol. XXI, p. 317.

174. *Ibid.*, p. 315.

Always to that (relative within three degrees) who is nearest to the (deceased) *sapiṇḍa* the estate shall belong, afterwards a *sakulya* shall be (the heir, then) the spiritual teacher or the pupil.

But on failure of all (heirs) brāhmaṇas (shall) share the estate (who are) versed in the three Vedas, pure and self-controlled; thus the law is not violated.[175]

The property of a brāhmaṇa must never be taken by the king, that is a settled rule, but (the property of men) of other castes the king may take on failure of all (heirs).[176]

But to the maiden (sisters) the brothers shall severally give (portions) out of their shares, each out of his share one-fourth part; those who refuse to give (it) will become outcasts.[177]

A son is even (as) oneself, (such) a daughter is equal to a son; how can another (heir) take the estate while such (an appointed daughter who is even) oneself lives?

But whatever may be the separate property of the mother, that is the share of the unmarried daughter alone; and the son of an (appointed) daughter shall take the whole estate of his (maternal grandfather) who leaves no son.[178]

He who takes care of his deceased brother's estate and of his widow, shall after raising up a son for his brother, give that property even to that (son).[179]

A mother shall obtain the inheritance of a son (who dies) without leaving issue, and if the mother be dead, the paternal grandmother shall take the estate.[180]

175. *Manu*, IX.186-8.
176. *Ibid.*, IX.189.
177. *Ibid.*, IX.118.
178. *Ibid.*, IX.130-1.
179. *Ibid.*, IX.146.
180. *Ibid.*, IX.217.

Aparārka comments while referring to the *śloka*s of Manu thus:

Firstly, he refers to *niyoga* whereby two views appear. Manu in chapter IX.145, 146 about *niyoga* and the order of inheritance but in chapter IX.143, 144, 147 he speaks to have a son by another through mere lust is not an heir. Thus, chastity for the widow is still kept in tact though *niyoga* is allowed under religious necessity and not as an act of adultery. This is why it is said that:

> The wife who is sonless and, being chaste, protects the bed of her lord (she) alone shall offer the *piṇḍa* and take the entire share of his wealth.[181]

So Aparārka's commentary on Yājñavalkya, punctuated with the verses contained in other Smṛtis speaks of two things:

1. That all *smṛtikāra*s speak of son as an heir but have not ignored the rights of women as a daughter, wife, mother or a widow. It speaks of the order of inheritance keeping in view the moral, social and economic aspects that covered the society then. Women were never ignored.
2. That the view of Yājñavalkya is that the ownership on the death of the (previous) owner of the wealth exists (already) in the wife and daughters and need not be created newly. However, it indicates that the inheritance of a wife or daughter is basically for sustenance and necessity for performance of religious duties cast on her and for daughter specifically to meet the marriage expenses.

However, two *śloka*s of Yājñavalkya throw further light on the rights of women, coupled with conditionalities:

> The *aurasa* and *kṣetraja* sons of these, however, take shares, if free from defects; the daughters also should be maintained until they are disposed off in marriage.
>
> Their sonless wives, conducting themselves alright must be supported; but such as one unchaste should be expelled, as also those who are hostile.[182]

181. *SBE*, Vol.2, p. 302, *GauDS*, ch. XXVIII.21-22, *Bṛhaspati*, ch. 25, p. 65.
182. *Yāj*, II.141-2.

Now we should proceed to the property of a woman called *strīdhana* which indicates that a woman was never without a property and that property was well protected. The texts relating to *strīdhana* are failry adequate and clear. The principle definition is contained in *Manu-smṛti*:

> What (was given) before the (Nuptial) fire, what (was given) on the bridal procession, what was given in token of love and what was received from her brother, mother or father, that is called the six-fold property of a woman.
>
> (such property) as well as a gift subsequent and what was given (to her) by her affectionate husband, shall go to her offsprings (even) if she dies in the lifetime of her husband.[183]

Viṣṇu and Yājñavalkya give a similar enumeration but add to the list the compensation which is given to a superseded wife.

Yājñavalkya says:

> What is given to a woman by her father, mother, husband or brother or received by her before her matrimonial fire or presented to her on her supersession, is denominated *strīdhana*.
>
> What is given to a woman by her relatives, *śulka* likewise and *anvadhiya*, the relatives take these if she dies without issue.[184]

**भाषा — पिता, माता, पति और भाई द्वारा दिया गया धन, विवाह में अग्नि के निकट मिला हुआ धन, आधिवेदनिक (दूसरा विवाह करते समय पति द्वारा पहली स्त्री के सन्तोष के लिये प्रदत्त) धन इत्यादि स्त्रीधन कहे गये हैं ।। १४३ ।।**

**भाषा — स्त्री के मातृपक्ष एवं पितृपक्ष के बन्धुओं द्वारा दिया गया धन, शुल्क (जो धन लेकर कन्या दी जाय), और अन्वाधेयक (विवाह के बाद पतिकुल या पितृकुल से प्राप्त) धन भी स्त्रीधन कहलाता है। स्त्री के बिना सन्तान (पुत्री, नाती, नाती के पुत्र आदि) मर जाने पर पति आदि बान्धव स्त्रीधन ग्रहण करते हैं ।। १४४ ।।**[185]

---

183. *Manu*, IX.194-5.

184. *Yāj*, II.143-44, see also *Viṣṇu*, XVII.18.

185. Dr. Umesh Chander Pandey's *Yājñavalkya-smṛti*, II.143-4.

Vijñeśvara who is the most important commentator on any Smṛti, declares in language, which is absolutely unambiguous that woman may acquire property by the very same eight modes which are open to a man and what she inherits is as much her *strīdhana* as the gift before the nuptial fire the ornaments on her person.[186] His explanation of the word च (*ca*) used in the verse means, 'etc.', which has been translated as 'इत्यादि' (*ityādi*) which he explained as property which she may have acquired by inheritance, purchase, partition, seizure, and finding.

Aparāka's commentary, reffering to Kātyāyana, Manu and Vyasa regarding *strīdhana* is:

> What is given to women at the time of their marriage before the sacred fire, is denominated by the sages their property *adhyagnikṛta*, i.e., given before the matrimonial fire. What a woman receives while she is led to the house of her husband, is called *adhyavahanikam* and it is (another kind of) property of a woman.[187]
>
> What a woman either after marriage or before it, either in the mansion of her husband and that which is given in return to her humble salutations, is called *pada vandinika* or *lāvaṇyarjita*, i.e., wealth gained by salutation or loveliness.[188]
>
> What a woman either after marriage or before it, either in the mansion of her husband or of her father, receives from her brothers or her parents, is called a gift from the affectionate kindred.[189]
>
> The gift by the affectionate kindred having by them (the donors) been presented in order that the woman possessing may live well, is declared by law to be her absolute property.[190]

---

186. *Mit*, II.IX.2.
187. Colebrooke's translation of Kātyāyana, Vol. II, pp. 585-6, *śloka*s, 464-6.
188. Aparārka's comment on above, MLJ, Vol.XXI, p. 428.
189. Colebrooke Vol.II, p. 594, *śloka*, 475.
190. *Ibid.*, p. 594, *śloka*, 475.

> Neither the husband nor the father nor the son nor the brothers are competent either in the taking or giving of a woman's wealth. If any among these appropriates by force a woman's wealth, he is to be made to repay it with interest and shall also be punished.[191]

Aparārka cites Vyāsa thus:

> That which is obtained by a maiden on the occasion of marriage, or after marriage, from the house of father and brother is called *saṇḍika*, i.e., from affectionate kindred.[192]

Nārada says:

> What has been given to a wife by her loving husband, that she may spend or give away as she likes, even after his death excepting immovables.[193]

Aparārka along with other commentators like Kamalākara, Bālambhaṭṭa, Nanda Paṇḍita, Rudra Deva and Vācaspati Miśra agree that the word *strīdhana* should bear its etymological and not a technical sense.

However, there is unanimity of views of all *smṛtikāra*s and their commentators about the concept of *strīdhana* and its legal existence and at no time, whether as a maiden, wife or widow has the woman been denied the use of her property as an absolute owner (apart from the husband's nominant position in respect of certain type of *strīdhana*).[194]

But the *smṛtikāra*s have differed from each other as to what items of property constitute her *strīdhana*. Manu recognised *strīdhana* and enumerates six kinds of *strīdhana* (IX.194), Viṣṇu enumerates four kinds of *strīdhana* (XVII.18), Kātyāyana speaks of six kinds of *strīdhana* but different as those enumerated by Manu (cited by Dāyabhāga, IV.1,19). Yājñavalkya gives a complete picture in (*Yāj*, II.143). He used the word 'and the like' which has been

191. Colebrooke Vol.II, p. 594, *śloka*, 475, *Manu*, VIII.29, IX.200.
192. As cited by Aparārka see *MLJ* (Journal), p. 428.
193. *Nārada*, I *śloka*, 38, *SBE*, Vol. 33, p. 50.
194. *Mitākṣarā*, II.9, 2.

enlarged by Vijñeśvara. Gautama explicitly recognised woman's right to hold and dispose of property (*GauDS*, XXVIII.24-6). However, Gooroodas Bannerji tried to resolve this difficulty saying:

> The difficulties besetting an enquiry into the question what constitutes *strīdhana*, arise from the fact that majority of sages and commentators give neither an exact definition of *strīdhana*, nor an exhaustive enumeration, and if the *Mitākṣarā* gives a simple and intellegible definition, that definition has been qualified and restricted in its application by our Courts, in consequence of its disagreement with the view of other authorities.[196]

Vijñeśvara's enlargement of the meaning of *strīdhana* including properties obtained by inheritance, purchase, partition, seizure and finding, was not accepted by the Privy Council in spite of the fact that it spoke in *Collectore of Madura* v. *Mootoo Ramalinga*[196] that the duty of a European Judge who is under the obligation to administer Hindu Law, is not so much to enquire whether a disputed doctrine is fairly deductible from the earliest authorities, as to ascertain whether it has been received by the particular school which governs the district with which he has to deal, and has been sanctioned by usage.

When the question, however, came before the Privy Council their Lordships could not rid their minds of certain preconceived notions. Western systems of Jurisprudence did regard sex as a disqualification and a married woman was not as a rule recognised to have dominion in her property. For English Judges it was difficult to conceive that an older system of Hindu Law had advocated a more Catholic doctrine and the Privy Council did not approve or was not prepared to accept the views propounded by Vijñeśvara and went into enquiry and from conflicting opinions of various scholars, came to a conclusion unhesitatingly that under the law of Mitākṣarā a widow's as well as a daughter's estate was but limited

---

195. Gooroodas Bannerjee, *Hindu Law of Marriage & Stidhana*, 3rd edn. p. 280.

196. 12 MIA 397.

and restricted and could not rightly be described a *strīdhana.*[197]

In another set of cases it was held that property inherited by female from females is also not *strīdhana.*[198] However, this law propounded by the Privy Council lacks legality under Bombay School where the property inherited by a woman from females is her *strīdhana.*[199]

Dr. Satish Chandra Bannerjee has said that there can be no doubt that the European Judges have transgressed their duty and deliberately overruled the Mitākṣarā. Sage Jaimini suggests no distinction between inherited and other property in the hands of a woman and it seems that it was Jimūtavāhana and not Vijñeśvara who modified the old law and the European Judges of India became familiar with the Bengal School of Hindu Law and hence this perverted decisions.

So much so that even the eminent Indian Judges followed suit blindly.[200] It is only in Madras which resisted this Judicial influence.[201]

It is sheer the influence of Nīlakaṇṭha of early *paṇḍit*s of Sir Michael Wertropp and Sri Raymond West that in Bombay the rights of female heirs have not been denied.

The concept of 'Women's right to limited estate' is not the law

---

197. *Thakoor Deybee* v. *Baluk Ram* [1866] 11 MIA 140; *Bhagwandeen* v. *Maya Baee* [1867] 11 MIA 487; *Chotay Lall* v. *Chunnoo Lalla* ILR 4 CAI 744 PC.

198. *Sheo Shankar* v. *Debi Sahai* ILR 25 All 468 PC; *Sheo Pratap* v. *Allahabad Bank* [1903] 30 IA 209.

199. *Kasserby* v. *Hunsraj* [1906] 30 Bom 431, *Gangadhar* v. *Chandrabhagabi* [1893] 17 Bom 690 (FB).

200. 1. *Jagat Narain* v. *Sheo Das* ILR 5 All 311.
 2. *Gauri* v. *Rukko* ILR 3 All 45.
 3. *Nanhi* v. *Gausi* ILR 28 All 187.
 4. *Jagan Nath* v. *Champa* ILR 28 All 307.
 5. *Koomud* v. *Seetha Kanth* WR, Sp No. FB 75.
 6. *Bhagwan* v. *Warubai* ILR 32 Bom 300, 312 (Per Chandavarkar J.).

201. 1. *Kutti Ammal* v. *Bada Kisina* 8 Mad HC 88.
 2. *Lakshamanammal* v. *Tiru Vengada* ILR 5 Mad 241.

propounded by the Smṛtis. It is the judiciary not knowing the ancient Hindu Law. Rather the concept of woman's property as propounded by the sages has been defamed, defiled and disfigured to ultimately destroy it. These judicial verdicts did not consider even for a moment that Hindu Jurisprudence has its foundation in *dharma* and those concepts based on *dharma* have been more misunderstood by Western Jurists. *Dharma* in Hindu Jurisprudence means righteous code of conduct, obligations, law and Justice by which all the members of a family, caste or class are bound together and were called *kula dharmāḥ sanātanaḥ*.

In *Bhagavad Gītā* it is said:

*kulakṣaye praṇaśyanti*
*kuladharmāḥ sanātanāḥ*
*dharme naṣṭe kulaṁ kṛtsnam*
*adharmo 'bhibhavaty uta*[202]

It is a pity that Hindus were attacked on two fronts. The Indians were made to accept of Macaulay's Minute on education in which all Indian thoughts in all ages were dismissed as 'dotages of Brāhmaṇical Superstition' and thus there was complete switch over to the exclusive study of Western thought. The system of education was designed to create, in the words of Macaulay, a class of people Indian in blood and colour but English in tastes, in opinions, in morals and in intellect. It did not succeed in making Indians Englishmen but completely succeeded in persuading Indians that they were an uncivilised people redeemed by the British. This was the first time that the Indian mind was thrown off its balance.[203] Every Western thinker thought about non-European concepts as mere 'dotages of Brāhmaṇical Superstition' and that the intellectual achievements, discipline, system of Jurisprudence or philosophy which is not European origin is useless so much so that even Marx and Engels, the founders of the philosophy of dialectical materialism, while recognising the idealist and materialist schools of Western philosophy, completely ignored Indian philosophy which

202. *Bhagavata Gītā*, I.40.

203. D.S. Sharma, "India Meets the West" quoted in D. Mackenzie Brown, *Indian Political Thought*.

holds that both matter and spirit are primary entities. This Western imperialist mentality is manifest from the remarks of Mr. Alan Gladhill in his *Republic of India* in which he quotes the remarks of Anglo-Indian Jurist by the name of Cowell:

> It is a record of experiments made by foreign rulers to govern alien races in a strange land, to adopt European institutions to Oriental habits of life and to make definite laws supreme among peoples who had always associated government with arbitrary and uncontrolled authority.[204]

The second attack on Indians came from Judiciary, where the English Judges, so far as India is concerned, not interpreted law but made law and one such derogative law is 'the limited estate of a woman', which was later on statutorily confirmed under the Hindu Women's Right to Property Act, 1937. Thus, this enactment deformed the Hindu Law when woman is never considered as playmate as European concept is but she is worshipped as mother and how mother can starve. How law can be based on *adharma* as to starve mother is *adharma*. Perhaps the English Judges forgot:

> Judges should be banished if they perpetrate injustice if they live on bribery and if they betray the confidence reposed in them.[205]

## Widow and satī

We find some desultory observations regarding Hindu widow, drawing conclusions that the condition of widow under religious ordinances was miserable and that there was a legal sanction for the self-immolation of a widow.

We find a mention in *Viṣṇu-smṛti* and in the code of Bṛhaspati. It is said:

> One of the duties of a woman is to preserve her chastity (*brahamacaryam*) after the death of her husband or to

204. A. Gledhill, *The Republic of India*, 2nd edn., 1964. H. Cowell, *History of the Constituion of the Courts and Legislative Authorities in India* TLL, 1872.

205. *Bṛhaspati-smṛti*, I.108, also I.98, *Kātyāyana*, 78.

ascend the funeral pile.[206]

> A wife is considered half the body of her husband, equally sharing the results of his good or wicked deeds, whether she ascends the pile after him, or chooses to survive him leading a virtuous life, she protects the welfare of her husband.[207]

To have legal appreciation of this concept, firstly we have to look to the chronology of the Hindu scriptures. Though it is difficult to locate exactly the period covered by these scriptures but still as a rough estimate the entire Hindu literature covers a periods of 6000 years. So Vedas can be during 4000 BC. The period of Dharma-sūtras begins from 700 BC. The age of the Smṛtis begins with Manu who is assigned to the second century BC.

Yājñavalkya is assigned to the first century AD, Viṣṇu lived in fourth century AD, Nārada and Bṛhaspati belong to sixth century AD, Medātithi, the commentator is assigned to the ninth century AD, Mitākṣarā, the eleventh century AD, Jimūtavāhana the twelfth century AD. The period of *Digest*, the fifteenth century AD, Nanda Paṇḍita, between sixteenth and seventeenth century, Dharmasindhu the eighteenth century. This being so the reference to self-immolation by the widow is during the period fourth to sixth centuries AD.

So we have to look to the Vedic period and the Dharma-sūtra period, *Manu-smṛti* and *Yājñavalkya-smṛti* which are earlier in time to Viṣṇu and Bṛhaspati. It is said that this custom of the self-immolation of a widow was in existence even in very earlier periods among tribesmen and races that had not imbibed Vedic culture. No text from any Śruti, except one in the *Atharvaveda*, or even Smṛti; before the fifth century AD sanctions this right.[208] But it is unbelievable as remarriage of a widow is permitted. It is said that:

> when a woman has had one husband before, and gets another, if they present *aja pañcaudana* offering, they shall

206. *Viṣṇu*, XXV.14.

207. *Bṛhaspati*, XXIV.11.

208. Shakuntla Rao Shastri, *Women in the Sacred Laws,* 1959, p. 119.

> not be separated. A second husband dwells in the same world with his rewedded wife if he offers the *aja pañcaudana*.[209]

If we look to *Gautama's Dharma-sūtra*, impliedly it speaks non-existence of the custom of self-immolation of a widow. We find in Gautama:

> A woman whose husband is dead, and who desires offspring (may bear a son) to her brother-in-law. Let her obtain the permission of her *guru*s and on failure of a brother-in-law (she may obtain offspring) by (cohabiting with) a *sapiṇḍa*, a *sagotra*, a *samāna pravara*, or one who belongs to the same caste.[210]

Gautama ordains the remarriage of a widow immediately after the death of her husband and no interval is enjoined but for a widow to have an offspring, it is not lust but necessity. Gautama thus declares:

> Some (declare) that she shall cohabit with nobody but a brother-in-law and not bear more than two sons.[211]

Now we turn to the *Dharam-sūtra of Baudhāyana* he says:

> A widow shall avoid during a year the use of honey, meat, spirituous liquor, and salt and sleep on the ground.[212]

He further says referring to Maudgalya:

> That she shall do so for six months. After the expiry of that time she may, with the permission of her *guru*s, bear a son to her brother-in-law, in case she has no son.

Here the stress is on two points. Firstly, that she is restricted for a specific period and ordained not to take lust breeding food and then she can have *niyoga*. Thus, the custom of self-immolation for a widow has no whisper at all.

---

209. *ṚV*, IX.5, 27, 28, (Muir).
210. *GauDS*, XVIII.4-6.
211. *Ibid.*, XVIII.7-8.
212. *BaudhDS*, II.2, 4, 7.

Āpastamba flourished when Buddhism was at its zenith and asceticism was the order of the day and good conduct and morals were expected from the society. So Āpastamba has to be understood in the light of the state of society then prevailing as man is not made for law but it is law that is made for man and such law when made is to be obeyed by a man. Āpastamba laid much stress on chastity. He gives preference to facing the punishment or reward in the next world rather than obtaining a son through the custom of *niyoga*.[213]

The next *sūtrakāra* is Vasiṣṭha. Vasiṣṭha speaks two types of *punarbhu*, and one of them is:

> She is called remarried who leaving an impotent, outcast, or mad husband, or after the death of her husband, takes another lord.[214]

Vasiṣṭha says that:

> A widow shall sleep on the ground for six months after the loss of her husband practising religious bows and abstaining from pungent condiments and salt. After the completion of six months she shall bathe and offer a funeral oblation to her husband. Then her father or brother shall assemble the *gurus* who taught or sacrificed for the deceased and his relatives, and shall appoint her to raise issue to her deceased husband but a mad, ill-conducted or diseased or aged widow is forbiddden to be appointed.[215]

He further says:

> The wife of an emigrant could marry after a lapse of five years. If she were unwilling to do so, she had to live like a widow.[216]

At another place he says:

> Exempted from taxes are the widow who return to their

213. *ĀpasDS*, II.10, 27, 7.

214. *VasDS*, XVII.20.

215. *Ibid.*, XVII.55-8.

216. *Ibid.*, XVII.75-7.

> former family, unmarried maidens and the wives of servants.[217]

If we read between the lines, three things are quite clear:

1. A widow can have a son by *niyoga*.
2. If so desires a widow can remarry.
3. If not she has to lead life of chastity.

But we cannot even smell a litle about the self-immolation of a widow. Even Kauṭilya recognises the remarriage of widows and the system of *niyoga*. But he puts a waiting period of seven months and also other conditions, though gives preference to a life of chastity.

He says:

> On the death of her husband a woman desirous of leading a pious life shall at once receive not only her endowment and jewellery but also the balance of *śulka* due to her. If after obtaining these two things, she remarries another, she shall be compelled to pay them back together with interest (on their value). If she is so desirous of a second marriage, she shall be given, on the occasion of her remarriage, whatever either her father-in-law or her husband or both had given to her. But if a widow marries any man other than of her father-in-law's selection, she shall forfeit whatever has been given to her by her father-in-law and her deceased husband.[218]

Kauṭilya furthers says:

> A widow remarrying shall forfeit what was given to her (late) husband. She shall use it if desirous of a pious life.

So Kauṭilya speaks of:

1. She is to lead a pious life.
2. She can have remarriage.

---

217. *VasDS*, XIX.24.

218. R.P. Kangle, *Kauṭilya Arthasasthra*, Bk III, ch. II, verse 19-23, 26-7.

3. She can have a son by *niyoga* if she has no son.

4. But the marriage is as per selection of father-in-law failing adverse consequences.

5. It is the will of the widow which shall prevail.

Now we look to *Manu-smṛti*. Manu's views on *niyoga* and remarriage of a widow are as below:

> At her pleasure let her emaciate her body (living on) pure flowers, roots and fruits; but she must never even mention the name of another man after her husband has died.[219]

> A virtuous wife who after the death of her husband constantly remains chaste, reaches heaven, though she have no son, just like those chaste men.[220]

> But a woman who from a desire to have offspring violates her duty towards her (deceased) husband, brings on herself disgrace in this world and loses her place with her husband (in heaven).[221]

The above verses speak about the chastity of a widow which must be kept sacred and from spiritual point of view it is impressed upon the widow to be chaste as their chastity will be the cause of attaining heaven even if she is sonless.

However, Manu in chapter IX speaks thus:

> By twice born men a widow must not be appointed to (co-habit with) any other (than her husband) for they who appoint (her) to another (man) will violate the eternal law.[222]

In the sacred texts which refer to marriage the appointment (of widows) is nowhere mentioned, nor is the remarriage of widows prescribed in the rules concerning marriage.[223]

---

219. *Manu*, V.157. *VasDS*, XVII.55-8, *BaudhDS*,II.2.4.7.
220. *Ibid.*, V.160
221. *Ibid.*, V.161.
222. *Ibid.*, IX.64.
223. *Ibid.*, IX.65.

He who takes care of his deceased brother's estate and of his widow, shall after raising up a (son) for his brother, give that property even to that son.[224]

If a woman (duly) appointed bears a son to her brother-in-law or to another (*sapiṇḍa*), that (son, if he is) begotton through desire, they declare (to be) incapable of inheriting and to be produced in vain.[225]

(If the widow) of (a man) who died without leaving issue, raises up to him a son, by a member of the family (*sagotra*), she shall deliver to that (son) the whole property which belonged to the (deceased).[226]

From the time of Manu, we find that utmost stress is laid on the chastity of a woman and thus even *niyoga* out of lust is forbidden. Marriage of a widow is not prescribed and rather she has been advised to remain chaste and true to her deceased husband. So even Manu does not subscribe to the concept of self-immolation of a widow.

Yājñavalkya and Parāśara who are also considered authorities on Hindu Law, also speak about widow:

Yajñavalkya says:

The younger brother of the husband, a *sapiṇḍa* or a *sagotra* being anointed with clarified butter, and with the permission of the *guru*, may go to sonless widow, when in season, with the desire of raising a son.[227]

She who does not go to another, whether her husband be alive or dead, obtains glory and becomes happy with Umā.[228]

Deprived of her husband, she should not reside apart from her father, mother, son or brother, from her mother-in-law

224. *Manu*, IX.146.

225. *Ibid.*, IX.147.

226. *Ibid.*, IX.190.

227. *Yāj*, I.68.

228. *Ibid.*, I.75.

> or father-in-law, or from her old maternal uncles, otherwise she becomes infamous.

पितृमातृसुतभ्रातृश्वश्रूश्वशुरमातुलैः ।
हीना न स्याद्विना भर्त्रा गर्हणीयाऽन्यथा भवेत्।। ८६ ।।[229]

Being *Yājñavalkya-smṛti* occupies an authoritative place in Hindu Law and *Mitākṣarā* by Vijñeśvara is also an authority on the comments on *Yājñavalkya-smṛti*, we have to study these verses critically.

There is a controversy between Viśvarūpa and Vijñeśvara on *śloka* I.68 of *Yājñavalkya-smṛti*. Vijñeśvara says that this verse relates to a widow whereas Viśvarūpa who was the teacher of Vijñeśvara says that this verse relates to betrothed girls (losing their would be husbands). But verse I.75 has made it very clear, as per *Mitākṣarā*, that chastity of a woman, wife or widow, brings her glory in this world and due to her holiness plays with (the goddess) Umā.

In verse I.86, Vijñeśvara in *Mitākṣarā* says that this is (the rule in case the widow wishes to pass her life) as a *brahmacārī* or celibate, because it is ordained in the *Viṣṇu-smṛti*, XXV.14, where Viṣṇu has said that there is great virtue in *anvarohna* (or self-immolation along with the deceased husband). Vyasa has shown the same thing in the form of the parable of the she-pigeon:

> Devoted to her husband she entered the raging fire, and thereafter she obtained her (dead) lord who was adorned with a variegated bracelet. Then afterwards the bird went in company with his wife to heaven and enjoyed it with her being honoured with all acts of service.[230]

To the same effect Śaṅkha and Aṅgirasa:

> So who follows her husband to another world, shall dwell in a region of joy for so many years as there are hairs on the human body, or thirtyfive millions.

---

229. *Yāj*, I.86.

230. *Vedavyasa-smṛti*, Ananda Asrama edn., p. 362.

To the same effect are Hārīta and Aṅgirasa:

> She who follows her husband (to death) by *anugamana* purifies three families, i.e., of her father, of her mother and of her husband where she is given.[231]

But these texts are not in consonance with the Vedic rule that *anugamana* is improper as it is opposed to the Śruti (Veda). The text "Desirous of heaven he should not die before the end of his natural life", means that one, who wishes to attain *mokṣa* (final emancipation) should not cut off the natural span of his life, with the object of getting heaven. Because so long as life remains, it is possible to attain *mokṣa* by reaching Brahmā who is ever lasting and eternal bliss, by removing mental impurities, through the performance of obligatory (*nitya*) and occasional duties and by self-knowledge through the hearing of scriptures pondering over the meaning and realising their sense by meditation.

Now we have to critically see what Viṣṇu and Bṛhaspati have said:

It will be seen that, though both Viṣṇu and Bṛhaspati allow a widow to lead a life of virtue and ascetioism, yet they have prescribed an alternative course of action also, that she may ascend the pile after him. It is a suggestive alternative and not an ordinance which these sages suggested thinking the widow may not keep her chastity intact and thus bring defame to the families.

Unfortunately, these views of Viṣṇu and Bṛhaspati have been misinterpreted by the Western scholars claim to have intense knowledge of Hindu Law. Sir Henry Maine has examined this institution and sought to trace its origin to the brāhmaṇa's dislike of enjoyment of property by women.[232]

This view of Sir Henry Maine appears to be out of time with the reality. Indian Jurispurdence was dismissed by Macaulay in the heyday of imperialism as 'dotage of Brāhmaṇical superstition'[233]

---

231. See *Parāśara Saṁhitā*, Prāyaścitta Kāṇḍam, Verse 30, 31. Also see Verse 32 & 33.

232. Sir Henry Maine, *Early Institutions*, p. 335.

233. Lord Macaulay, *Minute on English Education in India*, 1835.

and by Maine as 'an immense apparatus of cruel absurdities'. No doubt, the British Government at the instance of Raja Rammohun Roy and Pandit Ishwar Chander Vidyasagar brought two enactments Reg. XVII of 1829 and Act XV of 1856. By the Reg. of 1829, *satī* was abolished and by the Act of 1856 a statutory sanction was given to the remarriage of Hindu widows.

But the pertinent question is, whether there was the concept or custom of *anumaraṇa* ordained by Law? Medhātithi did not look upon *anumaraṇa* or the self-immolation of widows as a *dharma* or meritorious act at all and tolerated it only as a transgression in times of distress. Even this transgression in times of distress has been strongly objected to by Medhātithi while commenting on *Manu*, V.157.

However, the view of Sir Henry Maine is refutable for the simple fact that the ideal womanhood of India had unstinted and orthodox regard for chastity than death. For them the prospects of dishonour are worst than death as dishonour snatches away the idealism in woman. So the stray incidents of self-immolation can be traced to the natural devotion of the Hindu wife to the husband in particular and to the family in general. Instances have come where the wife could not bear the death of her husband and is so struck down by the bereavement that she also expired more or less simultaneously with her husband. It is no denial of fact and rather is conceivable that some women, out of pregnancy of their griefs and maddened by the despair in their souls, might have thrown themselves upon the funeral pyres of those whose demise had left their homes and hearts desolate. Even stray cases of such deaths do appear where women have committed suicide as found their lives unbearable to live after the death of their husbands. There is no authority in the scriptures to show that a woman, on the death of her husband, under compulsion or as a result of carrying out the tyrannical wishes of someone related to her, burnt herself on the funeral pyre of the deceased husband. It clearly appears that the Western Jurists, as told by the Christian missionaries misread and misinterpreted the Hindu Law and expended considerable logic, ingenuity and erudition to defile eand disfigure it and the view of Sir Henry Maine is not based on any authority in the original texts or in the practice of the country. It appears to be a figment of imagination and a blatant distortion of a simple fact that death can be licked when honour is at stake and such idealism, the Indian womanhood always cherished. Shakespeare, in the sixteenth century gave expression to this feeling when at one place in his famous drama, *As You Like It*, he said:

> Beauty provoketh thieves sooner than gold.

Thus, death and honour should be considered co-related concepts.

Another aspect should also not be ignored that widow marriage was never prohibited but chastity was expected from the widows and widow remarriage and chastity were also considered co-related but alternative concepts. In the first case 'the fear of dishonour' haunts and in the latter case 'the unsubdued senses' show their growing teeth.

However, remarriage of widow is not prohibitory in the scriptures and as such the concept of self-immolation need not be stretched unnecessarily so far.

To quote:

> When her husband is lost or dead or . . . these are the five causes of legal necessity in which a woman may be justified in taking an another husband.[235]

> When her husband is lost or dead or . . . under these five calamities, another husband is ordained.[236]

### Subjugation of women

There is another misconception that needs clarification that Hindu women have dependent position, i.e., subjugation of women. The distinguished jurist, clad with Western notions, was deeply imbued with ideas concerning the perpetual tutelage of women derived from a study of the ancient Law of Rome, and thought that the system survived in India in absolute completeness. "Its operation is so strict", he averred, "that a Hindu mother frequently becomes the

---

234. Sir Henry Maine, *Ancient Law*, World's Classic edn., 1931, pp. 16-27.
235. *Nārada*, XII.97.
236. *Parāśara*, IV.30.

ward of her own sons."[237] His authority being considered so great that other European jurists, unhesitatingly and without any demur, followed him and misinterpreted Hindu Law in all its aspects.

It is quite clear that there is nothing in Vedas to suggest the tutelage of a woman. Rather Vedas assigned a high place to woman in the society which includes family also. In the Vedas she is referred to as the queen and mistress of the household, holding full sway over her husband's family. In *Ṛgveda* it is said:

गृहान् गच्छ गृहपत्नी यथासो वशिनी त्वं विदथमा वदसि।
प्रति तिष्ठ विराडसि विष्णुरिवेह सरस्वती।। ऋ० १०।८५।२६[238]

सिनी वालि प्र जायतां भगस्य सुमतावसत्।। अथर्व० १४।२।१५[239]

There is another verse in *Atharvaveda* where she has been called as 'Bliss Bringer':

स्योनाभव श्वशुरेभ्यः स्योना पत्ये गृहेभ्यः।
स्योनास्यै सर्वस्यै विशे स्योना पुष्टायैषां भव।। अथर्व० १४।२।२७[240]

It is only when we come to some passages in Smṛtis which apparently imply to the subjection of women but those passages also seem to have been mis-interpreted and read in isolation and out of context. Some of the passages that appear in the Smṛtis are as below. According to Gautama

> Wife is not independent with respect to fulfilment of the sacred law. She should not violate her duty towards her husband. She should restrain her tongue, eyes and organs of action.

अस्वतन्त्रा धर्मे स्त्री ।। १ ।।
नातिचरेद् भर्तारम् ।। २ ।।
वाक्-चक्षुः-कर्म-संयता ।। ३ ।।[241]

Vasiṣtha says:

That a lady is not independent, but depends upon her

237. Sir Henry Maine, *Ancient Law*, p. 158.

238. *ṚV*, X.85, 26

239. *AV*, XIV.2, 15.

240. *Ibid.*, XIV.2, 27

241. *GauDS*, XVIII.1-3.

husband. She is to perform sacrifice with her husband. Her father protects her in her maidenhood, her husband in her youth and her sons in her old age. She does not desrve independence.

अस्वतन्त्रा स्त्रीपुरुषप्रधाना ।। १ ।।
अनग्निकाऽनुदक्या वा अनृतमिति विज्ञायते ।। २ ।।
पिता रक्षति कौमारे भर्ता रक्षति यौवने।
पुत्रश्च स्थविरे भावे न स्त्री स्वातन्त्र्यमर्हति ।। ४ ।।[242]

Baudhāyana says:

She is protected by her father in her girlhood, by her husband in her youth, by her sons in her old age. She does not deserve any idependent living. She should always look to the comforts of her husband. Thus, she would attain heaven.

न स्त्री-स्वातन्त्र्यं विद्यते ।। ५० ।।
पिता रक्षति कौमारे भर्ता रक्षति यौवने।
पुत्रस्तु स्थविरे भावे न स्त्री स्वातन्त्र्यमर्हतीति ।। ५२ ।।
भर्तृहिते यतमानाः स्वर्गं लोकं जयेरन् ।। ५४ ।।[243]

Yājñavalkya says:

Woman is to be respected by her husband, brother, father, kindred (*jñāti*), mother-in-law, father-in-law, husband's younger brother, and the *bandhus*, with ornaments, clothes and food.

When a maiden, her father, when married her husband, and when old, her sons, should protect her. In their absence, the kinsmen (should take care of her). The women are never independent.

Deprived of her husband she should not reside apart from her father, mother, son or brother, from her mother-in-law or father-in-law, or from her old maternal uncles. Otherwise she becomes infamous.

---

242. *VasDS*, V.1, 2, 4.
243. *BaudhDS*, 2.3.50, 52, 54.

> Devoted to the pleasure and to the good of her husband, of good conduct, with subdued passions (such a wife) obtains renown in this world, and after death attains the best end.
>
> भर्तृभ्रातृपितृज्ञातिश्वश्रूश्वशुरदेवरैः ।
> बन्धुभिश्च स्त्रियः पूज्या भूषणाच्छादनाशनैः ॥ ८२ ॥
>
> रक्षेत्कन्यां पिता विन्नां पतिः पुत्रास्तु बार्धके ।
> अभाव ज्ञातयस्तेषां न स्वातंत्र्यं क्वचित्स्त्रियाः ॥ ८५ ॥
>
> पितृमातृसुतभ्रातृश्वश्रूश्वशुरमातुलैः ॥
> हीना न स्याद्विना भर्त्रा गर्हणीयाऽन्यथा भवेत् ॥ ८६ ॥
>
> पतिप्रियहिते युक्ता स्वाचारा विजितेन्द्रियां ।
> सेह कीर्तिमवाप्नोति प्रेत्य चानुत्तमां गतिम् ॥ ८७ ॥[244]

Let us have some verses from Manu which throw light on the status aspect of a woman in respect of subjugation:

> Women must be honoured and adorned by their fathers, brothers, husbands and brothers-in-law, who desire (their own) welfare.
>
> Where women are honoured, there the gods are pleased; but where they are not honoured, no sacred rite yields rewards.
>
> The houses on which female relations not being duly honoured, pronounce a curse, perish completely, as if destroyed by magic.
>
> In that family, where the husband is pleased with his wife and wife with the husband, happiness will assuredly be lasting.
>
> यत्रनार्यस्तुपूज्यन्तेरमन्तेतत्रदेवताः ।
> यत्रैतास्तुनपूज्यन्तेसर्वास्तत्राफलाः क्रियाः ॥ ५६ ।
>
> शोचन्तिजामयोयत्रविनश्यत्याशुतत्कुलम् ।
> नशोचन्तितुयत्रैतावर्द्धतेतद्धिसर्वदा ॥ ५७ ॥
>
> जामयोयानिगेहानिशपन्त्यप्रतिपूजिताः ॥

244. *Yāj*, I.82, 85, 86, 87.

तानिकृत्याहतानीवविनश्यन्तिसमन्तः ।। ५८ ।।[245]

Another aspect of woman is described or ordained by Manu thus:

> Her father protects (her) in childhood, her husband protects (her) in youth and her sons protect (her) in old age, a woman is never fit for independence.[246]
>
> By a girl, by a young woman, or even by an aged one, nothing must be done independently, even in her own house.
>
> In childhood a female must be subject to her father, in youth to her husband, when her lord is dead to her sons, a woman must never be independent.

बालयावायुवत्यावावृद्धयावा पियोषिता ।
नस्वातंत्र्येणकर्त्तव्यंकिंचित्कार्यंगृहेष्वषि ।। १४७ ।।

बाल्येपितुर्वशेतिष्ठेत्पाणियाहस्ययौवने ।
पुत्राणाम्भर्त्तरिप्रेतेनभजेत्स्त्रीस्वतंत्रताम् ।। १४९ ।।[247]

Manu speaks the third aspect as duty of a wife which is being misinterpreted as subjugation of a woman.

> Until death let her be patient (of herdships), self-controlled, and chaste, and strive (to fulfil) that most excellent duty which (is prescribed) for wives who have one husband only.[248]
>
> A virtuous wife who after death of her husband constantly remains chaste reaches heaven, though she have no son, just like those chaste men.[249]
>
> By violating her duty towards her husband, a wife is disgraced in this world (after death) she enters the womb

---

245. *Manu*, III.56-8.
246. *Manu*, IX.3.
247. *Ibid.*, V.147-8, See *Manu*, IX.3, *Yāj*, I.85. *Viṣṇu*, XXVI.12-13.
248. *Ibid.*, V.158.
249. *Ibid.*, V.160.

of a jackal, and is tormented by diseases (the punishment of) her sin.[250]

She who controlling her thoughts, words and deeds, never slights her lord, resides (after death) with her husband (in heaven) and is called a virtuous wife.[251]

In reward of such conduct, a female who controls her thoughts, speech and actions, gains in this (life) highest renown, and in the next (world) a place near her husband.[252]

Whatever be the qualities of the man with whom a woman is united according to the law, such qualities even she assumes, like a river (united) with the ocean.[253]

He only is a perfect man who consists (of three persons united) his wife, himself, and his offspring; thus (says the Veda), and (learned) brāhmaṇas propound this (maxim) likewise,

The husband is declared to be one with the wife.[254]

The husbad receives his wife from the gods' (he does not wed her) according to his own will; doing what is agreeable to the gods, he must always support her (while she is) faithful.[255]

To be mothers were women created, and to be fathers men, religious rites, therefore, are ordained in the Veda to be performed (by the husband) together with the wife.[256]

Let mutual fidelity continue until death. This may be considered as the summary of the highest law for husband

---

250. *Manu*, V.164 and IX.30. See *VasDS*, XXI.14.

251. *Ibid.*, V.165 & IX.29.

252. *Ibid.*, V.166.

253. *Ibid.*, IX.22.

254. *Ibid.*, IX.45.

255. *Ibid.*, IX.95.

256. *Ibid.*, IX.96.

and wife.[257]

Before we make our critical comments on these three aspects, we should keep in view some verses as appear in other scriptures in this regard.

That lady called *parśuḥ* who gives birth to twenty children. She is ever prosperous. Her person is wonderful and her husband — Indra is better than others.

पर्शुर्ह नाम मानवी साकं ससूव विंशतिम् भद्रं भलत्यस्या ।
अभूद्यस्या उदरमामयद् विश्वस्मादिन्द्र उत्तरः ।।[258]

She should hear my words and realise me herself. Like an unbreakable needle she should strengthen the ties of love with me with her good behaviour and daily actions. She should give birth to a worthy, wealthy and heroic sons.

राकामहं सुहवां सुष्टती हवे शृणोतु नः सुभगा बोधतुत्मना ।
सीव्यत्वपः सूच्याच्छिद्यमानया ददातुवीरं शत दायुमुक्थ्यम् ।।[259]

Let wife speak words to her husband, giving mental peace to him.

जाया पत्ये मधुमतीं वाचं वदतु शान्तिवाम् ।[260]

Husband is a deity to a wife. Husband is her relative. Husband is her *guru*. To her husband is dearer that her own life. Therefore, he is to be obeyed primarily.

पतिर्हि देवता नार्याः पतिर्बन्धुः पतिर्गुरुः ।।
प्राणैरपि प्रियं तस्माद् भर्तुः कार्यं विशेषतः ।।[261]

Husband is a god to her. Husband is her *guru*. Husband is a pilgrimage to her. Her *dharma*, all her virtuous vows are her husband. Therefore, she, leaving aside everything, should worship her husband.

---

257. *Manu*, IX.101.
258. *AV*, 10.86.23.
259. *ṚV*, 2.32.4.
260. *AV*, 3.30.2.
261. *Balmi*, 7.48.17.

भर्ता देवो गुरुभर्ता धर्म-तीर्थ-व्रतानि च ।
तस्मात्सर्वं परित्यज्य पतिमेकं समर्चयेत् ।।[262]

That lady is called a wife, who has control over her passions, who can bear children, who is faithful to her husband, whose life is her husband. She is pioùs lady.

या नारी प्रयता दक्षा या नारी पुत्रिणी भवेत् ।
पतिव्रता पतिप्राणा सा नारी धर्मभागिनी ।।[263]

A lady who is called *jaya* is half of man.

यावन्न विन्दते जायां तावदधा भवेत् पुमान्[264]

A man is incomplete till he gets a wife.

अर्धो ह वा एष आत्मनो यज्जायेति ।।[265]

## Woman is never independent: What does it mean?

Manu and various other *sūtrakāras* and *smṛtikāras* have spoken that a woman should always be protected at all stages of life, rather from cradle to grave which has been interpreted by the Western jurists and followed by the modern interpreters perhaps prejudiced with the excellence of Hindu *dharma* or ignorance of Hindu *dharma* and their misleading interpretation is both out of context and as well as irrelevant as being inconsonance with the depth of Hindu thought. According to them 'never be independent' means always 'dependent' which has been taken as 'woman, a slave of man'. This interpretation indicates that woman is inferior to man. This is only a figment of imagination. Yājñavalkya has used the word रक्षेत् which has been explained by Vijñeśvara who points out that all that it means is that a woman is to be guarded from the performance of improper acts. Even the text of Aṅgirasa has gone to the extent that on the failure of both sides (the husband's and the father's relations), the king is the supporter and master of women. A careful study of the *Manu-smṛti* also makes it plain. Our saints and sages were clear in their mind that the preservation of the sanctity of

262. *Skanda Purāṇa*, 4.48.
263. *Viṣṇu-smṛti*, 3.322.11.
264. *ŚatBrā*, 5.2.3.10.
265. *Vyās Saṁhitā* 2. 14.

marriage and not being violated is also an act of *dharma* which is ordained as mandatory. Our *ṛṣis* took into consideration the temperamental aspect of a woman. Man differs from woman to a large extent. From a psychological viewpoint women are normally more emotional, while in man, the intellect dominates over the emotions. The difference is directly related to their nervous system and a critical psychological and physiological examination can prove very fruitful.[266]

Our sages knew well that woman is emotional by nature and in a tropical climate the flesh might sometimes prove too strong but they depricated all idea of physical coercion. Manu declares

> verily the man is cursed who confines the woman with a view to protect her.

Manu says:

> No man can completely guard women by force but they can be guarded by the employment of the (following) expedients.[267]

Manu at another place says:

> Women must particularly be guarded against evil inclinations, however, triffling (they may appear); for if they are not guarded, they will bring sorrow on two families.[268]

The whole concept of Manu and later on Yājñavalkya of 'never independent' is that a woman can be easily the victim of the vices which Manu has stated thus:

> Drinking (spirituous liquors), associating with wicked people, separation from the husband, rambling abroad, sleeping (at unseasonable hours) and dwelling in other men's house are the causes of the ruin of women.[269]

---

266. Dr. Shamsuddin Shams, *Socio-Legal Rights and Privileges of Women in Islam.*

267. *Manu*, IX.10. For expedients see *Manu*, IX.11.

268. *Ibid.*, IX.5.

269. *Ibid.*, IX.13.

Following it Manu says:

> Knowing their disposition, which the lord of creature laid in them at the creation, to be such, (every) man should most strenuously exert himself to guard them.[270]

This is why Manu has advised as follows:

> Let the (husband) employ his (wife) in the collection and expenditure of his wealth, in keeping everything clean, in (the fulfilment of) religious duties, in the preparation of his food and in the looking after the household utensils.[271]

So when our sages spoke of dependence of women, they have not spoken in terms of legal connotations.

Their whole emphasis was on the sanctity and the integrated existence of the family, considering that woman is mother and on her every act, the happiness of home depends, the prosperity of the society depends and the strength of the nation grows.

To quote Nārada, he says that —

> Only three persons are independent in this world, a teacher, a king and in every class throughout the whole system of classes, he who is the head of the family.[272]

So the dependence of women should not be stretched too far to call it subjugation of women. Even we have to look to the fact that the word protection has been used considering the physiological aspect of the woman. Physiology texts state that the structure of a man's body is different from that of a woman in all respects whether it he muscles, blood, bones, heart or brain. Whereas a man's brain weights 100 gm more than a woman's, his lungs weigh 300 gm more. The average weight of a male is 4000 gm more than that of a female body. Man's bones are heavier and stronger. Women's muscles are weaker and more delicate. The heart of an average man is nearly 50 gm heavier than that of an average woman. Hence

270. *Manu*, IX.16.
271. *Manu*, IX.11.
272. *Nārada*, I.32.

difference in physical structure is reflected in the mental capabilities of the two sexes.[273]

Historical perspective also contributes to the concept of 'protection' to the women at all stages because with the passage of time external contacts and its effect on society did affect this concept to save the motherhood, the foundation of civilisation.

About the close of the Vedic period, as a result of racial and cultural adjustment, *varaṇāśrama dharma* was conceived as the divinely ordained social framework and this *caluvarṇa* ensured the purity of the way of life. Besides, a well conducted individual life was divided into four stages, i.e., that of a student, a householder,

---

273. M.T. Mesbah, M.G. Bahonar and Lois L. Faruqi, *Status of Women* in *Islam*, Delhi, 1990, pp. 5-39.

Also see William Body's *Text Book of Pathology*, 7th. edn.

Arthur C. Guyton, *Text Book of Medical Physiology*, 8th edn.

Dr. Chandicharan Chatterji, *Human Physiology*.

*Heart*: The average weight is 300 gm in the male, 250 gm in the female but these figures will be considerably exceeded in a big muscular labourer or reduced in a tiny fragile woman.

*Lever*: The weight is 1400 to 1600 gm in the male, 1200 to 1400 gm in the female.

*Brain*: The average weight of the brain in the male is 1400 gm, in the female 1250 gm.

*Blood*: Red blood cells or Erythrocyte are 5.5 millions/Cumm of blood in males and 4.5 millions/Cumm in female. Specific gravity of blood is 1.053 (clinical average) in females whereas it is 1.057 in males.

Amount of Hemoglobin (Hb) in Males is 16 gm/dl of blood and in female 14/gm/dl. Blood volume is 7.5 per cent higher in males per sq. m of body surface than in the female.

*Respiratory System*: All pulmonary volumes and capacities are 20-25 per cent less in woman than in men.

*Kidneys*: The kidneys weigh 150 gm in males and 135 gm in females.

*General buildup*: The bones of the female are lighter and thinner. The bony markings are less prominent. The articular surfaces (acetabulum and on body of first sacral vertebra) are smaller.

*Menstrual tension*: This is seen in females just before the onset of menses. High extrogen level occur during this time and contribute to emotional stablility and mood swings. In some countries like Germany women during PMT are prohibited from driving vehicle.

a detached onlooker purusing a high purpose and lastly, an ascetic. For this planned social life, stability was essential. Stability implied protection but without slavery. To ensure stability, the concept of kingship, the enforcer of divine law and protector of *dharma*, took deep roots and every ordinance in scriptures was the clear manifestation of *dharma* oozing out of every 'do's and don'ts'.

Then we notice that between tenth and seventh century BC, there was a mighty upheaval of the human spirit. Waves of intense activity passed over many lands where man has emerged from the Bronze Age. Zoroaster gave a new creed to Iran; Confucius and Lao-tse taught in China; Jews in their Babylonian Captivity developed their tenacious faith in Jehove; Greece emerged as the pioneer of European culture and her philosophers began tackling the problems of life; Rome was founded. At that time, a highly complex civilisation and a noble culture had already been flourishing in India for centuries. The sages of India, did not ignore this historical and cultural upheaval in other parts of the globe and considering its impact assessment brought some evolutionary ordinances which apparently, on shallow basis, appear to be harsh restrictions, but in reality, these measures were to save the purity of our culture which was family based and society based, with the fulcrum point of individual life to be conducted on the touchstone of *dharma*.

Besides, two glittering stars in the personality of Lord Buddha and Lord Mahāvīra dominated the Indian social and religious scenario who ignored God and denied the Vedas. Though admitted the fourfold order of society but derided the four stages of life, stressing only the life of an ascetic and his *dharma* was the *aṣṭāṅga-mārga* and asceticism was the pivotal point in life wherein 'desire' has no place as being the source of all sorrows :

> Going further in 326 BC Alexander the Macedonian, with his thundering legions, entered north-western India, the erstwhile Satrapy of the Iranian empire. However, in a few months, he retreated from India, but latter on Seleucus tried to move towards India to recapture vanquished Alexander's lost possessions, somehow, could not succeed and once again India under Candragupta Maurya, became

an empire with stress on *dharma* as is reflected in Kauṭilya's *Arthaśāstra*.[274]

The impact of cultural upheaval elsewhere in the world, the influence of Buddhism and Jainism, was expected to affect the Hindu society and of course, to some extent, it did affect. So the period of *smṛtikāras* has to be looked from this viewpoint. Though there is difference of opinion among scholars about other Smṛti works, but they are almost unanimous about *Manu-smṛti* that the text was formulated sometime between 200 BC and AD 100. About other important Smṛtis the view of Jolly and Kane is as follows :

| *Smṛti* | *Jolly's view* | *Kane's view* |
|---|---|---|
| Yājñavalkya | 4th century AD | AD 100-300 |
| Nārada | AD 500 | AD 100-400 |
| Bṛhaspati | 6th or 7th century AD | AD 300-500 |
| Kātyāyana | Later than Bṛhaspati | AD 400-600[275] |

So the concept of 'protection' is purely based on the physiological aspect of a woman and the historical facts are looked from the angle of its social impact. The only fact to be noted is that the error into which European writers have fallen is evidently due to the fact that they assumed things on analogies and analogies are always misleading. They considered the texts in isolation apart from the context and such study will only be a piecemeal and not comprehensive. If the Smṛtis coupled with the commentaries and digests and in context with the situations and parallel study of the scriptures had been critically studied and analysed, the result would have been that a woman was always respected and protected.

It is worth noting that in Ancient India, the society regarded woman as the *sahadarmiṇī*.[276] The Hindu believes that a woman

274. The historical perspective is taken from *The History and Culture of the Indian People*, Vol.II, Bhartiya Vidya Bhavan Series.

275. Dr. B.K. Ghosh Translation of J.Jolly's *Hindu Law and Customs*. P.V. Kane, *History of Hindu Dharmaśāstras*, Vol. II, Part I, p. xi.

276. Sāyaṇa, Commenting on *Ṛgveda* (Verse 61.8) says: "The wife and the husband, being the equal halves of one substance, are equal in every respect, both should join and take equal part in all works religious and secular."

has a characteristic contribution meant for the society through her special duties inherently brought up in her and specifically ordained by the scriptures too. She is the source of the continuity of progeny. She is the foundation of the pillars of household. Whereas the husband was ordained to undertake worldly pursuits (*yajña prādhānya*), the wife was ordained to pursue *tapapradhayya*. She is to be one with the husband; be an embodiment of love and affection and self-control which means chastity. The stricter code of morality applied to wife is really a compliment to her as it shows the superiority of the women in all respects.

> सम्राज्ञी श्वशुरे भव, सम्राज्ञी श्वश्र्वां भव ।
> ननान्दरि सम्राज्ञी भव, सम्राज्ञी अधि देवृषु ।। ऋ० १०।८५।४६
> वीरसूः देवृकामा स्योना शं नो भव ।। ऋ० १०।८५।४४[277]

A woman was the cause of *dharma*, *artha*, *kāma* and *mokṣa*. *Kāma* was considered in terms of progeny. Fusion of wife and husband as one is *dharma*. The lifelong companionship of wife and husband and their daily cooperation in weal and woe, and the enshrined duties to sustain the glory of family life is the real *artha* and performance of religious *yajña* along with the husband is the cause of *mokṣa*. The words of Baudhāyana deserve mention to clear all doubts.

> *sarveṣām varṇanām dara rakṣyastama dhanāt* ।
>
> The wife is even more precious than wealth,

It is echoed long back in the sixteenth century in the Drama of Shaksepeare:

> Beauty provoketh thieves sooner than gold.[278]

To read verses of Manu in respect of 'duties of wife' in isolation is to neglect the concept of Hindu law. How we can forget that

> The mouth of a woman is always pure, likewise a bird, when he causes fruit to fall, a calf is pure on the flowing of the milk and a dog when he catches a deer.[279]

---

277. *Ṛ̣V*, X.85.46, 44.

278. *BaudhDS*, II.42; Shakespeare, *As you Like It*.

279. *Manu*, V.130.

Another sage has said:

> Strike not with a blossom a woman guilty of a hundred faults.

This saying is to be read with what is said in *Mitākṣarā* about Yājñavalkya's verse I.193

> What is spoiled by children what is handled by women and what is done in ignorance are always pure. This is the settled rule.[280]

Vivekānanda has summed up thus:

> The ideal woman in India is the mother, the mother first and the mother last. In the West the woman is wife. The idea of womanhood is concentrated there as the wife. To the ordinary man in India, the whole force of womanhood is concentrated in motherhood.[281]

Our sages looked woman from the vision of motherhood, the proud cause of sound and stalwart progeny and gave utmost respect.

Summing up the status of woman as largely considered is as follows:

> Hindu society had a flexible social structure. The concept of *ardhāngiṇī* suggests that there was equality between men and women, neither being superior to the other.[282]

> The word *patnī* in the *Brāhmaṇas* indicate her equal share in the social and religious side of the husband's life.[283]

> She is the sole mistress of the household".[284]

> She is the mistress of the home, partakes of the domestic

---

280. *Half of the Verse is from Vasiṣṭha*, III.45.
281. Svāmī Vivkānanda, *Our Women.*
282. Srikant Mishra, *Ancient Hindu Marriage Law and Practice.*
283. R.C. Majumdar, *The Vedic Age*, Vol.I.
284. *ṚV*, III.53.4.

> duties and religious rites along with her husband and takes part in family councils.[285]
>
> Wife is a friend.[286]
>
> The wife was never looked upon as a slave or a chattel but as a partner in religious matters, as a friend, a confident and guide.[287]

No doubt, there is a dissenting note of Usha M. Apte, wherein she cites *Śatapata Brahmāṇa*:

> The wife is virtually half of the husband and she should abide by the instruction of her husband and follow him like a shadow. She must be a friend, in all good activities and a servant at all his commands.[288]
>
> That woman is inferior to her husband as it requires her to eat after him and not with him.[289]

This view of the author seems to be too severe. Obedience to husband should be taken as a symbol of Harmony in family life. Bālambhaṭṭa gives an extract of some forty eight verses from *Skanda Purāṇa* (Kāśī-Khaṇḍa, IV Adhyāya) from the address of Bṛhaspati to Agastya wherein various qualities of Lopāmudrā, the wife of Agastya are given. If they are read with the duties of a wife as ordained by Manu chapter IX.1-30 read with chapter III.56-9.

> Where women are honoured, there the gods are pleased, but where they are not honoured, no sacred rite yields result.

followed by other sages, such an opinion of the author is not in tune with the dhārmic intentions of the sages and is just a version

---

285. *AV*, XIV.1.20 cited by N. Sen Gupta, *Sources of Law and Society in Ancient India*, 1914.
286. *AitBrā*, 33.
287. Jogiraj Basu, *India of the Age of the Brāhmaṇas*, p. 34.
288. *ŚatBrā*, V.1-6-10 cited by Usha M. Apte, *The Sacrament of Marriage* (Ph.D. Thesis).
289. *Ibid.*, I.9.2.12 cited by Usha M. Apte, *The Sacrament of Marriage* (Ph.D. Thesis)

misinterpreted in spirit and in contents as she has failed to read these verses in conjunction with other verses like:

> that the wife is the half of one's own self.[290]

This surely ranks wife on equal footing with her husband. So to read verses in isolation creates the confusion as one single verse may not convey the correct version.

In short, under the impact of images created from Vedic period to the Epic period and sustained in Hinduism, women were honoured, regarded and considered as an embodiment of purity and spiritual powers, and found in the motherhood the glimpses of mother goddess. Simultaneously, they are viewed as essentially weak creature physiologically and ordained to be protected at all stages of life which aspect has unfortunately been considered by many as a sign of tutelage and slavery.

In the Buddha period, completely the emphasis was on ethical values and also a reaction against orthodox Brāhmaṇism by which the position of women was highly elevated in the sense, that social and religious restrictions imposed on women evaporated and the main duty of both men and women was the upholding of *dharma*. But still her physiological and psychological traits were always kept in mind Buddha's saying is:

> Crying is the power of child; anger is the power of women.[291]

With the advent of Muhammadanism with Arab invasions beginning in AD 712, Hindu society's attitude towards women became more rigid and the society's main concern was the protection and preservation of women's honour and chastity and as such some practices did creep in which apparently were looked as degrading to women but in reality they were to save the women from dishonour. But in spite of these rigorous restrictions, still the Hindu women commanded respect due to their devotion, fidelity, love and fellowship. They were regarded as "Flaming torches of love and

290. *ŚatBrā.*
291. Buddha quoted by Albert Sehweit Zex, *Indian Thought and its Development*, Bombay, 1960, p. 95.

fellowship"[292], and admired for their single-minded devotion and fidelity.[293]

With the advent of the British rule, we find undisturbed traditional Indian social system as the aim of the Britishers was basically to rule the country and not to disturb the social and riligious equilibrium by taking any radical steps. However, in later stages, they started penetrating into the religious and personal law of the Hindus through the judicial decisions and started creating a class Indian in body but Britisher in taste and thought.

Though more or less the Britishers remained aloof or away from the personal laws of the Indians, but positively the effect of Mayne-Macaulay doctrine of colouring the Indians with Western culture, did show its manifestation. The emergence of modern Indian womanhood began to cast its direct impact on the society. Process of industrialisation, urbanisation, to a great extent Westernisation started to be working more rapidly. Its beginning can be attributed to the twentieth century. Various women organisations like, Women's Indian Association, The Seva Sadan, The Mahila Seva Samaj, The Indian Women's University Association, The Home Rule Leagers Branches were established. All-India Women's Conference (AIWC) at its inception had an aim to safeguard and protect the interests of Indian women.

In 1917 we found Indian women agitating under the leadership of Sarojini Naidu for the franchise. Not only that, they demanded expansion in the education of girls and drafted a plan for its dissemination and presented the plan in the shape of Memorandum to Lord Chelmsford, Viceroy and Governor-General of India and the Right Honourable E.S. Montague, Member Parliament, His Majesty's Secretary of State for India. This Memorandum had its effect that the Montague-Chelmsfrd Reform Act of 1919 gave women the right to vote in elections to all State Legislatures but not to the Council of State for Governor-General (Property and Educational Qualifications were still there). Subsequently, in 1926 women were given the right of membership of Provincial Legislatures.

Emboldened by these measures, in April 1931 a special meeting

292. Abul Fazl, *Akbarnama*, Vol. III, tr. by Henry Beveridge, 1984, p. 372.

293. *Tuzik-i-Jahangiri*, I, p. 150.

of AIWC was held in Bombay under the chairmanship of Sarojini Naidu. A memorandum supported by two other women's organisations, The Women's Indian Association and The National Council of Women was to be placed before the Franchise Sub-Committee of the First Round Table Conference in London. The main points of this Memorandum were :

(i) equal rights and obligations for All Indian Citizens without sex bar,

(ii) no disability to any citizen because of religion, caste, creed or sex in regard to public appointment to an office of powers or honour and in exercise of any trade,

(iii) Adult suffrage,

(iv) Women to contest on equal terms with men in mixed general elections, and

(v) no reservation of seats for women as such, no special monination or co-option.

Then came the great event of 1942 when women co-operated and struggled with men. Mrs. Sucheta Kriplani, Mrs. Aruna Asif Ali, Kamla Devi Chattopadhyaya are the names that shine like a beacon stars. Thus Indian women in general and Hindu women in particular stood in the forefront of every movement. Along with it, the Indian women fought for the rights of women. The Indian women's charter of Rights and Duties was prepared and was ratified by the Standing Committee of the All Indian Women's Conference at its meeting in Calcutta in July 1946 and this charter spoke of civil rights, health, moral standards, work, home making, property rights, marriage, women's place in the family and duties of women.

Pt. Jawahar Lal Nehru spoke so high of the women of India, taking leading part in the political movement and was so impressed that 14 women's found place in the Constituent Assembly of India formed in December, 1946 and the various Articles in the Constitution including Article 326 removed the sex barriers and sex discrimination.

With the dawn of freedom and a Sovereign Socialist Secular Democratic Republic Constitution, India marched towards progress and Indian women too. The status of women in Hindu society had changed from time to time as Hindu Law was always evolutionary in character. But the position of women has been variously estimated and diametrically opposite views are taken. One view was that she is little better than a slave or beast of burden, condemned to drudgery, bought as a chattel and treated as such.[294] The others considered women as the undisputed mistress of the family.[295] In the words of B. Kuppuswami:

> In fact, it would not be an exaggeration to say that the recent changes in the status of women in India is not a sign of progress but is really a recapturing of the position that they held in the early Vedic period.

The women of today are educationally advancing, socially, economically and politically have a say and thus have become to be called progressive. In their progressiveness it appears they are determined to shatter the yoke of domination of the male sex. It is a fact that the men are hesitant to abandon their die-hard habits and the women are determined to have a quantum jump. Both appear to be conflicting in outlook. It is ideology conflict. Women feel that they have been elevated in rhetoric but crushed in fact and it is unbearable to be a victim of man's many tyrannical cruelties and injustices. Perhaps this thinking is a fiction.

The fact is that in the past the woman was looked from only one angle, i.e., the stability of family and consequential happiness of the home, but now she has to be looked from various angles such as her position within the family, her rights to equality with men in different aspects of social life. So it is part of the total, far broader question regarding the direction of change that our society is taking. Now the goal is clear that the woman has to be looked from two angles, i.e., 'within the four walls' and 'outside the four walls'. The first concept is connected with the stability of the family and happiness of home and the other concept is equally relevant to the woman *versus* society. The second aspect is now being vigorously

---

294. David F. Peacock, "Change, Interaction and Comparison", *Contribution to Indian Sociology*, Vol. 7, March 1964, pp. 7-17.

295. B. Kuppu Swami, "Indian Social Values — Traditional and Modern", *Social Change in India*, pp. 67-89.

emphasised but social change simultaneously demands harmonious balancing because even progressiveness in women does not warrant any irresponsibility towards the duty which has been imposed on them to keep the stability of family protected and preserved.

The constitutional provisions and various enactments have improved the status of women and they are at par with men in every field. All steps are being taken and the national policy framed in 1996, has incorporated the essentials of the convention on the elimination of all Forms of Discrimination Against Women (CEDAW-1979) in 1993, The Mexican Plan of Action (1975), The Nairobi Forward Looking Strategies (1985), The Bejing Declaration as well as Platform for Action (1995) to improve the status of women educationally, socially, economically and politically.

Prabhu suggests that we should not go by extreme views and that a reasoned and balanced view of the whole matter need by taken.[297] Women constitute half the population of India. This half cannot be ignored as Svāmī Vivekānanda has said that a bird on one wing cannot fly. Wife is the half of a man as Hindu scriptures tell. Even then she cannot be ignored. Ignoring woman, in reality, is ignoring the half of the man.

Critically examining the researcher finds from Vedic period to the present day, various stands of ideologies such as unequal relationship between the sexes, gender stratification, ideological position of sex role, social reality and women's situation, norms governing the elimination of discrimination against women wherever it exists, development strategies and women's consideration and their role in them. All steps whether by way of religious ordinances and later on by statutory provisions were taken with one aim that she is a daughter, a wife, a mother and her status and protection is supreme. Law, today is channelised towards welfare of all and not to maintain supremacy of one sex over another In reality, there is no sex discrimination as constitution and statutory law manifest. If there are any misconceptions, they may be in mind which need to be removed. The need of the time is the change in the outlook which is coloured with Western cultural thoughts. This change can be brought not by law but by the concept

296. Prabhu, *Hindu Social Organisation.*

of *dharma* which can be practicable through the moral teaching. This is what we are lacking today. Materialism has brought changes and with the changes many problems. Spiritualism also brings, change in the soul and with it brings solution to all human problems because then the human being does not work in the lower strata of thinking but thinks of humanity. Woman of today is still the embodiment of love and sacrifice and her protection and exalted status was and is always the cherished desire of law and religion.

The old woman of India has been transformed into a new woman. Law can be a powerful force for social change only if a large majority of people favour of the new social norms. Hindu statutory enactments have institutionalised a new pattern of behaviour, manifesting new social values but to make it an active social force there should be a correlated cultural process which means internalisation of this new pattern of hehaviour in the society as institutionalisation and internalisation are closely related. If the women ask for their rights they should not forget their duties to the family. The women themselves have to redefine their role within the family in spite of their advancement and progressiveness and such redefined role should have to be compatible with the long cherished values of life that wife and husband have a unison in thought and action and this approach shall enhance her status more in society.

*Marriage is a sacred duty and whoever dislikes this way of life is not of me.*

— **Holy Prophet** quoted by Bhukhari

*Marriage is honourable in all, and the bed undefiled: but whoremongers and adulterers God will judge.*

— ***Hebrews*, 13:4**

*Marriage is an outward and visible sign of an inward and spiritual grace given unto us; ordained by Christ himself, as a means whereby we receive the same, and pledge to assure us thereof.*

— **Anglican Catechism**

*Marriage is one of the necessary saṁskāras or religious rites for all Hindus, whatever the caste, who do not desire to adopt the life of a perpetual brahmacārī or of a saṁnyāsī.*

— **John D Mayne**

# 2

# Hindu Marriage
## Concept and Nature

MARRIAGE is a significant event and an important aspect intermingled with woman which speaks of the religious and social aspect of life of a woman that reveals the culture and civilisation of the society and its exaltness.

It is said that womanhood is a precious jewel in the ornament of civilisation and motherhood is the ultimate truth wherein lies the continuity and spiritual salvation of mankind. Motherhood is the blended culmination of marriage and sonship and there lies the sacramental concept of life in terms of marriage and sonship. Manu has said:

> The production of children, the nurture of those born and the daily life of men (of these matters) woman is visibly the cause.
>
> Offsprings (the due performance of) religious rites, faithful service, highest conjugal happiness and heavenly bliss for the ancestors and oneself, depend on one's own wife.[1]

So Hindu scriptures speak very highly with a clear tinge of religious fervour about the idealship of marriage. Several words were employed in ancient India to denote the idea of marriage.[2]

Thus, the words *udvaha*, i.e., taking the girl out of her paternal home, *vivāha*, i.e., taking the girl for a special purpose, i.e., for

1. *Manu*, IX.27, 28.
2. Westermark, *History of Human Marriage*, Vol. I, p. 26.

making her one's wife, *pariṇaya* or *pariṇayana*, i.e., going round or making a *pradakṣiṇā* to fire, *upayāma*, i.e., to bring near and make one's own, and *pāṇigrahaṇa*, i.e., taking the hand of the girl, are employed to convey the sense of marriage.[3]

However, in general, the word is *vivāha* (marriage) which comes from the root *vaḥ prāpane* and its meaning is that one accepts the other with good thought.

However, various scholars tried to give varying thought to it and put forth their views through a social angle and whereas the pure Indian thought reflected in the scriptures depicts a concept deeply religious rooted, on which the superstructure of a well regulated society is raised.

Sir John Hanner in *Durham* v. *Durham* has said that the contract of marriage is a very simple one, which does not require a high degree of of intelligence to comprehend.[4]

Lord Penzence observed:

> I conceive that marriage as understood in Christiandom, may for this purpose be defined as the voluntary union for life of one man and one woman to the exclusion of all others.[5]

However, Vina Gradoff, contrary to Sir John Hanner, kept the matter in suspense when he remarked that marriage, being a complex phenomenon, cannot be explained by one single principle, idea or notion, as it represents a synthesis of several principles, ideas and notions and one cannot draw from it a perfectly logical set of rules.[6] Thus, he had kept the options open to define marriage as one looks at it from the angle one views it. So different shades of opinion can develop but the fulcrum point shall remain intact.

Margaret Puxon does not define marriage but dwells on its concept as an amalgam of tradition, religion, superstitions, instinct and reason which concerns us.[7]

3. P.V. Kane, *History of Dharmaśāstra*, Vol.II, p. 437.
4. [1885] 2 PD 130.
5. *Hyde* v. *Hyde* [1866] 1 PD 130.
6. Vina Gradoff, *Historical Jurisprudence*, Vol.I, pp. 163-6.
7. Margaret Puxon, *The Family and the Law,* p. 15.

Similarly, Lord Jowitt puts it in an oscillating way that what marriage means to different people will depend upon their upbringing, their outlook and their religious beliefs.[8]

So marriages can be defined in various ways. From religious or spiritual angle it is a *saṁskāra*. Materialistically, it is a contract but not confined or cabined into the four walls of a Contract Act; from matrimonial point of view it is a relation on which the foundation of a regulated society is based. It is a status which directly flows out of it or it is a social institution in which the interest of the society is paramount.

So the scholars, out of various facets of marriage chose one out of them, as their viewpoint. According to J.D.M. Derrett marriage is a status fulfilling a contract.[9] Marriage is a contract by which a man and a woman undertake to live together until one of them dies.[10] Sociologists view it from a different angle. Westermarck holds the view that marriage is more or less a durable connection between male and female lasting beyond the mere act of propagation or the birth of offsprings. But the sociologist at another place says that in the ordinary sense of the term, mrriage is a social institution which may be defined as a relation of one or more men to one or more women that is recognised by custom or law and involves certain rights and duties both in the case of parties entering the union and in case of the children born out of it. According to him marriage is also an economic institution which may in various ways affects the proprietary right of the parties.[11] However, this view of Westermarck appears to be clouded with thoughts of the Western civilisation where concept of marriage had undergone change unthoughtfully.

Bertrand Russell succinctly puts it that marriage differs, of course, from other sex relations by the fact that it is a legal institution. It is also in most communities a religious institution but it is the legal aspect which is essential.[12]

---

8. *Weatherley* v. *Weatherley* 1947 AC 628.
9. J.D.M. Derrett, *Introduction to Modern Hindu Law*, Bombay 1963, p. 136.
10. Tony Hanore, *Sex Law*, London 1978, p. 10.
11. Westermarck, *The Future of Marriage in Western Civilization London*, 1936, pp. 3-4.
12. Bertrand Russell, *Marriage and Morals*, London, 1930, p. 88.

In short, marriage may be defined from any angle, in any language, by the use of any idioms or phrases, the pivotal point cannot be ignored that it is a relationship, which was created either subscribing to the religious ordinances or by the solemn promises undertaken, or a superstructure raised on the edifice of sex, and that relationship must generate harmony compatible with the solemnity shown at the time of entering in this social knot, so that the society may not degenerate. It is immaterial, as to how we look at its sanctity and stability. But before we consider at length this concept of marriage, we may try to peep into the antiquity of various civilisations as to how this concept was evolved and how it is viewed.

We have a reference in *Mahābhārata* that Pāṇḍu, father of the five great Pāṇḍavas informs his wife that free sex of men and women like cattle continued till Śvetaketu, son of sage Uddālaka, and the first man, introduced the institution of marriage. So taking this reference as a benchmark, the earlier period of the history of mankind shall appear to be based on conjectures that it may be said that the social condition of primitive men was one in which no such institution existed. Perhaps the earliest form of such an institution was communal interlinking sexuality which is not marriage but a state of promiscuous intercourse and with the passage of time this promiscuous intercourse got moulded into a regulated and sanctified sexual intercourse within the framework of religious sanctions which later on got converted into social sanctions and then legal sanctions. Thus, marriage as a socio-religious institution clothed in legal garment took shape. Now this concept must be seen in its antiquity which may give us some thought provoking material to view it in its totality as it has an immense bearing on the society in which we live. Man, now is tied with the society, society is tied with law and law is meant for the man and his welfare.

We have before us the pictures of various civilisations which flourished and of course, except Indian civilisation, not a trace of their greatness remains and let us have a look one by one on them in this regard.

## Roman Law

To take the case of Roman Law, to which every European Jurist attaches great significance, we find that it is spread over three periods, i.e., (i) The monarchy, (ii) The Republic, and (iii) The Empire. From the founding of Rome (753 BC) to the Expulsion of the Tarquins (510 BC) is called the Monarchy. The period assigned to the Republic is (451 BC), i.e., Compilation of XII Tables to the battle of Actium (31 BC) and the Empire period is taken from Augustus to Justinian i.e., from 27 BC to 565 AD.

The Roman family is purely patriarchal, if there ever was a time when the more primitive matrilinear prevailed among any part of the population, it has left no traces in the legal system. It has been conjectured that the plebeians were of Etruscan origin and that the Etruscan system was matrilinear.[13] By the time of the XII Tables, the patriarchal system was crystallised and became differentiated so that its name varies according to the person over whom it was exercised. The normal marriage at this period is accompanied by *manus*, the woman passes out of her father's family and comes under the despotic rule of her husband. Apart from the question of *manus*, marriage was to the Romans as to the other people of antiquity, a *de facto* rather than a *de jure* matter, in the sense that two people held to be married, not because they had gone through any particular ceremony, but because they in fact lived together a man and wife.[14]

The state of affairs beings ordinarily with the bringing of the bride to the house of the bridegroom but no special legal significance attaches to this proceeding except in so far as it is the beginning of conjugal life. *Manus* would in early times normally result if such conjugal life was continued for a period and thus it may properly be said that marriage with *manus* was the rule and *manus* may arise in any one of the three ways by : (i) Confarreatio, (ii) Co-emptio or (iii) Usus.

Confarreatio was a religious ceremony in which the essential point was the transfer of the woman from the domestic cult of her

13. Muirhead, *Historical Introduction to Private Law of Rome*, 3rd edn., p. 32.

14. H.F. Jolowiez, *Roman Law*, p. 113.

father's family to that of her husband's.

Jorskunkel Says:

*nuptiae sunt coniunctio maris et feminae et consortium omnis vitae, divine et humani iuris communicatio.*

Co-emptio as oppossed to confarreatio is a secular form of marriage and is open to plebeians, the husband acquires *manus* over the wife by emancipation, i.e, by the formal act of purchase with the scales and copper in the presence of five citizen witnesses of full age, in the same way as a man acquires ownership over certain kinds of property but the words used differ from those of ordinary emancipation.[15]

Usus is another way of the arise of *manus*. If a woman remained married (*nupta perseverabat*) to a man for an unbroken year, she came under his *manus*. So this was a method of contracting marriage with *manus*.[16]

However, by the Time of the XII Tables, the marriage without *manus* was the rule and *manus* though it still existed, the exception. No ceremoney of any kind was required for contracting a marriage of this sort. All that was necessary was the consent of the parties if they were under power of their 'patres' together with the *de facto* beginning of conjugal life.

## Greek Law

The civilisation of the Greeks like Romans was a product of the special conditions of life which the Mediterranean reign imposes upon its inhabitants. The Greeks were a composite people, consisting in the main, of an indigenous mediterranean stock and of several intrusive elements from Asia Minor and the European continent. Their indigenous ancestors were the authors of a peculiar and precocious culture which had its chief seat in Crete. The prehistoric 'Cretans' or 'Minoans' were the first people to open up

15. *Gaius*, I.123. According to Boethius, the man asked the woman whether she would be his materfamiliar and she asked him whether he would be her paterfamiliar.

16. *Gaius*,I.111.

the Mediterranean by long seafaring voyages. Early contact with Egypt gave them the pattern of civilisation, which they, by their own, created a peculiar culture different from that of Egypt. About 2000 BC they were brought under the rules of a miniature pharaoh whose palace at Crossus was the earliest centre of political power in Greek lands.

The Greeks were originally organised in families of the Patriarchal type. These families were miniature states in themselves and they were held together by a rigid code under the authority of the 'Pater familias' The 'Pater familias' exercised over his household a power similar to the 'imperium' of an early Roman Consul. The woman was always under the bond of tutelage. So long as a woman remained unmarried, she stood under the authority of her father or some other male relative. A married woman passed into the power of her husband. The match was arranged over her head between her father or guardian and the bridegroom (or his parents) and in consideration of a sum paid to her family to compensate for the loss of her services. She was conveyed from one household to another.[17]

The patriarchal family organisation survived for a long time in the Greek marriage custom, but by the fifth century BC in Greek cities the law of marriage underwent an important change by which the women were also given the right of divorce on the ground of ill-treatment and adultery. It is said that during the Hellenistic period, women obtained more liberty.

But all this discussion leads us to only one point that the origin of marriage is still elusive. So even in 2000 BC there was a custom of marriage. It is a different matter as to how it worked and thus, irrespective of the status of women then, the concept of marriage had its roots and the society was a regulated one. It was no mere accident that the *Odyssey* an epic of conjugal fidelity, was the 'best seller' of the ancient world. Homer says outright that life can offer nothing better than a happy marriage. It is also an historical fact and still prevailing that wedding ceremonies began with an exchange of contract deeds and a sacrifice and prayer at the house

17. M. Cary and T.J. Haarhoof, *Life and Thought in the Greek & Roman World*, London, 1959, p. 142.

of the bride and ended at nightfall with a joyous procession in which the bride was conveyed to her new home.

## Jewish Law

A venture of probe in the Jewish civilisation will also be appropriate. The history of Jewish Law may be divided into the following periods:

| | |
|---|---|
| 1. Before Moses | 1300 BC |
| 2. Moses to Ezra | 444 BC |
| 3. Ezra to Hillel | 4 BC |
| 4. Hillel to R Judah | AD 217 |

Little is known definitely about the Israelites that their Pre-Mosaic history is largely guess work. About their cultural condition we can only hazard some general observations that one based more upon analogies drawn from similar semitic societies than upon any great store of fact or knowledge.[18] Being nomads, they had a body of customary law which like most primitive custom had the sanction of religion behind it. But generally the starting point is the Torah of Moses (The Pentateuch) as found in the first five books of the *Bible*: Genesis, Exodus, Leviticus, Numbers and Deuteronomy. This Torah was accepted from early times as the fundamental law of the Jewish people, because according to traditions, it had been given to them by God through Moses at Mount Sinai.

> Moses received the Torah from Sinai, and transmitted it to Joshua, Joshua to Elders, the Elders to the Prophets.[19]

It is said that there is no religion or nation in which the family occupies such an important place as in Judaism. In fact, according to *Bible* and Jewish tradition, the entire nation sprang and developed from a single family and furthermore the development proceeded not from all members of the family, but from those whose character displayed traits of nobility and righteousness.[20]

---

18. George Horowitz, *The Spirit of Jewish Law*.
19. *Mishnah*, I.1.
20. Meyer Waxman, *Judaism, Religion and Ethics*, London, p. 113.

Marriage is the basis and the source of all family life and the entire Jewish literature beginning with the Pentateuch speaks about it. According to the Book of Genesis, marriage was instituted by God himself at the very beginning of creation of man. The words are 'It is not good for a man to be alone'.[21] So this concept speaks of above the level of mere satisfaction of a biological necessity but emphasises on the element of companionship through their entire life. The Prophets often describe the relation between God and Israel symbolically as a marriage tie or covenant and constantly emphasise the element of love and the impossibility for a hosband to forget the wife of his youth, a figure which reflects the high conception of the marital tie.

The Jewish marriage is performed by observing various ceremonies like *Birkat Eursin*, *Kiddushin* and *The ketubah* is then read. The *Ketubah* is the formal marriage document in which the willingness of both parties to enter into the contract of marriage is expressed and some of the duties specified followed by *mohar* also known as *ketubah* money.

The history of Jewish civilisation dates back to 1300 BC but the view about marriage is that it exists since the creation of man by God. Thus, it shows that even in this civilisation the origin of marriage is not traceable.

### Christian civilisation

This is a religion-based civilisation, which took its birth 2000 years back. In Christian countries of the West, marriage is regarded by some as a sacrament, by others as a civil contract and by most as a mixture of the two. However, the existence of the institution of marriage was there when the Christianity had its birth. The early church based its attitude to sexual union on the doctrines of St. Paul:

> Now concerning the things whereof ye wrote unto me; It is good for a man not to touch a woman.
>
> Nevertheless, to avoid fornication, let every man have his own wife, and let every woman have her own husband.

21. Genesis, II.6.

> Let the husband render unto the wife due benevolence; and likewise also the wife unto the husband.
>
> The wife hath not power of her own body, but the husband and likewise also the husband hath not power of his own body, but the wife.
>
> Defraud ye not one the other, except it be with consent for a time that ye may give yourselves to fasting and prayer; and come together again, that *satan* tempt you not for your incontinency.
>
> But I speak this by permission, and not of commandment.
>
> For I would that all men were even as I myself. But every man hath his proper gift of God, one after this manner, and another after that.[22]

These verses again tell two things. Firstly, that the origin of marriage was there when Christianity took birth. Secondly, the marriage was basically to regulate sex. This is why in *Hyde* v. *Hyde*, Lord Penzence observed that marriage is the voluntary union for life of one man and one woman to the exclusion of all others.

**Pre-Islamic Arabia**

It is said that the concept of marriage was roughly known to the Arabians. The status of woman was not honourably recognised. They were treated as the cattle of the man. A young woman could be married to an old man. Women were sold in the society. The common prostitution was prevalent in Arab society but if prostitute conceived pregnancy she could decide the paternity among the frequent visitors. A man would purchase a girl from her parents or guardians on a fixed sum. *Muta* (temporary) marriages were prevalent prior to Islam. Thus, the concept of marriage was there but in a most crude form.

Prophet Mohammed recognised the institution of marriage and gave it a religious touch and sanction and according to *Hedaya*, it is a union of sexes. It is a contract for the sexual intercourse and legalisation of children.

---

22. Corinthians, VII, verses 1-7.

## Hindu civilisation

Now we turn our thoughts to Hindu civilisation which in reality is known as Vedic civilisation and history basing on conjectures merely estimates the existence of Vedic civilisation to 4000 BC, the oldest civilisation. Looking to Vedas, we find glorified mention of the concept of marriage in a most developed manner. This shows that the system of marriage is from time immemorial. It is the form of marriage which had undergone changes or the changes occurred in its concept. Hindu scriptures speak of marriage as *saṁskāra* and this concept is recognised also judicially.

## What is saṁskāra?

The question arises is as to what *saṁskāra* means in Hindu Law. The word *saṁskāra* means the performance which removes evils and creates good qualities in man. The Act of marriage uplifts the soul of the married. The purpose of this union is to inculcate disappearance of all harmful propensities in the two, bringing in them chastity, masculinity, restraint, pure love and the qualities of performing religious ceremonies, for the welfare of the progeny and society.[23]

Dr. S Ramaratnam's representation on "The philosophy of *gṛha* rituals" at the university seminar, spoke about *saṁskāra*s thus:[24]

1. *Saṁskāra*s refer to rituals by the performance of which the life of the Hindu performer is endowed with significant sanctity.
2. *Saṁskāra*s means, literally, 'making perfect'. Bhāṣya Śabara enunciates *saṁskāra*s that which being effected makes an object or a person eminently fit for a specified purpose. There are other definitions also.
3. Any person seeking to attain the 'highest reality' (*brahma sākṣātkāra*) must, necessarily, equip himself with the *sādhanā catuṣṭaya*, i.e., (i) discrimination between the

---

23. Pt. Nachiketa spoke on *Vivāha Saṁskāra* on 21-12-1992.
24. Appeared in *Indian Express*, Visakhapatnam edn., dated 23-10-1996.

permanent and the ephemeral (*nityānitya vastu viveka*), (ii) *vairāgya* (total dispassion), (iii) Tranquillity of mind (*sama*), control of sense faculties (*dama*) and faith (*śraddhā*), and lastly (iv) intense desire for liberation (*mumukṣutva*).

4. *Saṁskāras* encompass man's entire life right from his conception 'in the mother's womb till his death, and even later, to ensure, smooth passage for his soul into the other world.

5. Sage Aṅgirasa links poetically human personality development to the strict performance of the prescribed *saṁskāras* — just as a painting is embellished with picturesque colours so also the individual character is developed desirably by the enjoined performance of these *saṁskāras*.

6. In the book *Śāstras and Saṁskāras* by Shri V.A.K. Ayer it is said: In short, the whole gamut of *saṁskāras* is designed to channel the entire energies of man towards the creations of a perfect secular as well as spiritual life in himself in a manner that is not only ingenious but essentially practical, dignified and compulsory in the interest of all-round human welfare.[25]

7. V.A.K. Ayer quotes Max Müller: The prescription of these ceremonies by the ancients disclose the deep rooted tendency in the heart of man to bring the chief events of human life into contact with a higher power and to give to our joys and sufferings a deeper significance and religious sanctification.

8. That man must acquaint himself methodically with the prescribed texts imparting 'highest knowledge' through *śravaṇa* (hearing) and reading these, analyse in his mind what he has learnt (*manana*) and then meditate deeply upon the 'Supreme Self' (*nidhidhyāsana*).

---

25. V.A.K. Ayer, *Hindu Śāstra and Saṁskāras*, Bhavan's Book University Bombay, p. 24, 1993.

9. Mental purity of the highest order (*cittaśuddhi*) can be achieved through religious rites and practices performed with intense faith (*śraddhā*). All said and done, rituals are in essence, graded discipline taking man step by step from mundane considerations to the ultimate end of gaining the 'higher reality'.

10. Paradoxically, the purpose of rituals is to take man beyond rituals in pursuit of higher goals.

So just as gold or diamond that is dug out from the ore needs refining in order to shine in all its splendour, man too needs these *saṁskāras* or purificatory ceremonies in order to shine in his best form physically, psychically and spiritually.[26]

In the patriarchal society of *Ṛgveda* Hindu marriage was considered as a sacramental union and it continued to be so throughout the Hindu period. Sir Henry Maine has spoken about twelve *saṁskāras* of importance and *vivāha* (marriage) is one such important *saṁskāras*.[27]

Marriage is one of the necessary *saṁskāra* or religious rite for all Hindus, whatever the caste, who do not desire to adopt the life of a perpetual *brahmacārī* or of a *saṁnyāsī*, of course, there has never been any doubt as to its being a necessary *saṁskāra* for a Hindu woman of any caste.[28]

Manu says:

> Know that he for whom (the performance of) the ceremonies beginning with the right of impregnation (*garbhādhāna*) and ending with the funeral rites (*antyeṣṭi*) is prescribed, while sacred formulas are being recited, is entitled (to study) these institutes, but no other man whatsoever.[29]

This verse refers to the males of three *varṇas*. This verse is to be read along with another verse of Manu:

---

26. V.A.K. Ayer, *Hindu Śāstras and Saṁskāra*, 1993, pp. 22-23.
27. Mayne's *Hindu Law and Usage,* 1991 edn., Appendix I.
28. *Ibid.*, p. 118.
29. *Manu*, II.16.

> With holy rites, prescribed by the Veda, must the ceremony on conception and other sacraments be performed for twice born men, which sanctify the body and purify (from sins) in this (life) and after death.[30]

Then Manu again speaks about these ceremonies about women also He says:

> This whole series (of ceremonies) must be performed for females (also) in order to sanctify the body at the proper time, and in the proper order but without (the recitation of) sacred texts.[31]

> The nuptial ceremoney is stated to be the Vedic Sacrament for women (and to be equal to the initiation), serving the husband (equivalent to) the residence in (the house of the) teacher, and the household duties as the (daily) worship of the sacred fire.[32]

Yājñavalkya says about the ceremonies thus:

> The castes are the brāhmaṇas, the kṣatriyas, the vaiśyas and the śūdras. Only the first three (of these) are twice born, the performance of the ceremonies beginning with the rite of impregnation and ending (with the funeral rites) in the cremation ground, of these only, is prescribed with sacred formulas.[33]

This verse speaks of ceremonies (all) from *garbhādhāna* to *antyeṣṭi* which includes marriage too. He further says:

> By this the taint (derived from both parents, literally) produced from the seed and the embryo is destroyed. These ceremonies, in cases of women, are (to be) performed in silence, but however, their marriage is with (the recitation of) *mantras*.[34]

---

30. *Manu*, II.26.
31. *Ibid.*
32. *Ibid.*, II.67.
33. *Yāj*, I.10.
34. *Ibid.*, I.13.

*Mitākṣarā* propounds a special rule for women, 'these' ceremonies of birth, etc., of women are to be performed, at the proper time, 'in silence' without reciting sacred formulas. Their marriage (however), is (performed) with the *mantra*s, i.e., by reciting the sacred formulas.

This verse speaks, attaching great importance to the ceremony of marriage, as marriage being a *saṁskāra*s and this is why it has been ordained by Dakṣa that the twice born should not remain *anāśramī* (houseless or without belonging to particular order) even for a single day.[35]

The next question then haunts us as to why the marriage has been called a *saṁskāra*. The answer simply lies in the object and importance attached to the marriage as enshrined in the Hindu scriptures. Marriage is an initiation in the most important *gṛhasthāśrama*. Our sages introduced the *varṇāśrama* system which speaks of two things:

1. The *varṇa*s were created for the procurement of a general distribution of wealth, to expel want and misery from the country, promoting mental and moral progress, ensuring material efficiency, creating stable conditions for maintaining peace and tranquillity, to ensure harmonious development of the society and the nation.
2. The *āśrama*s speak of the individual and social aspects of life through the media of *karma* based on *dharma*, that speak of the period of learning, the period of *artha* and *kāma* based on *dharma*, the period of the attainment of the third aspect of life called *mokṣa*.

Manu says:

वेदानधीत्यवेदौवावेदंवा पियथाक्रमम्।
अविप्लुतब्रह्मचर्योगृहस्थाश्रममावसेत् ।। २ ।।

A student who had studied in due order the three Vedas, or two or even one only, without breaking the (rules of) studentship shall enter the order of householders.[36]

---

35. *Dakṣa*, I.10.
36. G. Bühler, *Manu*, III.2.

Manu another place says:

चतुर्थमायुषोभागमुषित्वाद्यंगुरौद्विज: ।
द्वितीयमायुषोभागंकृतदारोगृहेवसेत् ।। १ ।।

After dwelt with a teacher during the fourth part of (a man's) life, a brāhmaṇa, shall live during the second quarter (of his existence) in his house, after he has wedded a wife.[37]

Various Hindu scriptures speak about the *āśrama*s and one such scripture says:

ब्रह्मचर्याश्रमं समाप्य गृही भवेत्, गृही भूत्वा वनी भवेत्,
वनी भूत्वा प्रव्रजेत्। — शत० का० १४

So *gṛhasthāśrama* is the scond one and entry from the first *āshrama* to the second *āśrama* is an initiation which is based on the marriage ceremony to be solemnised and this initiation or marriage ceremony is called by the sages and the scriptures as one of the important *saṁskāra* and it is still continuing and its sanctity is preserved even under odd and adverse, so-called reformatory onslaughts.

The *āśrama* in the period of discharge of duties and debts which are as follows:

1. Duty to the family
2. The three natal debts.
3. Duties as householder as spoken in *Vaikhānasa Dharma-sūtras*.

### Duty to family

First of all we have to see the concept of family in general and then in particular as ordained in Hindu scriptures. It may not be impossible to define family but definitely it is a difficult preposition as it can have vast, varied and versatile meaning and can be looked from various angles such as religious, social and legal. In one sense it means all persons related by blood or marriage; in another it means all the members of a household. It is indeed a vastness of definition. So we should take a little narrower look at this concept

37. G. Bühler, *Manu*, IV.1.

by which the family may be regarded as a basic social unit constituted, firstly, at least by two persons having a relationship of wife and husband.

There can be other relationship such as parents living with one or more children or brothers and sisters and/or other blood relation or relation through marriage can also constitute a family. This social unit, as the minimum unit of the society is intertwined with religion as Hindu marriage is a *saṁskāra*, solemnised with due religious ceremonies and the marriage creates a legal relationship of status conferred on the spouses. So family embraces social, religious and legal parameters, three in one and none is ignorable. So the stability of the family, being a social unit, solemnised religiously, followed by the legal sanction accorded to it, is of paramount importance. The important question pertaining to marriage is not of the rights that accrue out of it but the duties imposed and the necessary rights should flow out of the discharge of such duties. In Hindu philosophy duty is a spiritual concept and the right flowing out of it is called the reward. So the family has to be seen from the concept of duty and not right.

Hindu scriptures have also taken a vast view of family as well as a narrower view of family.

In *Ṛgveda* there is a mention that:

अज्येष्ठासो अकनिष्ठास एते, सं भ्रातरो वाहघुः सौभगाय ।
युवा पिता स्वपा रुद्र एषां, सुदुघा पृश्निः सुदिना मरुद्भ्यः ।।

Let all these men who are brothers (to one another) advance forward unitedly for the attainment of prosperity for there being none high and none low (amongst them) God is their father. Let the earth pouring forth abundant milk (etc.) bring auspicious days for the living creatures.[38]

In *Atharvaveda* it is said:

मा भ्राता भ्रातरं द्विक्षन् मा स्वसारमुत स्वसा ।
सम्यञ्चः सव्रता भूत्वा वाचं वदत भद्रया ।।

Neither a brother should hate his brother nor a sister

38. *ṚV*, V.60.5.

should be unkind to her sister, you ought to speak with another most gently being united in your mind and keeping the same ideal before you.[39]

At another place it is said:

ज्यायस्वन्तश्चित्तिनो मा वियोष्ट संराधयन्तः सधुराश्चरन्तः।
अन्यो अन्यस्मै वल्गु वदन्तः एते सध्रीचीनान् वः संमनसस कृणोमि ॥

O ye mankind! who are respectable to the elders possessing noble hearts, friendly in their undertakings of acquiring wealth and walking in the same path bearing the common yoke together, be never dis-united with one another, come I make you single-intentioned and single-minded. Let each one of you speak sweetly to the other.[40]

सध्रीचीनान् स संमनसस्कृणोम्येकश्नुष्टीन्त्संवननेन सर्वान् ।
देवा इवामृतं रक्षमाणाः सायं प्रातः सौमनसो वो अस्तु ॥

O ye mankind! I (God) enjoin on all of you to be mutually helpful to one another, to be united in your mind and to have common ideal of life for benefiting one another like the enlightened person who ever take care of the immortal principle (in their life) may be friendly feelings amongst you increase morning and evening.[41]

The *Yajurveda* says:

तं पत्नीभिरनु गच्छेम देवाः पुत्रै र्भ्रातृभिरुत वा हिरण्यैः ।
नाकं गृभ्णानाः सुकृतस्य लोके तृतीये पृष्टेऽअधि रोचने दिवः ॥

O learned persons! Just as ye, mastering that fire, engaged in the performance of virtuous Vedic deeds, residing in a beautiful knowable pleasant place, built scientifically, attain the happiness with your wives, sons, brothers, other relatives and with gold, so may we, also be happy in all these respects.[42]

39. *AV*, III.30.3.
40. *Ibid.*, III.30.5.
41. *Ibid.*, III.30.7.
42. *YV*, XV.50.

Kauṭilya says:

> अपत्यद मातापितरौ भ्रातृनप्राप्तव्यवहारान् भगिनीः कन्या विधवाश्चाविभ्रतः
> शक्तिमतो द्वादशपणो दण्डः, अन्यत्र पतितेभ्यः, अन्यत्र मातुः ।। २८ ।।
>
> If a person with means does not maintain his children and wife, his father and mother, his brothers, who have not come of age, and his unmarried sisters and widowed sisters, a fine of twelve *paṇa*s (shall be imposed) except when these have become outcasts, with the exception of mother.[43]

The above cited verses speak of family in terms of *kula*. As per Pāṇini *kula* has a bigger congregation. It includes of several members.

But we also find verses where a narrower concept of family is also taken. In *Atharvaveda* we find:

> अनुव्रतः पितुः पुत्रो मात्रा भवतु संमनाः ।
> जाया पत्ये मधुमतीं वाचं वदतु शान्तिवाम् ।।
>
> Let the son be obedient to his father and in accordance with the mind of his brother. Let the wife speak to her husband, calm, gentle and sweet words as honey.[44]

It is said that the husband and wife are, so to speak, two horses tied round the same yoke. There should be perfect harmony between them. They have to march together step by step, tied by that invisible rope of conjugal love than which nothing is stronger.[45]

In *Ṛgveda* we find:

> इहैव स्तं मा वियौष्टं विश्वमायु व्यश्नुतम् ।
> क्रीडन्तौ पुत्रै र्नप्तृभि र्मोदमानौ स्वगृहे ।।
>
> O bride and bridegroom! You two stay here. Never be disunited (i.e., be faithful, never think of any other man or woman). Enjoy the full span of life. Play with children and grandchildren. By happy in your home.[46]

---

43. *Kauṭilya*, 2.1.28.
44. *AV*, III.30.2.
45. Dr. Veda Mitra, *India of Dharma-sūtras*, pp. 65-6.
46. *RV*, 10.84.52.

In this regard Manu says:

> He only is a perfect man who consists (of three persons united), his wife, himself and his offsprings; thus (says the Veda), and (learned) brāhmaṇas propound this (maxim) likewise. The husband is declared to be one with wife.[47]

This narrow concept of family can be taken as a part of the one whole. For our matter under discussion we take this narrow concept of family consisting of husband, wife and children as the bedrock of society. Concept of society in any sense is an *āśrama* which only devotes and indicates duties and nothing else and such duties imposed, speak of the essence of *saṁskāra* and a brief picture of the duties is given below.

**Duties of a householder**

We shall only refer to the scriptures which speak of the duties of the householder and the nature of the duties which lay emphasis on the religious and spiritual aspect of life individually and in relation to society.

*Ṛgveda* says:

सङ्गच्छध्वं सं वदध्वं सं वो मनांसि जानताम् ।
देवा भागं यथा पूर्वे सञ्जानाना उपासते ।।

> O ye mankind! Let all your activities lead to one common goal (for which) let there be a common language for all of you and let your mind be all of one accord, to acquire the knowledge of various sciences fully and like the enlightened seers who lived before you. You ought to worship me alone, who is the only real object of your devotion.[48]

It is further said that:

समानो मन्त्रः समितिः समानी समानं मनः सह चित्तमेषाम् ।
समानं मन्त्रमभि मन्त्रये वः समानेन वो, हविषां जुहोमि ।।

47. *Manu*, IX.45. See also *Āpastamba*, II.14, 16: *Vājasaneyi Brāhmaṇa*.
48. *RV*, X.191.2.

O ye mankind! let the object of your thought be the same, the place of your assembly ought to be common, your mind should be of one accord and let your hearts be united together. I (God) initiate you in common inspired hymn and provide all of you with common objects of accepting and offering.[49]

समानी व आकूतिः समाना हृदयानि वः ।
समानमस्तु वो मनो यथा वः ससहासति ।।

O ye mankind! Let your object of life be one and the same, let your hearts be equal (in feeling) and let your minds be united together so that there may be an excellent common status of life for all.[50]

*Atharvaveda* says:

सहृदयं सांमनस्यमविद्वेषं कृणोमि वः ।
अन्यो अन्यमभिहर्यत वत्सं जातमिवाध्न्या ।।

O ye mankind! I ordain for you to have concordance in your heart, unanimity in your minds and freedom from hatred in your dealings. Everyone of you ought to love one another in every way just as the violable cow loveth the calf which she hath born.[51]

*Yajurveda* says:

मित्रस्याहं चक्षुषा सर्वाणि भूतानि समीक्षे ।

May I look upon all beings with a friend's eye.[52]

These duties are of general nature which speak of purity of mind, heart and soul and their manifestation in general terms to create love and affection among all as a consequence of righteous conduct. Now we come to the specific duties imposed on the householder from a social, moral and cultural angle. One specific thing to be

---

49. *RV*, X.191.3.
50. *Ibid.*, X.191.4.
51. *AV*, III.30.1.
52. *YV*, 36.18.

noted is that though the duties imposed are basically religious or moral in character but law as intertwined with religion and morals, these duties can be aptly called as legal duties also.

Householder is of four kinds as revealed in the scriptures, i.e.,

1. *Vārtā-vṛttis* is one who lives on agriculture, tending of cows and trade.

2. *Śālīna-vṛttis* who is practising *niyamas* performing the *pāka-yajñas* and establishing the sacred fires, is performer of *darśapūrṇamāsya* sacrifices, full moon and new moon sacrifices every fortnight, *cāturmāsya* sacrifice every four months, *paśubandha* sacrifice every six months and some sacrifice annually.

3. *Yayavara* is he, who performs himself sacrifices — *haviryajñas*, *somayajñas* and causes others to perform the above sacrifices, who reads the Vedas himself and teaches the Vedas to others, who donates and takes donations from others, who is busy in the six duties every-day and who performing Agnihotra, entertains the guests and other visitors with food, etc.

4. *Ghoracārika* is one who is practising *niyamas*, performs sacrifices for himself and not for others, studies the Veda himself but does not teach it to others, gives but does not receive alms and lives by gleaning, devoted to the worship of 'Nārāyaṇa' and offering sacrifices in the sacred fires both morning and evening and performing the sword-edge-vow (*asidhara vrata*) during the months of *Mārgaśīrṣa* (November-December) and *Jyeṣṭha* (May-June). He performs *homa* in the sacred fire with faggots from the woods.

*Vaikhānasa Dharma-sūtra* gives a vivid description of householder as follows:

गृहस्थाश्चतुर्विधा: वार्तावृतिः, शालीन वृति र्यायावरो घोरव्ध्रिकश्चेति ।। १ ।। वार्तावृतिः कृषिगोरक्ष्यवाणिज्योपजीवी ।। २ ।। शालीनवृति र्नियमै र्युतः पाकयज्ञै रिष्ट्वाग्नीनाधाय पक्षे पक्षे दर्श पूर्णमास याजी, चतुर्षु चतुर्षु मासेषु चातुर्मास्ययाजी पद्षु षद्सु मासेषु पशुबन्धयाजी, प्रतिसंवत्सरं सोमयाजी च ।। ३ ।। यायावरो हविर्यज्ञैः सोमयज्ञैश्च यजते

याजयत्यधीते ऽध्यापयति ददाति प्रतिगृह्णाति षट्कर्मनिरतो नित्यमग्निपरिचरणमतिथिभ्यो ऽभ्यागतेभ्यो ऽन्नाद्य च कुरुते ।।

घोराचारिको नियमैर्युक्तो यजते न याजित, अधीते नाध्यापयति, ददाति न प्रतिगृह्णाति-इत्युञ्छ वृत्तिमुपजीवति नारायण पारायणः सांय प्रातरग्निहोत्रं हुत्वा मार्गशीर्ष ज्येष्ठ मासयोरसि-धारा व्रतं वनौषधिभिरग्निपरिचरणं करोति ।। ५ ।।[53]

*Vaikhānasa Dharma-sūtra* further states that after taking a wife and even after thus becoming householder one should, observing, *niyamas* and performing *upāsanā pākayajñas* after *vaiśvadeva homa*, receive and saluting, offer seats and water for washing feet and sipping (*ācamana*) to the teacher who has come to his house and the religious student who is entering the householder's stage, also, after giving them *madhuparka*, he feeds them with cooked rice and other things according to his ability. (This indicates the respect for the teacher who is the spiritual *atithi* and this is the foremost duty of every householder as the teacher is solely responsible for bringing enlightenment of knowledge to the householder when he was a student and making him worthy to discharge his household duties with wisdom).[54]

दारान् संगृह्य गृहस्थोऽपि स्नानादि नियमाचारो नित्यमौपासनं हुत्वा पाकयज्ञयाजी वैश्वदेवहोमान्ते गृहागतं गुरु स्नातकं च प्रत्युत्थायाभिवाद्यासनपाद्याचमनानि प्रदाय मधुना तोयेन वा दधिघृतक्षीर मिश्रं पधुपर्कं च दत्वा न्नाद्यैर यथाशक्ति भोजयति ।। १ ।।

It further says of an other duty that possessing kindness being truthful and observing the customary practices, he should satisfy the *ṛṣis* by reciting the Vedas and by oblation of water, the gods, by performing *homa* and offering things like water and flowers; the father's *pitṛs* by *śrāddhas* and by begetting sons, living creatures by offering *bali* and human beings by giving cooked rice, etc., freed him from the three debts, he owes and becomes debtless. (So five types of *yajñas* are prescribed as religious rites which encompass the whole universe.[55]

दयासत्य शौचाचार युतः स्वाध्याय तर्पणाभ्यामृषीन्,
यज्ञ बलिहोम जलपुष्पाद्यै र्देवान्, श्राद्धैः पत्रैश्च

53. *VaikhāDS*, 1.5.1-5.

54. *Ibid.*, 1.4.1.

55. *Ibid.*, 1.4.4-5.

पितृन्, बलिना भूतान्, अन्नाद्यैर् मनुष्यांश्च नित्यं तर्पयेत् ।। ४ ।।
ऋणत्रयै मुक्तो ऽनृणी भवति ।। ५ ।।

Now a brief description of the five *yajñas* will show the exaltness of the householder (*gṛhasthāśrama*) from a Universal and Cosmos angle which can be performed by the householder after he has taken a wife and entered this *gṛhasthāśrama*. These five *yajñas* have been described in *Taittiriya Āraṇyaka* which says:

पञ्च वा एते महायज्ञाः सतति प्रतायन्ते सतति सन्तिष्ठन्ते
देव यज्ञः पितृ यज्ञो भूत यज्ञो मनुष्य यज्ञो ब्रह्मयज्ञः ।।[56]

These five *yajñas* are a prominent feature of *Manu-smṛti*. Manu says:

> By the study of Vedas, by vows, by burnt oblations, by (the recitation of) sacred texts, by the (acquisition of the) threefold sacred science, by offering (to the gods, *ṛsis* and manes), by (the procreation of) sons, by the great sacrifices and by (*śruta*) rites this (human) body is made fit for (union with) *Brahman*.[57]

Manu then speaks of five great sacrifices thus:

> With the sacred fire, kindled at the wedding, a householder shall perform according to the law the domestic ceremonies and the five (great) sacrifices, and (with that) he shall daily cook his food.[58]

He again says:

> In order to successively expiate (the offences committed by manes) of all these (five) the great sages have prescribed for householders the daily performance of the five great sacrifices.[59]

तासां क्रमेणः सर्वासां निष्कृतयर्थं महर्षिनिः ।
पञ्च क्लृप्ता महायज्ञाः प्रत्यहं गृहमेधिनाम् ।।

56. *Taitirīya Āraṇyaka*, 2.10.7.
57. *Manu*, II.28.
58. *Ibid.*, III.67.
59. *Ibid.*, III.69.

Then Manu gives the vivid picture of the sacrifices thus:

> Teaching (and studying) is the sacrifice (offered) to *Brahman*, the (offerings of water and food called) *tarpaṇa*, the sacrifice to the manes, the burnt oblations the sacrifice offered to the gods, the *bali* offering that offered to the *bhūta*s and the hospitable reception of guests the offering to men.[60]

अध्यापनं ब्रह्मयज्ञः पितृयज्ञस्तु तर्पणम् ।
होमो दैवो बलिर्भौतो नृ यज्ञोऽतिथि पूजनम् ।।

He further says:

> They call (these) five sacrifices also, *ahuta*, *huta*, *prahuta*, *brahmya-huta* and *prasita*.[61]

Then Manu says:

> Let him worship, according to the rule, the sages by the private recitations of the Veda, the gods by burnt oblations, the manes by funeral offerings (*śrāddha*), men by (gifts of) food, and the *bhūta*s by the *bali* offering.[62]

स्वाध्यायेनार्चयेदृषीन् होमैर्देवान् यथाविधि ।
पितृन् श्राद्धैश्चान्नै र्भूतानि बलि कर्मणा ।।

Manu then repeats it in different perspective:

> Let him never, if he is able (to perform them) neglect the sacrifices to the sages, to the gods, to the *bhūta*s, to men and to the manes.[63]

ऋषियज्ञं देवयज्ञं भूतयज्ञं च सर्वदा ।
नृयज्ञं पितृयज्ञं च यथाशक्ति न हापयेत् ।।

These five sacrifices briefly are:

1. *Ṛṣi-yajña*: This ceremony is the reading and teaching of

---

60. *Manu*, III.70.
61. *Ibid.*, III.73.
62. *Ibid.*, III.81.
63. *Ibid.*, IV.21.

the Vedas and scriptures, meditation and prayer and the practice of introspection or *yoga*.

2. *Deva-yajña*: The company of the sages, their service, purity and requirement of angelic and holy qualities, the charity, the pursuit of knowledge. These two *yajña*s, i.e., *ṛṣi-yajña* and *deva-yajña* are to be performed morning and evening.

3. *Pitṛ-yajña*: It consists of serving the elderlies, the learned, the teachers, the father, the mother and other elderly scholars and eminent spiritualists and clairvoyants.

4. *Bhūta-yajña*: It is a duty to nature. The food being ready, a portion of viands made of clarified butter and sugar should be taken out, leaving out such as is sour, saltish and alcholic and separating a part of fire, it should be offered into it as is ordained by Manu.

5. *Atithi-yajña*: It is the duty of hospitality. An oblation to the fire of the hearth and to all the gods of nature and part of food to be offered to the miserable, hungry persons, or dogs, crows, cows and other animals. A householder before eating the food himself prepared in his household kitchen should share it by offering to others as mentioned above. A householder should always remember that the creator of the vast universe created it as a compact whole and that he is a particle in it.[64]

Baudhāyana laid great stress on these *yajña*s with specific emphasis on *atithi-yajña*.

He says that these are the five great sacrifices. These also are the great sacrificial sessions. Sacrifice to Gods, sacrifice to *pitṛs*, sacrifice to elementals, sacrifice to men, sacrifice to Veda. Then he says that one would eat the sins of others, who eats alone. He should first feed the guests, then the youngsters, the poor beggars and especially the sick persons. If he eats his food without giving to others, then he eats nothing, rather is eaten up by others. This he vividly explains in the Dharama-sūtra.[65]

---

64. Dr. Ved Mitra, *India of Dharma-sūtras*, pp. 120-1.

65. *BaudhDS*, 2.6.7-8, 2.7.6, 9, 23, 27-28.

Āpastamba says that:

> By way of laudation, they are called great sacrifices and then he explains the meaning and manner of the performance of these sacrifices and also lays great stress on giving food first to his guests and to infants, old or sick people, female relations and pregnant women.[66]

Yājñavalkya says:

> The *bali-karma*, the *śrāddha*, the *homa*, the study of the Vedas and honouring the guests are the great sacrifices to the *bhūtas* the *pitṛs*, the gods, the *Brahman* and men.[67]

Mitākṣarā has explained this verse thus:

> *Bali karma* is *bhūta-yajña*. The *śrāddha* (giving of food after pronouncing the word *śrāddha*) is *pitṛ-yajña*. (Sacrifice of food to fire) is *deva-yajña* (sacrifice to gods), *svādhyāya* (study of the Vedas) is *brahma-yajña*. The honouring of guest is *mānuṣya-yajña*. These five great *yajñas* should be daily performed because they are permanent duties (*nitya*).

About *atithi-yajña* Yājñavalkya says:

> Children, the bride, the old, the pregnant, the sick, the damsel, the guest and the servants are to be fed, the couple (husband and wife) eating last.[68]

Mitākṣarā explains 'eating last' as eating last or the remainder.

If we critically examine the duties of householder, which are multifacet, one clearly understands the depth of our sages that such duties are only imposed on the householder. To enter *gṛhasthāśrama*, the prerequisite is marriage and Hindu marriage is called a *saṁskāra* which means, Hindu marriage is sacrament which means a religious act that is sacred as a sign or symbol of a spiritual reality and the *saṁskāra* of marriage is to prepare the couple in the best form physically, psychically, spiritually and it is

---

66. *ĀpasDS*, I.4.12.14-15, 1.4.13.1, 2.2.3.16.20, 2.2.4.8,11-14.

67. *Yāj*, I.102.

68. *Yāj*, I.105.

an early means by which the couple is helped to develop moral virtues so that they become conscious of their moral upliftment over material benefits and be ready to perform their duties as good householder as *gṛhasthāśrama* is the foundation of all other *aśrama*s, though it is second in sequence.

So naturally the Hindu marriage, being a *saṁskāra* has to be performed religiously so that the couple develops the energy towards creating a perfect secular as well as spiritual life, practical, dignified and humanly social, in the interest of all-round human welfare and all creations of the creator.

Thus, the marriage, is solemnised with the performance of various ceremonies by reciting *mantra*s, which is a preparation for entry into *gṛhasthāśrama*, conscious of duties to be discharged and thus it is but essential to have a picture of some of the essential ceremonies and the *mantra*s that are recited to have the feel of the real sense of *saṁskāra*.

### Hindu marriage — Ceremonies and mantras

Marriage rites are common for all forms of marriage. Since marriage is a sacrament, the ceremonies of solemnisation of marriage commence with the invocation of God's mercy and ancestral blessings by means of prayer and food to seven brāhmaṇas as worship of *saptarṣi*. So the marriage ceremony starts with *abhyudayika* and ends with a concluding ceremony called *kuśaṇḍika*. The intermediate ceremonies are in four parts.[69]

### The first ceremony is 'maṇḍapa ceremony'

This ceremony is solemnised at the respective houses of the bride and bridegroom separately which consists of invocation of God's blessing, serving food as worship to the *saptarṣi*s and later turmeric powder mixed with wheat flour and oil and making a special dough like thing and to be rubbed on the body of the bride and bridegroom and then giving them bath. This ceremony is known as *gotra-haridra* (besmearing the body with turmeric powder). The primary object is to prepare them for the performance of the duty of holy *kāma*

69. Dr. Ved Mitra, *India of Dharma-sūtras*, p. 78.

which is the *sine qua non* of the marriage to redeem the debt which one owes to the manes. It is to generate in the sense-organs an irresistible power. It is said that the woman is like a pot of *ghī* and the man like live coal. Therefore, a wise man should not bring together *ghī* and fire. The sense-organs are so powerful that they can even over power the learned person. It is said:

घृत कुम्भसमा नारी तप्ताङ्गार समः पुमान्।
तस्माद् घृतं च वह्निं च नैकत्र स्थापयेद् बुधः।। १ ।।

मात्रा स्वस्रा दुहित्रा वा न विविक्तासनो भवेत्।
बलवानिन्द्रियग्रामो विद्वांसमपि कर्षति।। २ ।।

**The scond part is known as 'dvāra-pūjā'**

At the time when bridegroom reaches along with his party and enters the house of the bride the bridegroom and his party are welcomed through the following manner of *madhuparka*, etc.

It may be mentioned here that *madhuparka* is a mixture of honey, *ghī* and curd. These three things inspire to build a happy life. Honey signifies sweetness. Sweetness comes from affection. Sweetness is essential for married life. *Ghī* signifies mildness. If there is no mildness in a man, he can never find peace. Curd signifies coolness. As the curd removes heat of the body, in the same manner coolness is essential to make life successful and for improvement of family.

Thus, there is conversation between the bride and bridegroom which speaks of invocation and prayer for the union of the two and the offering of *madhuparka*.

ओं साधु भवानास्तामर्चयिष्यामो भवन्तम्।।

Bride: Please be seated well. We shall adore you.

ओं अर्चय।।

Bridegroom : Yes, your cordial reception is accepted

ओं विष्टरो विष्टरः प्रतिगृह्यताम्।।

Bride: It is a nice seat, kindly be seated.

ओं प्रतिगृह्णामि।।

Bridegroom : Thanks, I accept it.

Then the Bridegroom takes the seat and utters a *mantra*:

Amongst my equals like the sun amongst shining planets and stars, I hold superiority. To him who tries to humiliate me, I will tread down in the manner I sit on this seat.

ओं वर्ष्मोऽस्मि समानानामुद्यतामिव सूर्यः।
इमन्तमभितिष्ठामि यो मा कश्चाभिदासति।।

Bride : Please accept this water to wash your feet.

ओं पाद्यं पाद्यं पाद्यं प्रतिगृह्यताम्।।

Bridegroom : Thanks, I accept it.

ओं प्रतिगृह्णामि।।

Then the bridegroom takes the full pot of water and washes his feet and pronounces the following *mantra*:

ओं विराजो दोहोऽसि सिराजो दोहमशीय मयि पाद्यायै विराजे दोहः।।

Bridegroom : This water is the essence of various shining matters. It is good fortune that the same water has been given to me for washing my feet.

Then the bride gives a small pot, full of water in the hand of bridegroom and say:

ओ अर्घोऽर्घोऽर्घः प्रतिगृह्यताम्।।

Bride : Please accept this water to wash your face.

ओं प्रतिगृह्णामि।।

Bridegroom : Thanks I accept it.

The bridegroom washes his face and pronounce the following *mantras*:

ओं आप स्थ युष्माभिः सर्वान्कामानवाप्नवानि।
ओं समुद्रं वः प्रहिणोमि स्वां योनिमभिगच्छत्।
अरिष्ठास्माकं वीरा मा परासेचि मत्पयः।।

Through this water I fulfil my aspirations. I send this water to the atmospheric ocean. This would reach its primal source. May our children enjoy health and happiness. By grace of God this water may not forsake us.

Again the bride offers the full pot of water to the bridegroom and utter.

ओं आचमनीयमाचमनीयम्प्रतिगृह्यताम्।।

Bride: Please accept this water for sipping.

ओं प्रतिगृह्णामि।।

Bridegroom : Thanks, I accept it.

The bridegroom sips the water thrice after reciting the following *mantra*:

ओं आ मागन् यशसा स सृज वर्चसा।
तं मा कुरु प्रियं प्रजानामधिपतिं पशूनामरिष्टिं तनूनाम्।।

O water! You have come to me, accomplish me with glory and strength. By your grace, may I be affectionate to my children master of animals like cow, horse, etc., and let my body and limb be free from diseases.

Then the bride offers *madhuparka* and says:

ओं मधुपर्को मधुपर्को मधुपर्कः प्रतिगृह्यताम्।।

Bride : Here is *madhuparka*, please accept it.

ओं प्रतिगृह्णामि।।

Bridegroom : Thanks, I accept it.

Then the bridegroom pronounces the following *mantra* and minutely look at the *madhuparka:*

ओं मित्रस्य त्वा चक्षुषा प्रतीक्षे।।

Bridegroom : I look at you with the eye of a friend.

Then the bridegroom takes the pots of *madhuparka* and pronounce the following *mantra*:

ओं देवस्य त्वा सवितुः प्रसवेऽश्विनोर्बाहुभ्यां।
पूष्णो हस्ताभ्यां प्रतिगृह्णामि।।

Thereafter, the bridegroom pronounces the following *mantras*:

ओं भूर्भुव स्वः। मधु वाता ऋतायते मधु
क्षरन्ति सिन्धवः माध्वीर्नः सन्त्वोषधीः।। १ ।।

ओं भूर्भुवः स्वः। मधु नक्तमुतोषसो मधु-
मत्पार्थिवं रजः। मधु द्यौरस्तु नः पिता।। २ ।।

आं भूर्भुवः स्वः। मधुमात्रो वनस्पतिर्मधुमा
अस्तु सूर्यः। माध्वीर्गावो भवन्तु नः।। ३ ।।

Bridegroom : O God, to enjoy the peaceful and truthful life let the sweet wind blow, let the water of rivers flow gently, the herbs be full of sweetness, let the night and dawn be sweet, let the earth and heaven which is protector of all, be sweet, let the vegetables, rays of sun and all domestic animals like cow, etc., be full of sweetness.

Then the bridegroom mixes the honey into curd thrice with second finger and thumb of the right hand and pronounce the following *mantra*:

ओं नमः श्यावास्यायान्नशने यत्त आविद्ध तत्ते निष्कृन्तामि।।

Bridegroom : This *madhuparka* is energy giving food for health. If there is anything unacceptable mixed herein, I take away from it.

Now the bride sprinkles this *madhuparka* in all directions with the following *mantras*:

ओं वसवस्त्वा गायत्रेण छन्दसा भक्षयन्तु।।
ओं रुद्रास्त्वा त्रैष्टुभेन छन्दसा भक्षयन्तु।।
ओं आदित्यास्त्वा जागतेन छन्दसा भक्षयन्तु।।
ओं विश्वे त्वा देवा आनुष्टुभेन छन्दसा भक्षयन्तु।।
ओं भूतेभ्यस्त्वा परिगृह्णामि।।

Thereafter the bridegroom pronounces the following *mantra* and takes the *madhuparka* from each of the three pots:

ओं यन्मधुनो मधव्यं परम रूपमन्नाद्यम्।
तेनाहं मधुनो मधव्येन परमेण रूपेणान्नाद्येन परमो मधव्योऽन्नादोऽसानि।।

Bridegroom : O God! As the honey contains sweetness

present in an ideal food — so I should be able to take that *madhuparka*.

Then the bridegroom takes water and sips it twice after uttering the following *mantra*s and then takes some water in his left palm and dip the middle and ring finger into the water and touch his different organs with *mantra*s:

ओं वाङ्मऽआस्येऽस्तु।।
ओं नसोर्मे प्राणोऽस्तु।।
ओं अक्ष्णोर्मे चक्षुरस्तु।।
ओं कर्णयोर्मे श्रोत्रमस्तु।।
ओं बाह्वोर्मे बलमस्तु।।
ओं ऊर्वोर्मऽओजोऽस्तु।।
ओम् अरिष्टानि मेऽङ्गानि तनूस्तन्वा से सह सन्तु।

Afterwards, stretching right palm of the bridegroom, the guardian of bride put the palm of bride thereon and utter the following sentence:

ओम् . . . . गोत्रोत्पन्नाम् इमाम् . . . . नाम्नीम् अलंकृतां कन्यां . . . . प्रतिगृह्णातु भवान्।

Kindly accept this girl named . . . . in your . . . . family.[70]

ओ प्रतिगृह्णामि।।

Bride: Thanks, I accept her.

Then comes the ceremony of offering of clothes (*vastra-dāna*). The bridegroom gives to bride cloth and *upavastra* with the following *mantra*:

ओं जरां गच्छ परिधत्स्व वासो भवा कृष्टीनामभिशस्ति पावा। शतं च जीव शरदः सुवर्चा रयिं च पुत्राननु संव्ययस्वायुष्मतीदं परिधत्स्व वासः।। ओं या अकृन्तन्नवयन् या अतन्वत याश्च देवीस्तन्तुनभितो ततन्थ। तास्त्वा देवीर्जरसे संव्ययस्वायुष्मतीदं परिधत्स्व वासः।।

O Bride! you put on this cloth and enjoy long and lustrous life. Becoming the mother wish your family well, O bride! The ladies who have woven this cloth, should wish you long life and they may provide good clothes for you all along.

70. In the blank space the name of the bride and the *gotra* of the bridegroom is to be filled.

Then the bridegroom also dresses himself with the *vastra* and *upavastra* with the reciting of the following *mantra*:

> ओं परिधास्यै यशोधास्यै दीर्घायुत्वाय जरदष्टिरस्मि।
> शतं च जीवामि शरदः पुरुची रायस्पोषमभिसंव्ययिष्ये।।
>
> ओं यशसा मा द्यावापृथिवी यशसेन्द्राबृहस्पती।
> यशो भगश्च मा विदद्यशो मा प्रतिपद्यताम्।।

I am putting on this cloth for fame and long life. May I live hundred years with all essences. May the earth and heaven enrich me with fame and may fame always visit me.

Then comes the prayer of the bride and bridegroom and they pronounce the following *mantra*:

> ओं समञ्जन्तु विश्वे देवाः समापो हृदयानि नौ।
> सं मातरिश्वा सं धाता समु देष्ट्री दधातु नौ।।

Let all the learned persons present here should know that we are accepting each other voluntarily and pleasantly. Our hearts should be calm and united like water. We should be happy like breath of life and love each other.

Thereafter, the bridegroom holds the right hand of the bride with his right hand and are uttered the following *mantra:*

> ओं यदैषि मनसा दूरं दिशोऽनुपवमानो वा।
> हिरण्यपर्णो वैकर्णः स त्वा मन्मनसां करेतु असौ।।

O bride! or bridegroom! you voluntarily accept me like sun which reaches powerful water, substances and directions from a great distance. May God permit him/her to be favourable to each other.

> ओं भूर्भुवः स्वः। अघोरचक्षुरपतिघ्न्येधि शिवा पशुभ्यः सुमनाः सुवर्चाः।
> वीरसूर्देवृकामा स्योना शन्त्री भव द्विपदे शं चतुष्पदे।।

O bride! you who do not create any opposition with the bridegroom, should obtain pleasant vision by the grace of God — the protector of all, life giver and remover of all miseries. You should be vigorous producer of heroic son, well-wisher of *devara* (brother of husband), man and cattle, etc.

ओं भूर्भुवः स्वः। सा नः पूषा शिवतमामैरय सा न उरू उशती विहर। यस्यामुशन्तः प्रहराम शेफं यस्यामु कामा बहवो निविष्ट्यै।।

O God, the source of energy, you transmit this well wisher bride to me. She should think of our happiness and be herself happy. Let her fulfil the desire of son, virtue and wealth of this family.

After reciting the above *mantras*, bridegroom and bride circle round the *yajña-kuṇḍa* and take their seats at previously fixed places facing in the east. The bride on the right side of the bridegroom and the bridegroom on the left of the bride. The bride then pronounces the following *manta* thereafter:

ओम् प्र मे पतियानः पन्थाः कल्पताꣳ शिवा अरिष्टा पतिलोकं गमेयम्।

May this path of my husband would be the same to me. Desiring unobstructed happiness I enter my husband's home.

Then starts the beginning of the main *homa* of marriage ceremony. Main *yajña*, *rāṣṭravṛt-yajña, jāyā homa, abhatna homa* and then the *ajyāhuti*, which all are done by reciting *mantras*.

The starting of the marriage ceremonies of the *yajña*, the *purohita* (the priest who conducts the marriage ceremony), the bride and the bridegroom, after initial beginning participate in the Main *yajña*.

## Main yajña

During the *yajña* the bride touches the right shoulder of bridegroom and offer fine oblations with the following *mantras*:

ओं भूर्भुवः स्वः। अग्न आयूंषि पवस आ सुवोर्जमिषं च नः।
आरे बाधस्व दुच्छुनां स्वाहा।। इदमग्नये पवमानाय-इदन्न मम।। १ ।।

ओं भूर्भुवः स्वः। अग्निऋषिः पवमानः पाञ्चजन्यः पुरोहितः।
तमींमहे महागयं स्वाहा।। इदमग्नये पवमानाय-इदन्न मम।। २ ।।

ओं भूर्भवः स्वः। अग्ने पवस्व स्वपा अस्मे वर्चः सुवीर्यम्।
दधद्रयि मयि पोषं स्वाहा।। इदमग्नये पवमानाय-इदन्न मम।। ३ ।।

ओं भूर्भुवः स्वः। प्रजापते न त्वदेतान्यन्यो विश्वा जातानि परिता बभूव।

यत्कामास्ते जुहुमस्तन्नो अस्तु वयं स्याम पतयो रयीणां स्वाहा।।
इदं प्रजापतये-इदन्न मम।। ४ ।।

ओं भूर्भुवः स्वः। त्वमर्यमा भवसि यत्कनीनां नाम स्वधावन्गुह्यं बिभर्षि। अञ्जन्ति मित्रं सुधितं न गोभिर्यद्दम्पती समनसा कृणोषि स्वाहा।। इदमग्नये-इदन्न मम।। ५ ।।

O omnipotent and ever joyful God, the upholder of happiness and wealth, who is the arbiter of the life of the daughter or who as potential within, nourishes and allows the pair to think themselves one, and who behaves like an intelligent friend, be pleased.

**Rāṣṭravṛt-yajña**

It consists of making twelve oblations to be offered with the following *mantas*:

ओं ऋताषड् ऋतधामाग्निर्गन्धर्वः। स न इदं ब्रह्म क्षत्रं पातु तस्मै स्वाहा वाट्।।
इदमृताषाहे ऋतधाम्ने अग्नये गन्धर्वाय-इदन्न मम।। १ ।।

ओं ऋताषाड् ऋतधामाग्निर्गन्धर्वस्तस्यौषधयोऽसरसो मुदो नाम। ताभ्यः स्वाहा।।
इदमोषधिभ्योऽप्सरोभ्यो मुद्भ्यः-इदन्न मम।। २ ।।

ओं सँहितो विश्वसामा सूर्यो गन्धर्वः। स न इदं ब्रह्म क्षत्रं पातु तस्मै स्वाहा वाट्।। इदं सꣳहिताय विश्वसाम्ने सूर्याय गन्धर्वाय-इदन्न मम।। ३ ।।

ओं सꣳहितो विश्वसामा सूर्यो गन्धर्वस्तस्य मरीचयोऽप्सरसऽआयुवो आम। ताभ्यः स्वाहा।।
इदं भरीचिभ्योऽप्सरोभ्य आयुभ्यः-इदन्न मम।। ४ ।।

ओं सुषुम्णः सूर्यरश्मिश्चन्द्रमा गन्धर्वः। स न इदं ब्रह्म क्षत्रं पातु तस्मै स्वाहा वाट् इदं सुषुम्णाय सूर्यरश्मये चन्द्रमसे गन्धर्वाय-इदन्न मम।। ५ ।।

ओं सुषुष्णः सूर्यरश्मिश्चन्द्रमा गन्धर्वस्तस्य नक्षत्राण्यप्सरसो भेकुरयो नाम। ताभ्यः स्वाहा।।
इदं नक्षत्रेभ्योऽप्सरोभ्यो भेकुरिभ्यः-इदन्न मम।। ६ ।।

ओं इषिरो विश्वव्यचा वातो गन्धर्वः। स न इदं ब्रह्म क्षत्रं पातु तस्मै स्वाहा वाट्।।
इदमिषिराय विश्वव्यचसे वाताय गन्धर्वाय-इदन्न मम।। ७ ।।

ओं इषिरो विश्वव्यचा वातो गन्धर्वस्तस्यापोऽअप्सरसऽऊर्जो नाम। ताभ्यः स्वाहा।।
इदमद्भ्योऽप्सरोभ्य ऊर्ग्भ्यः-इदन्न मम।। ८ ।।

ओं भुज्युः सुपर्णो यज्ञो गन्धर्वः। स न इदं ब्रह्म क्षत्रं पातु तस्मै स्वाहा वाट्।। इदं भुज्यवे सुपर्णाय यज्ञाय गन्धर्वाय-इदन्न मम।। ९ ।।

ओं भुज्युः सुपर्णो यज्ञो गन्धर्वस्तस्य दक्षिणा अप्सरस स्तावा नाम। ताभ्यः स्वाहा।। इदं दक्षिणाभ्योऽप्सरोभ्यः स्तावाभ्यः-इदन्न मम।। १० ।।

ओं प्रजापतिर्विश्वकर्मा मनो गन्धर्वः। स न इदं ब्रह्म क्षत्रं पातु तृणैस्म स्वाहा वाट्।। इदं प्रजापतय विश्वकर्मण मनस गन्धर्वाय-इदन्न मम।। ११ ।।

ओं प्रजापतिर्विश्वकर्मा मनो गन्धर्वस्तस्य ऋक्सामान्यऽप्सरस एष्टयो नाम। ताभ्यः स्वाहा।। इदमृक्सामेभ्योऽप्सराभ्य एष्टिभ्यः-इदन्न मम।। १२ ।।

## Jāyā homa

After offering oblations to (*rāṣṭra-vṛt*) *āyjāhuti* with the above twelve *mantras*, *jaya homa* should be performed by the following *mantras*:

ओं चित्तं च स्वाहा।। इदं चित्ताय-इदन्न मम।। १ ।।

ओं चितिश्च स्वाहा।। इदं चित्त्यै-इदन्न मम।। २ ।।

ओं आकूतं च स्वाहा।। इदमाकूताय-इदन्न मम।। ३ ।।

ओं आकूतिश्च-स्वाहा।। इदमाकूत्यै-इदन्न मम।। ४ ।।

ओं विज्ञातं च स्वाहा।। इदं विज्ञाताय-इदन्न मम।। ५ ।।

ओं विज्ञातिश्च स्वाहा।। इदं विज्ञात्यै-इदन्न मम।। ६ ।।

ओं मनश्च स्वाहा।। इदं मनसे-इदन्न मम।। ७ ।।

ओं शक्वरीश्च स्वाहा।। इदं शक्वरीभ्यः-इदन्न मम।। ८ ।।

ओ दर्शश्च स्वाहा।। इदं दर्शाय-इदन्न मम।। ९ ।।

ओं पौर्णममासं च स्वाहा।। इदं पौर्णमासाय-इदन्न मम।। १० ।।

ओं बृहच्च स्वाहा।। इदं बृहते-इदन्न मम।। ११ ।।

ओं रथन्तरञ्च स्वाहा।। इदं रथन्तराय-इदन्न मम।। १२ ।।

जीवन में सफल होने के लिए इन शक्तिओं का आह्वान कर जाया होम से आहुति दी जाती है।

The above twelve oblations are given to have strength for heart, determination, science, mind and for the *yajña* at the time of full moon and *amāvasyā* as well as greatness and regarding *Sāmaveda*.

Oblations offered in the *jāyā-homa* is meant for invitation of powers to make successful life. Then the last oblation is performed with the *mantra*:

ओं प्रजापतिर्जयानिन्द्राय वृष्णो प्रायच्छदुग्रः पृतनाजयेषु।
तस्मै विशः समनमन्त सर्वाः स ग्रः स इ हव्यो बभूव स्वाहा।।
इदं प्रजापतये जयानिन्द्राय-इदन्न मम।। १३ ।।

The God has given the hymns of victory to man for fulfilment of desire through the *yajña*. The influence of *jāyā-homa*, strength is furiously increased to have celebrated victory upon the foes. It is why all the subjects of this world bow down before him and that is acceptable.

## Abhatana homa

Thereafter the oblations of *abhatana-homa* should be performed by reciting *mantras*:

ओं अग्निभूतानामधिपतिः स मावत्वस्मिन् ब्रह्मण्यस्मिन् क्षत्रेऽस्यामाशिष्यस्यां पुरोधायामस्मिन् कर्मण्यस्यां देवहूत्यांं स्वाहा।। इदमग्नये भूतानामधिपतये-इदन्न मम।। १ ।।

The fire is the main among the 'five primary elements' that should save me. The fire should protect the bride in this auspicious act and in this place are called the *devas*, our protector:

ओं इन्दो ज्येष्ठानामधिपतिः स मावत्वस्मिन् ब्रह्मण्यस्मिन् क्षत्रेऽस्यामाशिष्यस्यां पुरोधायामस्मिन् कर्मण्यस्यां देवहूत्याथ्ठं स्वाहा। इदमिन्नद्राय ज्येष्ठानामधिपतये-इदन्न मम।। २ ।।

ओं यमः पृथिव्याऽअधिपतिः स मावत्वस्मिन् ब्रह्मण्यस्मिन् क्षत्रेऽस्यामाशिष्यस्यां पुरोधायामस्मिन् कर्मण्यस्यां देवहूत्याथ्ठं स्वाहा।। इदं यमाय पृथिव्याअधिपतये-इदन्न मम।। ३ ।।

ओं वायुरन्तरिक्षस्याधिपतिः स मावत्वस्मिन् ब्रह्मण्यस्मिन् क्षत्रेऽस्यामाशिष्यस्यां पुरोधायामस्मिन् कर्मण्यस्यां देवहूत्याथ्ठं स्वाहा।। इदं वायवे अन्तरिक्षस्याधिपतये-इदन्न मम ।। ४ ।।

ओं सूर्यो दिवोऽधिपतिः स मावत्वस्मिन् ब्रह्मण्यस्मिन् क्षत्रेऽस्यामाशिष्यस्यां पुरोधायामस्मिन् कर्मण्यस्यां देवहूत्याथ्ठं स्वाहा।। इदं सूर्याय दिवोऽधिपतये-इदन्न मम ।। ५ ।।

ओं चन्द्रमा नक्षत्राणामधिपतिः स मावत्वस्मिन् ब्रह्मण्यस्मिन् क्षत्रेऽस्यामाशिष्यस्यां पुरोधायामस्मिन् कर्मण्यस्यां देवहूत्याथ्ठं स्वाहा।। इदं चन्द्रमसे नक्षत्राणामधिपतये-इदन्न मम ।। ६ ।।

ओं बृहस्पतिर्ब्र ह्मणोऽधिपतिः स मावत्वस्मिन् ब्रह्मण्यस्मिन् क्षत्रेऽस्यामाशिष्यस्यां पुरोधायामस्मिन् कर्मण्यस्यां देवहूत्याथ्ठं स्वाहा।। इदं ब्रहस्पतये ब्रह्मणोऽधिपतये-इदन्न मम ।। ७ ।।

ओं मित्रः सत्यानामधिपतिः स मावत्वस्मिन् ब्रह्मण्यस्मिन् क्षत्रेऽस्यामाशिष्यस्यां पुरोधायामस्मिन् कर्मण्यस्यां देवहूत्याथ्ठं स्वाहा।। इदं मित्राय सत्यानामधिपतये-इदन्न मम।। ८ ।।

ओं वरुणोऽपामधिपतिः स मावत्वस्मिन् ब्रह्मण्यस्मिन् क्षत्रेऽस्यामाशिष्यस्यां पुरोधायामस्मिन् कर्मण्यस्यां देवहूत्याꣳ स्वाहा।। इदं वरुणायापामधिपतये-इदन्न मम।। ९ ।।

ओं समुद्रः स्त्रोत्यानामधिपतिः स मावत्वस्मिन् ब्रह्मण्यस्मिन् क्षत्रेऽस्यामाशिष्यस्यां पुरोधायामस्मिन् कर्मण्यस्यां देवहूत्याꣳ स्वाहा।। इदं समुद्राय स्त्रोत्यानामधिपतये-इदन्न मम।। १० ।।

ओं अन्नꣳ साम्राज्यानामधिपतिः तन्मावत्वस्मिन् ब्रह्मण्यस्मिन् क्षत्रेऽस्यामाशिष्यस्यां पुरोधायामस्मिन् कर्मण्यस्यां देवहूत्याꣳ स्वाहा।। इदमन्नाय साम्राज्यानामधिपतये-इदन्न मम।। ११ ।।

ओं सोमऽओषधीनामधिपतिः स मावत्वस्मिन् ब्रह्मण्यस्मिन् क्षत्रेऽस्यामाशिष्यस्यां पुरोधायामस्मिन् कर्मण्यस्यां देवहूत्याꣳ स्वाहा।। इदं सोमाय ओषधीनामधिपतये-इदन्न मम।। १२ ।।

ओं सविता प्रसवानामधिपतिः स मावत्वस्मिन् ब्रह्मण्यस्मिन क्षत्रेऽस्यामाशिष्यस्यां पुरोधायामस्मिन् कर्मण्यस्यां देवहूत्याꣳ स्वाहा।। इदं सवित्रे प्रसन्नानामधिपतये-इदन्न मम ।। १३ ।।

ओं रुद्रः पशुनामधिपतिः स मावत्वस्मिन् ब्रह्मण्यस्मिन् क्षत्रेऽस्यामाशिष्यस्यां पुरोधायामस्मिन् कर्मण्यस्यां देवहूत्याꣳ स्वाहा।। इदं रुद्राय पशूनामधिपतये-इदन्न मम।। १४ ।।

ओं त्वष्टा रूपाणामधिपतिः स मावत्वस्मिन् ब्रह्मण्यस्मिन् क्षत्रेऽस्यामाशिष्यस्यां पुरोधायामस्मिन् कर्मण्यस्यां देवहूत्याꣳ स्वाहा।। इदं त्वष्ट्रे रूपाणामधिपतये-इदन्न मम।। १५ ।।

ओं विष्णुः पर्वतानामधिपतिः स मावत्वस्मिन् ब्रह्मण्यस्मिन् क्षत्रेऽस्यामाशिष्यस्यां पुरोधायामस्मिन् कर्मण्यस्यां देवहूत्याꣳ स्वाहा।। इदं विष्णवे पर्वतानामधिपतये-इदन्न मम।। १६ ।।

ओं मरुतो गणानामधिपतयस्ते मावत्वस्मिन् ब्रह्मण्यस्मिन् क्षत्रेऽस्यामाशिष्यस्यां पुरोधायामस्मिन् कर्मण्यस्यां देवहूत्याꣳ स्वाहा।। इदं मरुद्भ्यो गणानामधिपतये-इदन्न मम।। १७ ।।

ओं पितरः पितामहाः परेऽवरे ततास्ततामहाः इह मावन्त्वस्मिन् ब्रह्मण्यस्मिन् क्षत्रेऽस्यामाशिष्यस्यां पुरोधायामस्मिन् कर्मण्यस्यां देवहूत्याꣳ स्वाहा।। इदं पितृभ्यः पितामहेभ्यः परभ्योऽवरेभ्यस्ततामहेभ्यश्च-इदन्न मम।। १८ ।।

Like the omnipresent Agni, Indra and Vāyu in the world and the parents in the family, grandfather, grandmother and relations, near and distant ones, should save me.

## Ājyāhutis

After this, eight *ājāyāhutis* for removal of death and troubles are to be offered with the recitation of *mantras*:

ओं अग्निरैतु प्रथमो देवतानाथ्ठं सोऽस्यै प्रजां मुञ्चतु मृत्युपाशात्। तदयं राजा वरुणोऽनुमन्यतां यथेयं स्त्री पौत्रमघं न रोदात् स्वाहा।। इदमग्नये-इदन्न मम।। १ ।।

First, (Agni) the fire, the governor among all the physical elements. Let the fire come and save her offsprings from premature death. Let not this bride regret over her child.

ओं इमामग्निस्त्रायत्तां गार्हपत्यः प्रजामस्यै नयतु दीर्घमायुः। अशून्योपस्था जीवतामस्तु माता पौत्रमानन्दमभिविबुध्यतामिय स्वाहा।। इदमग्नये-इदन्न मम।। २ ।।

May the fire of household save the bride and may it allow her offspring towards long life. May she be free from all defects of barrenness and be the mother of living child. May she ever enjoy the pleasures from her children.

ओं स्वस्ति नोऽग्ने दिवा पृथिव्या विश्वानि धेह्ययथा यजत्र। यदस्यां मयि दिवि जातं प्रशस्तं तदस्मासु द्रविणं चेहि चित्रं स्वाहा।। इदमग्नये-इदन्न मम।। ३ ।।

Plenty of wrongs has been performed by me. Let me have good intellect to correct them and the praiseworthy qualities on my possession be, properties-like:

ओं सुगन्नु पन्थां प्रदिशं न एहि ज्योतिष्मध्ये ह्यजरं न आयुः।
अपैतु मृत्युरमृतं म आगाद्वै वस्वतो नो अभयं कृणोतु स्वाहा।। इदं वैवस्वताय-इदन्न मम।। ४ ।।

O God! please guide us the easily accessible path of prosperity and bless us long life without suffering from oldage. Death should depart from us and we attain salvation. Let the sun make us fearless.

ओं परं मृत्यो अनुपरेहि पन्थां यत्र नोऽअन्य इतरो देवयानात्। चक्षुष्मते शृण्वते ते ब्रवीमि मा नः प्रजाथ्ठंरीरिषो मोत वीरान्त्स्वाहा।। इदं मृत्यवे-इदन्न मम।। ५ ।।

This is my desire and prayer to God that by your blessing our children should not sustain any loss.

ओं द्यौस्ते पृष्ठं रक्षतु वायुरूरू अश्विनौ च। स्तनन्धयस्ते पुत्रान्त्सविताभिरक्षत्वावाससः परिधानाद् बृहस्पतिर्विश्वे देवा अभिरक्षन्तु पश्चात् स्वाह।। इदं विश्वेभ्यो देवेभ्यः-इदन्न मम।। ६ ।।

O bride! Let the sun protect you, let the learned like doctors protect you from ailments. Let the God save your children who are sucking the breast and let the saint and the elders in society protect you.

ओं मा ते गृहेषु निशि घोष उत्थादन्यत्र त्वद्रदत्यः संविशन्तु। मा त्व ः रुदत्युरऽआवधिष्ठा जीवपत्नी पतिलोके विराज पश्यन्ती प्रजाꣳ सुमनस्यामानाꣳ स्वाहा।। इदमग्नये-इदन्न मम।। ७ ।।

Let there not be wailing or shouting of any kind except that of the children in your home at night. Let the bride live happily with her children in the family of husband.

औ अप्रजस्यं पौत्रमर्त्य पाप्मानमुत वाऽअधम् । शीर्ष्णः स्रजमिवोन्मुच्य द्विषद्भयः प्रतिमुञ्चामि पाशः स्वाहा ।। इदमग्नये-इदन्न मम ।। ८ ।।

O bride! Let me promise to clear off the envious people and to remove your unhappiness over offsprings like throwing off the old garment.

After the above oblations the following four *ājyāhuti*s should be offered:

ओं भूरग्नये स्वाहा ।। इदमग्ये इदन्न मम ।। १ ।।
ओं भुवर्वायवे स्वाहा ।। इदं वायवे इदन्न मम ।। २ ।।
ओं स्वरादित्याय स्वाहा ।। इदमादित्याय इदन्न मम ।। ३ ।।
ओं भूर्भवः स्वरग्निवायवादित्येभ्यः स्वाहा ।।
इदमग्निवाय्वादितेभ्यः इदन्न मम ।। ४ ।।

## Pāṇigrahaṇa

Then comes the oath taking ceremony of *pāṇigrahaṇa* which is also known as (*pratijñā vidhi*). The bridegroom standing in front of the bride sitting east facing should keep his face in western direction and taking the right palm of the bride by his left hand should lift up and the so lifted right palm of bride along with thumb should accept and pronounce the *mantra*s to take oaths:

ओं गृभ्णामि ते सौभगत्वाय हस्तं मया पत्या जरदष्टिर्यथासः।
भगो अर्यमा सविता पुरन्धिर्मह्यं त्वादुर्गार्हपत्याय देवा ।। १ ।।

O bride I hold your hand for wealth, prosperity and good progeny. May you live up to oldage with your husband in pleasures.

God, the master of all prosperity, the upholder of justice, the creator of the universe and the learned persons present in this assembly are offering you to me for fulfilment of the obligations of household life.

ओं भगस्ते हस्तमग्रभीत् सविता हस्तमग्रभीत्।
पत्नी त्वमसि धर्मणाहं गृहपतिस्तव ।। २ ।।

O bride! I being a respected person accept your hand. I with all inspirations of religious deeds already accepted your hand. You are my wife by the virtue of *dharma* and I thus become your husband accodingly.

ममेयमस्तु पोष्या मह्यं त्वादाद् बृहस्पतिः।
मया मत्या प्रजावति शं जीव शरदः शतम् ।। ३ ।।

O bride! The protector of the universe who has given you to me and you would be worth supporting wife in this world to me. O ye my wife! May you live hundred autumns happily with your husband.

त्वष्टा वासो व्यऽदधाच्छुभे कं बृहस्पतेः प्रशिषा कवीनाम् ।
तेनेमां नारी सविता भगश्च सूर्यमिव परि धत्तां प्रजया ।। ४ ।।

O bride! The relation of husband and wife is established in this world through the teachings of God and the learned. Just as the light is present everywhere so you have from me good dresses, ornaments and happiness for the sake of my pleasure. May God fulfil the wishes of both.

इन्द्राग्नी द्यावापृथिवी मातरिश्वा मित्रावरुणा भगो अश्विनोभा ।
वृहस्पतिर्मरुतो ब्रह्म सोम इमां नारीं प्रजया वर्धयन्तु ।। ५ ।।

O ye our relatives! Just as light and fire, sun and earth, atmospheric air, breath, wealth, physician and true preacher, cultured men, supreme being, the moon and herbs enhance the progeny so you should entrance progeny.

## Mounting on the small stone

Then comes the ceremony of mounting on the small stone. The mother or the brother of the bride should lift bride's right foot and put it on small piece of stone near by. At that moment the bridegroom pronounces the following *mantra*:

> ओं आरोहेममश्मानमश्मेव त्वँ स्थिरा भव ।
> अभितिष्ठ पृतन्यतोऽवबाधस्व पृतनायतः ।।

> O bride! You mount on this stone and assume firmness like rock. Resist quarrelsome persons.

In order to make the wife firm in her devotion and fidelity to him the husband makes her to mount on a mill stone situated at the north of the fire.[71]

According to Āśvalāyana, stone here is symbolical of firmness and strength in crushing the enemies.[72] Rajbali Pande in his thesis agrees with the finding of Āśvalāyana[73]. This rite has been mentioned in *Atharvaveda*, *Baudhāyana*, *Bhardvāja* and *Mānava-sūtra*.[74]

Sengupta assumes that evidently the rite symbolises the very natural desire of making the union firm and strong and may have its origin in the ancient custom of oath taking on a stone.[75] *Atharvaveda* also mentions "Tread the foes down and turn away the enemies".[76]

> अहं वि ष्यामि मयि रूपमस्या वेददित्पश्यन्मनसः कुलायम् ।
> न स्तेयमद्मि मनसोदमुच्ये स्वयं श्रध्नानो वरुणस्य पाशान् ।। ६ ।।

> O bride! Just as I mind the increase of my family and this is obtained with love through your pervading beauty, so also you will be attracted in me just as I would not conceal anything from you and I would not enjoy anything stealthily, so also you are expected to act accordingly.

---

71. *ParGS*, I.7.
72. *ĀśvaGS*, I.7.7.
73. Rajbali Pande, *Hindu Saṁskāra*, 1969, p. 219.
74. *AV*, XIV.1.4.7, *BaudhGS*, I.4.24, *BharadvājaGS*, I.16, *ManGS*, 1.10.16.
75. Sengupta N., *Evolution of Hindu Marriage*, 1965.
76. *AV*, II.13.4.

## Promise for circle-round

Then comes the ceremony of 'promise for circle round', which is performed with the chanting of the following *mantra*:

> ओं अमोऽहमस्मि सा त्व ँ सा त्वमस्यमोहम् । सामाहमस्मि ऋक्त्वं द्यौरहं पृथिवी त्वं तावेव विवहावहै सह रेतो दधावहै। प्रजां प्रजनयावहै पुत्रान् विन्दावहै बहून्। ते सन्तु जरदष्टयः सं प्रियौ रोचिष्णू सूमनस्यमानौ। पश्येम शरदः।
>
> O bride! I accept with all my knowledge and intentions and so you have done. I am like *Sāmaveda* and you are *Ṛgveda*. I am like the sun, you are the earth. Both of us should marry each other pleasantly. We should uphold the essence of lives together, produce sons. The children should live long and love, admire, be good at heart to each other, let them live long with happiness and listen to pleasant words.

## Homa with roasted paddy and circle round

The roasted paddy has been taken here symbolically to express the meaning of union of the daughter with husband.

The paddy is first sown in a particular place and then reaped in another place for flourish and fruits, so the daughter is reared in her parent's home in her early life and then is offered to husband's home for his progeny. In the contact with fire the paddy takes the form of roasted paddy which signifies that the daughter in contact with her husband is to lead a life full of pleasantries and happiness. Thus, a woman becomes complete and perfect only in marriage. At the end of *lājā homa* through circling-round the *yajña-kuṇḍa*, it is indicated that the bride would join her husband's family and be initiated by the husband in the completion of their household duties in unison only to be perfect in keeping up with their promises.

In the performance of *lājā homa* the bride and bridegroom should stand keeping their faces in the east direction. The bride and bridegroom being united in their palms in the posture of offerings to fire, thereafter the brother or mother of the bride would stand, by taking a basket full of roasted paddy and give on their palms. Now the bride and bridegroom should offer these roasted paddy in the fired *agnikuṇḍa* with the following mantras:

ओं अर्यमणं देवं कन्या अग्निमयक्षत ।
स नोऽअर्यमा देवः प्रेतो मुञ्चतु मा पतेः स्वाहा ।।
इदमर्यमणे अग्नये-इदन्न मम ।। १ ।।

Worshipping the fire as God the bride prays that the God should separate me from my parental family but never separate me from my husband's family.

इयं नार्युपब्रूते लाजानावपन्तिका ।
आयुष्मानस्तु मे पतिरेधन्तां ज्ञातयो मम स्वाहा ।।
इदमग्नये-इदन्न मम ।। २ ।।

This lady offering the oblations of roasted paddy in the fire with the prayer that by the grace of God let my husband attain long life and the members of the nearest relations flourish in happiness and prosperity.

ओंइमाँल्लाजानावपाम्यग्नौ समृद्धिकरणं तव ।
मम तुभ्यं च संवननं तदग्निरनुमन्यतामियँ स्वाहा ।।
इदमग्नये-इदन्न मम ।। ३ ।।

O bridegroom! I offer these roasted paddy in the fire for your prosperity. May there be a great affection between you and me and God should be helpful in our cause.

Thereafter the bridegroom pronounces the following *mantras*:

ओं सवस्वति प्रेदमव सुभगे वाजिनीवति।
यान्त्वा विश्वस्य भूतस्य प्रजायामस्याग्रतः।
यस्यां भूतँ समभवद्यस्यां विश्वमिदं जगत्।
तामद्य गाथां गास्यामि या स्त्रीणामुत्तमं यशः।।

Afterwards the bridegroom holding the right palm of bride into his own right palm pronounces the following *mantras* and circle round:

ओं तुभ्ययग्रे पर्यवहन्त्सूर्या वहतुना सह।
पुनः पतिभ्यो जायां दा अग्ने प्रजया सह ।। १ ।।

ओं कन्यला पितृभ्यः पतिलोकं यतीयमय दीक्षामयष्ट।
कन्या उत त्वया वयं धारा उदन्या इवातिगाहेमहि द्विषः ।। २ ।।

Thus completing the four circles-round as in the above procedure the bridegroom and bride should stand in the west of the *yajña*-

*kuṇḍa* facing the east. Thereafter the mother, brother of the bride should give the remaining grains of roasted paddy of the basket in the *añjali*[77] of the bride. Reciting the following *mantra* the bride should offer the oblation by *ghī*.

> ओम् भगाय स्वाहा । इदं भगाय-इदन्न मम ।।
> ओम् प्रजापतये स्वाहा । इदं प्रजापतये-इदन्न मम ।।

**Release of tied hair**

It is also known as *keśa vimocana* or hair loosening ceremony. The bridegroom takes the bride and unties the knot of the hair of her head with the verses:

> प्रत्वा मुञ्चामि वरुणस्य पाशाद्येन त्वाबध्नात्सविता सुशेवः ।
> ऋतस्य योनौ सुकृतस्य लोकेऽरिष्टान्त्वा सह पत्या दधामि ।। १ ।।[78]

> प्रेतो मुञ्चामि नामुतः सुबद्धाममुतस्करम् ।
> यथेयमिन्द्र मीढ्वः सुपुत्रा सुभगासति ।। २ ।।[79]

> I free thee from restrictions of the law by which thy good father hitherto bound thee, i.e., the life of celibacy. Now I am marrying you and thy maidenhood comes to an end by my touch of your hair. With me, thy husband, thou shall live a life of righteousness and charity. I free her from her obligations here, i.e., in her father's family and not there, i.e., in the husband's family. Now that she stands well bound with her husband, she might have good luck in worthy progeny.

**Sapta-padī**

The next step is tying into a knot and seven steps. At this juncture 'scarf' of the bride should be tied with the *upavastra* of the bridegroom. This is the conjugal tie. Leaving their seats the bride and bridegroom both should stand up. Then the bridegroom holding the right hand *añjali* of the bride in his right hand should go in the north side of the *yajña-kuṇḍa*. Thereafter the bridegroom should

---

77. *Añjali* means 'palm'.

78. *Ṛ̥V*, X.85.24.

79. *Ibid.*, X.85.25.

put his hand on the right shoulder of the bride and both stand together side by side facing north. After this the bridegroom pronounces:

मा सव्येन दक्षिणमतिक्राम ।।

Let not thy left foot out do thy right foot (i.e., be constant and consistent).

Then starts the *sapta-padī*. Each step has separate vows:

FIRST STEP

ओं इष एकपदी भव सा मामनुव्रता भव विष्णुस्त्वा नयतु
पुत्रान् विन्दावहै बहूँस्ते सन्तु जरदष्टयः ।। १ ।।

O bride! please take the first step towards securing of food and daily necessaries and be determined to help me always. Let the supreme being confirm you in this meritorious act and allow you to produce better sons who would be helpful in old days.

SECOND STEP

ओं ऊर्ज्जे द्विपदी भव सा मामनुव्रता भव विष्णुस्त्वानयतु
पुत्रान् विन्दावहै बहूँस्ते सन्तु जरदष्टयः ।। २ ।।

O bride! Please take the second step to imbibe courage and three noble virtues and be determined to help me always. Let the supreme being confirm you in this meritorious act and allow you to produce better sons who would be helpful in old days.

THIRD STEP

ओं रायस्पोषाय त्रिपदी भव सा मामनुव्रता भव विष्णुस्त्वानयतु
पुत्रान् विन्दावहै बहूँस्ते सन्तु जरदष्टयः ।। ३ ।।

O bride! Please take the third step for acquiring of wealth and property and be determined to help me always. Let the supreme being. . . .

FOURTH STEP

ओं मयोभवाय चतुष्पदी भव सा मामनुव्रता भव विष्णुस्त्वानयतु
पुत्रान् विन्दावहै बहूँस्ते सन्तु जरदष्टय: ।। ४ ।।

O bride! Take the fourth step to inspire in me the strength to enjoy wealth and property and be determined to help me always. Let the supreme being. . . .

FIFTH STEP

ओं प्रजाभ्य: पञ्चपदी भव सा मामनुव्रता भव विष्णुस्त्वानयतु
पुत्रान् विन्दावहै बहूँस्ते सन्तु जरदष्टय: ।। ५ ।।

O bride! Please take the fifth step to produce children and their upbringing and be determined to help me always. Let the supreme being. . . .

SIXTH STEP

ओं ऋतुभ्य: षट्पदी भव सा मामनुव्रता भव विष्णुस्त्वानयतु
पुत्रान विन्दावहै बहूँस्ते सन्तु जरदष्टय: ।। ६ ।।

O bride! Please take the sixth step to conduct your family in obedience to the behaviours of the different seasons with all their different ceremonies and necessaries and be determined to help me always. Let the supreme. . . .

SEVENTH STEP

ओं सखे सप्तपदी भव सा मामनुव्रता भव विष्णुस्त्वानयतु
पुत्रान् विन्दावहै बहूँस्ते सन्तु जरदष्टय: ।। ७ ।।

O bride! Please take the seventh step to be my real friend and guide throughout my life and be determined to help me always. Let the supreme being. . . .

Completing the procedure of seven step ceremony the bridegroom and bride should take their previous seats. Thereafter the water should be sprinkled on the head of bridegroom with the following *mantra*:

ओम् आपो हि ष्ठा मयोभुवस्ता न ऊर्ज्जे दधातन ।
महे रणाय चक्षसे ।। १ ।।

Let this water help us to increase our strength of life and help us to see this world as a place of beauty and happiness.

यो वः शिवतमो रेसस्तस्य भाजयते ह नः ।
उशतीरिव मातरः ।। २ ।।

Let this water bestow on us the eternal welfare like the milk of respected mother.

तस्मा अरङ्गमाम वो यस्य क्षयाय जिन्वथ ।
आपो जनयथा थ नः ।। ३ ।।

Let us have this water which nourishes the medicinal plants for the sustenance of lives and which invigorates fertility in the animal world.

ओम् आपः शिवाः शिवतमाः शान्ताः शान्ततमास्तास्ते कृण्वन्तु भेषजम् ।। ४ ।।

Let us have this water as a cure of disease which is bringing us welfare, happiness and strength.

Thereafter the bride and bridegroom look at the sun and pronounce the *mantra*:

ओं तच्चक्षुर्देवहितं पुरस्ताच्छुक्रमुच्चरत्। पश्येम शरदः शतं जीवेम शरदः शतँ शृणुयाम
शरदः शतं प्र ब्रवाम शरदः शतमदीनाः स्याम शरदः शतं भूयश्च शरदः शतात् ।।

After this act, the bridegroom and bride would touch each other's chests by their right hands and pronounce the *mantra*:

ओं मम व्रते हे हृदयं दधामि मम चित्तमनु चिंत्त ते अस्तु।
मम वाचमेकमना जुषस्व प्रजापतिष्ट्वा नियुनक्तु मह्यम्।।

Let me wish you to behave in favour of the desires of my heart. Let my heart play in your wishes too. Let you listen to my words in all attention. The supreme being, the protector of subjects, appoints you to perform my deeds.

After this the bridegroom touches the bride's forehead and addresses the visitors and friends attending:

सुमङ्गलीरियं वधूरिमां समेत पश्यत।
सौभाग्यमस्यै दत्त्वायाथास्तं वि परेतन।।

Let these persons assembled here behold in unison this well meaning bride. Let she have blessings of you all to be ever in prosperity.

The persons assembled here should bless with the following sentence:

ओं सौभाग्यमस्तु। ओं शुभं भवतु।।

Afterwards the bride and bridegroom should perform the *yajña*, main *homa* and *ājyāhutis* with the following *mantras*:

ओं यदस्य कर्मणोऽत्यरीरिचं यद्धा न्यूनमिहाकरम्।
अग्निष्टत्स्विष्टकृद्विद्यात्सर्वं स्विष्टं सुहुतं करोतु मे। अग्नये
स्विष्टकृते सुहुतहुते सर्वप्रायश्चित्ताहुतीनां कामानां समर्द्धयित्रे
सर्वान्नः कामान्त्समर्द्धय स्वाहा। इदं अग्नये स्विष्टकृते-इदन्न मम।।
ओं भूरग्नये स्वाहा। इदमग्नये-इदन्न मम।।
ओं भुवर्वायवे स्वाहा। इदं वायवे-इदन्न मम।।
ओं स्वरादित्याय स्वाहा। इदमादित्याय-इदन्न मम।।
औं भूर्भुवः स्वरग्निवाय्वादित्येभ्यः स्वाहा।
इदमग्निवाय्वादित्येभ्यः-इदन्न मम।।

प्रधान-होम

ओं लेखासन्धिषु पक्ष्मस्वावर्त्तेषु च यानि ते। तानि ते पूर्णाहुत्या सर्वाणि शमयाम्यहं स्वाहा। इदं कन्यायै इदन्न मम ।। १ ।।

ओं केशेषु यच्च पापकमीक्षिते रुदिते च यत्। तानि ते पूर्णाहुत्या सर्वाणि शमयाम्यहं स्वाहा। इदं कन्यायै इदन्न मम ।। २ ।।

ओं शीलेषु यच्च पापकं भाषिते हसिते च यत्। तानि ते पुर्णाहुत्या सर्वाणि शमयाम्यहं स्वाहा। इदं कन्यायै इदन्न मम ।। ३ ।।

ओं आरोकेषु दन्तेषु हस्तयोः पादयोश्च यत् । तानि ते पुर्णाहुत्या सर्वाणि शमयाम्यहं स्वाहा। इदं कन्यायै इदन्न मम ।। ४ ।।

ओं ऊर्वोरूपस्थे जङ्घयोः सन्धानेषु च यत्। तानि ते पूर्णाहुत्या सर्वाणि शमयाम्यहं स्वाहा। इदं कन्यायै इदन्न मम ।। ५ ।।

ओं यानि कानि च घोराणि सर्वाङ्गेषु तवाभवन। पर्णाहतिमिराज्यस्य सर्वाणि तान्यशीशमं स्वाहा। इदं कन्यायै इदन्न मम ।। ६ ।।

४ आज्याहुति

ओं भूरग्नये स्वाहा । इदमग्नये इदन्न मम ।।

ओं भुवर्वायवे स्वाहा ।। इदं वायवे इदन्न मम ।।
ओं स्वरादित्याय स्वाहा ।। इदमादित्याय इदन्न मम ।।
ओं भूर्भुवः स्वरग्निवाय्वादित्येभ्यः स्वाहा ।।
इदमग्निवाय्वादित्येभ्यः इदन्न मम ।।

Then the ceremony of pointing out the pole star, wherein the bridegroom tells the bride to look at the pole star and the bride looks at the pole star and then bride says:

ओं ध्रुवं पश्य।

The pole star is constant. May I be Dhruva, constant in my husband's family.

ओं पश्यामि । ओं ध्रुवमसि ध्रुवाहं पतिकुले भूयासम्, गौरवस्य प्रियानाम्नी अहम् ।

Then the bridegroom showing the *arundhatī* (the star bearing this name) says to the bride to look at it. The bride looks at the *arundhatī* star and says:

ओं पश्यामि।
ओं अरुन्धत्यसि रुद्धाहमस्मि, गौरवस्य प्रिया नाम्नी अहम्।

This *śloka* is pertaining to the story that the wife of Vasiṣṭha who followed him after death to the sky and is having a place near the Vasiṣṭha star in the *saptarṣimaṇḍala*. So the bride referring to Arundhatī, speaks of firmness in conjugal life with her husband.

Then the bridegroom should touch on her forehead and pronounce the following *mantras*:

ओं ध्रुवा द्यौर्ध्रुवा पृथिवी ध्रुवं विश्वमिदं जगत् ।
ध्रुवासः पर्वता इमे ध्रुवा स्त्री पतिकुले इयम् ।। १ ।।

औं ध्रुवमसि ध्रुवन्त्वा पश्यामि ध्रुवैधि पोष्ये मयि ।
मह्यं त्वादाद् बृहस्पतिर्मया पत्या प्रजावती संजीव शरदः शतम् ।। २ ।।

Just as the other world, this world, mountains are fixed so also you remain fixed in my family. As you have appointed by the supreme being I would wish you to be fixed in my family and to enjoy hundred years of life in company with the meritorious sons.

After this act, the bride and bridegroom should perform *samādhi-homa*, *agharapajyabhagāhuti*, *vyāhṛti āhuti* and thereafter the oblations with cooked rice should be offered in the *agni-kuṇḍa* by the following *mantras*:

ओम् अग्नये स्वाहा ।। इदमग्नये-इदन्न मम ।। १ ।।
ओं प्रजापतये स्वाहा ।। इदं प्रजापतये-इदन्न मम ।। २ ।।

ओं विश्वेभ्यो देवेभ्यः स्वाहा ।।
इदं विश्वेभ्यो देवेभ्यः-इदन्न मम ।। ३ ।।

ओम् अनुमतये स्वाहा ।। इदमनुमतये-इदन्न मम ।। ४ ।।

Thereafter the bridegroom and bride should offer *siṣṭakṛtāhuti* and then after all these acts the bridegroom should put *ghī* on the remaining cooked rice and keep his right hand on it and pronounce the following *mantras*:

ओं अन्नपाशेन मणिना प्राणसूत्रेण पृश्निना ।
बध्नामि सत्यग्रन्थिना मनश्च हृदयं च ते ।। १ ।।

ओं यदेतद्धृदयं तव तदस्तु हृदयं मम ।
यदिदं हृदयं मम तदस्तु हृदयं तव ।। २ ।।

ओं अन्नं प्राणस्य षड्विध शस्तेन बध्नामि त्वा असौ ।। ३ ।।

Thereafter the bridegroom takes the cooked rice and a portion of it is left to be taken by the bride and then the *mahāvāmadevyagāna* and closing of wedding ceremony by the reciting of *mantras* takes place:

*Mahāvāmadevyagāna* and closing of wedding ceremony:

ओं भूर्धुवः स्वः। कया नश्चित्र आ भुवदूती सदा वृधः सखा। कया शचिष्ठया वृता ।। १ ।।

ओं भूर्भवः स्वः। कस्त्वा सत्यो मदानां मथ हिष्ठो मत्सदन्धसः। दृढा चिदारुजे वसु ।। २ ।।

ओं भूर्भुव स्वः। अभीषुणः सखीनामविता जरितॄणाम् शतम्भवास्यूतये ।। ३ ।।

Then finally, there is recitation of peace *mantra*. It is *mantra* for universal peace and also covers every aspect of life and all creations of the creator.

Recitation of peace *mantra*:

द्यौः शान्तिरन्तरिक्षꣳ शान्तिः पृथिवी शान्तिरापः शान्तिरोषधयः शान्तिः। वनस्पतयः शान्तिर्विश्वे देवाः शान्तिर्ब्रह्म शान्तिः सर्वꣳ शान्तिः शान्तिरेव शान्तिः सा मा शान्तिरेधि।।

ओं शान्तिः। शान्तिः। शान्तिः।

After the solemnisation of marriage, the bride goes to the house of the bridegroom. Though there reaching, many ceremonies are performed because her coming into the house is synonymous with the coming into the plenty,[80] yet the words of the father to the daughter at the time of departure speak about the essence of marriage and the essence of her duty in the new *parīvāra*:

> O daughter! May this fortunate husband, after marrying you, take you in a chariot with his brother to his house. Darling! you go there. You are the mistress of that house. You are to keep them in your control. Speak always charming and pleasing words to them.

भगस्त्वेतो नयतु हस्तगृह्याश्विना त्वा प्रवहतां रथेन।
गृहान् गच्छ गृह पत्नी ययासो वशिनी त्वं विदयमा वदासि।।
अथर्व० १४।१।२०

We have gone through the various ceremonies and rituals pertaining to the solemnisation of marriage. All these rituals show that marriage is not a mere legal abstraction but a social institution constituting a religious duty and purificatory rite. So a marriage under old Hindu Law is a sacrament, a religious rather than a secular institution.

Of all the *saṁskāra*s performed for a Hindu from the womb to the grave, from *garbhādhāna* (conception) to *antyeṣṭi* (cremation) marriage is given paramount status among *saṁskāra*s. It is the last of the *saṁskāra*s because with it starts the entry into *gṛhasthāśrama*. Manu says:

> The nuptial ceremony is stated to be the Vedic sacrament for women (and to be equal to the initiation) serving the husband (equivalent to) the residence in (the house of the) teacher and the household duties (the same) as the (daily) worship of the sacred fire.[81]

Manu says further:

> Because men of three (other) orders are daily supported by

---

80. Srinivasa M.N., *Marriage and Family in Mysore*, Bombay, 1942.
81. *Manu*, II.67.

the householder with (gifts of) sacred knowledge and food, therefore, (the order of) householder is the most excellent order.[82]

Yājñavalkya says:

> By this the taint (derived from both parents, literally) produced from the seed and the embryo is destroyed. These ceremonies, in cases of women, are (to be) performed in silence, but, however, their marriage is with (the recitation of) *mantra*.[83]

The importance of marriage as *saṁskāra* is well illuminated in the verse:

> गुभ्णामि ते सुप्रजास्त्वाय<br>
> हस्तं मया पत्या जरदष्टिर्यथाऽसः।<br>
> भगो आर्यमा सविता पुरंधि-<br>
> र्मह्यं त्वाऽदुर्गार्हपत्याय देवाः।।

> I seize thy hand to have a fine progeny, that thou mayest live with me, thy lord, till thou shall attain decay. The Gods — Bhaga, Aryaman, Savitri and Purandhi — have given thee to me for householdship.[84]

This *mantra* indicates the main object of marriage, i.e., *suprajātva*, the generation of a fine progeny. This result will accrue from the union of a man and a woman joining together in dose companionship for the whole life and duly performing, from the very day of the marriage onward, the duties of the householder's life — duties which they as husband and wife owe to the Gods, to man and to lower animals. Invocation of God in every *mantra* speaks of the divine ordinance behind every duty imposed upon the householder.

The next *mantra* of importance is:

> सखा सप्तपदा भव, सखायो सप्तपदा बभूव, सख्यं ते गमेयं, सख्यात्ते मा योषं. सख्यान्मे मा योष्ठाः । समयाव संकल्पावहै सं प्रियो रोचिष्णू सुमनस्यमानौ । इषमूर्जमभि सं वसानौ सं नौ मनांसि सं व्रता समु चित्तान्याकरम् ।।

---

82. *Manu.*, III.78.

83. *Yāj*, I.13.

84. *Taittirīya Ekāgnikāṇḍa*, I, iii.3.

> A friend shall thou be, having paced these seven steps with me. Nay having paced together the seven steps, we have become friends. May I retain thy friendship and never part from thy friendship. Let us unite together; let us propose together. Loving each other and ever radiant in each other's company, meaning well towards each other, sharing together all enjoyments and pleasures, let us join together our aspirations, our vows and our thoughts.[85]

This *mantra* signifies the ideal relationship of husband and wife, with meeting of minds, living in harmony and loving spontaneously, with a divine motto to bring forth a fine, manly and spiritual progeny and thereby forward the advance of humanity. These *mantra*s only speak of duty and the concept of right is totally missing because of the nature of marriage which is a *saṁskāra*.

Even the judicial opinion seems to favour the sacramental concept of Hindu marriage and its indissolubility which is the essential corollary of the sacramental concept of marriage. It is a permanent stable union. It is a tie, once tied, is never untied. Wife regarding husband as God and wife verily the half of the husband, ordained to discharge religious duties, is nothing but *saṁskāra*. Judicial view gives it full recognition.

1. *Binda* v. *Kausilia*[86]

It is a suit for restitution of conjugal rights, wherein the concept of Hindu marriage was also discussed, and the honourable Court referred to Shyam Charan Sarkar's *Vyavasthā Çandrikā*, Vol. II, p. 480.

The effect of marriage is the union of the bride and bridegroom, upon the performance of the nuptial ceremonies and rites, more especially by the recitation of this text of Veda: "Bones (identified) with bones, flesh with flesh and skin with skin", the husband and wife became as it were one person. So Manu Says: 'The husband is even one person with his wife' so also Bṛhaspati

In scriptures, and in the code of Law as well as in popular

85. *Taittirīya Ekāgnikāṇḍa*, I, iii, 14.

86. [1890] 13 ILR All 126.

> practice, the wife is declared to be half the body of her husband, equally sharing the fruits of pure and impure acts. Of him whose wife is not deceased, half the body survives.

So being the legal contemplation of the effects of marriage, the same learned author sums up the results of the authorities by laying down that 'marriage' properly contracted by the performance of the nuptial rites is indissoluble and the reciprocal relation of the married pair endures even after the natural death of one or both of them. The basis of this conclusion is especially on the text of Manu (Ch. IX.46)

> Neither by sale nor desertion can a wife be released from her husband; thus we fully acknowledge the law enacted of old by the Lord of Creatures.

2. *Venkatacharyulu* v. *Rangacharyulu*[87]

It is a case of a brāhamaṇa bride given in marriage by her mother without her father's consent and the validity of marriage was agitated. The honourable Court relying upon *Brindabun Chandra Kurmokar* v. *Chundra Kurmoka* ILR 12 Cal 140 held that when the marriage rite was duly solemnised and there was no fraud or force, the doctrine of factum valet applied and the marriage was irrevocable and further said that as a religious ceremony it becomes complete when the *saptapadī* is performed and the honourable Court referred several Smṛtis to that effect.

Manu says:

> The relation of wife is created by the texts pronounced when "the girl is taken by hand". Be it known that those texts end, according to the learned, with the texts prescribed "for walking seven steps".

Yama says:

> Not by the pouring of water nor by the words of gift is the

87. [1890] 14 ILR Mad 316.

> relation of husband and wife formed, but it is formed by the rite of taking the bride by hand and when they walk together the seventh step.

Nārada says:

> Once is a partition ordained, once is a girl given in marriage and once does a man say, "I give".

The author of *Smṛti Candrikā* says and forbids a second *saṁskāram* or marriage for the *kali-yuga*.

Thus, the theory is that when a legal relation is once consecrated by *mantra* or Vedic texts, it is permanently fixed. Then the Court held:

> There can be no doubt that a Hindu marriage is a religious ceremony. According to all the texts it is a *saṁskāram* or sacrament, the only one prescribed for a woman and one of the principal religious rites prescribed for purification of the soul. It is binding for life because the marriage rite completed by *saptapadī* or the walking of seven steps before the consecrated fire creates a religious tie, and a religious tie, when once created, cannot be untied. The person married may be a minor or even of unsound mind, and yet, if the marriage rite is duly solemnised, there is a valid marriage.

3. In the matter of *Ramkumari*[88]

It is a case of bigamy under section 494 of IPC where a conversion of Hindu wife to Mohammedanism and married to a Mohammedan. The honourable High Court held the petitioner guilty of bigamy and reasoned that it is argued that the Hindu Law would regard the apostate wife as beyond its pale and as a person that is civilly dead. That may be so as regards her civil rights but we find no authority in Hindu Law for the position that a degraded person or an apostate is absolved from all civil obligations incurred before degradation or apostasy. So far as the matrimonial bond is concerned, such a view would, we think, be contrary to the spirit of

88. [1891] XVIII ILR Cal 264.

the Hindu which regards that bond as absolutely indissoluble. The honourable Court referred *Manu-smṛti* V.156-85, IX.46 and relied upon;

(i) the *Govt. of Bombay* v. *Ganga* ILR 4 Bom 330

(ii) *Administrator of Madras* v. *Anandachari* ILR 9 Mad 467 and

(iii) In re. *Millard* ILR 10 Mad 218

4. *Tekait Mon Mohini Jemadai* v. *Basanta Kumar Singh*[89]

It is a suit for enforcement of conjugal rights wherein the nature of Hindu marriage was discussed and the Court said that it may be premised that though marriage under the Hindu Law is a contract, it is also a sacrament, it is more religious than secular in character; the union is indissoluble, for it is a 'union of flesh with flesh, bone with bone'. During the life of the husband, he is to be regarded by the wife as a god and the wife is declared to be half the body of her husband, equally sharing the fruits of pure and impure acts and no sacrifice or religious rite is allowed to her apart from the husband's. Hence, it is that after the husband's death, the widow is regarded as the surviving half of his body, the union is a sacred tie and subsists even after the death of the husband. The Court relied upon and referred *Manu*, II.67, III.43, V.154-8, 160, 165, IX.29, *Dāyabhāga*, IV.14, IX.1.2 and *Hindu Law on Marriage* by Dr. Banerjee, p. 131.

5. *Govindarajulu Narasimham* v. *Devara Bhotla Venkatanarasayya*[90]

It is a case of sale by father of family lands for expenses of one son's marriage for which there was no accent of other sons. The question agitated before the Court is as to whether it is a moral or religious duty of the father to bring about the marriage of his son.

The Court held that the sale of land was therefore invalid so far as the share of the other brothers are concerned as there is no moral or religious duty of the father to bring about the marriage of

89. [1901] XXVIII ILR Cal 751 at 758.

90. [1903] XXVIII ILR Mad 206.

his son. So it is not a legal necessity. The Court relied upon the Smṛti texts.

Laws of *Manu*, II.36-47, 169, 179 S.B.E. In these verses directions are given as to the initiary ceremonies to be performed in the case of brāhmaṇas and it is laid down that he who has not been initiated is on a level with śūdra (II.172). Nowhere, however, is marriage in the case of a male included among the initiatory ceremonies. Dr. Jolly, the learned translator and editor of *Nārada* writes:

> There appears to be some doubt as to what is meant by the term *saṁskāra*, initiary ceremonies or sacramental ceremonies, some commentators including the ceremony of marriage in that term and others declaring the initiatory ceremonies to terminate with the investiture with the sacred thread.

The honourable Court then referred to *Mitākṣarā* (chapter I section I, para 29) and various references from Stokes' *Hindu Law Books*, Colebrook's *Digest of Hindu Law*, and *Smṛti Candrikā* and held that there is a complete absence of authority for the proposition that omission to perform the ceremony of marriage in the case of a male brāhmaṇa curtails a forfeiture of his caste or status and such being the case, there is no moral or religious obligation on a father to bring about the marriage of his son.

Thus, the honourable Court came to a conclusion that marriage by the father of his son is neither a moral nor a religious duty and marriage, resultantly, is not a *saṁskāra* and is not a ceremony, which falls within the ambit of initiation ceremony. However, without going into the merits of the conclusions arrived at it is sufficient to state that this decision has been overruled in subsequent decisions.

6. *Sundra Bai* v. *Shivnarayana*[91]

It is a debt contracted for the marriage of a coparcener in a joint Hindu family and is binding on the other coparcener as a debt

91. [1907] XXXI ILR Bom 81.

contracted for a family purpose and, therefore, for the benefit of the family. In this case the concept of marriage as a *saṁskāra* was also discussed in detail and *Govindrajulu* v. *Venkatanarasayya* was dissented from and held that under the *Mitākṣarā* as well as the *Mayūkha* the word *saṁskāra* ordinarily includes marriage. Various scriptures were referred such as the text of Yājñavalkya, cited and expounded in the *Mitākṣarā* and a text of Bṛhaspati quoted in *Vyavahāra Mayūkha*, wherein sacramental ceremonies have been called as *saṁskāras*. Even *Nārada-smṛti* is to the same effect. In all these texts the original word used for 'ceremonies' is *saṁskāra*. Dr. Jolly had shown some doubt whether *saṁskāra* includes marriage or only ends with the investiture with the sacred thread. Though it is not expressly stated but the text of Yājñavalkya and Bṛhaspati implies that marriage was meant to be included in the word 'ceremonies' and thus the honourable Court said that the word *saṁskāra* (sacramental ceremonies) occurring in these texts means all such ceremonies as are, according to the Śāstras, applicable to males where the question is about males, and all such ceremonies as are applicable, according to the same Śāstras, to females where the question is about females. Even Bālambhaṭṭa's Gloss speaks on *Mitākṣarā* on *Yājñavalkya*, I.15, that

> A female child has the same liberty as the uninitiated boy, so long as she is not married.

It clearly shows that marriage is also an initiation ceremony.

The honourable Court referred to the Smṛti of Vyāsa quoted at page 78 of *Vivādāraṇav Setu* and Yājñavalkya's text in *Madana Pārijāta* and referred to the explanation added that the word, *asaṁskṛta,* used by Yājñavalkya means 'uninitiated' in the *saṁskāras* (sacramental ceremonies) which end with marriage.

Then the honourable Court differed with the decision in *Govindarajulu* v. *Venkatanarasayya* [1903] ILR 27 Mad 206 stating that the learned Judge's decision rests on the misapprehension of the texts of the law expounded by Vijñeśvara in *Mitākṣarā* and by the author of *Smṛti Candrikā*.

The honourable Judges in this case relied upon the text of Gautma which is an express authority on the proposition that marriage is the only obligatory order of life in the case of a male and if he does not become a *gṛhastha*, he forfeits his caste and status. However, Gautma believes only in two *āśrama*s whereas Manu and Yājñavalkya believe in all the four *āśrama*s and referring to them the honourable Court held that it is sufficient to say from the works of commentators to whom this Court constantly refers in construing either the *Mitākṣarā* or the *Vyavahāra-mayūkha* that there is none among them who has interpreted these texts in the sense of excluding marriage from the meaning of the word *saṁskāra*.

7. *Kameshwar Shastri* v. *Veeracharlu*[92]

It is a case of contracting debt for the marriage of a son, binding on the coparceners, as being legal necessity and on this issue the marriage as a *saṁskāra* was also discussed.

In this case, the honourable Judges referred to various scriptures such as *Yājñavalkya* (I.13) *Aparārka*, *Saṁskāra Mayūkha* of Nīlakaṇṭha, *Saṁskāra Bhāskara*, *Yama* and held that it is necessary to point out that amongst śūdras marriage is an initiary ceremony or *saṁskāra* and perhaps the most important *saṁskāra* performed for them.

The great commentator Aparārka observes that for the śūdra the *saṁskāra*s are without *mantra*s but the śūdras shall have the marriage *saṁskāra* alone. Banerjee in his *Tagore Lectures*, first edn., p. 31, speaks of marriage as the only sacrament for women and śūdra. Thus, held that Marriage is one of the necessary *saṁskāra*s or religious rites, in the case of śūdras, as well as the twice born classes and thus *Govindarajulu* v. *Venkatanarasayya* ILR 27 Mad 206 dissented from?

8. *Gopalkrishnam Raju* v. *Venkatarasa Raju*[93]

The question before the Court was whether a debt contracted for the marriage of a male member is binding on the family.

The honourable Court referred to various judgements like:

92. 34 ILR Mad 422.

93. [1911] 37 ILR Mad 273 (FB).

(i) *Govindarajulu* v. *Venkatanarasayya* [1904] ILR 27 Mad. 206.

(ii) *Kameshvara Shastri* v. *Veeracharlu* [1911] ILR 34 Mad 422.

(iii) *Sundra Bai* v. Shivnarayana [1908] ILR 32 Bom 81.

(iv) *Malayandi Gounder* v. *Subharaya Vanavaraya Gounder* [1906] and held that marriage is obligatory on Hindus who do not desire to adopt the life of a perpetual *brahmacārī* or of a *saṁnyāsī*.

Thus, the honourable Court overruled [1904] ILR 27 Mad 206 and approved [1911] ILR 34 Mad 422.

9. *Bhagwati Saran Singh* v. *Kumar Parameshwari Nandan Singh*[94]

It was a property matter wherein the validity of marriage was challenged that the marriage of a lunatic was invalid.

The point raised was that Hindu marriage is not only a *saṁaskāra* but is also a contract and a lunatic being unable to give his consent, consent being a necessary element of contract, his marriage is invalid.

In this case various scriptures, authorities on Hindu Law and judicial pronouncements were referred to hold that Hindu marriage is a sacrament and those references are herein repeated:

Mayne's *Hindu Law*, 10th edn.:

> While marriage is according to Hindu Law a sacrament, it is also a civil contract which takes the form of a gift in Brahmā, a sale in the *asura* and an agreement in the *gāndharva*. —pp. 143-4

> The marriage of a lunatic, an idiot or an impotent person is invalid under Hindu Law. —p. 150

> Medhātithi inclines to the view that impotent persons and lunatics are not entitled to marry, as they are not entitled to the performance of any religious rites. —p. 151

94. AIR 1942 All 267.

> Whereas archaic rules of Hindu Law very plainly transgress the rules of justice, equity and good conscience, they cannot be enforced. The marriage of an impotent person, not being merely sterile, or of a lunatic or of an idiot, clearly tends to promote immorality and may also be regarded as contrary to public policy. — p. 153

Stuart C.J. in *Deo Kishen* v. *Budh Prakash*[95] took the view that such a marriage is invalid, does not appear to be the view which was originally held by Mr. Mayne at least as regards females and said:

> It is not suggested that the insane person who is a woman was so from her birth, and even if she was, such insanity of a Hindu woman does not appear to disqualify her for marriage.

On this subject Mayne basing his opinion on the Institutes of Manu chapter II, verses 66-7 says:

> A Hindu marriage is the performance of a religious duty, not a contract, adding therefore, the consenting mind is not necessary, and its absence, whether from infancy or incapacity, is immaterial.

In Macnaughten's *Hindu Law*, p. 57 the learned author says:

> Marriage among the Hindus is not merely a Civil Contract, but a sacrament forming the last of the ceremonies prescribed to the three regenerate classes and the only one for śūdras.

In Strange's *Hindu Law*, p. 44 there is the following passage:

> The essence of the rite (of marriage) consists in the consent of the parties . . . that is of the man on the one hand, and on the other of the father or who-ever else gives away the bride.

In *Vyavasthā Candrikā*, Vol.2, p. 432, it is said:

> Marriage amongst us, Hindus, though essentially a

95. [1883] AWN 105 (FB).

> religious sacrament (being the part of the initiary rites prescribed for men of regenerate classes and the only one for women and śūdras) partakes also of the nature of a civil contract.

In *Muthusami Mudliar* v *Masilamani*,[96] Sankaraj J., says:

> A marriage, whatever else it is, a sacrament, an institution, is undoubtedly, a contract entered into for consideration with correlative rites and duties.

In Gooroodas Banarjee's *Hindu Law of Marriages and Strīdhana*, 5th edn. at p. 37 the learned author says:

> I shall consider first the question who are incompetent to marry? Here you will bear in mind that marriage is regarded in Hindu Law not only as a civil contract, but also as a sacrament, being one of the ten *saṁskāra*s or regenerating ceremonies necessary for men of the twice born classes and the only one necessary for śūdras and that in consequence of this religious necessity, the grounds of disqualification for marriage are fewer in the Hindu Law than in any other polished system of Law.

At page 39 after stating that the consent of the father or other guardian of a minor boy is necessary, the learned author says:

> The want of the guardian's consent would not, however, invalidate a marriage otherwise legally contracted.

At page 40 we read:

> Persons of unsound mind — that is idiots and lunatics — though disqualified for civil purposes generally have not been declared incompetent to marry. On the contrary there are indications in the law from which it would appear that they are considered to be competent to marry.

*Dabychurn Mitter* v. *Radhachurn Mitter*[97]

The author citing the above case says that:

---

96. 33 Mad 342.

97. 2 Morely's Digest 99.

> It should be noticed that the idiot and the lunatic being, where the loss of reason is complete, incompetent to accept the gift of the bride which is a necessary part of the ceremony of marriage, it is not easy to understand how their marriage in such cases can be regarded as marriage at all. And I may add here that Hindu Law permits the wife to neglect a mad husband.

Then he cites *Manu*, IX.89 and concludes in an ambiguous state but favours the marriage for some reasons. Stating that the rule which declares them valid and legal can be justified only on the ground that the opposite rule would be hard against the unfortunate offsprings and would deprive the unhappy wife of her legitimate conjugal status without giving her any compensating advantage.

In Mandlik's *Hindu Law* at pp. 426-7. The author has made an observation referring to the old texts and finally says that how can an idiot be capable of accepting a bride and yet the marriages of such idiots appear to have been contemplated by Yājñavalkya when he declares that the blameless sons of idiots are qualified for inheritance. The author further says that according to usage, such marriages are reckoned quite proper and sanctioned by the community, although they are opposed to the old text laws.

A question arose in *Dabychurn Mitter* v. *Radhachurn Mitter* 2 Morley's Digest 99

> Is the marriage of lunatic without the consent of his family valid?

The answer was that under every circumstances, if such a marriage be contracted, it is valid.

Various cases were referred in this regard such as:

(i) *Myna Boyee* v. *Ootaram* [1856-61] 8 MIA 400.

(ii) *Inderun Valung Porly Talaver* v. *Ramaswamy Pandia Talaver* [1869] 13 MIA 141.

(iii) *Collector of Madura* v. *Moottoo Ramling Sathupathy* [1868] 12 MIA 397.

(iv) *Mouji Lal* v. *Chandravati* 38 Cal 700

In 38 Calcutta 700 it was held that man's unsoundness of mind was not such as would render the marriage invalid by reason of his being incapable of accepting the bride during the ceremony and of understanding what was going on and finally the Court after referring to various authorities and the old textbooks held that the person married may be a minor or even of unsound mind and yet if the marriage rite is duly solemnised, there is a valid marriage.

10. *Amirthammal* v. *Vallimayil Ammal*[98]

In this case the validity of the marriage of a congenital idiot was considered. The honourable Court referred to various old texts.

> Mayne's *Hindu Law*, at p. 106, 6th edn.:
>
> As the great and primary object of marriage is the procuring of male issue, physical capacity is an essential requisite, so long as mere selection of bridegroom is concerned; but a marriage with a eunuch is not an absolute nullity as with us. Mental capacity stands in the same position. While the matter rested in contract, no Court, I imagine, would treat a promise to marry a lunatic or an idiot as binding, but the marriage, if celebrated, would be valid.

The Court referred to *Venkatacharyulu* v. *Rangacharyulu*[99] where it is stated that

> the person married be a minor, even of unsound mind, and yet, if the marriage rite is duly solemnised, there is a valid marriage.

Then the Court held:

> It is undoubtedly abhorrent to a modern mind that a congenital idiot should be allowed to marry, but the Court here can only have regard to the personal law and the personal law of Hindus undoubtedly regards such a marriage as being possible.

98. AIR 1942 Mad 693 FB.

99. 14 Madras 316.

11. *Ratan Moni Debi* v. *Nagendra Narain Singh*[100]

In this case the Court held that the marriage of an impotent person is a nullity and referred to various texts.

Mayne has referred to *Yājñavalkya* at pp. 151-2 of Mayne's *Hindu Law*, 10th edn:

> Neither an impotent man nor a sexless woman can marry.

*Nārada-smṛti* speaks thus:

> The man must undergo an examination with regard to his virility; when the fact of his virility has been placed beyond doubt, he shall obtain the maiden otherwise not.
>
> Women have been created for the sake of propagation, the wife being the field and the husband the giver of the seed. The field must be given to him who has seed. He who has no seed is unworthy to possess the field.

*Parāśara-smṛti*:

> Another husband is ordained for women in five calamities, i.e., if the husband be unheard of, or be dead, or adopt a religious order or be impotent or become an outcast.

*Hindu Law* by Sir Earnest Trevelyan, 3rd edn., p. 38, The author observes:

> The ancient authorities permitted a eunuch to marry on the ground that his wife could raise up a son to him by a man legally appointed, but now that the system of *niyoga* is obsolete, it may be a question whether the Courts will not declare the marriage of an impotent person to be void.

In this case the Court held that under Hindu Law the marriage of a female with a male who is impotent and has never been able to consummate the marriage is a nullity.

It appears that the English Judge relied upon the interpretations given by the European Jurists and the English cases favouring nullity of marriage on such ground but it is regretted

100. AIR 1949 Cal 404.

that the learned Judge did not go into the sacredness of marriage and his more reliance was on *Rayden on Divorce*, p. 69 where it is said that even when a husband and wife refuse to submit to inspection, the Court may grant a decree. The learned Judge decided the case from the angle of English Law and not the personal law of the Hindus.

12. *Ratneshwari Nandan* v. *Bhagwati Saran*[101]

The case came from Allahabad High Court wherein the marriage with a lunatic was held valid once it is solemnised. The judgement of the High Court was challenged in the Federal Court. The Court held that it cannot be disputed that none of the early Smṛti writers have mentioned lunacy is a disqualification for purposes of marriage, though insanity and various other physical and mental ailments are sufficient grounds for excluding a person from inheritance.

The honourable Court held that the texts which have been quoted and relied upon by all the leading authorities of the different schools of Hindu Law, that obtain in India, apparently imply that lunatics and similar other disqualified persons are competent to marry.

13. *A* v. *B*[102]

It was a case of divorce under Bombay Hindu Divorce Act, 1947 or alternatively a suit for declaration that the marriage be held void on the ground that his wife was impotent at the time of marriage and still continued to be so.

The honourable court dissented (i) AIR 1942 All 267 and (ii) AIR 1942 Mad 693 (FB) and approved AIR 1949 Cal 404 and held that marriage under Hindu Law was both a sacrament and civil contract, that the husband was in this case entitled to a declaration that the marriage is null and void and that even if the husband was not entitled to a declaration of nullity, he could still be granted a decree for divorce under the provisions of the Bombay Divorce Act, 1947.

101. AIR 1950 FC 142.

102. AIR 1952 Bom. 486.

In this case original texts from Manu, Yājñavalkya, Nārada, Kātyāyana, Kauṭilya, Vīramitrodaya were cited and examined.[103-12]

This decision of the honourable Court is erroneous as it clearly depends upon misinterpretation of various *śloka*s finding place in various scriptures and their treatment in isolation. Marriage being a *saṁskāra* and preparing the couple for the discharge of duties of an householder and for the progeny worthy and clad in qualities for the development of purity and strength of the race various qualities are needed to be seen in the man and woman to be united in wedlock and great emphasis is laid on those qualities. Manu in chapter III verses 5-10 speak about as to what is to be seen in the bride and her family. Yājñavalkya also speaks about it in Book I verses 52-5. This is why matching of horoscope, the ceremony of betrothal, are the steps taken to ensure the satisfaction of both the parties and thus leading the path clear for the solemnisation of marriage. This is why in *Umedkika* v. *Nagivdas*[113] and *Ganpat Narain Singh* v. *Rajan*[114] it was decided that specific performance of such a promise is not enforceable by a suit. However, in another case *Atmaram* v. *Sheolal Mulookchand*[115] and *Mt. Ruliyat* v. *Madhowjee Panachund*[116] taken a contrary view.

But once the marriage is solemnised, with due religious rites, then the *saṁskāra* aspect of marriage is complete and hence it is indissoluble. The Court relied on the defects in the bride and

---

103. *Sacred Books of the East* (*SBE*), Vol.XXXII, Chap. III, Vers 18-19.
104. *Yāj*, I.52.
105. *Manu*, VIII.226.
106. *Smṛtimuktafala* quoting *Candrikā*.
107. *SBE*, Vol. XXXIII, ch. XII, p. 97.
108. Kātyāyana quoted in *Vīramitrodaya*.
109. Vasiṣṭha quoted in *Madana Pārijāta* at p. 153.
110. *Manu*, IX.73.
111. *Kauṭilya*, ch. XV.
112. *Yājñvalkya*, I.66. Commentary in *Vīramitrodaya*.
113. 7 Bom OCJ 122.
114. ILR 1 Cal 74.
115. 1 Borr 358.
116. 2 Borr 680.

bridegroom, pointed out in the scriptures and had drawn an inference that such a marriage even if solemnised is bad in law. Such inference is unwarranted because every Hindu marriage is arranged by the parents after due deliberations and complete satisfaction based on *dharma*. Hence, the decision is not in tune with the spirit and sanctity of the marriage as disintegration of marriage is not provided anywhere in any scripture though references of second marriage are there under restricted conditions.

14. *Kantilal Motichand* v. *Vimla and Others*[117]

In this case the Court held that under Hindu Law a marriage of a person with a woman who is impotent cannot be treated as void or a nullity nor can it be dissolved.

In this regard the honourable Court reviewed various case laws and old texts on Hindu Law and finally followed AIR (29) 1942 All 267(2) Stating that these references only refer to disqualifications for marriage and not marriage in itself. The honourable Judge referred to the *Preface to the Work of Hindu Law* by Sir W. Maenaughten which says:

> It by no means follows that because an act has been prohibited, it should, therefore, be considered as illegal. The distinction between the 'Vinculum Juris' and the 'Vinculum Pudoris' is not always discernible.

15. *Devivanai Achi* v. *R.A.M.A.I Ct. Chidambaram Chettiar*[118]

In this case the question about the validity of marriage in the case of non-performance of ceremonies was agitated. The Court held that marriage has two aspects, i.e., secular and religious. The secular aspect consists of the gift of the bride, i.e., *kanyādāna* and the religious aspect which is prescribed by the *Gṛhyasūtra*s of the nature of ceremonies and rites and both are essential for the validity of marriage so much so that ceremonies are essential in the case of all the eight forms of marriage and this rule applies even to śūdras and this is the strict Hindu Law regarding the mode by which a

117. AIR 1952 Saurashtra.

118. AIR 1954 Mad 657.

valid marriage could be effected. Thus, the emphasis placed on the religious aspect of marriage, i.e., the *saṁskāra*. The honourable Court examined various case laws and Hindu scriptures to arrive at the decision.

*Nirṇaya Sindhu*[119]

> Even in *gāndharva* and other forms of marriages, gift preceded by pouring of water is insisted upon.

In this context Yama says:

> A man is not to be called the husband of a girl merely by pouring water in his hand or by declaring him her husband. But only by *pāṇigrahaṇa* ceremony (catching hold of the hands of the girl) and having taken seven steps with her.

Devala says in *Parāśaramādhavīya*:

> In the marriage the *gāndharva*, the marriage ceremony should again be performed by the people of the three castes by competent men having the fire as witness. Here by three castes is signified the three castes other than brāhmaṇas which three castes are eligible for *gāndharva* marriage.

In the *Pariśiṣṭa* (or reminder chapter of *Parāśaramādhavīya*) it is said as follows:

> In the marriages *gāndharva*, *asura*, *paiśāca* and *rākṣasa* the girl is to be accepted first and then a *homa* (ritual in fire) is ordained. So if the *homa* is not performed, the girl does not attain wifehood and therefore she may be given in marriage to another man.

Vasiṣtha and Baudhāyana say in that context:

> If a girl who was carried away by force was not purified by marriage *mantra*s of ceremony, she may be given to any other man according to rules as if she was a *kanyā* (unmarried girl). (Here the commentator says by carrying away by force is meant *gāndharva* and other marriages.) Here (a question arises): If a girl is not married with the

119. Appendix attached to AIR 1954 Mad 657.

chanting of *mantras*, she may be given to any other person in any form of marriage. That being so, special mention in the case of girl being carried away by force in *rākṣasa* and *paiśāca* (forms) is meaningless.

The reply is as follows:

> A girl who does not accept the man who carried her away by force as her husband, may be given in marriage once again and it is immaterial in those marriages whether she is purified by *saṁskāra* or otherwise.

*Nārada* says in *Madanapārijāta*:

> The *mantras* for marriage are considered to be essential to make a girl a wife, and the seventh step taken along with that girl is the culmination of that ceremony.

The same is said in *Aparārka* and *Smṛti Candrikā* also.

In the *Śūdra Kamlākara*[120]

Then the *saṁskāra* of the śūdra.

Yama: The śūdra should be purified by ceremonies in the following manner without *mantras*. The above-stated *ślokas* speak about the *saṁskāras* to be done without reciting of *mantras* but the *vivāha saṁskāra* with the recitation of *mantras*. *Pāṇigrahaṇa* is common to all *varnas* without making any distinction. Thus, the honourable Court expressly laid stress on the religious aspect of marriage and secular aspect too.

The judicial view is crystal clear that Hindu marriage is a *saṁskāra* and *saṁskāra* is indissoluble.

Now we have to look to the Hindu Marriage Act, 1955, which it is said that it has made inroads in the religious aspect of Hindu marriage and it has brought in a contractual content. To understand the contractual content whether it is there or not, we have to necessarily go into the two sections of Hindu Marriage Act, 1955 and they are section 5 and section 7.

120. Appendix attached to AIR 1954 Mad 657.

Section 5 of Hindu Marriage Act, 1955

It deals with the conditions of a Hindu marriage. A marriage may be solemnised between any two Hindus; if the following conditions are fulfilled, namely:

(i) neither party has a spouse living at the time of the marriage;

This section5(1) of the said Act, 1955 is to be read with section 11 and section 17 of the said Act, 1955 also.

Section (11) stipulates

> Any marriage solemnised after the commencement of this Act shall be null and void and may, on a petition presented by either party thereto, against the other party; be so declared by a decree of nullity if it contravenes any one of the conditions specified in clauses (*i*), (*iv*) and (*v*) of section 5.

Section 17 stipulates

> Any marriage between two Hindus solemnised after the commencement of this Act is void if at the date of such marriage either party had a husband or wife living, and the provisions of sections 494 and 495 of the Indian Penal Code (45 of 1860) shall apply accordingly.

These provisions are to be further read with section 4 and section 29(1) of the said Act, 1955.

Section 4 stipulates

Save as otherwise expressly provided in this Act, —

(*a*) any text, rule or interpretation of Hindu Law or any custom or usage as part of that law in force immediately before the commencement of this Act shall cease to have effect with respect to any matter for which provision is made in this Act;

(*b*) any other law in force immediately before the commencement of this Act shall cease to have effect in so

> far as it is inconsistent with any of the provisions contained in this Act.

Section 29(1) stipulates

> A marriage solemnised between Hindus before the commencement of this Act, which is otherwise valid, shall not be deemed to be invalid or ever to have been invalid by reason only of the fact that the parties thereto belonged to the same *gotra* or *pravara* or belonged to different religions, castes or sub-divisions of the same caste.

The object of this Act is to amend and codify the law relating to marriage among Hindus. The expression used is 'to amend and codify'. A codifying statute is one which purports to state exhaustively the whole of the law upon a particular subject and when the law is codified, it becomes binding on the Court to remain within the parameters fixed and as such the Court is not at liberty to go outside the statute but the earlier law may be referred to get the ambiguity cleared if it appears to enable the Court to have true interpretation. So the previous law does not meet its death but its use becomes negligible or remote and only remains a source of light if needed.

The Act is also an amending Act. It clearly shows that if the Act is silent on a particular aspect of old law and no provision is made in the new Act, then the provisions of old law are applicable and as such to understand the codified law, we have to necessarily look to the old law also as to whether the old law is retained as such or amended, etc.

Section 5(1) introduces the principle of monogamy among Hindus as enshrined by the use of expression, 'Neither party has a spouse living at the time of marriage'. To sanctify this principle of monogamy, the statute provided stringent cover in section 11 and section 17 read with sections 494 and 495 of IPC. So to appreciate this provision, section 5(1), we will go to this principle under Hindu uncodified Law.

We find a few references to polygamy or plurality of wives. *Ṛ̥V*, X.145 is a charm for winning husband's love from the co-wives. In *Ṛ̥V*, X.159 Śaci, i.e., Indra's wife claims to have vanquished all co-wives. In *Ṛ*V, 1.105, 8 "Tṛta" compares the sides of the well to co-wives. But all these verses are about gods or lords or kings. On the other hand the word *dampati* which occurs very frequently in *Ṛgveda* conveys the idea of a monogamous marriage. Hence, it shows that polygamy was common among very rich people and not amongst the common masses.[121] There are other various instances in *Ṛgveda* about the concept of polygamy.[122]

There are also references in *Atharvaveda*. The word *mahaṣi* which means chief of the queens, suggests that king had more than one wife.[123]

*AV*, II.18, 2 says that the lady concerned should be favoured amongst the co-wives. It is desired that the co-wives should be destructed. *AV*, VII.11, 3, 2 uses the word *parivṛkta* which means the neglected wife. So even during Vedic time we get references of polygamy but stress was always laid on monogamy. The entire hymn X.85 of the *Ṛgveda* is a discourse on monogamous marriage between Sūryā the daughter of the sun God and Soma (moon). B.S. Upadhyaya tries to interpret this verse as an evidence of monogamy and he argues that this was possible only if a single wife was the object of this address, by the priest, for his authority in her new dominion which she acquired through marriage was uncontrolled and undivided, wholly absolute.[124] Apart from the above references some other hymns of *Ṛgveda* also inform about the singular number of wife.[125]

*Aitareya Brāhmaṇa*, 12.11 is the first authoritative reference to polygamy. It says that one man may have many wives but one woman cannot have many husbands. Thus, it nagatives the existence of polyandry also. This passage has been later on quoted many a time by Smṛtis in favour of polygamy.

*Aitareya Brāhmaṇa*, 33 contains the story of Hariścandra. It

---

121. Usha M. Apte, *The Sacrament of Marraige in Hindu Society*, p. 13.

122. See *Ṛ*V, V.2.2, 37.3, 102.11, *Ṛ*V.VII.18.2.

123. *AV*, II.36.3.

124. B.S. Upadhyaya, p. 110.

125. *Ṛ*V, I.124.7, IV.3.2, X.71.4, 85.36, etc. Cited in Srikant Misra's *Ancient Hindu Law and Practice*.

says the king had hundred wives but was unlucky enough not to get a son from any of them.

*Śatapata Brāhmaṇa*, XIII.4, 1, 8, 9 say that the king had four wives, Mahiṣi, Vavata, Parivṛkta and Palagali. Mahiṣi was the first wife. Vavata was the favoured one, Parivṛkta was the unfavoured one and Palagali was the daughter of the officials. *Śatapata Brāhmaṇa*, XIII.2, 6, 7 also refers to plurality of wives (*patnyaḥ*). Usha M. Apte had drawn a conclusion that during the period of *Brāhmaṇas* and the Upaniṣadas, even this practice had percolated to common masses. A person who had no male offspring married many-a-wife in order to get one.[126]

Then we come to the period of Dharmaśāstras and Smṛtis. We find a verse in *Āpastamba Dharma-sūtra* that if the wife bears a son to the husband and is ready to perform religious ceremonies one need not marry again.[127]

Various verses in *Manu-smṛti* throw much light on the aspect of monogamy and polygamy.

> Having thus, at the funeral, given the sacred fires to his wife who dies before him, he may marry again, and again kindle (the fires).[128]
>
> She who drinks spirituous liquor, is of bad conduct, rebellious, diseased, mischievous or wasteful, may at any time be superseded (by another wife).[129]
>
> A barren wife may be supreseded in the eighth year, she whose children (all) die in the tenth, she who bears only daughters in the eleventh, but she who is quarrelsome without delay.[130]
>
> If twice born men wed women of their own and of other (lower castes), the seniority, honour, and habitation of those

126. Usha M. Apte, *The Sacrament of Marriage in Hindu Society*, pp. 40-1.
127. *ĀpasDS*, 11.5.11.12.
128. *Manu*, V.168.
129. *Ibid.*, IX.80.
130. *Ibid.*, IX.81.

> (wives) must be (settled) according to the order of the castes (*varṇa*).[131]
>
> Among all (twice born men) the wife of equal caste above, not a wife of a different caste by any means, shall personally attend her husband and assist him in his daily sacred rites.[132]
>
> But he who foolishly causes that (duty) to be performed by another, while his wife of equal caste is alive, is declared by the ancients (to be) as (despicable) as *kandala* (sprung from the) brāhmaṇa (caste).[133]

These verses speak of polygamy but in other verses, the inference can be clearly drawn of monogamy:

> The husband receives his wife from the gods, (he does not wed her) according to his own will; doing what is agreeable to the gods, he must always support her (while she is) faithful.[134]
>
> Let a mutual fidelity continue until death, this may be considered as the summary of the highest law for husband and wife.[135]
>
> Let man and woman, united in marriage constantly exert themselves, that (they may not be) disunited (and) may not violate their mutual fidelity.[136]

Then in one of the verses Manu speaks of polygamy:

> If among all the wives of one husband one have a son, Manu declares all (to be) mothers of male children through that son.[137]

---

131. *Manu*, IX.85.
132. *Ibid.*, IX.86.
133. *Ibid.*, IX.87. *Kandala* means *ayogava* read *Manu*, X.12.
134. *Ibid.*, IX.95.
135. *Ibid.*, IX.100.
136. *Ibid.*, IX.101.
137. *Ibid.*, IX.183. Also refer *Vas*, XVII.11, Viṣṇu, XV.41.

Now we have to look to various other Smṛtis and Dharmaśāstras as to what they speak:

Yājñvalkya says:

> The liquor drinker, the diseased, the cunning, the barren, the killer of wealth, the unpleasant spoken, who bears female children should be superseded, so also (one) who hates people.[138]

This verse basically speaks of another wife, when the first wife is living and thus speaks of impliedly polygamy. *Mitākṣarā* explains the meaning of *adhivedana* means taking another wife.

Then we go to the next verse of Yājñavalkya which clearly speaks of polygamy:

> When there exists a wife of the same class (*savarṇa*), religious works are not to be performed by a wife of another class when there are wives of the same class, then religious duties are to be performed by the eldest and not by the others.[139]

Kātyāyana quoted in the *Chāndogya Pariśiṣṭa* in various verses speaks about as to who should participate with the husband for performance of religious rites, in case there are many wives which indicates plurality of wives.[140]

Viṣṇu also speaks about it that if many wives of his own class be living, with the eldest alone should the husband conduct business relating to acts of religion though his younger wives be dearer to him, but if there be no wife of equal class, the business may, in case of distress, be executed by that wife only who is of the class next below him, yet let not a twice born ever perform holy rites with the aid of a śūdra wife.[141]

Dakṣa says:

> The first is the wife married from a sense of duty: the second

138. *Yāj*, I.73.

139. *Yāj*, I.88.

140. *Kātyāyana-smṛti*, II.19, 3-8.

141. *SBE*, Vol.VII; *Viṣṇu*, XXVI.1-3.

promotes sensual gratification; sensible, not moral effects proceed from her. The first wife is called the wife whom acts of duty concern, provided she be faultless; but if she be faulty, there is no offence in employing another wife endued with excellent qualities.[142]

Dakṣa another place says:

दुःखासिकाङ्क्षनिर्वेदच्छिद्रं पीडापरस्परम्।
प्रतिकूलकलत्रस्य द्विदारस्य न संशय।।

Polygamy, however, is not very desirable as it leads to constant frictions.[143]

*Critical appreciation*: In whatever spirit or manner these verses are said, they do give and manifest three propositions:

1. Monogamy is the Law.
2. Polygamy is permissible.
3. That polygamy is permissible under some specific situation. It is not a blanket cheque.

Then the question comes, that if this is the position under Hindu Law, then section 5(1) has not brought any revolutionary change by which we can say that Hindu Law has been defiled. It has only statutorily recognised the old Hindu Law. So this provision can be read now as follows:

1. Monogamy is the law.
2. Polygamy is not permissible under any circumstances.
3. It is (second marriage) void under section 11, punishable under section 17 of the Hindu Marriage Act, 1955 and is also subject to sections 494 and 495 of IPC as applicable.

Thus, the framers have brought reformation in this aspect of marriage. Polygamy was a curse and was never considered desirable and moreover, it was a symbol of degradation of women's honour and dignity and any act done in degradation of the honour of women

---

142. *Dakṣa*, IV.14-15.

143. *Ibid.*, IV.7.

is *ultra vires* of the Constitution as it violates Article 51A(e). So the provision of monogamy is the finest contribution to law.

But some jurists see in it the content of contract which is not understandable. In particular, section 5(1) does not speak anything like contract except the expression 'void' used in section 11 which is read with section 5(1).

Looking to the definition of 'void' in the Contract Act, "An agreement not enforceable by law is said to be void", its import in the matrimonial law does not mean the import of Contract Act in the Hindu Marriage Act, 1955. It is well settled law that whenever there is any ambiguity about any expression used in the enactment, its meaning is to be found out in the Act itself; if not available reference to be made to the General Clauses Act; if not found there then its meaning be searched in any other enactment with reference to the context. So the expression 'void' explained in the Contract Act simply refers to the matters of commerce exclusively and conclusively and its import in the matrimonial law is only to state that the marriage while the first spouse is living, is not a marriage in the eye of law.

To quote Manu:

> Once is the partition (of the inheritance) made, (once is) a maiden given in marriage, (and) once does (a man) say, 'I will give', each of those three (acts is done) once only.[144]

This verse of Manu clearly throws an unqualified light on monogamy and also simultaneously the sacramental nature also, as sacraments need not be performed on the second marriage.

Even the Judiciary has not viewed it as contract. In *Rani Bala* v. *Ram Krishna*[145] it is said that the two statutes, The Hindu Marriage Act, 1955 and the Contract Act, 1872 are not *pari materia*. The former deals with marriages. The latter deals with contracts and commerce. A Hindu marriage is neither a contract nor a commerce. It is a sacrament. Sacrament apart, a marriage can never be regarded as a mere contract. The parties who enter into contract

144. *Manu*, IX.47.

145. [1969] 73 CWN 751.

can at their Will dissolve it but the parties who contract a marriage cannot. The Hindu Marriage Act, no doubt made an inroad into the close preserve of that ancient law but the concept of a sacrament still goes strong.

The words of Martin Luther are noteworthy:

> Marriage is a divine institution and the highest of all human callings.

The philosopher Hegel defines it as morality in a natural form.[146]

Section 5(2) attracts more attention as it appears to be in consonance with section 12 of the Contract Act, 1872. The essence of section 12 of the Act is that the law in regard to contracts made by parties, affecting their rights and interests is that there must be full and free consent in order to bind the parties. Consent is an act of reason accompained by deliberation. It is upon this ground that there is lack of rational and deliberable consent that transactions of persons of unsound mind are held to be void.

Section 5 (2) stipulates

> At the time of marriage, neither party —
>
> (*a*) is incapable of giving a valid consent, to it in consequence of unsoundness of mind; or
>
> (*b*) though capable of giving a valid consent, has been suffering from mental disorder of such a kind or to such an extent as to be unfit for marriage and the procreation of children; or
>
> (*c*) has been subject to recurrent attacks of insanity or epilepsy.[147]

The main object of marriage, according to Indian ideals, is the obtainment of a son who would be competent to offer gifts and oblations and perform religious ceremonies for the forefathers and a religious institution whereby the entry in the *gṛhastha* is opening

146. Eversley's *Domestic Relation*, p. 5 as cited in Hindu Marriage from Sacrament to Contract *A Conceptual Analysis* by Ratan Lal Jat.

147. Substituted by Act 68 of 1976, section 2 for clause (*ii*).

of the doors of the discharge of multifarious duties as a householder. Thus, it is expected that physical and mental capacity is an essential requisite and our sages laid great stress on this aspect as the procreation of son is the continuity of generation.

Āpastamba has said:

> These (sons) who live, fulfilling the rites taught (in the Veda) increase the fame and heavenly bliss of their departed ancestors.[148]

Yājñavalkya says:

> Because continuity (of family) in this word and getting of heaven in the next, are through sons, grandsons and great-grandsons, therefore, women ought to be attended to and should be guarded carefully.[149]

Āpastamba at another place says:

> He should go to his wife and not another woman, for the sake of religion and progeny.[150]

So the physical and mental capacity of a man is of paramount consideration and of women too so that the union becomes divine and good progeny is secured. So we have to first see what the Śāstric law on this aspect is

MANU ON MARRIAGE

Manu speaks on Marriage and says that "Let him carefully avoid the ten following families" and then states about them.

> One which neglects the sacred rites, one in which no male children (are born), one in which the Veda is not studied, one (the members of) which have thick hair on the body, those which are subject to hemorrhoids, plithisis, weakness of digestion, epilepsy or white and black leprosy.[151]

---

148. *Āpastamba praśna*, II.9.24.3.
149. *Yāj*, I.78.
150. *Āpastamba* II.5.11-12.
151. *Manu*, III.7.

Let him wed a female free from bodily defects, who has an agreeable name, the (graceful) gait of a *haṁsa* or of an elephant, a moderate (quantity of) hair on the body and on the head, small teeth and soft limbs.[152]

Though (a man) may have accepted a damsel in due form, he may abandon (her if she be) blemished, diseased or deflowered and (if she have been) given with fraud.[153]

If anybody gives away a maiden possessing blemishes without declaring them, (the bridegroom) may annual that (contract) with the evil-minded giver.[154]

But she who shows aversion towards a mad or outcast (husband), a eunuch, one destitute of manly strength or one afflicted with such diseases as punish crimes, shall neither be cast off nor be deprived of her property.[155]

(But) the maiden, though marriageable, should rather stop in (the father's) house until death, than that he should ever give her to a man destitute of good qualities.[156]

In *Viṣṇu Purāṇa* it is said:

He must not marry a girl who is vicious or unhealthy, of low origin or labouring under disease, one who has been ill brought up, one who talks improperly, one who inherits some malady from father or mother.[157]

Gautma Says:

A girl should be given to one who is educated, and a man of character.[158]

---

152. *Manu*, III.10.
153. *Ibid.*, IX.72.
154. *Ibid.*, IX.73.
155. *Ibid.*, IX.79.
156. *Ibid.*, IX.89.
157. *Viṣṇu Purāṇa*, Book III, Ch. 10.
158. *GautDS*, IV.5.

Here the expression 'Character' is all embracing. It speaks of body, mind and soul.

Yama Says:

> The wise should give their daughter after investigating the seven qualities — family, mentality, health, age, education, wealth and support.

Yājñavalkya says:

> She should be of a great family of *śrotriyas* whose ten ancestors are renowned, but not of a family, though prosperous, that has any hereditary disease or taint.[159]

Vijñeśvara in *Mitākṣarā* has explained:

> The expression 'hereditary disease', is such as leprosy, epilepsy, and the rest.

Yājñavalkya puts the same conditions for the bridegroom when he says:

> The bridegroom too should possess these qualifications (and free from the same defects) and be of the same class (or of a higher), be a *śrotriya* (himself), young, wise, beloved of all, and one whose virile power has been well examined.[160]

Bālambhaṭṭa commenting on this verse speaks of twelve rules to be applied regarding the fitness of bride and two of them are

> 'not suffering from any incurable disease' and 'not having any hereditary taint'.

In *Āśvalāyana Gṛhya-sūtra* it is said:

> The girl should be free from disease, i.e., she should be healthy.[161]

---

159. *Yāj*, I.54.
160. *Yāj*, I.55.
161. *ĀśvaGS*, I.V.3.

In *Āpastamba Gṛhya-sūtra*:

> A detailed description about the choice of the bride is given and one of the defects given is "avoid one who has withered limbs".[162]

He also mentions the qualities of a bridegroom, such as

> Possessing brothers and purity of character, learning and freedom from diseases are the qualities of a bridegroom.[163]

In *Mānava Gṛhya-sūtra*:

> Five qualities of the bridegroom are mentioned. They are: wealth, handsomeness, knowledge, intelligence and relatives. The last two qualifications appear to be mandatory. Intellectually dull person may be dull to perform the duties of a householder and other duties of sharing marriage.[164]

The above verses have laid down rules, to be looked into before fixing the marriage Subramia Iyer J. in *Raghavendra Rao* v. *Jayanana Rao*[165] has said that a glance at the numerous rules laid down by the Ancient Hindu Legislators with reference to the selection of the bride is enough to show that they are, with very few exceptions, rules of caution and advice.

Later on in the case of *Ramachandra* v. *Gopal*[166] the same view was affirmed and also opined that they are only hortatory and not mandatory.

Thus, the viewpoint is very simple to comprehend. The ancient sages laid stress on the qualifications of the bride and bridegroom, keeping in mind:

1. Stability of marriage.

---

162. *ĀpasGS*, I.3.11-14.
163. *Ibid.*, 1.3.20.
164. *ManGS*, 1.7.6-7.
165. 20 Mad 283.
166. 32 Bom 619 at p. 267.

2. Fitness of the couple physically and mentally to discharge the duties of the household.
3. to have good progeny.

Harīta says: "Children are born according to their families" and families have been described to be free from hereditary disease or taint.

The framers of the Hindu Marriage Act, 1955 brought the Ancient Law under section 5(2) of the said Act and made it to be read with section 12 of the said Act. Such a marriage under the cover of such defects has been made voidable and not void. Keeping in view that the great and primary object of marriage of procreation of male issue, i.e., a good progeny. Physical and mental capacity is considered a good prerequisite and the same was provided in section 5(2). It is not provided keeping in view section 12 of the Contract Act but the stability of the marriage and to have a good progeny.

Sir John Hannen in *Durham* v. *Durham*[167] says the contract of marriage is a very simple one, which does not require a high degree of intelligence to comprehend. So it is not the concept of 'consent' which is in view but the ancient law in view and the same was provided with utmost care and caution without disturbing the sanctity of the ancient law. Rather utmost respect was given to the ancient law, coupled with the various decisions of the Courts like *Amrithammal* v. *Vallimavil* ILR (1942) Mad 807 FB and *Parameshwari Nandan* v. *Bhagwati Saran* 1942 All 267 and AIR 1950 FC 142. Thus, section 5 (2) of the said Act should not be clothed in the sheet of Contract Act, simply because the word 'voidable' is used. Hindu marriage is still considered even statutorily as *saṁskāra*, but by way of reformation, this clause which was a piece of utmost advice in ancient law, has been recognised as legal provision, giving discretion.

Section 5(3) stipulates:

> The bridegroom has completed the age of twenty-one years and the bride the age of eighteen years at the time of the marriage.

---

167. [1885] PD 80.

However, the law-makers did not put the violation of this clause under section 11 or section 12 of the said Act. It is neither void nor voidable.

It is generally said that this clause is in semblance with section 11 of the Contract Act, 1872 which stipulates:

> Every person is competent to contract who is of the age of majority according to the law to which he is subject. . . .

The age of majority is governed by the provisions of the Majority Act, 1875 in terms of its section 3.

Bringing in section 11 of the Contract, by way of comparison, to call clause (*iii*) of section 5 of Hindu Marriage Act, 1955, appears to be legally superfluous having no relevance at all. However, to clear such misinterpretation, we have to refer to the aims and objects of the Child Marriage Restraint Act, 1929 (Act 2 of 1978).

This Act was enacted with a view to prevent child marriages, namely, a marriage to which either of the contracting parties is under a specified age. Originally the age limit for a male was eighteen years and for a female fifteen years. The age limit was subsequently raised in the case of females from fifteen years to eighteen years. (See section 5(*iii*) of Hindu Marriage Act, 1955.)

The question of increasing the minimum age for males and females has been considered in the present context when there is an urgent need to check the growth of population in the country. Such increase of the minimum age will result in lowering the total fertility rate on account of later span of married life. It will also result in more responsible parenthood and in better health of the mother and child.

Thus, the object of this Amendment as introduced in section 5(*iii*) is social and not contractual. Now it needs to be seen as to what the ancient Hindu Law says about it as we find a wide fluctuation in different periods, perhaps due to changing social scenario but any amendment with regard to change in the age specified for marriage even in future need not to be tagged to the contractual content as it is purely social in concept.

In the Vedic age we find various references which give indication about the age of the bride.[168] Various words are used for the bride such as *kanyā*, *duhitā*, *yoṣā*, *yuvatī*, *nārī*, etc., which means a grown up, mature and young maiden. C.K. Chatterjee holds the view, after reviewing the various hymns of *Ṛgveda*, that bride was a youthful lady.[169]

In *Ṛgveda* there is a hymn:

आधेनवो धुनयन्तामीशांश्वीः, शवर्दुघाः शशया अप्रदुग्धाः।
नव्या नव्या युवतयो भवन्तीर् महद्देवानामसुरत्वमेकम्।।

ऋग्० ३/५५/१६

Let girls, who are virgins, resembling cows that have never been milked before, who have passed the period of childhood and are about to leave single lives, are well educated and cultured, fit to bear all the responsibilities of married life and are in the full bloom of youth, who by their practice *brahamcarya*, have reached a state of excellence and wisdom, which only those of great learning and high virtues can attain, marry husbands of mature age and bear children by them.

In another hymn, the same view is expressed about a man who enters married life in the full bloom of youth is as if born again (in knowledge and wisdom).[171]

युवा सुवासाः परिवीत आगात्, स उ श्रेयान् भवति जायमानः।
धीरासः कवय उन्नयन्ति, स्वाध्यो मनसा देवयन्तः।।

In *Atharvaveda*, various hymns like VI.89.2, VI.13., XX.126.10 also give some indications, according to Usha M. Apte these reference suggest that the bride is grown up.[172]

To support this viewpoint we refer to *ṛṣi* Dhanvantari, the author of *Suśruta*, who forbids men and women of underage from

---

168. *ṚV*, I.48.6, I.124.3, IV.58.5, VII.2.5, X.168.2, 69.11.
169. C.K. Chatterjee, *Studies in the Rites and Rituals of Hindu Marriage in Ancient India*, 1978, Ph.D.Thesis, Calcutta University.
170. *ṚV*, III.55.16.
171. *Ibid.*, III.8.4.
172. Usha M. Apte, *The Sacrament of Marriage in Hindu Society*, pp. 24-5.

attempting procreation. The impregnation of a woman less than sixteen years of age by a man less than 25 years of age is subject to misfortune.[173]

ऊन षोडश वर्षायामप्राप्त पञ्च विंशतिम्।
यदाधत्ते पुमान् गर्भः कुक्षिस्थ स विपद्यते ।। ४७ ।।

He further says that if it fruits in the birth of a child, the child will not live long, but if it lives long, it will be weak in constitution. So the conception of a minor should not be encouraged.[174]

जातो वा न चिरञ्जीवेद् जीवेद्वा दुर्बलेन्द्रियः।
तस्मादत्यन्त बालायां गर्भाधानं न कारयेत् ।। ४८ ।।

He has further spoken about the four stages of human body, i.e.,[175]

1. Period of Adolescence from 16th to 25th year.
2. Period of manhood from 25th to 40th year.
3. Period of maturity about the 40th year.
4. Period of loss.

So he advises celibacy for man up to 25, 30, 36, 40 or 44 and for a woman up to 16, 17, 18, 20 or 24 years respectively.

Usha M. Apte draws inference from hymns: of *Yajurveda*: (*YV*, 11.49)

> Which says that he was to shoulder the responsibility of a household and was supposed to protect his wife from disease and enemy, he was required to give her a descent household and comfortable living, that to fulfil all these expectations required of him it appears that the groom's age was about 22 years.[176]

Then we come to the period known as Sūtra period wherein the views of Gautama, Vasiṣṭha, Baudhāyana and Āpastamba are of much importance on this subject.

---

173. *Śusruta*, Nirnaya Sagar Press, Bombay, 1930, 10.47, Ch. 10.
174. *Ibid.*, 10.48, ch. 10.
175. *Ibid.*, ch. 35.
176. Usha M. Apte, *The Sacrament of Marriage in Hindu Society*, p. 35.

Gautama says:

> That the father of a girl had to give his daughter in marriage as soon as she attained puberty. Any negligence on the part of the father was considered a sin. The daughter should wait for three months after she starts menstruating. Then she should find her own partner giving away ornaments given to her by her father.

Usha M. Apte referring to verse IV.1 that a householder should get a wife who is similar in qualities to him, the use of word householder or *gṛhastha* suggests that the groom is quite mature and has finished his studentship.[177]

Vasiṣṭha says:

> If through the father's negligence, a maiden is given away after the suitable age has passed, she, who was waiting for a husband, destroys him, who gives her away . . . out of fear of the appearance of menses, let the father marry his daughter while she still goes about naked, for if she stays in the house after the age of puberty, sin falls upon the father.[178] .

Baudhāyana says:

> One should give one's daughter, while she still goes nacked, to a man who has not broken the bow of chastity and who possesses good qualities or even to one destitute of good qualities. He should not keep the maiden in his house after she has reached the age of puberty.[179]

Baudhāyana further repeats that

> he who does not give away a marriageable daughter within three years of the puberty, doubtlessly contracts a guilt to that of killing an embryo.[180]

---

177. Usha M. Apte, *The Sacrament of Marriage in Hindu Society*, p. 141.
178. *VasDS*, 17.61-2.
179. *BaudhDS*, 4.1.12.
180. *Ibid.*, 4.1.12-13.

Coming to the period of Smṛtis, reference to be made to Manu, the law-giver:

> To a distinguised, handsome suitor (of) equal (caste) should (a father) give his daughter in accordance with the prescribed rule, though she have not attained (proper age).[181]

> Three years let a damsel wait, though she be marriageable but after that time he let her choose for herself a bridegroom (of) equal caste and rank.[182]

> A man aged thirty years, shall marry a maiden of twelve who pleases him, or a man of twenty-four a girl eight years of age; if (the performance of) his duties would (otherwise) be impeded, (be must marry) sooner.[183]

Commenting on this verse Medhātithi and Kullūka say that this verse is not intended to lay down a hard and fast rule, but merely to give instances of suitable ages. However, Kullūka, Nārāyaṇa and Rāghavānanda, the commentators say that if (the performance of) his duties would be impeded, i.e., if he has finished his studentship earlier, be must marry at once in order to be able to fulfil his duties as a householder.

Yājñavalkya says that:

> Without breaking (the rules) of studentship, let him marry a woman with auspicious characteristics who has not belonged to another man, who is lovely, who is not a *sapiṇḍa* and who is younger (than himself).[184]

> If they fail to give her away in marriage, they incur the sin of killing the embryo at every menstruation, in the absence of persons who can give her away in marriage, the girl herself may elect a proper bridegroom.[185]

---

181. *Manu*, IX.88.
182. *Ibid.*, IX.90.
183. *Ibid.*, IX.94.
184. *Yāj*, I.52.
185. *Ibid.*, I.64.

The other *smṛtikāra*s have spoken too about it. According to Bṛhaspati, a man of thirty should marry a girl of ten, while a person of twenty-one years of age should marry a girl of seven years of age. Bālamabhaṭṭa has though spoken like this but does not, however, prove it.[186]

*Viṣṇu Purāṇa* lays down a universal rule that bride should be one-third of the age of man. If he marries he must select a maiden who is of a third of his age.[187]

*Parāśara-smṛti* says:

> A girl at the age of eight is called *gaurī*, at nine *rohiṇī*, at ten *kanyā*, thereafter she is called *rajasvalā*. If she is not married before she becomes *rajasvalā* (till the tenth year), her father, mother and elder brother, all of them shall go to hell.[188]

अष्टवर्षा भवेद् गौरी नववर्षा च रोहिणी ।
दशवर्षा भवेन् कन्या तत ऊर्ध्वं रजस्वला ।। १ ।।
माता चैव पिता तस्या ज्येष्ठो भ्राता तथैव च ।
त्रयस्ते नरक यान्ति दृष्ट्वा कन्यां रजस्वलाम् ।। २ ।।

If we critically examine the various verses and hymns we can safely say that no age is prescribed for a valid marriage, but the age of the bride went on changing with evolution in society. The fact remains that the girl should be married when she attained puberty and it is only by way of utmost precaution that she should be married earlier as the father may not come to know about the attainment of puberty by the girl. However, it is seen that even when the marriage of the girl is solemnised when being a minor, she was not sent to the family of the husband till she got puberty and that custom of northern India is called *muklāvā*. So, the marriage of the girl, being a heavy responsibility on the shoulders of the parents, every parent tried to discharge this duty as early as possible and perhaps also due to outer influence on Indian soil, the marriage of a minor girl was preferred but there is no such sanctity about it and as such if

186. Cited by Bālambhaṭṭa in his commentary on *Yāj*, I.52.

187. Cited by Bālamabaṭṭa, Bk III, ch. X 16.

188. Dr. Ved Mitter, *Parāśara Smṛti* cited in *India of Dharma Sūtra*, p. 22.

in the Hindu Marriage Act, 1955, the age is fixed, it has nothing to, do with section 11 of the Contract Act, 1872 and the judicial position is as below:

In *Ram* v. *Chand*:[189] It is held that such marriages below the age prescribed though restrained under law, yet are not invalid.

In *Venkataraman* v. *State*:[190] Andhra Pradesh High Court overruling AIR 1975 AP 193[191] and dissenting from *Krishna Devi* v. *Tulsam Devi*[192] held that the marriage in contravention of the age limits can neither be void nor voidable though it is punishable under section 18 of the Act.

However, the Supreme Court in *Lila Gupta* v. *Lakshminarayana*[193] observed that a reference to the Child Marriage Restraint Act would show that it was enacted to carry forward the reformist movement of prohibiting child marriages and while it made a marriage in contravention of the provisions of that Act punishable, it did not render the marriage void. The same reasoning would apply to a marriage contravening section 5(*iii*) of the Act.

After the decision of the Supreme Court, various High Courts held that such a marriage is neither void nor voidable as the legislature excepted that provision from the purview of sections 11 and 12 of the Act.[194]

So even this provision does not fall under the shadow of the contractual content. We have seen that from Vedic age to Smṛti period, change in the marriage age of the bride was undergoing due to the changing social scenario but the age of the bridegroom remained constant, i.e., after completion of his studies. Similarly, a change effected in section 5 (*iii*) is not to be read too much into, to say that it smells a provision of the Contract Act. Bengal School of

---

189. ILR [1937] 2 Cal 764.
190. AIR 1977 AP 43 (FB).
191. *Suramma* v. *Ganapathi*.
192. AIR 1972 Pb. 142.
193. AIR 1978 SC 1351 at 1358.
194. AIR 1977 Ori 36, 1980 HLR 166 (Raj), 1978 HLR, 547 (Punj).

Hindu Law fixed the age of majority as fifteen years and sixteen years as interpreted by the Mitākṣarā School.[195]

However, if still some doubt is persisting in the minds that a contractual content has entered in the Hindu marriage, it should vanish with the provision (section 7) of the said Act which overrides section 5 completely.

Section 7 of Hindu Marriage Act, 1955 stipulates:

1. A Hindu marriage may be solemnised in accordance with the customary rites and ceremonies of either party thereto.
2. Where such rites and ceremonies include the *saptapadī* (that is, the taking of seven steps by the bridegroom and the bride jointly before the sacred fire), the marriage becomes complete and binding when the seventh step is taken.

This section is clearly mandatory in nature though the word 'may' is used. And customary rites and ceremonies of either party thereto is also mandatory and this provision is supplemented with the expression 'solemnised' used in the section. In the words of Usha M. Apte[196] the sacrament of marriage is a very important *saṁskāra* from various points of view. It gives a religious and legal sanction to the matrimonial relations of the persons concerned. Particularly to the Hindu mind, it is sacrament which lends a sort of permanency to the wedlock. The religious aspect of the Hindu Marriage is very important from this point of view. The rites give a special meaning to sexual intercourse which otherwise would be a simple gratification of the sex-instinct.

The *vivāhasūkta* of *Ṛgveda*, X.85 gives first clear picture of the primary marriage ritual. According to Rajbali Pandey[197] the rites of marriage mentioned in *Ṛgveda* have been bodily taken in *Atharvaveda* but with some important changes. The Sūtras and Śāstras give a fully developed marriage rituals prescribing as

195. *Nār*. I.35, *Vyavcandrikā*, II.590. *Kullūka and Narāyaṇa Commenting on Manu*, VIII.27 say that the minority ends with the sixteen year.
196. Usha M. Apte Preface to *The Sacrament of Marriage in Hindu Society*.
197. Rajbali Pande, *Hindu Saṁskāra*, p. 205.

number of details to be followed. The Gṛhyasūtras mainly deal with the rituals of marriage, though there is some variation in details. The principal Gṛhya-sūtras are *Āśvalāyana Gṛhya-sūtra*, *Gobhila Gṛhya-sūtra*, *Āpastamba Gṛhya-sūtra*, *Mānava Gṛhya-sūtra*, *Parāśara Gṛhya-sūtra*.

These rituals and ceremonies are not only having religious significance but also social significance and the invocation of God is to confer strength to discharge the duties of a householder and as Manu said:

> As all living creatures subsist by receiving support from air, even so (the members of) all orders subsist by receiving support from the householder.[198]
>
> Because men of the three (other) orders are daily supported by the householder with (gifts of) sacred knowledge and food, therefore, (the order of) householders is the most excellent order.[199]

So marriage is the foundation of *gṛyhasta* and *gṛyhasta* is the foundation of the society and as such utmost sanctity is to be bestowed on marriage as its stability is the *sine qua non* of the harmony of the society.

In *Kunta Devi* v. *Siri Ram Kaluram*[200] it is said that the performance of *homam*, the *pāṇigrahaṇa* or taking hold of bride's hand and going round the fire with Vedic *mantras*, the treading on the stone and the seven steps or *saptapadī*, these are the more important rites.

Supreme Court in *Bhau Rao* v. *State of Maharashtra*[201] it is said that the word 'solemnised' means to celebrate the marriage with proper ceremonies with the intention that the parties should be considered to be married. Merely going through certain ceremonies with the intention that the parties be taken to be married would not make the ceremonies prescribed by law or

198. *Manu*, III.77.
199. *Ibid.*, III.78.
200. AIR 1963 Punj 235.
201. AIR 1965 SC 1564.

approved by any established custom. The Supreme Court reiterated the same view in *Kanwal Ram* v. *H.P. Administration.*[202]

However, Kerala High Court in *Chakki* v. *Ayyappan*[203] observed that if the essential ceremonies of *saptapadī* and invocation before sacred fire were observed, the absence of some customary ceremonies neither ancient nor definite nor obligatory does not invalidate a marriage. The stress of the High Court is clearly to solemnise the marriage with the essential and obligatory ceremonies.

So non-performance of essential and obligatory ceremonies and rites renders the marriage 'no marriage in the eye of law'. Even the Courts have taken the stand that if it is proved that no valid ceremony was performed, restitution of conjugal rights cannot be granted.[204]

In *Rajaihi* v. *Selliah*[205] Mr. Justice Satyanaryana Rao of the Madras High Court said that it may be laudable object to simplify the marriage ceremonies as laid down in Śāstras and custom but it will be a dangerous doctrine to lay down that a community should have liberty to prescribe the requisites of a valid marriage without any statutory authority.

Thus, in essence, Hindu Marriage Act, 1955 which was enacted to codify and amend the ancient Hindu Law, the intention of the legislature is never there to destroy the sacrament character of Hindu marriage.

In *Rani Bala* v. *Ram Krishna*[206] a clear picture has been thus given. The two statutes, the Hindu Marriage Act, 1955 and the Contract Act, 1872 are not pari-material. The former deals with marriages. The later deals with contracts and commerce. A Hindu marriage is neither a contract nor a commerce. It is a sacrament.

---

202. AIR 1966 SC 614.

203. AIR 1989 Ker 89.

204. *Deivanai* v. *Chidanbaram* AIR 1954 Mad 657. *Parbia* v. *Thopli* AIR 1966 HP 20.

205. [1966] 2 MLJ 40.

206. [1969] 73 CWN 751.

Sacrament apart, a marriage can never be regarded as a mere contract. The parties who enter into contract can at their will dissolve it, but the parties who contract a marriage cannot. The Hindu Marriage Act has no doubt made an inroad into the close preserve of that ancient law, but the concept of a sacrament still goes strong.

However, the propounders of the theory that Hindu marriage is a contract, base their assertion on divorce, which dissolves marriage.

Even this view does not appear to be sound and any such statement being made, is incorrect and untenable statement in law. To quote J.D.M. Derrett:[207]

> The introduction of Divorce has not interfered with the *saṁskāra* still less abolished it . . . as too many jurists have pathetically and incautiously observed. Marriage performed according to Śāstra is still a *saṁskāra* and judicial divorce cannot end that aspect of marriage. It merely terminates (subject to orders, relating to alimony, matrimonial property and custody of children) secular rights of one spouse against the other and frees each other to enter into another. . . . The Śāstric concept of marriage as a *saṁskāra*, a Union of two persons for all purposes spiritual . . . has been trimmed but not destroyed by the legislature.

So it needs to be seen as to how the introduction of divorce in Hindu Marriage Act, 1955 has affected the sacrament character of Hindu marriage or it is a mere fantasy. So a detailed study of the concept of divorce from ancient Hindu Law to the present Act is to be examined.

---

207. J.D.M. Derrett, *A Critique of Modern Hindu Law*, 1970, p. 348. Also see *Introduction to Modern Hindu Law*, 1963.

*Where they are no more twain, but one flesh. What therefore, God hath joined together, let not man put asunder.* **— St. Matthew 19 : 6**

*In every parting there is an image of death.*
**— George Eliot**

# 3

# Divorce under Hindu Śāstric Law

PARADOXICAL though it may appear, nevertheless it is true that while sometimes words are employed to hide thoughts, at other times they contain more meaning than is apparent to an ordinary observer.

Divorce is also a great paradox, though seemingly contradictory yet perhaps is true. The French word is 'Diverter' and Latin word is 'Divortium' which means 'to divert'. But it is commonly said that Divorce is a word of Roman Origin from 'dis', apart and 'verter', to turn — but this expression gives a meaning full of suspense as to whether it singnifies a separation between man and wife permanently or temporarily. Whether it is partial or complete.

Webster's *Third New International Dictionary* states it to mean amongst other things:

1. Legal dissolution in whole or in part of a marriage relation usually by a Court or other body having competent authority.

2. An absolute dissolution of a valid marriage made by decree of Court for lawful cause arising after the marriage (distinguished from annulment).

3. A formal separation of man and wife by the act of one party or by consent according to established custom.

The *Law Lexicon* by Ramanatha Aiyer (1990) says:

1. Divorce is a judicial act by which the marriage relation is either dissolved or partially suspended.

2. *Divortium dicitur a divertendo quia vir divertitur ab uxore.*

   "Divorce is said to be from divertendo because a man is diverted from his wife."

3. 'Mensa et thoro' dissolveth not the marriage, it only suspends the marriage relation.

'A Vinculo Matrimonii' absolutely dissolves marriage and makes it void.

The writings of Sir Henry Sumnen Maine, who made a deep study of the institutions of early society do give a picture of the origin of the power of repudiation of the marriage tie which the then inchoate law entrusted to the husband against the wife. But this phenomenon is connected with that archaic state of society, where the family and not the individual was the fulcrum around which rights, obligations, duties, etc., were gathered.

Firstly, we have to base or presume our study merely on conjectures because the making of marriage and breaking of marriage has its roots in infinity. It has to be imagined that the remotest early period was the period of unwritten law and the principle of evolution must have brought forth many institutions including the one institution of marriage by which the weaker section to have a safe shelter must have felt the necessity of bringing them within the arms of the stronger. Thus, it can be imagined the society of man and beast alike but then innate inclinations, regulated satisfaction of biological urges and nearness and emotional touch with the offsprings must have brought the concept of one man and wife.

Then sharing of that state of life must have produced some conflicting and contradictory tastes which tended to loosen the state of nearness or the closeness of tie by which the destructive aspect of life in the shape of repudiation came forth.

In order to channalise the unhappy unions, unsuitable closeness, bad tempers, varying tastes, must have come some regulations that gave a shape to repudiation as to how this union of one man and wife should come to an end amicably whereby some restrictions and limitations have been imposed according to the nature of the society then and such development both constructive and destructive in nature continued with the evolution of society.

Leaving these conjectures we come to reality and some authenticated history of divorce as it manifested in various civilisations.

**Divorce and Roman Law**

Considered historically, among the Greeks of Homeric Age, divorce was seldom practised in Greece. In the Periclean age it became somewhat common, but practically speaking it is from the time of Romans that we can follow the development of divorce historically. Roman Law is divided into four periods.

1. The Monarchy from 753-510 BC. The era 753 BC is significant as it coincides with the founding of Rome.
2. The Republic from 451-50 BC when there was compilation of Twelve Tables.
3. The Principate from 27 BC to AD 235.
4. The Dominate from AD 284 to 565 which is the reign of Diocletian to Justinian.

We find that among the Romans the word 'divorce' had two significations. First is the complete abrogation of the marital tie by which each party was liberated from the other and had perfect right to re-marry. This the Romans used to term 'vinculo matrimonii'.

Secondly, the incomplete severance by which the man and wife were separated but not so as to enable either to re-marry and this the Romans called a divorce 'a mensa et thoro'.

The Roman family is purely patriarchal; if there ever was a time when the more primitive matrilinear prevailed among any part of the population it has left no traces in the legal system. 'Patria Potestas' or the power of the head of the family was supreme over all its members. The individual members of a family had no life of their own. They lived for and in the family and it was the family that was unit of society and this conception of society produced a unique effect on the concept of divorce.

By marriage the girl was transferred from the family of the father to the family of the husband and the husband acquired two controls over his wife, i.e., as father being the concept of 'Patri Potestas' and as husband as the transfer of the right of 'Patri Potestas'.

But the father even after transfer of power, still had the right to retract the powers which he had once vested in the husband.

Thus, the father was still instrumental in the divorce of the daughter. It is reflected from a constitution of Antonius Pius which prohibited the fathers from disturbing harmonious union. It is stated that, however, fathers were given some concession in the time of Marcus Aurelius by which a father could interfere between the girl and the husband for a just and strong cause which is known as 'Magna et justa causa interveniente'.

There is a curious collection of enactments and counter enactments in Roman Law about Divorce by which the powers given to husbands at different times, were afterwards limited or withdrawn. The XII Tables gave freedom of divorce. It was entirely at the option of the husband. Though it is asserted that for nearly 500 years, the public opinion of society and custom deterred husband from the pronouncement of wanton divorces, still it is true that the husbands took full advantages of their legal rights and divorces were no rare happenings. Cicero, the greatest Roman Orator is to be held liable for this unbecoming act for his informal dismissal of his wife Terentia.[1]

However, the most important legislation came in AD 331, in the time of Constantine when for certain specified causes, a husband or wife could divorce each other. One notable circumstance connected with the legislation of Constantine is that the pecuniary punishment, attendant on a divorce for the specified causes was abolished.

Then in AD 421 the Emperors Honorius and Theodosius enacted further laws of divorce which imposed still greater penalties for wanton divorces or for divorces on slight causes.

---

1. *The Development of Divorce before Christianity*, 14 ALJ 147.

Then came the law on divorce by Theodosius and Valentinian which made the law on divorce simple by which she can divorce her husband under either of the twelve grounds and any violation, she forfeited her dowry and could not marry again for five years.

Similarly, the husband can divorce his wife on specified grounds only and if he divorced his wife for any other cause, he lost all claims to her dowry. These enactments are before Christianity took roots in the Roman Empire.

**Divorce and Jewish Law**

Next we come to the History of Jewish Law which may be divided into the following periods:

1. Before Moses, i.e., 1300 BC
2. Moses to EZRA, i.e., 444 BC
3. EZRA to Hillel, i.e., 4 BC
4. Hillel to R. Judah, i.e., AD 217

Generally, the starting point is the Torah of Moses (The Pentateuch) as found in the first five books of the Bible: Genesis, Exodus, Leviticus, Numbers and Deuteronomy. This Torah was accepted from early times as the 'Fundamental law' of the Jewish people, because, according to tradition, it had been given to them by God through Moses at Mount Sinai.

Little is known definitely about the early Israelites and that their Pre-Mosaic history is largely guesswork. About their cultural tradition we can only hazard some general observations that are based on analogies drawn from similar sematic societies than upon any great store of fact or knowledge. Being nomads, they had a body of customary law which like most primitive custom had the sanction of religion behind it.[2]

The bill of 'divorcement', 'keritut' (let 'cutting') of Deut 24, 1-4 is the first mention of what came to be known later by the Talmudic term 'get', a word which signified broadly any formal written instrument like a deed, bond, bill of sale, etc., However, it is narrow

2. George Horowitz, *The Spirit of Jewish Law.*

and specialised meaning in post Talmudic times was 'Bill of Divorce'. In the period of Mishnah, its form seems to have been very simple and the significance was that the wife had been already divorced and was, therefore, 'sui juris' and free to marry another man.

Later in the Babylonian academies minute details were developed with respect to the preparation, form and the language of the 'get'.

However, it is worth mentioning that Mishnah declares:

> Moses received the Torah from Sinai, and transmitted it to Joshua, Joshua to the Elders, the Elders to the Prophets.

Thus, the law of Divorce is from time immemorial and being an integral part of Torah, was never divorced from ethics or religion. So Jewish Law is interpreted with morality piety and equity. Thus, for law of Divorce we should only look to Deut (Biblical Book).

1. Moses commanded that the wife should be given a written 'bill of divorcement'.
2. The husband should have no right at all to put her away (Deut 22, 13-19, 28-9).
3. A wife could not be put away while she was a minor, a captive or insane.
4. By the year 1000, it was enacted by Rabbinical Ordinance that a man could no longer put away his wife except by her own consent unless she be at fault.

> To assimilate the right of the woman to the right of the man, it is decreed that even as the man does not put away his wife except of his own free will, so shall the woman not be put away except by her own consent.

## Divorce and Pre-Islamic Arabia

Now we shall have a picture of divorce very briefly as prevalent in Pre-Islamic Arabia and its development. Arabia is one of the hottest and driest countries in the world. There is variation in climatic and geographical condition, which led to the formation of two different kinds of inhabitants. Some of them were more or less of the nomadic kind. The Arabics were divided in various tribes.

Each tribe was governed by their own law. The religion of the Arabians was essentially a plenatory one. Star-worship was the essential basis of their religion. The tribes being nomads, they were wandering from place to place. Their main business was to wage war, enjoy woman and wine. The status of woman was worse than animals. To be precise, the institution of marriage was not there in real concept, even if it was there, it was a mere myth. There is a mention of one type of marriage called *'Baal'* marriage where husband paid a sum of money to the wife's parents as a consideration of marriage. So to say that a limit of marriage and divorce was not controlled by any law or religion. Since the pre-Islamic period was known as the period of 'Jahilliya' or the period of ignorance, thus no legal inspiration is to be drawn on the concept of divorce.

It is only after Holy Prophet got enlightenment that he established the institution of marriage and two traditions of Holy Prophet are worth mentioning:

> The Prophet declared that marriage is a sacred duty and whoever dislikes this way of life is not of me.
>
> — Bukhari

> When a man got married, he has made his Islam half perfect. Then let him fear Allāh for the remaining half.[3]
>
> — Baihaqi

Regarding divorce three verses from Holy Korān will sum up the concept of divorce:

> If ye take a dislike to them
> It may be that ye dislike
> A thing, and God brings about
> Through it a great deal — IV: 19

> If ye fear a breach

3. Cited in the Thesis of H.D. Kohli, *Maintenance of Muslim Wife — A Mythical Realism*.

Between them twain
Appoint (two) Arbiters,
One from his family,

And the other from hers
If they wish for peace
God will cause
Their reconciliation —IV: 35

Then if they obey you
take no further action against them
All is high. Supreme. —IV: 34

Thus, concept of divorce was clear in the Islamic Arabia and pre-Islamic Arabia, throwing away the women, as and when desired, like dumb driven cattles. It was the barbarian concept and not divorce as such. However, prophet brought some regulation in it.

## Divorce and Hindu Law

Now we should look to the concept of divorce under Hindu Law. But before we take up this concept under Hindu Law, it is but essential that we should also take note of this concept as the statutes present and the meaning of this concept as to whether it amounts to dissolution of marriage or it is merely a dissolution of status. So we have to go through the various enactments dealing with divorce such as:

1. Section 13 of the Hindu Marriage Act, 1955.
2. Section 27 of the Special Marriage Act, 1954.
3. Section 32 of the Parsi Marriage and Divorce Act, 1936.
4. Section 1 of the Matrimonial Causes Act, 1950.
5. Section 2 of the Dissolution of Muslim Marriage Act, 1939.
6. Sections 10 and 22 of the Indian Divorce Act, 1869.

These enactments do speak about divorce but has not defined divorce as to what it is and what it caters to. Does it dissolve marriage? Or does it dissolve only status and the consequences of marriage still remain tagged to it?

**What is divorce**

The word 'divorce has been used in some enactments and whereas in some other enactments the word 'dissolution of marriage' has been used.

> Section 13 of the Hindu Marriage Act, 1955 stipulates:
>
> Subject to the provisions of this Act and to the rules made thereunder, a petition for divorce may be presented to the District Court either by the husband or the wife on the ground that the respondent. . . .

Section 27 of the Special Marriage Act, 1954 states:

> Subject to the provisions of this Act and to the rules made thereunder a petition for divorce may be presented to the District Court by the husband or wife on the ground that the respondent. . . .

Section 32 of the Parsi Marriage and Divorce Act, 1936 speaks:

> Any married person may sue for divorce on any one or more of the following grounds, namely. . . .

Even section 1 of the Matrimonial Causes Act, 1950 has used the word 'divorce':

> Subject to the provisions of the next following section, a petition for divorce may be presented to the Court either by the husband or the wife on the ground that the respondent. . . .

But in section 2 of the Dissolution of Muslim Marriages Act, 1939 the word 'dissolution of marriage' is used:

> A woman married under Muslim Law shall be entitled to obtain a decree for the dissolution of her marriage on any one or more of the following grounds, namely. . . .

However, a peculiar situation arises in the Indian Divorce Act, 1869, wherein both the words are used but under different provisions. Section 10 of the Act says:

> Any husband may present a petition to the District Court or to the High Court, praying that his marriage may be dissolved on the ground that his wife has, since the solemnisation of, been guilty of adultery.
>
> Any wife may present a petition . . . praying that her marriage may be dissolved on the ground that, since the solemnisation thereof, her husband has exchanged his profession of Christianity for the profession of some other religion, and gone through a form of marriage with another woman. . . .

Section 22 of the said Act says:

> No decree shall hereafter be made for a divorce a 'mensa et toro' but the husband or wife may obtain a decree of judicial separation. . . .

Now the question that legally haunts is as to whether 'divorce' and 'dissolution of marriage' are two distinct concepts or they are synonymous. To find the answer we have to look for guidance in judicial pronouncements.

In *Chadburn* v. *Chadburn*[4]

This is a petition for judicial separation on the ground of desertion for three years and upwards immediately preceding the presentation of the petition wherein the matter was agitated under Supreme Court of Judicature (Consolidation) Act, 1925 amended by the Matrimonial Causes Act, 1937 whereby section 5 of the Act is substituted for sub-sections 1 and 2 of the Judicature Act of 1925. In this case Hodson J. defined divorce in terms of Matrimonial Causes Act, 1937 as divorce clearly means throughout this Act, unless it otherwise appears, divorce 'a vinculo'.

*In Re. Miles*:[5] The case was for the proceeds of a certain policy of Insurance on the life of a person to be paid to the deceased's wife who was the wife of the deceased at the date of the issue of the policy of Insurance but who subsequently obtained a decree absolute dissolving her marriage with the deceased.

4. [1941] P. 66.
5. [1951] 4 DLR, 359.

Laidlaw J., commenting on the word 'divorced' used in section 169(1) of the Insurance Act R.S.O. 1950 said that I think the word 'divorced' in section 169(1) was intended to apply in the larger sense to all actions for dissolution of marriage, whether based upon grounds existing at the time of marriage or because of events subsequent thereto. It was intended to mean the dissolution by law of the bond of matrimony.

Later on, in *Deacock* v. *Deacock*, Hodson LJ[6] said that in my view the word 'dissolution' relates to the marriage bond itself, whereas the word 'divorce' relates to the parties to the marriage bond and it is apt to refer to 'divorce' when speaking of parties and 'dissolution' when speaking of the bond.

However, in *Zohara Khatoon* v. *Mohd Ibrahim*,[7] which was a case under section 125(1) *Explanation* clause (*b*) and section 127(3) of CrPC and dissolution of Muslim Marriages Act, 1939. In the said Act of 1939 the word 'dissolution of marriage' is used whereas in section 125(1) *Explanation* (*b*) the phrase used is — 'Wife includes a woman who has been divorced by or has obtained a divorce and has not remarried'.

Thus, to resolve this distinction, Koshal J. explained this distinction stating

> As ordinarily understood, therefore, divorce is nothing more nor less than another name for dissolution of marriage whether the same results from act of parties or is a consequence of proceeding at law, and it would, in our opinion, be wrong to regard the two terms as not being synonymous with each other unless the legislature makes a direction to the contrary.

We need hardly point out that section 125 of the code contains no such direction.

Thus, according to Mr. Justice Koshal, the expression 'divorce' and 'dissolution' were really two facets of the same situation. Still it is felt that the legislature has provided different expressions like divorce and nullity of marriage which shows that the legislative intention has something in mind.

In section 11 of the Hindu Marriage Act, 1955, the expression 'decree of nullity' was used. In section 12 of the said Act, the expression 'marriage may be annulled by a decree of nullity' was used. However, in section 13 of the said Act, the word 'be dissolved by a decree of divorce' was used.

In any case, the legal consequence is the dissolution of marriage. In nullity of marriage, it is the inherent impediment in the marriage itself and whereas in divorce, the marriage is valid and it is in the sharing of marriage that some impediments occur leading to the breaking of marriage by a decree of divorce. It is appropriate to quote what Mr. Justice S Murtaza Fazal Ali in AIR 1981 SC 1243 has said:

> By obtaining a decree from a Civil Court for dissolution of marriage under section 2 of the Act of 1939 which also amounts to a divorce (under the law) obtained by the wife.

After the resolution of this distinction, it is but necessary to have a comprehensive picture of the concept of divorce as envisaged in the Hindu Law.

## Divorce and Hindu Law

Hindu Law in its complete comprehensiveness is the law from time immemorial to the present-day punctuated by custom and dominated by the continually changing social scenario.

Thus, Hindu Law can be conveniently divided into three categories:

1. Divorce and Śāstric Law
2. Divorce and Customary Law.
3. Divorce and Hindu Marriage Act, 1955

## Divorce and Śāstric Law

Hindu Law may be described to be the ancient law of the Hindus rooted in the Vedas and announced in the Smṛtis, as explained and enlarged in recognised commentaries and digests and as supplemented and varied by usage. Hindu Law, it is generally agreed, has the most ancient pedigree of any known system of Jurisprudence.[8]

So from the researches of the scholars of Hindu Law as well as from the Hindu scriptures, it is now abundantly clear that the rules of *vyavahāra* or Civil Law, relating to Marriage, Adoption, Partition, Inheritance, in the Smṛtis were, in the main, drawn from actual usages then prevalent, to an appreciable extent, they were modified or supplemented by the opinions of Hindu Jurists.[9] This is why the various scriptures which flourished at varied intervals of time spoke about marriage and about its dissolution in different connotations but on the touchstone of unity in diversity, there appears to be clear and solemn semblance in the approach drawing inspiration from *Manu-smṛti*. In the Vedas itself the pre-eminence of Manu is declared in these terms.

Whatever Manu says is medicine[10] *Smṛticandrikā* and *Vīromitrodaya* cited by Ganga Nath Jha declare that where there is conflict between the code of Manu and another Smṛti, the former is to be accepted.[11]

Now if we go through the various Hindu scriptures, we find three expressions uttered by the divine sages and learned and versatile scholars and they are: 'abandonment', 'supersession', and 'remarriage'. But it is only the *Arthaśāstra* of Kauṭilya which contains some interesting observations bearing on divorce. However, there appears to be unanimity among the law-givers and commentators that divorce was unknown to Ancient Hindu Law. As they draw their legal inspiration from *Manu-smṛti*, so a peep into the verses of *Manu-smṛti* has to be made to get a radiant view.

**पाणियहणिकामंत्रानियतन्दारलक्षणम्।**
**तेषान्निष्ठातुविज्ञेयाविद्वद्भिःसप्तमेपदे।। २२७ ।।**

---

8. Mayne, *Hindu Law*.
9. *Anirudh Jagdeorao* v. *Baba Rao Irabji* 1983 HLR 446 Bom.
10. P.V. Kane, *History of Dharma-Śāstra*, vol. I, 1930, pp. 136-7.
11. Ganga Nath Jha, *Hindu Law in its Sources*.

The nuptial texts are a certain proof (that a maiden has been made a lawful) wife; but the learned should know that they (and the marriage ceremony) are complete with the seventh step (of the bride around the sacred fire).

— *Manu*, VIII. 227

एतावानेवपुरूषोयज्ञायात्माप्रजेतिह।
विप्राःप्राहुस्तथाचैतद्योभर्त्तासास्मृताङ्गना।। ४५ ।।

He only is a perfect man who consists (three persons united) his wife, himself, and his offsprings; thus (says the Veda) and (learned) *Brāhmaṇa*s propound this (maxim) likewise, 'The husband is declared to be one with the wife'.

— *Manu*, IX.45

पतिंयानाभिचरतिमनोवाग्देहसंयता
साभर्तृलोकमाप्नोतिसद्भिःसाध्वीतिचोच्यते ।। १६४ ।।

She, who, controlling her thoughts, words and deeds, never slights her lord, resides (after death) with her husband (in heaven) and is called a virtuous wife. — *Manu*, V.165

सकृदंशोनिपततिसकृत्कन्याप्रदीयते
सकृदाहददानीतित्रीण्येतानिसंतासकृत् ।। ४७ ।।

Once is the partition (of the inheritance), made, (once is) a maiden given in marriage, (and) once does (a man) say, 'I will give', each of those three (acts is done) once only.

— *Manu*, IX.47

ननिष्क्रयविसर्गाभ्याम्भर्त्तुर्भार्य्याविमुच्यते ।
एवंधर्म्मंविजानीमःप्राक्प्रजापतिनिर्म्मितम् ।। ४६ ।।

Neither by sale nor by repudiation is a wife released from her husband, such we know the law to be, which the Lord of Creatures (Prajāpati) made of all. — *Manu*, IX.46

तथानित्यंयतेयातांस्त्रीपुंसौतुकृतक्रियौ ।
यथानाभिचरेतान्तौवियुक्तावितरेतरम ।। १०२ ।।

Let man and woman, united in marriage, constantly exert themselves, that (they may not be) disunited (and) may not violate their matual fidelity. —Manu, IX.102

अन्योन्यस्याव्यभिचारोभवेदारणान्तिकः ।
एषधर्मःसमासेनज्ञेयःस्त्रीपुंसयोःपरः ॥ १०१ ॥

Let mutual fidelity continue until death, this may be considered as the summary of the highest law for husband and wife. —Manu, IX.101[12]

The cumulative inference that we can draw is that a man who has not taken a wife, has not fully perfected himself, his personality both socially and religiously is incomplete and imperfect. To this effect, in *Śatpatha Brāhmaṇa* it is said that. 'The wife is verily the half of the husband'. The *Taittirīya Saṁhitā* also speaks that, 'Half is she of the husband that is wife'. Derrett puts in crystal clear manner that the intention of the sacrament is to make the husband and wife one, physically and psychically, for secular and spiritual purposes, for this life and for after lives.[13]

In *Tekait Mon Mohini Jemadai* v. *Basanta Kumar Singh*[14] though the suit was for enforcement of conjugal rights, but a detailed discussion on Hindu Law was made wherein it is said that it may be premised that though the marriage is a contract, it is also a sacrament, it is more religious than secular in character, the union is indissoluble, for it is a union of flesh with flesh, bone with bone. During the husband's lifetime, he is to be regarded by the wife as god and the wife is declared to be half the body of her husband equally sharing the fruit of pure and impure acts, and no sacrifice or religious rite is allowed to her apart from the husband's. Hence, it is that after the husband's death, the widow is regarded as the surviving half of his body, the union is a sacred tie even after the death of the husband.

Thus, looking to these verses, we may add other verses to strengthen the conclusions drawn that Hindu marriage is a tie, once tied, cannot be united [15] and divorce was unknown to ancient Hindu Law.

---

12. G. Bühler, all the verses are taken from *The Laws of Manu*.
13. J.D.M. Derrett, *Death of Marriage Law*.
14. ILR [1901] 28 Cal 751.
15. Dr. Paras Diwan, *Modern Hindu Law*.

Manu says:

> To be mothers were women created and to be fathers men; religious rites, therefore, are ordained in the Veda to be performed (by the husband) together with wife.
>
> — *Manu*, IX.96

Husband and wife are enjoined to live in perpetual love, bliss and happiness. A passage in *Rgveda* runs

> Be thou (wife) mother of heroic children, devoted to God, be thou queen in thy father-in-law's household. May all Gods unite the hearts of us two into one.[16]

It is further supported by a hymn in *Atharvaveda* which reads:

> Be not divided, O husband and wife; live together all your lives, sporting with sons and grandsons; rejoicing in your happy home.[17]

But there are certain verses in *Manu-smṛti* and other Smṛtis which do speak of abadonment of wife under certain circumstances. Then naturally the question ariese as to how to reconcile the two views, i.e., 'indissolubility of marriage' and 'abandonment of wife'.

> विधिवत्प्रतिगृह्यापित्यजेत्कन्यांविगर्हिताम् ।
> व्याधितांविप्रदुष्टांवाछद्मनाचोपपादिताम् ।। ७२ ।।
>
> Though (a man) may have accepted a demsel in due form, he may abandon (her if she be) blemished, deseased deflowered and (if she have been) given with fraud.
>
> —*Manu*, IX.72

> यस्तुदोषवर्तींकन्यामनाख्यायोपपादयेत् ।
> तस्यतद्वितथंकुर्य्यात्कन्यादातुर्दुरात्मनः ।। ७३ ।।
>
> If anybody gives a maiden possissing blemishes without declaring them (the bridegroom) may annual that contract with the evil-minded giver. — *Manu*, IX.73

---

16. *Ṛ̣V*, IX.85.
17. *AV*, XIV.1, 21,22.

मद्यपान्साधुवृत्ताचप्रतिकूलाचयाभवेत् ।
व्याधितावात्तधिवेऽत्तव्याहिंस्त्रात्तर्थधोचसर्वदा ॥ ८० ॥

She who drinks spirituous liquor, is of bad conduct, rebellious, diseased, mischievous or wasteful, may at any time be superseded (by another wife). —*Manu,* IX.80

बन्ध्याऽष्टमेऽधिवेद्याऽच्देदशमेतुमतप्रजा ।
एकादशेस्त्रीजननीसद्यस्त्वप्रियवादिनी ॥ ८१ ॥

A barren wife may be superseded in the eighth year, she whose children (all) die in the tenth, she who bears only daughters in the eleventh, but she who is quarrelsome without dalay. — *Manu*, IX.81

Apparently, if we look at these verses, they do give an inference, but rebuttable that some traces of the concept like divorce did exist.

Manu at another place says that:

नान्योत्पन्नाप्रजास्तीहनचाप्यन्यपरिमहे ।
नद्वितीयश्चसाध्वीनांकृचिद्भर्त्तोपदिश्यंते ॥ १६२ ॥

Offsprings begotten by another man is here not (considered lawful) nor (does offsprings begotten) on another man's wife (belong to the begetter) nor is a second husband anywhere prescribed for virtuous women. —*Manu*, V.162

This verse does indirectly point out that if the wife is blemished, then she can be discarded and this view is already there in other verses of Manu. But if we go deep into the matter, that though these verses do speak of discarding of the wife under some situations this discarding does not give any inference of the existence of divorce in ancient Hindu Law.

P.K. Virdi is of the opinion that there was no evidence as to the practice of divorce as such during the Vedic and post-Vedic periods. It was a holy union of mind, body and soul of the spouses and it was believed that death did not put an end to it, for the wife remained linked with her husband in soul after death in the next world. He further says that non-existence of nuptial ceremonies for a second marriage and prohibition of remarriage of women are evidence against the recognition of divorce in the matrimonial system known to Śāstra.[18]

However, to clear the confusion, immaterial how mild it is, we should refer to the various views of other versatile sages who are either the law-givers or they were the exponents of law.

Gautama, who has been assigned to the Sāmavedic school says that strict discipline in life and fidelity to her husband are demanded from a woman.

> Let her not violate her duty towards her husband and let her restraint her tongue, eyes and actions. In case the husband renounced the world, she had, then to lead a life of strict discipline and self-restraint, but where the husband had disappeared, the wife had to wait for six years before she could marry again, and if at the end of six years, the husband returned, she had to go back to him.[19]

These verses lay more stress on the duties of the wife towards husband and family to ensure bliss and happiness. However, it has spoken of one exception in case of the husband's disappearance and to be unheard of for six years. It is deemed a case of presumption of death and the echo of this presumption can be seen in the Evidence Act; of course, where the period mentioned is seven years[20] and the same presumption finds place in the Hindu Marriage Act,[21] 1955; hence, this exception points out three things:

1. If the husband disappears.
2. Not heard of for six years.
3. She can remarry. But there is a rider that if the husband returned at the end of six years, she had to go back to him.

It clearly shows:

1. That she should try to apply self-restraint on her sensual

---

18. P.K. Virdi, *The Grounds for Divorce in Hindu and English Law*.
19. *GauDS*, XVIII.2, 3, 16, 15.
20. Section 108 of the Evidence Act, 1872.
21. Section 13(1) (*vii*) of Hindu Marriage Act, 1955.

urges even if the husband disappeared and not heard of for six years.

2. There is a rider that in case the husband returned then she had to go back to him.

3. Thus, if at all any inference has to be drawn it is not an element of divorce but shows a titling tendency towards remarriage and a conclusion need not be drawn that remarriage presupposes divorce.

Baudhāyana is also the law-giver of considerable importance and antiquity who belonged to the Black Yajurvedic School. He says that under certain conditions a man could abandon his wife and marry again. The conditions are:

> Let her abandon a barren wife in the tenth year; one who bears daughers (only) in the twelfth year, one whose children die in the fifteenth; but her who is quarrelsome, without delay.[22]

Another place Baudhāyana has said that the aim of existence of a woman was to be the mother of sons; duaghters were not desirable and the extraordinary importance given to a son is evident from the fact that a wife who bore only duaghters should be abandoned. But still this dictum does not refer to any inference of divorce but shows beyond doubt that monogamy was the prevailing order of the society and polygamy, an exception under oxtraordinary situations.

Āpastamba says that :

> If he has a wife who is willing and able to perform her share of the religious duties and who bears sons, he shall not take a second. If a wife is deficient in one of these two qualities, he shall take another, but before he kindles the fires of the Agnihotra. For a wife who assists at the kindling of the fires becomes connected with those religious rites of which that fire-kindling forms a part.[23]

---

22. *BaudhDS*, II.2, 4, 6 (See *Manu*, IX.81).

23. *ĀpasDS*, II.5, II.12-14.

At another place Āpastamba says that the sanctity of the marriage vow was not to be violated and if the marriage vow is transgressed, both husband and wife certainly go to hell.[24] About abandonment of wife, he says that a wife could not be abandoned unjustly and any violation of that rule merited severe punishment.

> He who has unjustly forsaken his wife shall put on an ass's skin, with the hair turned outside, and beg in seven houses saying, 'Give alms to him who forsook his wife'. That shall be his livlihood.[25]

Here one important factor needs to be kept in mind that Āpastamba's date as per mention in the *Sacred Books of the East*, has been considered to be not later than the third century BC and that time Buddhism was at its zenith and the importance of conduct and morals, which Buddhism demanded and set forth, had its repercussions on Hindu society as a whole and the concept of *aṣṭāṅga-mārga* of Buddhism was the fulcrum point at that given time. So *Āpastamba Dharma-sūtra* reflects the law as to what is right and as to what is to be followed by the people and as such the laws which were hitherto considered good and beneficial to the society, had to be discarded as unfit.[26]

Vasiṣṭha is claimed to be sage Vasiṣṭha and the commentators considered his works as most authentative though the Western scholars discard this concept on linguistic grounds. But whatever may be the fact, he speaks about the general rules for society and general laws that are applicable for all.

He admits the remarriage of women and gives legal recognition to their sons. He gives two definitions of the term 're-marriage'.

> She is called re-married (*punarbhu*), who, leaving the husband of her youth and, having lived with others, re-enters his family. And she is called re-married who having an impotent, outcast, or mad husband, or after the death of her husband, takes another Lord.[27]

---

24. *ĀpasDS*, II.10, 27, 6.
25. *Ibid.*, II.10, 28, 19.
26. Shakuntla Rao Shashtri, *Women in the Sacred Laws*, p. 38.
27. *VasDS*, XVII.19, 20.

Another place he says that the wife of an emigrant could marry after a lapse of five years. If she were unwilling to do so, she had to live like a widow.

For a brāhmaṇa and kṣatriya wife, she has to wait for five years, four years for a vaiśya and three years for a śūdra, after which the abandoned wives could marry again.[28] But another place Vasiṣṭha says that a wife could never be abandoned by a man on any account,

> though tainted by sin, whether she be quarrelsome or has left the house or has suffered criminal force or has fallen into the hands of thieves, a wife must not be abandoned, for, to forsake her is not prescribed by the sacred law.[29]

This view is quite contradictory to what has been said previously that a woman should be abandoned under similar circumstances. A scholar of renown has tried to reconcile the views by saying that abandonment of wife under the accusation of blemish is the original view of Vasiṣṭha and non-abandonment under any circumstances is a later addition.[30]

Parāśara as a legislator, has been upheld by some to be the highest authority of the fourth age. He confines himself to two aspects of Hindu Law, i.e., *ācāra* and *prāyaścitta.* His account of household is meagre. However, from *Parāśara Saṁhitā,* we find that

> a maiden becomes one with her husband in *piṇḍa* and *gotra* and is detached from the *gotra* of her father on the completion of the seventh step.[31]

Then he further states that

> when the husband of a woman has disappeared, is dead, has turned a recluse, is impotent or has been ex-

28. *VasDS*, XVII.75-7.
29. *Ibid.*, XX.VIII.2-3.
30. Shakuntala Rao Shashtri, *Women in the Sacred Laws*, p. 46.
31. *ParS*, Ācārakāṇḍam, I.2, 63.

> communicated, under these five calamities, another husband is permitted to women.[32]

Nārada also says to the same effect.

Shakuntala Rao Shashtri in her book *Women in The Sacred Laws* states that Parāśara mentions that divorce is allowed on easy terms under certain circumstances and refers to the five such calamities as mentioned earlier.

Ancient Hindu Law is of dynamic evolution. We find modifications in law accoring to the changing social scenario. Parāśara has positively taken a sympathetic view about the women and that must be according to the state of the society then and as per changed conditions, provisions had to be made in confirmity with the altered conditions. Madhvācārya wrote a gloss on the *Parāśara Saṁhitā* which period is being considered as fourteenth century, by which time Hindu society seems to have changed rapidly. So in the light of other verses of *Parāśara Saṁhitā* a great stress on the virtue of chastity of a woman is laid.

> She who follows her husband will abide in heaven for as many years as there are hairs on a human being, that, three thousand crores and half.

As a snake-catcher takes out a snake from a hole by force, in the same manner the wife (who immolates herself) taking out her husband (from hell) enjoys (heavenly bliss) with him.[33]

In view of this, it has to be understood that it is only speaking some changes that have taken place at that material time which cannot be termed by the name 'divorce'. It is only a presumption that where the remarriage of a woman is mentioned, divorce should be presumed to be a prerequisite. In reality the whole stress is on the husband and wife to be unblemished and virtuous to stick sincerely to the vow taken during the solemnisation of marriage.

Besides we find some reference in Kauṭilya's *Arthśāstra*: Nine verses are worth mentioning:

---

32. *ParS*, Ācārakāṇḍam, Prāyaścitta Kāṇḍam, IV.30; *Nārada*, XII.37.
33. *Ibid.*, Prāyaścitta Kāṇḍam, verses, 32-3.

अमोक्ष्या भर्तुरकामस्य द्विपती भार्या, भार्यायाश्च भर्ता । १५ । परस्परं द्वेषान्मोक्षः । १६ । स्त्रीविप्रकारद्वा पुरुषश्चेन्मोक्षमिच्छेद् यथागृहीतमस्यै दद्यात् । १७ । पुरुषविप्रकाराद्वा स्त्री चेन्मोक्षमिच्छेन्नास्यै यथागृहीतं दद्यात् । १८ । अमोक्षो धर्मविवाहानाम् । १९ । इति द्वेषः ।

A disaffected wife is not to be granted divorce who is unwilling. — III.3, 15

By mutual disaffection (alone) a divorce (shall be granted) — III.3, 16

Or, if the husband seeks divorce because of the wife's offence, he shall give to her whatever he may have taken. — III.3, 17

Or, if the wife seeks divorce because of the husband's offence, he shall not give her whatever may have been received. — III.3, 18

There is no divorce in pious marriage. Thus ends (the topic of) disaffection. — III.3, 19

वर्षाण्यष्टावप्रजायमानामपुत्रां वन्ध्यां चाकाङ्क्षेत, दश निन्दुम्, द्वादश कन्याप्रसविनीम् । ३८ । ततः पुत्रार्थी द्वितीयां विन्देत । ३९ । तस्यातिक्रमे शुल्कं स्त्रीधनमर्धं चाधिवेदनिकं दद्यात्, चतुर्विंशतिपणपरं च दण्डम् । ४० ।

The (husband) shall wait for eight years if the wife does not bear offsprings or does not bear a son or is barren, for ten if she bears dead offsprings, for twelve if she bears only daughters. — III.2, 38

After that, he may marry a second wife with the object of getting a son. — III.2, 39

In case of transgression of that (rule), he shall handover the dowry, the women's property and half (that) as compensation, and (pay) a fine of twenty-four *paṇa*s maximum. — III.2, 40

नीचत्वं परदेशं वा प्रस्थितो राजकिल्विषी ।
प्राणाभिहन्ता पतितस्त्याज्यः क्लीवोऽपि वा पतिः ।। ४८ ।।

> A husband, who has become degraded or gone to a foreign land or has committed an offence against the king or is dangerous to her life or has become an outcast or even an impotent, one may be abandoned.[34] — III.2, 48

In Kauṭilya's *Arthaśāstra*, translated by Dr. R. Shamasastry, we find the same concept of law, though the translation is little bit different by the use of different words to interpret the verses. He says:

> A woman, who hates her husband, cannot dissolve her marriage agaist his will. Nor can a man dissolve his marriage with his wife against her will. But from mutual enemity, divorce may be obtained (*parasparam dveṣanmokṣaḥ*). If a man, apprehending danger from his wife, desires divorce (*mokṣamicchet*), he shall return to her whatever she was given (on the occasion of the marriage). If a woman, under the apprehension of danger from her husband, desires divorce she shall forfeit her claim to the property; marriages contracted in accordance with the customs of the first four kinds of marriages cannot be dissolved.[35]

P.V. Kane says that:

> In the Vedic literature there are at least some texts capable of being interpreted as relating to the remarriage of widows and we have the word *punarbhu*. But as regards divorce there is absolutely nothing in the Vedic texts nor is there much in post-Vedic literature.[36]

The position of the writers on Dharma-śāstra is that marriage is *saṁskāra*, that the status of wifehood arises from that *saṁskāra*, that even if the husband or wife become *patita*, the *saṁskāra* already performed is not annulled by that fact, that even if a wife committed adultery, she still remains a wife and that when she performs a penance for her lapse, it is not necessary to have a fresh *saṁskāra*

---

34. R.P. Kangle, these verses have been taken from *Kauṭilya's Arthaśāstra*.
35. R. Shamashastri, *Kauṭilya's Arthaśāstra*, pp. 176-7.
36. P.V. Kane, *History of Dharma-Śāstra*, p. 619.

of marriage performed on her. To support it P.V. Kane refers to the following verse:

> केचित्तु परिव्यक्तासु पारदार्थप्रायश्चित नैवेच्छन्ति संबन्धिनिमित्तत्वाद दारशब्दस्य। तथाच सति विधवास्वपि पारदार्थं न स्यात। न च व्यभिचारादिभिस्तम्यापगमो युक्तः संस्कारनिमित्त वाद दारशब्दस्य तस्य च पतनेऽप्यनमयमात्। अत एव पतिता योषितः कृतप्रायश्चित्तः पुनर्ग संस्क्रियन्ते। अन्यथा तु पतनेन संस्कारस्यापगमात् कृतप्रायश्चिता अप्यदाराः स्युः। अतो व्यभिचारिणीप्यप्यस्त्येव पारदार्यम।

He further explains that a man was allowed to supersede a wife and marry another or others or to abandon his wife altogether in certain circumstances as stated by many writers. But that does not amount to divorce, the marriage is still there intact. Even speaking about the views of Nārada and Parāśara and a few others a woman was allowed to remarry in case of various calamities but according to the digests and commentaries these rules apply to former *yuga* (age). Therefore, divorce in the ordinary sense or word, i.e., divorce a *vinculo matrimonii*, has been unknown to the Dharmaśāstras and to Hindu society except on the ground of custom among the lower castes. Thus, the conclusion derived at is that the word *tyāga* used in the scriptures was not only no divorce a *vinculo* at all but was not even a divorce a *mensa et thoro* and to further support his view he relies upon the following decisions:[37]

1. *The Govt. of Bombay* v. *Ganga*.[38]

2. In the matter of *Ram Kumari*.[39]

3. *Budansa* v. *Fatmabi*.[40]

These are the decisions of Indian Courts which have held that mere change of faith or apostasy by a Hindu wife or husband does not *ipso facto* dissolves the marriage. P.V. Kane refers to Kauṭilya's Arthaśāstra as below:[41]

> अमोक्ष्या भर्तुरकामस्य द्विपदी भार्या, भार्यायाश्च भर्ता। १५ । परस्परं द्वेषान्मोक्षः। १६ ।

---

37. P.V. Kane, *History of Dharma-Śāstra*, p. 620.
38. ILR 4 Bom 330.
39. ILR 18 Cal 264.
40. 26 MLJ 260.
41. P.V. Kane, *History of Dharmaśāstra*.

स्त्रीविप्रकाराद्वा पुरुषश्चेन्मोक्षमिच्छेद् यथागृहीतमस्यै दद्यात्। १७ । पुरुषविप्रकाराद्वा स्त्री चेन्मोक्षमिच्छेन्नास्यै यथागृहीतं दद्यात्। १८ । अमोक्षो धर्मविवाहानाम्। १९ । इति द्वेष:।

But he has avoided to make any comments on it but indirectly an inference can be drawn that perhaps under really extraordinary circumstances divorce might have been possible.

But according to Shakuntala Rao Shastri, divorce is permissible by mutual consent under Buddhist Law. When one party contracts some incurable disease, such as leprosy, divorce is immediately granted. It is well established that when Buddhism was a living religion in India, it influenced, not to small extent, Hindu culture and legal literature. Kauṭilya admits divorce by mutual consent as did the Buddhists.[42]

It is on record that Nārada, Parāśara, Vasiṣṭha and Kauṭilya authorise a woman to take another husband in five cases as already enumerated.[43] Even Nandana and Devala of later period are of the opinion that she could take another husband and in doing so there would be no sin.[44]

Now the main question that has arisen for consideration is as to what is meant by 'abandonment' and 'supersession' and also what is meant by *tyāga* and *mokṣa* as have been used in orginal Smṛtis and in their English translations by the renowned scholars.

Many scholars on Hindu Law have spoken much on this aspect. Dr. Jayaswal says that *tyāga* denotes separation from conjugal intercourse, as opposed to *mokṣa* the technical divorce.[45] It has been echoed when Prof. S. Venkataraman said that *tyāga* is only withdrawal from the society of the other spouse whereas *mokṣa* is the termination of the marriage itself.[46]

Since the right to abandonment has been considered as being tantamount to a right to divorce even under Śāstric Law, then we must examine as to what abandonment means and in what respect

42. Shakuntala Rao Shastri, *Women in the Sacred Laws*, p. 9.
43. *Nārada*, XII.97, *Parāśara*, IV.30, *Vasiṣṭha*, XVII.75-7.
44. R.M. Das, *Women in Manu and his Seven Commentators*.
45. Jayaswal, *Manu and Yājñavalkya*, p. 230.
46. [1962] 1 MLJ Journal-1.

this phrase has been used. The word used is *tyāga* translated as 'abandonment'. Even Steele after going through the legal aspect of the scriptures and in particular the sayings of Vasiṣṭha considered abandonment as equal to divorce. But this view will get frustrated if we look to the comprehensive concept of Hindu marriage that for a Hindu, marriage is mandatory so that he can discharge his debt to his ancestors — the debt of begetting offsprings and that marriage is also obligatory because without a wife a man cannot perform his religious and spiritual duties. So marriage has two aspects, worldly and spiritual. The former purpose would be frustrated where a wife was addicted to drink, was of bad conduct, was diseased, insane, guilty of adultery, had attempted to kill her husband or committed other crimes including procuring abortion. The latter purpose of the marriage would be frustrated if she was barren, bore daughters only and had reached menopause. Therefore the husband would be justified in ceasing to co-habit with such a wife but this abandonment never had the effect of divorce.[47] Both the phrases 'abandonment' or 'supersession' appear to be sysnonymous. The wife retained her status of a wife and had to be maintained. This is why a penance has been prescribed for a woman and after its performance, she is restored to her former position. Even unjust abandonment was punishable.

Prof. Indra[48] on the authority of *Dakṣa-smṛti* (IV.45) asserts that the wife even though she be fallen should not be abandoned and a man violating this principle is born as a woman in his next life and bears the agony of barrenness. To quote Manu: Yājñavalkya:

> But she who shows aversion towards a mad or outcast (husband), a eunuch, one destitute of manly strength, or one afflicted with such diseases as punish crimes, shall neither be cast off nor be deprived of her property.
>
> — *Manu*, IX.79

> The unchaste wife should be deprived of authority, should be unadorned, allowed food barely sufficient to sustain her body, rebuked, and let sleep on low bed and thus allowed to dwell. — *Yājñavalkya*, III.70

47. P.K. Virdi, *The Grounds for Divorce in Hindu and English Law*, p. 27.
48. Indra, *The Status of Women in Ancient India*, p. 94.

The above discussion, though speaks of at times conflicting opinions among law-givers and commentators, but unambiguously speaks that divorce was, though known, but not prevalent and applicable among regenerate classes who were governed by the Śāstric Law.

To conclude, we may refer to P.V. Kane who has said:

> Law was based on a two-tier system, one for the intellectuals or cultural elite and the other for the less sensitive or ill-informed. Accordingly, Hindu Law approved the divorce which was applicable to non-caste Hindus, the lowest rung of the ladder in the socio-cultural hierarchy.

There is almost unanimity among scholars that *Manu-smṛti* dates back to the period 200 BC and that of Yājñavalkya AD 100 and there is also semblance of views that next to *Manu-smṛti*, *Yājñavalkya-smṛti* is an authoritative work on Śāstric Law and as such his views along with light on this aspect and the following verses are relevant for the purpose herein:

> One who gives away a girl without mentioning her defects, is to be punished with *uttama sahasa* and he who abandons a wife who is without blemish is similarly punishable. Again one who falsely blames a girl is to be punished with one hundred (*paṇa*s). —*Yāj*, III.66

> She, on whom the sacrament of marriage is again performed, is called a *punarbhu* (again sanctified), whether she be a virgin or deflowered. She is called a *svairiṇī*, who abandoning a husband, takes protection under a person of her own caste, through lust. —*Ibid.*, III.67

> The purification from unchastity is at the season; in case of conception her abandonment is ordained so also in case of causing abortion or killing a husband or committing a heinous crime, and the rest. —*Ibid.*, II.72

> The liquor drinker, the diseased, the cunning, the barren, the killer of wealth, the unpleasant spoken who bears female children should be superseded, so also (one) who hates people. —*Ibid.*, III.73

The superseded should be maintained, otherwise great sin is caused. When the husband and wife live in harmony the three *vargas*[49] prosper there. —*Ibid.*, III.74

Because continuity (of family) in this world and getting of heaven in the next, are through sons, grandsons and great grandsons, therefore, women ought to be attended to and should be guarded carefully. —*Ibid.*, III.78

When there exists a wife of the same class (*savarṇa*) religious works are not to be performed by a wife of another class. When there are wives[50] of the same class, then religious duties are to be performed by the eldest and not by the others.[51] —*Ibid.*, III.88

In these verses we find the expressions used such as *punarbhu*, 'abandonment', 'superseded', 'superseded should be maintained', 'continuity of family', 'heaven in the next world', 'wives and performance of religious duties'. Cumulatively, if we examine they do speak of remarriage, polygamy and also abandonment but the superseded wife should be maintained, is sufficient to show that abandonment or supersession only means to deprive the wife of worldly pleasures till she goes through the penance and there is no trace of any inference of divorce. So discarding of wife is only meant not to allow her to participate in the performance of religious duties and nothing more.

Vasiṣṭha, Parāśara and Nārada authorise a woman to take another husband in certain situations. Now let us see how Nārada speaks about it. There are many verses in this regard:

The man must undergo an examination with regard to his virile; when the fact of his virile has been placed beyond doubt, he shall obtain the maiden (but not otherwise).[52] —*Nārada*, XII.8

---

49. *Vargas* means religion, wealth and pleasure.
50. This verse speaks of performance of sacred rites and also indirectly speaks of polygamy also.
51. Srisa Chandra Vidyarnava, translator of *Yājñavalkya-smṛti*.
52. *Sacred Books of the East*, Vol. XXXIII, chap. XII, tr. by Jolly.

> If a man is potent with another woman but impotent with his own wife, his wife shall take another husband. This is a law promulgated by the creator of the world.
>
> —*Nārada*, XII.18

> Women have been created for the sake of propagation, the wife being the field and the husband the giver of the seed. The field must be given to him who has seed. He who has no seed is unworthy to possess the field.
>
> —*Ibid.*, XII.19

> When the husband is lost or dead, when he has become a religious ascetic, when he is impotent, and when he has been expelled from caste, these are the five cases of legal necessity, in which a woman may be justified in taking another husband. —*Ibid.*, XII.97

Now these verses are to be read in conjunction with what Devala and Nārada have said:[53]

> When husband and wife leave one another, from mutual dislike, it is a sin, except when a woman, who is kept under supervision, commits adultery. When a married woman commits adultery, her hair shall be shaved, she shall have to lie on a low couch, receive bad food and bad clothing and the removal of the sweepings shall be assigned to her as her occupation. One who wastes the entire property of her husband under the pretence that it is (her own) *strīdhana*, or who procures abortion or who makes an attempt on her husband's life, he shall banish her from the town. One who always shows malice to him or who makes unkind speeches or eats before her husband, he shall quickly expel her from his house.

> Let not a husband show love to a barren woman or to one who gives birth to female children only, or whose conduct is blamable, or who constantly contradicts him; if he does (have conjugal intercourse with her) he becomes liable to censure (himself).

53. *Nārada*, XII.90-4.

So if we critically examine these verses, we come to only one conclusion that even under worst situations the wife has been deprived of her worldly/spiritual rights to perform certain duties and also subjected to penance and that is the end. Even by a figment of imagination divorce under Śāstric Law cannot be contemplated.

In short, if we refer to *Nārada* (XII.97, 98); *Parāśara* (IV.30); *Vasiṣṭha* (XVII.74, 78, 79); *Gautama* (XVIII.15, 17); *Manu* (IX.76); *Yājñavalkya* (III.74), wherein all these law-givers only refer to abandonment or supersession but not to divorce as Kauṭilya has propounded. Since Hindu marriage is sacrament and its object is continuity of progeny and performance of religious duty, the provision to have another wife is positively contemplated under certain situations but not divorce as contemplated in the modern Law.

**Divorce under Customary Law**

There is a unanimity of views that divorce is not known to the general Hindu Law. The reason being that a marriage, from the Hindu point of view creates an indissoluble tie between the husband and wife and as also judicially stressed in

1. *Kudomee* v. *Joteeram*[54]
2. *Shankarlingam* v. *Subban*[55]

But there is also a clear semblance in views that customary divorce was prevalent and recognised. So before we take a deep look on the aspect of customary divorce, it is but essential to first have a picture of what custom is. How it was recognised by the General Hindu Law and under what conditions and constraints it was acceptable judicially.

A custom may be briefly described or defined as a continuing course of conduct which by the acquiescence, or expressed approval (though not in a statutory form) of the community observing it, has come to be regarded as fixing a rule or norm of conduct for the members of the community. Custom grows by conduct, from practices

54. [1878] 3 Cal 305.
55. [1894] 17 Mad, 479.

adopted for the convenience of society and the individual. Their roots go down deep into the soil of national ideas and institutions. So what prevails amongst a set of people as the result of their consensus of opinion and approval is custom.[56] It is said that custom is to the society what law is to the state. However, custom is the creation of the society by its own long drawn out expression considering it fit as being tested on the principle of right and justice and followed it from antiquity uninterrupted and law recognised it as such.

A custom is a particular rule which has existed either actually or presumptively from time immemorial, and has obtained the force of law in a particular locality although contrary or not consistent with the general common law of the realm.[57] However, all customs are purely local and confined to particular places. There cannot be a custom in one place to do something in another. The land in a particular place and the inhabitants in respect thereof, may be charged by custom, for matters within the place, but custom will not apply to matters out of it.[58]

In *Black's Law Dictionary* by Henry Campbell Black 5th edn., it is stated that a usage or practice of the people, which, by common adoption and acquiescence, and by long and unvarying habit, has become compulsory, and has acquired the force of law with respect to the place or subject-matter to which it relates. It results from a long series of actions constantly repeated, which have, by such repetition and by uninterrupted acquiescence, acquired the force of a tacit and common consent.[59]

This definition leads us to another aspect also which needs explanation 'custom' and 'usage' are two different concepts. They are not synonymous terms though they are often used interchangeably. Strictly speaking there is a clear distinction between the two. 'Usage' represents the twilight stage of custom — custom begins where usage ends.[60] Butterworth explained it saying that a

56. P.S. Atchuthen Pillai, *Jurisprudence and Legal Theory*, pp. 104-5.

57. Halsbury's *Law of England* by Lord Simonds, 3rd edn.

58. *R.* v. *Ecclesfield* (*Inhabitants*) [1818] IB & Ald 348 per Lord Ellenborough C.J. at p. 360.

59. Taken from *Louisville & N.R. Co.* v. *Reverman* 243 Ky 702.

60. Mayne's *Hindu Law and Usage*, 13th edn., p. 457.

custom in the intendment of law is such a usage as hath obtained the force of law.[61] So 'custom' implies practice from time immemorial while 'usage' does not. It was, however, observed that section 3(*a*) of the Hindu Marriage Act, 1955, does not preserve this distinction but places both in the same terms.[62]

Beside, these definitions we should turn our attention to its legal sense from Śāstric viewpoint and as judicially pronounced.

Manu, in various verses has spoken about custom as follows:

> The Veda, the sacred tradition, the custom of virtuous men and one's own pleasure, they declare to be visibly the fourfold means of defining the sacred law.
>
> — *Manu*, II.12

To the same effect *Yājñavalkya-smṛti* speaks:

> The Śruti, the Smṛti, the conduct of good men, what appears pleasant to one's ownself and the desire which springs from a good resolution, are said to be the roots of *dharma*.
>
> — *Yāj*, I.7

> The custom handed down in regular succession (since time immemorial) among the (four chief) castes (*varṇa*) and the mixed (races) of that country, is called the conduct of virtuous men. — *Manu*, II.18

> Let him walk in that path of holy men which his fathers and grandfathers followed; while he walks in that, he will not suffer harm. — *Ibid.*, IV.178

> The rule of conduct is transcendent law, whether it be taught in the revealed text or in the sacred traditions, hence a twice born man who possess regard for himself should be always careful to (follow) it. — *Ibid.*, I.108

> Daily (deciding) one after another (all cases) which fall

---

61. Butterworth, *Word and Phrases Legally Defined*, 2nd edn., Vol. I, p. 392 — taken from *Stark's International Law*, 6th edn., p. 34.

62. *Jagdeo Rao* v. *Irhaji* 1983 HLR 446 (FB).

> under the eighteen titles (of law) according to principles drawn from local usages and from the institutes of the sacred law. —*Ibid.*, VIII.3
>
> (A king) who knows the sacred laws, must enquire into the laws of castes (*gati*) of districts, of guilds and of families and (thus) settle the peculiar law of each.
>
> —*Ibid.*, VIII.41
>
> What may have been practised by the virtuous, by such twice born men as are devoted to the law, that he shall establish as law, if it be not opposed to the (customs of) countries, families and castes (*gati*).[63] —*Manu*, VIII.46

Other authorities of General Hindu Law, have also spoken about custom. Gautama, the most ancient of the *sūtrakāra*s whose aphorisms on law are extant, states at the very outset of his work:

> The Veda is the source of the sacred law, and the tradition and practice of those who know the Veda.
>
> — *GauDS*, I.1,2
>
> The custom of countries, castes and families, which are not opposed to the sacred records have also authority.[64]
>
> — *Ibid.*, XI.20

Bṛhaspati has spoken:[65]

> *deśa jāti kulanām ca ye dharma prāk pravartitaḥ* ।
> *tathaiva te plalanīyaḥ prajā prakṣubhyatenyathā* ॥
>
> — *SBE*, XXIII, II.28

Āpastamba has also spoken:[66]

> *athataḥ sayamacarikan dharman vyakhyāsyamaḥ*
> *dharmana samayaḥ pramāṇam vedaśca* ॥
>
> — *ĀpaDS*, I.1-2

---

63. All the verses taken from the *Laws of Manu* tr. by G. Bühler.
64. Taken from *Sacred Books of the East* (Vol. II).
65. *SBE*, Vol. XXIII.
66. Cited in *Mīmāṁsā*.

All these above verses speak about the legal significance of custom but the question still remains that if there is specific prohibition in the sacred laws about a particular aspect of a usage or custom, then how far its legality will be acceptable judicially or otherwise. K.L. Sarkar is of the opinion that it is enough if it is not positively condemned by the Smṛtis[67] and he further refers to Colebrooke's *Misc. Essays* and Jaimini's rule 'without reference to causes, usages prevail'.[68] It is said that the exact legal status of custom as itself a rule of Smṛti which has been emphatically laid down by Medhātithi the commentator of Manu, is almost conclusive on this question. And the *Mitākṣarā* quotes texts to the effect that even practices expressly inculcated by the sacred ordinances may become obsolete and should be abandoned if opposed to Public Opinion.[69]

That being the position a look at the judicial pronouncements, will add more clarity to it.

1. *Collector of Madura* v. *Moottoo Ramalinga*:[70] The judicial committee of the Privy Council said, under the Hindu system of Law, clear proof of usage will outweigh the written text of law.

2. *Neelkisto Deb* v. *Beerchunder*:[71] That a custom may be in derogation of Smṛti law and where proved to exist may supersede that law.

3. *Hurpurshad* v. *Sheo Dyal*:[72] A custom is a rule which, in a particular family or in a particular district, has from long usage obtained the force of law. It must be ancient, certain and reasonable and being in derogation of the general rules of law must be construed strictly.

4. *Parbati* v. *Jagdish*:[73] The tenacity of family custom even under the strain of migration has been repeatedly recognised in the

67. K.L. Sarkar, *Mīmāṁsā*, 247-8.

68. *Ibid.*, p. 444.

69. Mayne's, *Hindu Law and Usage*, pp. 45-6.

70. [1868] 12 MIA 397, 436.

71. [1868] 12 MIA 523, 542.

72. [1875] 3 IA 259, 285.

73. [1902] 29 IA 82.

decisions of the Courts.

5. *Kali Prashad* v. *Amund Roy*:[74] That though local and family custom, if proved to exist, will supersede the general law, the general law will in other respects govern the relation of the parties outside that custom.

6. *Mookka Kone* v. *Ammakutti Ammal*:[75] In this case their Lordships discussed threadbare every aspect of custom and said that in order to give effect to a custom which is set-up and which is at variance with the ordinary Hindu Law, it should be ancient, invariable, continuous, notorious, not expressly forbidden by the legislature and not opposed to morality or public policy and as regards instances in support of the custom they should be established by clear and unambiguous evidence and must be conclusive what is ordinary understood as Hindu Law is not the Customary Law of the country like the common Law of England. Neither it is a Statute Law in the sense that some king or legislature framed the law and enforced its acceptance by the people. The Hindu Law as is commonly understood is a set of rules contained in several Sanskrit books of authority on the law governing Hindus. There are several treatises on law and they are not of equal authority in all the provinces. So Hindu Law as understood by the Judges and the legal profession is applicable to all Hindus and a custom not in accordance with the general Hindu Law has to be proved by the party setting it up. The custom is not an exception to the general Hindu Law but a course of conduct adopted in variance with the law which governs them.

7. The Supreme Court in *Gokalchand* v. *Parvin Kumar*,[76] while dealing with section 5 of the Punjab Laws Act, 1872 on the question of Customary Law of Punjab and how to be dealt with, laid down seven general principles in particular reference to *riwāj-i-ām*, and one of them is:

A custom in order to be binding, must derive its force from the fact that by long usage it has obtained the force of law, but the

74. [1887] 15 IA 18.

75. AIR 1928 Mad 299 (FB); AIR 1915 PC 30.

76. AIR 1952 SC 231.

English Rule that "a custom in order that it may be legal and binding, must have been used so long that the memory of man runneth not to the contrary", should not be strictly applied to Indian conditions. All that is necessary to prove is that the usage has been acted upon in practice for such a long period and with such invariability as to show that it has, by common consent, been submitted to as the established rule of a particular locality.

The Supreme Court in a catena of decisions stressed on the concept of custom with reference to its continuity, consistency, invariability, reasonableness and its antiquity.[77]

The judicial organ of this country looked to every aspect of custom with regard to every aspect of general Hindu Law, may it be inheritance, adoption, marriage, maintenance, impartible estate or divorce or any other aspect of Hindu Law and recognised the custom where it was pleaded and strictly proved on the touchstone of principles laid down in this regard. A variety of decisions of the Privy Council, High Courts and the Supreme Court recognised the legal supremacy of custom when it had attained the force of law as revealed in the Śāstric Law and as per modern Hindu Law as amended and codified. The sacred books on Hindu Law spoke about custom and insist repeatedly that custom must be enforced and that either it may override or supplement the Smṛti rules and modern law did not lag behind in this regard.

Section 29(2) of Hindu Marriage Act, 1955 postulates:

> Nothing contained in this Act shall be deemed to affect any right recognised by custom or conferred by any special enactment to obtain the dissolution of a Hindu marriage, whether solemnised before or after the commencement of this Act.

This section has to be read with section 3(*a*) of the said Act:

> The expressions 'custom' and 'usage' signify any rule which, having been continuously and uniformly observed for a long

77. *Siromani* v. *Hemkumar* AIR 1968 SC 1299; *Kochan Kani Kunjuraman Kani* v. *Mathevan Kani Sankaran* AIR 1971 SC 1398.

time, has obtained the force of law among Hindu in any local area, tribe, community, group of family:

> *Provided* that the rule is certain and not unreasonable or opposed to public policy:
>
> *Provided further* that in the case of rule applicable only to a family it has not been discontinued by the family.

These stipulations are to be further read with Article 13(3)(*a*) of the Constitution of India:

> 'Law' includes any ordinance, order, bye-law, rule, regulation, notification, custom or usage having in the territory of India the force of law.

These statutory provisions were incorporated with due regard to the Śāstric Law and the various decisions of the higher Courts which laid down rules earlier for recognition of the custom pleaded and proved.

This takes us further to the cases where the parties to the marriage sought customary divorce and when challenged, how they were viewed by the judiciary:

1. *Khemkor* v. *Umiashankar*:[78] In this case the question was whether a Sompura brāhmaṇa woman who has contracted a marriage with a man of that caste, during the lifetime of her husband and without his consent, is entitled to maintenance.

Held that among Sompura brāhmaṇa *natras* or remarriages are allowed among them but with the consent of the first husband but since consent was lacking, it was held that the second marriage in not valid as per custom of her caste, relying upon 2 BHCR 124.

2. *Sundor* v. *nihala*:[79] Held that it was found that by the custom of jāṭs of the district of Siālkoṭ a woman who has received a written divorce from her husband was free to contract a second marriage.

3. *Kudomee Dossee* v. *Joteeram Kolita*:[80] It is a case where a

78. [1873] BHCR 381.

79. [1889] 84 PR 1889. See also *Jasan* v. *Nihala* [1884] 78 PR 1884.

80. [1877] ILR 3 Cal. 305.

Hindu husband sued his wife for restitution of conjugal rights and the defendant pleaded divorce. It was held that though the Hindu Law does not contemplate divorce, still in those districts where it is recognised as an established custom, it would have the force of law. There can be no doubt that the Hindu Law has been affected in particular districts by particular usages and these usages have hitherto been respected unless clearly repugnant to the Principles of Hindu Law. Referring to Sham Churu's *Vayvasthā Darpaṇa*, p. 387, where it is said that reason and justice are more to be regarded than mere texts and that wherever a good custom exists, it has the force of law.

4. In [1870] 7 BHCR 133 also the question arose about *natra* marriage and it was held that a custom which authorises a woman to contract a *natra* marriage without a divorce, on payment of a certain sum to the caste to which she belongs is an immoral custom and one which shall not be judicially recognised.

5. *Sankaralingam Chetti* v. *Subban Chetti and Another*:[81] The question in issue is whether there has been a valid and legal divorce between plaintiff and second defendant and the only point argued is that whether the caste custom is valid as it was contended that it is immoral and that the courts will not recognise it. It was held that divorce in this form is consistent with the 'original' custom of the potters and if this be so, the custom is sufficiently ancient and it is not immoral since it does not ignore marriage as a legal institution but provides a special mode by which it may be dissolved.

6. *Keshav Hargovan* v. *Bai Gandi*:[82] In this case the Court held that a custom by which the marriage tie can be dissolved by either husband or wife, against the wish of the divorced party and for no reason but out of mere caprice, the sole condition being the payment of a sum of money fixed by the caste, is opposed to public policy and is also repugnant to Hindu Law and, therefore, cannot be judicially recognised. In this case the custom pleaded was not recognised by the Court.

81. [1894] 17 ILR Mad. 479.

82. AIR 1915 Bom 197. See also (1875-7) 1 Bom. 347 *Reg* v. *Shambhu Raghu*, *Jukni* v. *Queen Empress* [1892] 19 Cal 627, *Reg* v. *Karsan Goja* [1864-66] 2 BHCR, *Narayanan Bharti* v. *Laving Bharti* [1877-78] 2 Bom 140, *Uji* v. *Hathi Lalu* [1870] 7 BHCR 133.

7. *Bai Ganga* v. *Emperor*:[83] It was a case under section 494 of IPC. The Court held that Courts do not recognise the authority of a caste to dissolve a marriage or to declare it void or give permission to a married woman to remarry.

8. *Basant Singh and Another* v. *Bhagwan Singh and Another*:[84] Held that according to the customary law of the Siālkoṭ district among Hindus, divorces must be in writing and in the absence of such writing the oral relinquishment by a jāṭ of his wife would not be sufficient under the custom binding on his tribe.

9. *Jina Magan Pakhali* v. *Bai Jethi*:[85] In this case the custom was pleaded. It was a case for restitution of conjugal rights wherein the plea of customary divorce was taken to resist the case. It was held that custom of divorce in Pakhali community does exist and if the consent of the husband has been given it would not be against the spirit of Hindu Law.

In this case reliance was also placed, besides the judicial precedents, on treatises that divorce is not contemplated by the Hindu Law but it is not repugnant to its principles, and if there be a well established custom in its support, it may override the general provisions of that law.[86] Also that in the lowest classes divorce is attainable between a husband and wife provided it is allowed by the custom of the caste.[87]

10. *Thangammal* v. *Gengayammal and others*:[88] In this case the validity of custom was challenged. It was held that there is no invalidity in a custom by which married couple being unable to live together, by consent seek divorce and are divorced by the parties, approaching the headman and other relations, paying certain amount and taking away the *tāli* from round the neck of the wife and giving it back to the husband. It is only where the divorce is

83. AIR 1916 Bom 97.

84. AIR 1933 Lah 755.

85. AIR 1941 Bom 298.

86. Tagore Law Lectures 1908, *Customs and Customary Laws in British India*.

87. Sir William Strange, *Treatise on Hindu Law*.

88. AIR 1945 Mad 308.

enforced against the wish of the wife that the custom permitting the divorce may be illegal.

In Mayne's *Hindu Law*, para 37, p. 50, 13th edn., November 1991, it is said that it was doubted whether a custom authorising her to marry again during the lifetime of her husband and with her consent, would have been valid.[89]

11. *Kodu and another* v. *Lola and another*:[90] It was a case of dispute about property wherein the custom of marriage and divorce was pleaded. Held that the presumption under Hindu Law is that marriage should be deemed to be in an approved form and that a *pat* marriage in *curi* form is no exception but herein it does not and cannot by any stretch of reasoning support the contention that Mt. Sita's *curi* marriage with Lola was in an unapproved form. Evidence clearly shows that the remarriage and earlier divorce were as per approved custom and valid.

12. *Pujam Liklai Singh Bhabando Singh* v. *Moiranthem Maipak Singh and another*:[92] It was a case for declaration for entitlement to the properties specified in the plaint wherein the question of divorce by custom was raised. It was held that according to the report of the customs prevailing in Manipur, divorce or *khainaba* is permissible amongst the Hindus of Manipur and it can be from husband's side or from the wife's side. There is no condition attached and it can be done at pleasure. It is done even at a slight pretex. *Gāndharva* form of marriage is also recognised in Manipur. The union of a man with a divorced woman is also recognised as a local valid marriage. It is also held that the performance of ceremony of *loukatpa* is not a condition for a marriage to be legal and valid.

13. *Shivalingiah* v. *Chowdamma*:[92] The case was regarding legitimacy of the appellant where marriage as per custom was pleaded. The Court held that separation by mutual consent and dissolution of the marital tie so as to enable the woman to marry

---

89. *Khemkar* v. *Umiashankar* [1873] 10 BHC 381; *In re. Gedula Narayana* AIR 1932 Mad 561.
90. AIR 1948 Nagpur 141.
91. AIR 1956 Manipur 18.
92. AIR 1956 Mysore 17.

another man in what is called *kudike* form and have the full status of a wife, are proved to be possible in the community to which the parties belong and the Court also relied upon the evidence adduced regarding the doctrine of *factum valet*.

14. *Mt. Savitri Devi* v. *Naukhi ram*:[93] In this case the lower Court granted divorce on the basis of custom wherein no custom was pleaded. The Court held that it is nobody's case that the marriage had been or was to be dissolved in accordance with custom and in the second place it is not the function of the Court constituted under the Hindu Marriage Act, 1955 to grant a decree of divorce or a declaration of divorce on the basis of custom.

15. *Rapeti Bulli Tatayya* v. *Rapeti Nookaraju*:[94] In this case the Court held that Hindu Law does not permit divorce. If a plaintiff relies upon customary divorce, he must allege and prove incidents of that custom. The mere writing of a letter cannot dissolve a legal marriage unless it is established that the customary method of divorce of that particular community could be achieved by the mere writing of a letter.

16. *Nallathangal* v. *Nainan Ambalam*:[95] The case was under section 488 of CrPC, 1898 wherein the point of divorce by custom was agitated. The Court held that though Hindu Law does not recognise divorce between husband and wife, nevertheless the custom in certain communities may permit a valid divorce by means of a caste, *pañcāyat* or similar tribunal. Even after passing of the Hindu Marriage Act, 1955, customary rights of divorce were saved and such divorces continue to have the force of law among the communities where the custom prevailed.

17. *Kishenlal* v. *Mst. Prabhu*:[96] It was a case of customary divorce and the Court held that Courts do not recognise the authority of the caste to dissolve a marriage or to give permission to a married woman to remarry. Therefore, a custom by which a caste *pañcāyat* can grant a divorce whenever it thinks fit irrespective

93. AIR 1958 HP 15.

94. AIR 1958 AP 611.

95. AIR 1960 Mad 179.

96. AIR 1963 Raj 95.

of the mutual consent of the parties cannot be countenanced by Court of law as valid custom. It is incumbent on the plaintiff to state with precision and clarity what the custom is.

18. *Sudhia Alial Gulabi* v. *Sankappa Raj*:[97] In this case section 10 of the Madras Aliya Santhana Act was challenged as *ultra vires* of Art. 14 of the Constitution wherein the point of customary divorce was agitated. The Court held that a marriage which is purely contractual in character cannot be said to be against public policy. Though it is not desirable that matrimonial ties should be broken at the caprice of one of the parties to the marriage and that neither the society nor the parties to the marriage will be benefited by yoking together two persons who pull in opposite directions there is no virtue in making a mockery of married life. Views on this question, as in most other questions differ. Oftentimes those views are the product of customs, habits and environments. It is not proper to elevate those views to the position of absolute truth.

19. *Premanbai* v. *Channoolal Punao*:[98] It is a case wherein the validity of customary divorce was challenged. The Court held that divorce is unknown to Hindu Law and is a creature of custom amongst the communities in which it obtains. Where a custom permits a divorce between *paṭva*s with the mutual consent of the spouses, the age of discretion under the Mitākṣarā School of Hindu Law does not govern the case and a wife in a *paṭvā* community can, at the age between 14 and 15 years, when she has attained sufficient maturity of understanding to comprehend the nature of the act she is doing, validly consents to her divorce from her husband in a caste *pañcāyat* held for the purpose and a consent so given is binding on her according to the caste custom.

20. *Gurdit Singh* v. *Mst. Angrej Kaur and others*:[99] In this case the point regarding customary divorce and the remarriage of the wife during the lifetime of the first husband was in issue. The Court held that a custom exists among the Hindu jāṭs of the Jalandhar distirict which permits a valid divorce by a husband of his wife which dissolves the marriage. On the dissolution of such marriage

---

97. AIR 1963 Mys 245.

98. AIR 1963 MP 57.

99. AIR 1968 SC 142.

the divorced wife can enter into a valid marriage with a second husband in the lifetime of the first husband. In this case the Supreme Court affirmed [1962] 64 Punjab LR 1179.

21. *Mal Singh* v. *Ram Kaur*:[100] Another case of the same nature came before the Punjab and Haryana High Court where it was held that there is a custom in *tarkhan* community of divorcing a woman by repudiation and the repudiated woman is free to remarry in the lifetime of her first husband.

A catena of cases have been cited above to show that custom is not cabined or confined within a particular locality but is prevalent throughout the country having force of law.

Bṛhaspati thus speaks in two of his verses:

> When a decision is passed in accordance with local custom, logic or the opinion of the traders (living in that town), the issue of the case is overruled by it. — *Bṛhaspati*, II.26

> The time honoured institutions of each country, caste and family should be preserved intact otherwise the people would rise in rebellion, the subject would become disaffected towards their ruler and the army and treasure would be destroyed.[101] — *Ibid.*, II.28

It is well settled that legal importance of custom is supreme as the whole legal concept flows from *dharma*. In the *Mahābhārata* it is explained why *dharma* is so-called:

> They call it *dharma* because it is a force which supports or holds together — because it holds the people or society together.[102]

Manu says:

> That is (1) the Veda, (2) the Smṛtis, (3) *sadācāra* that is, the righteous conduct established by custom and public opinion and (if these three provide no guidance), (4) conduct

---

100. AIR 1973 P & H 124.

101. These verses (tr. by Julius Jolly) have been taken from *SBE*, Vol. XXXIII.

102. *Mahābhārata*, Karna Parva.

> according to one's own conscience; these are the four attributes of *dharma*. — *Manu*, II.12

In Indian Jurisprudence the concept of *dharma* is not static. It regards all laws, including even the fundamental law, as subject to the law of change — that is, a concept which evolves with the evolution of society.[103] In Indian Jurisprudence law derives its sanction and its sanctity from the needs of social life. Then what will happen if social conditions which gave validity to law, change? The answer is that if social conditions change, our laws must change. Both Parāśara and Manu say,

> The laws of men in the *kṛta-yuga* are other than those in the *tretā* and *dvāpara* and in the *kali-yuga* different from all other ages — the laws of each age being in keeping with the distinctive character of that age.[104]

However, the concept under Manu changed and by the time of *Mahābhārata* the content of *dharma* was enlarged to include the pursuit of material welfare in worldly life. Thus, the concept of *dharma* became (1) *sadācāra*, (2) the injunction of the Veda, (3) the Smṛti, and (4) the *artha* (the pursuit of material welfare). It is different from the order, Veda, Smṛti, *sadācāra* in Manu. The emphasis had shifted to custom.

Later on Dr. Ganganath Jha said that the principle was canvassed that custom should be regarded as of equal authority to the Śruti itself, and still later on custom came to be regarded as more authoritative than anything else and it was declared that the custom of a region (*deśācāra*) should be given the first consideration and in every region custom alone should be observed.

But in spite of the supremacy of a custom, it clearly appears that law was based on two-tier system, one for the intellectuals or cultural elite and the other for the less sensitive or ill-informed. Accordingly, Hindu Law approved the divorce which was applicable to non-caste Hindus, i.e., the lowest rung of the ladder in the socio-

103. S.S. Dhavan, Secularism in Indian Jurisprudence — An Article in, *Secularism, its Implications for Law and Life in India.*

104. *Parāśara-smṛti*, I.22; *Manu*, I.85.

cultural hierarchy[105] and perhaps this lowest rung of the ladder was in vast majority. Derrett while talking to Late Pt. Jawaharlal Nehru regarding divorce as antithesis to marriage got an answer that 80 per cent of the Hindus are already covered by the customary divorce.[106] But now the present trend is quite different. Custom has almost started giving way to statutory provisions. There are two reasons for that:

Firstly, Bṛhaspati's edict is:

> Where the king disregarding established usage, passes a sentence (according to his own inclination), it is (called) an edict from the king and local custom is overruled by it.[107]

Kauṭilya has also spoken to the same effect, that is —

> The four pillars of the legal system are the *dharamaśāstra*, *caritra*, *vyavahāra* and *rājaśāsanam*. The supremacy of each being in the reverse order.

Thus, according to Kauṭilya, the decrees of the secular authority were to prevail over the injunctions of the sacred texts. Thus, now the custom is at the mercy of the edicts of the king, which in turn means, in modern parlance the statutory provisions, i.e., legislation. Wherever the legislation provides, the custom shall prevail. Section 4 of the Hindu Marriage Act has an overriding effect which is as follows:

> Any text, rule or interpretation of Hindu Law or any custom or usage as part of that law in force immediately before the commencement of this Act shall cease to have effect with respect to any matter for which provision is made in this Act.

And such custom must be in consonance with section 3 of Hindu Marriage Act, 1955. So we have to now peep into the statutory provisions governing divorce.

---

105. P.V. Kane's *History of Dharmasūtra*, chapters III and IV.
106. Derrett, *The Death of a Marriage Law*.
107. *Bṛhaspati*, II-27; *SBE*, Vol. XXXIII, tr. by Julius Jolly.

## Divorce under Statutory Law

Before we take up divorce under Statutory Law as covered by Hindu Marriage Act, 1955, it is but incumbent to deal with the historical perspective of matrimonial law and its evolution leading to the enactment of Hindu Marriage Act, 1955 and subsequent amendments thereto.

The Britishers came to India as traders. By employing all types of means both fair and file, they went on acquiring trading rights. Then by taking advantage of the rivalry between the States, they started siding one State against the other and extracting the self-suited mileage which culminated in the Battle of Plassey (1757). In 1765 East India Company got the Dīwānī of Bengal and Orissa from Shāh Ālam, the Moghul Emperor. The year 1765 is the founding year of the territorial domination and sovereignty of the Company and the beginning of real territorial expansion and annexation and also the administration of Civil and Revenue cases. Various regulations were promulgated, particularly in the matter of personal laws which speak of exclusiveness.

Mr. Justice Field[108] said that the British Rule at the outset of its authority in this country recognised the rule as applicable to Hindus and Mohammedans.

(i) Regulation of 21st August, 1772 which laid down the exact scope of the application of the Hindu and Mohammedan Laws and the omission to provide for the cases which do not fall within the rule was supplied by the;

(ii) Regulation of the 5th July, 1781 which directed that 'in all cases for which no specific directions are hereby given, the judges do act according to justice, equity and good conscience'.

(iii) The latter part of the rule was reproduced in section 21 of the Reguloation III of 1793 and re-enacted in section 15 of Regulation IV of 1793 which laid down:

that in suits regarding succession, inheritance,

108. *Regulations of Bengal Code*, pp. 169-71. Also see *A code of Gentoo Laws* by N.B. Halhed.

marriage and caste and all religious usages and institutions, the Mohammedan Laws with respect to Mohammedans and the Hindu Law with regard to Hindus, are to be considered as the general rules by which the judges are to form their decisions.

(iv) To the two-fold rule so laid down, addition was soon after, made by RegulationVIII of 1795 which enacted that in cases in which the plaintiff shall be of a different religious persuasion from the defendant, the decision to be regulated by the law of the religion of the latter excepting where Europeans or other persons, not being either Mohammedans or Hindus, shall be defendants, in which cases the law of the plaintiff is to be made the rule of the decision in all plaints and actions of a civil nature.

(v) The next important piece of legislation on the subject was Regulation VII of 1832, section 9 of which, while affirming the rules to which reference has already been made, added a new preposition as an injunction to the Courts administering justice under the East India Company. The section ran thus —

> It is hereby declared, however, that the above rules are intented and shall be *bona fide* professors of those religions at the time of application of the law of the case and were designed for the protection of the rights of such persons — not for the deprivation of the rights of the others.

This being the case of earlier period personal law of the Hindus and Muslims was not interfered with, perhaps at that time, the Britishers were more concerned to consolidate their political gains. But the British Jurists of the Macaulay-Maine type, due to sheer ignorance, imperialist self-interest and contempt for Indian thought, which was a part of the Imperialist outlook dominated. British Jurist, historians and thinkers in the heyday of Imperialism started penetrating in the exclusive domain of personal laws both legislatively and judicially.

In *Moonshee Buzloor* v. *Shumsoonissa*,[109] the Privy Council held

109. [1867] MIA 551.

that restitution of conjugal rights is a species of suit for specific performance. Thus, the procedure of restitution of conjugal rights recognised in England by the Ecclesiastical Courts, was introduced in India at least from the time of the decision in the above-cited case.

Even in *Tekait Manmohini* v. *Basanta Kumar*,[110] it is said that where the marriage is once completed, if either party refuses to live with the other, the remedy is by a suit for restitution of conjugal right. Thus, judicial intervention in personal law made a beginning countrary to Bengal Regulations.

Even statutorily, though sparingly legislative intervention also started showing its supremacy in the personal matters after 1857 when the Matrimonial Causes Act, 1857 was passed in England and this Act perpetuated the old ecclesiastical practice with regard to nullity and judicial separation (divorce *a mensa et toro*), thereby the jurisdiction of the Ecclesiastical Courts dealing with matrimonial matters got transferred to Civil Courts.

So the history of Statutory Law in India, particularly in matter of marriage, divorce, and inheritance, etc., took birth and then almost it became a movement perhaps to deform the Hindu Law. The important statutes are as under:

1. Caste Disabilities Removal Act, 1850.
2. Hindu Widows Remarriage Act, 1856.
3. Convert's Marriage Dissolution Act, 1866.
4. Hindu Disposition of Property Act, 1916.
5. Hindu Inheritance (Removal of Disabilities) Act, 1928.
6. Hindu Law of Inheritance (Amendment) Act, 1929.
7. Hindu Gains of Learning Act, 1930.
8. Hindu Women's Right to Property Act, 1937.
9. Arya Marriage Validation Act, 1937.

110. [1901] 28 Cal 751.

10. Hindu Married Women's Right to Separate Residence and Maintenance Act, 1946.
11. Hindu Marriage Disabilities Removal Act, 1946.
12. Hindu Marriage Validity Act, 1949.

Coming events cast their shadow before. Another three Acts, i.e., Indian Divorce Act, 1869, Dissolution of Muslim Marriage Act, 1939 and Parsi Marriage and Divorce Act, 1936, do point out what is in store for Hindus. It is only a matter of time. So the Britishers along with their consolidated political supremacy started deforming the divine personal laws when it is said that between man and god, state has no business to be there.

However, taking cue from these statutes, Indian States at their own level showed initiative either at the instance of so-called liberals or due to extraordinary overzealousness of men in power and brought out legislations bringing in statutory divorce. In the Legislative Assembly of British India H.S. Gaur's Bill to introduce Divorce was rejected several times between 1928 and 1933.

However, Baroda, small State having a small brāhamaṇa population in proportion to its numbers of 'lower' castes governed by much less strict customs, the humane idea of allowing judicial divorce first came to fruition in the "Hindu Lagna Viccheda Nibandha" of 1931, repealed and replaced by sections 147-54 of the (Baroda) Hindu Nibandha (Hindu Act) 37 of 1937.[111]

Section 148 of the said Act made judicial dissolution of marriage available to those who were not covered by the customary divorce. Judicially divorce was on the following grounds of the respondent:

1. disappearance for seven years or more;
2. becoming a recluse;
3. changing his/her religion by conversion;
4. being guilty of cruelty so as to cause danger to (*a*) life, (*b*) limb, or (*c*) bodily or mental health so as to give rise to a reasonable apprehension of such danger;

---

111. J.D.M. Derrett, *The Death of a Marriage Law*.

5. being guilty of desertion without reasonable cause for more than three years after cohabitation commenced;
6. being addicted to intoxicants for more than three years and thus unable to fulfil marital obligations;
7. committing adultery; or
8. marrying a second time during the lifetime of the petitioner.

Moreover, the wife had additional grounds if her husband:

1. was impotent;
2. habitually committed an unnatural offence, or
3. refused to allow the wife to stay with him for more than three years without reasonable cause.

The husband on his part had additional grounds:

1. If the wife was pregnant at the time of the marriage by a person other than himself, and the fact was unknown to him or, if he was a minor, to the guardian in marriage, or
2. failed to stay with him for more than three years without reasonable cause.

Derrett observed that under the social conditions, all or most of these grounds amounted to a statutory relief for the wife against aberrations on the part of her husband.

Though this enactment, being a pioneer work attracted the attention of many and in particular allured Mysore and being allured Mysore Act 10 of 1933 was legislated and many other States followed suit:

1. Bombay Hindu Divorce Act, 1947.
2. Madras Hindu (Bigamy & Divorce) Act, 1949.
3. Saurashtra Hindu Divorce Act, 1952.
4. Madhya Pradesh Divorce Act, 1955.

But this historical perspective shall remain incomplete without the Hindu Code Bill which was passed by the Parliament, but could not get the assent of the President and lapsed.

In 1937, the Hindu Women's Rights to Property Act was passed. This affected the views of Mitākṣarā relating to woman's right of inheritance. Thereafter, a committee was appointed by the Government of India to examine the said Act and to amend the Act so as to —

1. resolve the doubts felt as to the construction of the Act.
2. also to clarify the nature of the right conferred upon the widow.
3. to remove any injustice that may have been done by the Act to the daughter.

On June, 19, 1941 the committee submitted their report and contended that piecemeal legislation will not be beneficial to society. The time had now come to attempt a codification of Hindu Law but that it should be taken up one by one, first the law of succession, then the law of marriage and so on. On this, the Government of India appointed a committee for drafting the Hindu Code and the report was finalised on February, 21, 1947. After giving final touches to the draft Bill. It was placed before the Parliament for its approval.

Broadly speaking the Code[112] consists of nine parts with seven Schedules. The provisions contained in the Code are distributed into 139 sections. Part II is relevant for our present study.

Part II, chapter I, deals with marriage — here two kinds of marriages are mentioned — the sacramental and the civil. The civil marriages is in the form of a contract; a certificate of marriage is an essential feature of a civil marriage. Sacramental marriages can be registered if the parties so desire.

Part II, chapter II deals with void and voidable marriage and section 30 of the same deals with dissolution of marriage on special grounds, whether it is solemnised before or after the commencement of the Code.

---

112. *The Bombay Law Reporter*, vol. 53, p. 94.

The grounds on which marriage can be dissolved:

1. Impotency of either party at the time of marriage and if it continues.
2. The husband keeping a concubine or the wife becoming a concubine of any other man.
3. If one of the parties changes his or her religion.
4. If either paty is of unsound mind and continuously under treatment for a period of five years.
5. If either party is suffering from a virulent form of leprosy.

Part II, chapter III deals with the restitution of conjugal rights and avoidance of marriage. Section 33 mentions the grounds for judicial separation and they are:

1. Desertion for at least two years.
2. If one party is so cruel that it is not safe for the other to live with him or her.
3. If the other party suffers from an incurable venereal disease and in a communicable form not contracted from the petitioner for a period not less than one year immediately before the presentation of the petition.
4. If the other party is suffering from a virulent form of leprosy.
5. Has been habitually of unsound mind since the date of marriage.
6. Has committed adultery during the marriage.

Section 36 deals with dissolution of marriage and section 38 gives additional specific grounds for such dissolution. These provisons are somewhat similar to the provisions of the Corresponding Bomaby Act XXIII of 1947. Sections 39 to 44 deal with the questions of procedure and jurisdiction in regard to the applications for judicial separation or dissolution.

This Code, though could not become an Act, but still it was hailed by many celebrated authorities on Hindu Law like B.P.

Gajendrabadkar.[113] He, while supporting it has said that

> I do not for a moment suggest that the provisions for the divorce of a Hindu marriage which are included in the Hindu Code can claim to receive consistent and uniform support from the Hindu texts. I am only concerned to show that similar provisions are found in some texts.

Then he refers to Parāśara, Devala and Nārada and says that:

> The point which I wish to make is that it is not correct to say that in permitting divorce the Hindu Code makes an encroachment upon Hindu religion.

Shakuntala Rao Shashtri said:[114]

> It is heartening to see modern India attempting to re-establish the time honoured laws of this ancient country, which were, however, forgotten during these changing centuries.

Whatever the reaction may be, favourable or otherwise, the orthodox element in Hinduism became triumphant but the rebellious element in liberalism did not sleep over the matter. Realising the irritated thinking of highly religious Hindus and even deep thinking patriots, towards the marriage part of the code, it was better thought to split the Hindu Code into four parts and bring them one by one. Not only that, real political manipulative game was played to test the patience of orthodoxism and thought it practicable to reform the Special Marriage Act and then using that as the thin end of the wedge, to proceed to amend the Hindu Law of marriage.[115]

So the Special Marriage Act, 43 of 1954 came into the statute book. In this garb, repealing and replacing the Act of the same name of 1872, the whole range of matrimonial remedies was introduced. So an advantage was taken of the fact that respectable Hindus may be few to get involved in it, while fashionable folk

---

113. B.P. Gajenderagadkar, two lectures delivered by him before the Karnataka University, December 15, 1951.

114. Shakuntla Rao Shastri, *Women in the Sacred Laws*.

115. Derrett, *The Death of Marriage Law*, p. 22.

would find no difficulty in cross-communal marriages. So it encouraged the propounders of the reforms in Hinduism or to deform Hinudism and paved the way for introducing the Hindu Marriage Bill in the Parliament next year and it became Hindu Marriage Act, 1955.

**Hindu Marriage Act, 1955**

The object of the Act is to amend and codify the law relating to marriage among Hindus. Herein we are concerned with the provisions governing divorce for the purpose of this thesis. Section 13 deals with divorce.

> 1. Any marriage solemnised, whether before or after the commencement of this Act, may, on a petition presented by either the husband or the wife, be dissolved by a decree of divorce on the ground that the other party —
>
> (*i*) is living in adultery; or
>
> (*ii*) has ceased to be a Hindu by conversion to another religion; or
>
> (*iii*) has been incurably of unsound mind for a continuous period of not less than three years immediately preceding the presentation of the petition; or
>
> (*iv*) has, for a period of not less than three years preceding the presentation, been suffering from a virulent and incurable form of leprosy; or
>
> (*v*) has, for a period of not less than three years immediately preceding the presentation of the petition, been suffering from venereable disease in a communicable form; or
>
> (*vi*) has renounced the world by entering any religious order; or
>
> (*vii*) has not been heard of as being alive for a period of seven years or more by those persons who would naturally have heard of it, had that party been alive; or

(*viii*) has not resumed co-habitation for a space of two years or upwards after the passing of a decree for judicial separation against the party; or

(*ix*) has failed to comply with a decree for restitution of conjugal rights for a period of two years or upwards after the passing of the decree.

2. A wife may also present a petition for the dissolution of her marriage by decree of divorce on the ground :

(*i*) in the case of any marriage solemnised before the commencement of this Act, the husband had married again before such commencement or that any other wife of the husband married before such commencement was alive at the time of the solemnisation of the marriage of the petitioner:

*Provided* that in either case the other wife is alive at the time of the presentation of the petition; or

(*ii*) that the husband has, since the solemnisation of the marriage, been guilty of rape, sodomy or bestiality.

## Amendments in 1964

In 1964, section 13(1) was modified by omitting the last two clauses, i.e., clause (*viii*) and (*ix*) and the said two omitted clauses were brought in section 13(1A). Transfer of these clauses from section 13(1) to a newly created section 13(1A) is significant as it indirectly brings in the theory of irretrievable breakdown of marriage, because two years period was in reality a period for change of mind to save the marriage.

Section 13(1A) stipulates:

Either party to a marriage, whether solemnised before or after the commencement of this Act, may also present a petition for the dissolution of marriage by a decree of divorce on the ground —

(*i*) has not resumed cohabitation for a space of two years or upwards after the passing of a decree for judicial separation against the party, or

(*ii*) has failed to comply with a decree for restitution of conjugal rights for a period of two years or upwards after the passing of the decree.

But this amendment did raise a judicial controversy as to mere expiry of the specified period of the decree of judicial separation or restitution of conjugal rights is sufficient to grant divorce or it is only a prerequisite for creation of a ground for applying for divorce and the divorce is to be granted or not depends upon the merits of a case and in such cases section 23(1)(*a*) has been invoked which reads as follows:

> In any proceeding under this Act, whether defended or not, if the court is satisfied that —
>
> (*a*) any of the grounds for granting relief exists and the petitioner [except in cases where the relief is sought by him on the ground specified in sub-clause (*a*), sub-clause (*b*), or sub-clause (*c*) of clause (*ii*) of section 5] is not in any way taking advantage of his or her own wrong or disability for the purpose of such relief, and —

When section 13(1A) was introduced by the Amendment Act of 1964, section 23 was already there. So the question arises as to whether the Legislature was knowing fully well the implications of section 23 in regard to section 13 (1A) and kept section 23 untouched or the Legislature failed to appreciate the implications of section 23 with regard to section 13(1A).

However, this point was repeatedly agitated before the higher Courts and the Apex Court.

In *Laxmibai Laxmi Chand Shah* v. *Laxmichand Ravaji Shah*,[116] the Court held that sectin 13(1A) is subject to section 23(1)(*a*) of the Act. It is said that there is no warrant in the language of sub-section (1A) of section 13 for holding that it confers right on a party to apply for and obtain a decree of divorce. It is open to the Court to

116. AIR 1968 Bom 332.

consider whether provisions mentioned in sub-section (1) of section 23 are satisfied but the Court is under obligation to consider that question. Section 23 is in the nature of an overriding provision.

In *Ram Kali* v. *Gopal* Khanna C.J[117] (as he then was) observed in different way that it would not be practical and realistic, indeed it would be unreasonable and inhuman to compel the parties to keep up the facade of marriage even though the rift between them is complete and there are no prospects of their ever living together as husband and wife. His trend of thinking is towards irretrievable break-down of marriage and two years period (now reduced to one year) is a period of reconciliation that has not fructified.

This point was alos agitated in *Bimla Devi* v. *Singh Raj*[118] and the Court held that the only reasonable way of construing the provision and giving effect to legislative intent is to say that section 23(1)(*a*) applies to cases based on the concept of wrong or disability and not to section 13(1A) which is not based on that concept. At any rate the wrong or disability contemplated in section 23(1)(*a*) is not the non-resumption of co-habitation or the non-restitution of conjugal rights which is the basis of section 13(1A).

The Supreme Court in *Dharmendra* v. *Usha*,[119] adopted a middle course that in order to be a wrong within the meaning of section 23(1)(*a*) the conduct alleged has to be something more than a mere disinclination to agree to an offer of Union, it must be misconduct serious enough to justify denial of relief to which the husband or wife is otherwise entitled. So the Supreme Court kept the question open and made it to depend upon the facts and circumstances of the case.

So in *Anil Jayanti Vyas* v. *Sudhaben*,[120] the Court took the stand that mere non-compliance *per se* would not amount to taking advantage of his own wrong. Husband is not precluded from claiming divorce. The Court held that the marriage has foundered and there was no scope of reconciliation. So the inference is not

117. ILR [1971] 1 Delhi 6 FB.

118. AIR 1977 P & H 167.

119. AIR 1977 SC 2218.

120. AIR 1978 Guj 74.

towards application of section 23(1)(*a*) but it is directed towards irretrievable break-down of marriage.

The same trend of thinking can be seen in *N. Varalaxmi* v. *N.V. Hanumantha Rao*[121] where the Court held that the fact that the wife's attempts at resumption of co-habitation has been thwarted by the husband would be immaterial. Volition of both parties is needed.

In *Soundarammal* v. *Sundara Mahalinga Nadar*,[122] the High Court referring to various rulings observed that in order to be a wrong within the meaning of section 23(1)(*a*), the conduct alleged has to be something more than a mere disinclination to agree to an offer of re-union. However, held that law can never give a helping hand to a wrong-doer. To prevent the wrong-doer from seeking relief under section 13(1A) Parliament had left section 23(1)(*a*) untouched in spite of the amendments effected under the Acts 44 of 1964 and 68 of 1976 and held that section 13 including sub-section (1A), however, continues to be subject to the provisions of section -23.

Andhra Pradesh High Court in *Akkama* v. *Jagannadham*[123] has said that a marriage which has irretrievably broken down should not be allowed to continue and that a marriage buried in fact should also be buried in law.

The Supreme Court in *Saroj Rani* v. *Sudershan*[124] again took a stand that when the marriage has broken down and the parties can no longer live together as husband and wife, if such is the case, it is better to close the chapter.

The above cited cases point out two things:

(i) It is no use of keeping the empty shell of marriage intact which in fact has completely dried up of its juice.

(ii) However, the wrong-doer should not be allowed to take advantage of its wrong doing.

---

121. AIR 1978 AP 6.

122. AIR 1980 Mad 294.

123. AIR 1981 AP 269.

124. AIR 1984 SC 1562.

Thus, these views when read together, tend to create uncertainty.

In *R.* v. *Jackson*[125] it is said that conjugal rights cannot be enforced by the act of either party and a husband cannot seize and detain his wife by force.

But Order 21 Rule 32(1)[126] says:

> where the party against whom a decree for specific performance of a contract, or for restitution of of conjugal rights, or for an injunction, has been passed, has had an opportunity of obeying the decree and has wilfully failed to obey it, the decree may be enforced in the case of a decree for restitution of conjugal rights by the attachment of his propety or . . . by his detention in the civil prison or by the attachment of propety or by both. In this case two 'words' are significant, i.e., 'the party against whom a decree has been passed' and 'by the attachment of his property'. It clearly shows that it is applicable only to the husband and the wife under special protection of Article 15(3) shall be saved.
>
> So it suggested that:
>
> 1. Sub-section (1A) though kept under separate sub-section, it must be statutorily considered as a mandatory period of reconciliation and the party may be free to approach the Court, after the expiry of period without reconciliation, under section 13B.
> 2. If the party is not inclined to avail section 13B, then it can approach the Court by way of petition under section 13 which will be subject to section 23(1)(*a*) and necessary provision be made to section 13(1A).

And the Court should always bear in mind what Viscounts Simon L.C. has said in *Blunt* v. *Blunt*[127] and recommends to the Courts:

125. [1891] IQB 671.
126. *Code of Civil Procedure*, 1908.
127. [1942] 3 AllER 76.

> . . . I would add a fifth, of a more general character which must indeed be regarded as of primary importance, viz., the interest of the community at large, to be judged by maintaining a true balance between respect for the binding sanctity of marriage and the social considerations which make it contrary to Public Policy to insist on the maintenance of a union which has utterly broken down.

**Law Commission (59th Report)**

The Minister of Law, Justice and Company Affairs addressed a communication to the Chairman of the Law Commission suggesting a revision on top priority basis, in Hindu Marriage Act and the Special Marriage Act and also forwarded to the Law Commission a draft Bill prepared by the Ministry, changes to be effected concerning divorce in the draft Bill as follows:

1. In section 10 of the Hindu Marriage Act, 1955, in sub-section (1) for clause (*b*), the following clause shall be substituted, namely:

   "(*b*) has, after the solemnisation of the marriage treated the petitioner with cruelty; or.

2. In section 13 of the Hindu Marriage Act: in sub-section (1),

   (a) in clause (*v*), after the words 'in a communicable form', the words 'the disease not having been contracted from the petitioner' shall he inserted.

   (b) After clause (*vii*), the following clause shall be inserted, namely:

   "(*viii*) has, after the solemnisation of the marriage treated the petitioner with cruelty;"

3. In sub-section (1A), in clauses (*i*) and (*ii*) for the words 'two years', the words 'one year' shall be substituted.

4. In sub-section (2):

   (a) in clause (*ii*), the word 'or' shall be inserted at the end;

(b) after clause (*ii*) the following clause shall be inserted namely:

"(iii) that an order has been passed against the husband by a magistrate awarding separate maintenance to the petitioner, and the parties have not had marital intercourse for three years or more since such orders."

5. In section 14 of the Hindu Marriage Act, —

(a) for the words 'three years have elapsed', in both the places where they occur, the words 'one year has elapsed' shall be substituted;

(b) for the words 'Three years', wherever they occur the words 'One year' shall be substituted.

Law Commission looked to these provisions of the draft Bill (only provisions concerning divorce are taken here) and also looked to the desirability of introducing other changes made the following recommendations in its 59th Report which are as follows:

1. Section 10(1) should be revised so as to refer to section 13(1).

2. Section 13(1)(*i*) of Hindu Marriage Act (living in adultery as a ground of divorce) should be revised so as to read as follows:

   "(*i*) has, after the solemnisation of the marriage, had voluntary sexual intercourse with any person other than his or her spouse."

3. The minimum period of three years, imposed on the right to seek divorce, should be done away with in section 13(1)(*iii*), Hindu Marriage Act.

4. The proposal to add a restriction that a venereal disease was not contracted from the petitioner, is not accepted. In section 10(1)(*d*)—(Judicial Separation) also this restriction should be removed.

5. The fact that the respondent has treated the petitioner with cruelty should be a ground for divorce, in the Hindu Marriage Act.

6. (a) In section 13(1) of Hindu Marriage Act, a new clause should be added as follows:

   "has deserted the petitioner for a period not less than two years immediately preceding the presentation of the petition, or"

   (b) The following *Explanation* should be inserted at the end of section 13(1) of the Hindu Marriage Act:

   "*Explanation*: In this section, the expression 'desertion' means the desertion of the petitioner by the other party to the marriage without reasonable cause and without the consent or against the wish of such party, and includes the wilful neglect of the petitioner by the other party to the marriage, and its grammatical variations and cognate expressions shall be construed accordingly."

7. The suggestion to add, as a ground of divorce under the Hindu Marriage Act, wilful refusal to consummate a marriage, is not accepted.

8. In section 13(1A) of Hindu Marriage Act, the period should be reduced from two years to one year.

9. In section 13(2) of Hindu Marriage Act, provision for divorce at the instance of wife after obtaining a decree or order for maintenance should be inserted on the lines recommended:

   "that in a suit under section 18 of the Hindu Adoption and Maintenance Act, 1956 or in a proceeding under section 125 of the Code of Criminal Procedure, 1974 a decree or order, as the case may be, has been passed against the husband awarding maintenance to the wife notwithstanding that she was living apart and that since the passing of such decree or order, cohabitation between the parties has not been resumed for one year or more."

10. A new section should be inserted in the Hindu Marriage Act to empower the Court in any proceeding on a petition for a decree of divorce, to pass instead a decree for judicial separation, in certain cases:

"13A. In any proceeding on a petition for a decree of divorce, except where the petition is founded on the ground mentioned in clause (*ii*), clause (*vi*) or clause (*vii*) of sub-section (1) of section 13, the Court may, if it considers just to do so having regard to the circumstances of the case, pass instead a decree for judicial separation."

11. Section 14 of Hindu Marriage Act should be deleted.

12. The provision to section 15 of Hindu Marriage Act should be deleted.

On the strength of Draft Bill sent by the Ministry of Law, Justice and Company Affairs and the recommendations thereto by the Law Commission, we had The Marriage Laws (Amendment) Act, 1976, provisions concerning divorce and as a result of which the provisions concerning divorce and other allied matters stand as below:

SECTION 13

(1) Any marriage solemnised, whether before or after the commencement of this Act, may, on a petition presented by either the husband or the wife, be dissolved by a decree of divorce on the ground that the other party . . .[128]

(*i*) has, after the solemnisation of the marriage, had voluntary sexual intercourse with any person other than his or her spouse; or

(*ia*) has, after the solemnisation of marriage treated the petitioner with cruelty; or

(*ib*) has deserted the petitioner for a continuous period of not less than two years immediately preceding the presentation of the petition; or

(*ii*) has ceased to be a Hindu by conversion to another religion; or

(*iii*)[129] has been incurably of unsound mind, or has been

---

128. Substituted by Act 68 of 1976, section 7, for the former clause.

129. Substituted by Act 68 of 1976.

suffering continuously or intermittently from mental disorder of such a kind and to such an extent that the petitioner cannot reasonably be expected to live with the respondent.

*Explanation*: In this clause:

(*a*) the expression 'mental disorder' means mental illness, arrested or incomplete development of mind, psychopathic disorder or any other disorder or disability of mind and includes schizophrenia;

(*b*) the expression 'psychopathic disorder' means a persistent disorder or disability of mind (whether or not including subnormality of intelligence) which results in abnormally aggressive or seriously irresponsible conduct on the part of the other party, and whether or not it requires or is susceptible to medical treatment; or

(*iv*)[130] has been suffering from a virulent and incurable form of leprosy; or

(*v*)[131] has been suffering from venereal disease in a communicable form; or

(*vi*) has renounced the world by entering any religious order; or

(*vii*)[132] has not been heard of as being alive for a period of seven years or more by those persons who would naturally have heard of it, had that party been alive.

[133]*Explanation*: In this sub-section, the expression 'desertion' means the desertion of the petitioner by the other party to the marriage without reasonable cause and without the consent of such party and includes the wilful neglect of

130. Substituted by Act 68 of 1976.

131. *Ibid.*, certain words omitted by section 7.

132. *Ibid.*, word 'or' is omitted.

133. Inserted by section 7 of Act 68 of 1976.

the petitioner by the other party to the marriage and its grammatical variations and cognate expressions shall be construed accordingly.

[134](1A) Either party to a marriage, whether solemnised before or after the commencement of this Act, may also present a petition for the dissolution of the marriage by a decree of divorce on the ground.

(*i*)[135] that there has been no resumption of co-habitation as between the parties to the marriage for a period of one year or upwards after the passing of a decree for judicial separation in a proceeding to which they were parties; or

(*ii*)[136] that there has been no restitution of conjugal rights as between the parties to the marriage for a period of one year or upwards after the passing of a decree for restitution of conjugal rights in a proceeding to which they were parties.

(2) A wife may also present a petition for the dissolution of her marriage by a decree of divorce on the ground —

(*i*) in the case of any marriage solemnised before the commencement of this Act, that the husband had married again before such commencement or that any other wife of the husband married before such commencement was alive at the time of the solemnisation of the marriage of the petitioner:

*Provided* that in either case the other wife is alive at the time of the presentation of the petition; or

(*ii*)[137] that the husband has, since the solemnisation of the marriage, been guilty of rape, sodomy or bestiality; or

---

134. Inserted by Act 44 of 1964, section 2.
135. Substituted by Act 68 of 1976, Section 7 for '2 years'.
136. Substituted by Act 68 of 1976, section 7 for '2 years'.
137. Substituted by Act 68 of 1976, 'or' is added after bestiality.

(*iii*)[138] that in a suit under section 18 of Adoptions and Maintenance Act, 1956 (78 of 1956) or in a proceeding under section 125 of the Code of Criminal Procedure, 1973 (2 of 1974) or under the corresponding section 488 of the Code of Criminal Procedure, 1898 (5 of 1898), a decree or order, as the case may be, has been passed against the husband awarding maintenance to the wife notwithstanding that she was living apart and that since passing of such decree or order, cohabitation between the parties has not been resumed for one year or upwards; or

(*iv*) that her marriage (whether consummated or not) was solemnised before she attained the age of fifteen years and she has repudiated the marriage after attaining that age but before attaining the age of eighteen years.

*Explanation*: This clause applies whether the marriage was solemnised before or after the commencement of the Marriage Laws (Amendment) Act, 1976 (68 of 1976).

[139]13A. *Alternate relief in divorce proceedings*: In any proceeding under this Act, a petition for dissolution of marriage by a decree of divorce, except in so far as the petition is founded on the grounds mentioned in clauses (*ii*), (*vi*) and (*vii*) of sub-section (1) of section 13, the Court may, if it considers it just so to do having regard to the circumstances of the case, pass instead a decree for judicial separation.

13B. *Divorce by mutual consent*: (1) Subject to the provisions of this Act a petition for dissolution of marriage by a decree of divorce may be presented to the district Court by both the parties to a marriage together, whether such marriage was solemnised before or after the commencement of the Marriage Laws (Amendment) Act, 1976, on the ground that they had been living separately for a period of one year or more, that they have not been able to live together and

---

138. Inserted by Act 68 of 1976.

139. Inserted by Act 68 of 1976.

that they have mutually agreed that the marriage should be dissolved.

(2) On the motion of both parties made not earlier than six months after the date of presentation of the petition referred to in sub-section (1) and not later than eighteen months after the said date, if the petition is not withdrawn in the meantime, the Court shall, on being satisfied, after hearing the parties and after making such enquiry as it thinks fit, that a marriage has been solemnised and that the averments in the petition are true, pass a decree of divorce declaring the marriage to be dissolved with effect from the date of the decree.

**Section 14**

By section 9 of Marriage Laws (Amendment) Act, 1976 changes were brought in section 14 of Hindu Marriage Act, 1955 by which the period of three years has been reduced to one year. So wherever in the section 'three years' was mentioned, it was substitued by 'one year', but under the provision, the Court is conferred a discretionary power to entertain the petition before one year if it finds on the allegations in the affidavit in support of the petition that *prima facie* there is exceptional hardship to the petitioner or exceptional depravity on the part of the respondent. This section 14 has a special bearing on the petition for divorce.

We have taken the historical perspective of divorce under Statutory Law. Hindu Marriage Laws (Amendment) Act, 1976 is a step forward to make the divorce easy and quick, though the social awakening has not reached that stage warranting such changes. It is perhaps a wrong notion that Western civilisation is superior to Indian civilisation and that we have to take inspiration from Western ideas where woman is considered a mere playmate. Without making much comment at this stage, it is worthwhile stating that we feel proud in forgetting our own exalted culture and civilisation and to imitate that culture which if takes root in our country, we shall definitely be heading for creation of millions of broken houses, deserted wives and neglected children. Lord Evershed M.R.[140] said,

> If men and women of a hundred years ago had been told that in the enlightened days of their great grandchildren, 30,000 marriages would be dissolved by the civil Courts in each year — in the majority of cases upon the petition of the wife — they would, I do not doubt, have been greatly shocked. And if they have asked the natural question what becomes of the tens of thousands of innocent children of those marriages, they would have raised one of the most important and most perplexing problems that is now presented to us.

Greavson: himself observes as follows:

> For the present we may, perhaps, rejoice in the opportunities for easier divorce as one of the outstanding feature of the past century. But we cannot forget that 'if the divorce as is no longer a disgrace, it remains a tragedy. Ten per cent is a high mortality rate for marriage. The victory of emancipation has its shadow of Greek tragedy. For emancipation, in so far as it connotes easy divorce, carries in its train disintegration of family as a unit of the society and so ultimate of the society itself.[141]

Since the concept of divorce in Hindu Law is a pure act of imitation, so necessarily we have to glance through the global perspective firstly, and then to see as to how we have destroyed our own ethics and ethos of which we were always proud of and how we have defiled our own *dharma* which was the foundation of Hindu society. In support of this Prof. Derrett in his book on *Death of Marriage Law* remarked that the Hindu Marriage Act, and its Amendment Act, 1976 in particular destroyed Hindu Law of Marriage (the Dhārmic Law). See for details Derrett's *Death of Hindu Law of Marriage*.

---

140. In his Foreword to R.R. Greavson and F.R. Grane's *A Century of Family Law*.

141. R.R. Greavson, *A Century of Family Law*, 1957, p. 412. It refers to Matrimonial Causes Act, 1857 (English Law).

*Marriage is not merely a contract between the parties. It is the foundation of the family. It is a social institution of the highest importance. . . . The Commonwealth has a deep interest that its integrity is not jeopartised.*

**— Joseph Cummings**

*If divorce is no longer a disgrace, it remains a tragedy.*

**— Greavson**

# 4

# Emerging Global Perspective

ALL the writers on Hindu Law are of the unanimous opinion that a Hindu marriage, being a sacrament, once performed before the nuptial fire with the sacred texts, becomes irrevocable on the completion of the ceremony of taking seven steps by the couple.[1] There is no evidence as to the practice of divorce as such during the Vedic and post-Vedic periods.[2] It was a holy union of mind, body and soul of the spouses and it was believed that even death did not put an end to it, for the wife remained linked with her husband in soul after death in the next world.[3] Hindus conceived their marriage as a union primarily meant for the performance of religious and spiritual duties. Such a marriage cannot take place without the performance of sacred rites and ceremonies. Secondly, it is a permanent union, being sacramental. Being sacramental it is an eternal union. Marriage is a tie which once tied cannot be untied.[4] Such being the case, marriage being indissoluble, naturally the concept of divorce is bound to be unknown to Hindu Law which means dissolution of marriage. Then from where this concept has been brought into the Hindu Marriage Act, 1955. Was it the demand of the Hindu society? Or was it an Act of imitation overshadowed by the influence of Western culture to which we are addicted to consider superior to our Hindu culture under the magic spell of Mayne and Macaulay? To know it, it becomes necessary to scan

1. *Manu*, VIII.227.
2. P.K. Virdi, *The Grounds for Divorce in Hindu and English Law*, p. 19.
3. *Tekait Mon Mohini* v. *Basanta* [1901] 28 Cal 751 at 758.
4. Dr. Paris Diwan, *Modern Hindu Law*, p. 65.

the concept of divorce in its global perspective, especially the English Law and its adoption in Hindu Law.

**English Law of divorce**

The Anglo-Sexon Law before the Norman Conquest allowed divorce by mutual consent or on the ground of the wife's infidelity and recognised a right to remarry.[5] The Ecclesiastical Courts during the reign of Queen Elisabeth[6]· have granted a divorce *a vinculo matrimonii* as distinguished from divorce *a mensa et thoro* on the ground of adultery and permitted the parties to marry again.[7] As early as the tenth century the law of marriage and divorce was cast in a rigid mould because of the complete dominance of the church over matrimonial matters. The Ecclesiastical Courts could pronounce a marriage void *ab initio* but they had no power to pronounce a divorce *a vinculo* if there had been a valid marriage (see 1 Holdsworth, *A History of English Law*, 7th edn., 1956).

So the procedure to obtain divorce during the seventh century till 1857 was that the husband seeking divorce on the ground of his wife's adultery was first to obtain a decree of divorce *a mensa et thoro* from the Ecclesiastical Court and then petition the Parliament for divorce *a vinculo*.[8] But before he could obtain the decree from the Ecclesiastical Court, he had to file a suit against the adulterer in an action for criminal conversion and after having proved the charge against his wife and the co-respondent, he could obtain the decree from the church's Court. The procedural formalities, the expenses involved and the time consumed was so alarming that divorce became the luxury of the rich people.[9] However, the demand

5. See 2 Holdsworth, *A History of English Law* 90 (4th edn. 1936), Pollock and Maitland *The History of English Law* (2nd edn. 1959), Kitchin, *A History of Divorce*, 171 (1912), Worsley Boden, *Mischief of the Marriage Law*, 217 (1932).

6. First Report of the Royal Commission, *The Law of Divorce* (1853) makes mention of it.

7. McGregor, *Divorce in England*, I.34 (1957), J. Jackson, *The Formation and Annulment of Marriage* (2nd edn., 1969).

8. See Morris, *The End of Marriage*, 16 (1971).

9. Hartley, *Divorce (Today and Tomorrow)* 6 (1957), Don Flood, *The Dissolution of Marriage*, 751 (1962).

for cheaper and simpler form of divorce started during the years following Waterloo.[10] But one fact is noteworthy that the canonical theory of indissolubility of marriage was sacrosanct and it allowed divorce *a mensa et thoro* on the ground of adultery which was considered as a serious breach of marriage law.[11]

Then came the Matrimonial Causes, Act, 1857 which made the first inroad in the ecclesiastical divorce law. A Royal Commission was appointed in 1850 to look into the question of reforms in the matrimonial law. The Commission recommended cruelty and desertion in addition to adultery as ground upon which divorce could be granted. The Act was passed in the teeth of opposition.

Gladstone, a powerful antagonist to liberal divorce spoke so strongly —

> It is opposed to the law of Church, to the law of nature, and to the law of God.[12]

Even Lord Cranworth who recommended the passage of the Bill had his own reservations. He struck a note of caution and expressed fear by stating:

> I think recognition of the sanctity of marriage underlines the essentials of our quality as a people. No measure could be more injurious or more calculated to interfere with the social welfare of the country than one which tended to shake the solidarity of marriage and the strength of the marriage tie.[13]

Dicey called it the triumph of individualistic liberalism and of common justice. It did away the inequity of law which theoretically permitted divorce but in reality conceded to the rich a right denied to the poor.[14] However, this comment of Dicey 'individualistic liberalism' speaks much about individual as the smallest unit of

---

10. Greaveson, *The Century of Family Law.*
11. See *Rye* v *Fuliambe*, Moor's Report 683 (1602).
12. As quoted by Lord Merrivale in *Marriage and Divorce* at 37 (1936).
13. *Ibid.*, at 37-8 (1936).
14. Dicey, *Law and Public Opinion in England During Nineteenth Century*, (2nd edn., 1920) at p. 347.

society and not family. Thus, in his comments he ignored the concept of family for which the foundation is marriage.

However, the purpose of the Act appears simply to take away the jurisdiction of the Ecclesiastical Courts over matrimonial matters and gave powers to the Secular Courts to dissolve the marriage. The ground for divorce was that the husband could obtain divorce on the ground of adultery simpliciter, whereas a wife had to prove adultery coupled with incest, bigamy, cruelty or alternatively rape or an unnatural offence.[15] This distinction was already there prior to this Act and the Matrimonial Causes Act, 1857 retained this distinction.

This distinction was, however, removed by the Matrimonial Causes Act, 1923 by which this strange distinction between the position of the husband and that of the wife was the symbol of inequity. This Act brought the husband and wife on an equal footing by permitting the latter to petition on the grounds of adultery alone.[16]

Then came the A.P. Herbert's Matrimonial Causes Act, 1937 by which further grounds were added for seeking divorce. Under the Act.[17] Divorce or judicial separation could be obtained for cruelty or desertion without cause for three years or incurable insanity.

From that time onward various Royal Commissions were appointed to enquire into the law of matrimonial causes because the English Law believed in matrimonial guilt and how insanity was added is not understood as insanity is not based on the principle of matrimonial guilt but was added as a ground for divorce. So the divorce law needed reforms. Thus, after 1939 the Matrimonial Causes (War Marriages) Act, 1944 gave the Court temporary jurisdiction to entertain petitions for divorce or nullity where the husband was, at the time of the marriage domiciled outside the United Kingdom and the wife was immediately before the marriage domiciled in England and the parties did not reside together in the

---

15. See Matrimonial Causes Act, 1857, section 27.
16. McGregor, *Divorce in England*, pp. 20-1 (comments on the distinction), L.J. Blom-Cooper, *A Century of Divorce* (1958) 25.
17. Matrimonial Causes Act, 1937, sections 2 and 3.

country in which the husband was then domiciled. Then came the Law Reform (Miscellaneous Provisions) Act, 1949 by which an extensive permanent enlargement of jurisdiction was effected. However, this Act was repealed and replaced by the Matrimonial Causes Act, 1950. It can be said that by a touch here and a twist there the law was altered and consolidated in the Matrimonial Causes Act, 1950. The law as further amended, repealed and finally consolidated in the Matrimonial Causes Act, 1965.

Matrimonial Causes Act, 1965 contained 46 sections and Schedule I and Schedule II. Section 1 dealt with grounds of divorce.

(1) Subject to the next following section, a petition for divorce may be presented to the High Court (hereinafter in this Act referred to as 'the Court') —

(*a*) by the husband or the wife on the ground that the respondent —

(*i*) has since the celebration of the marriage committed adultery; or

(*ii*) has deserted the petitioner without cause for a period of at least three years immediately preceding the presentation of the petition; or

(*iii*) has since the celebration of the marriage treated the petitioner with cruelty; or

(*iv*) is incurably of unsound mind and has been continuously under care and treatment for a period of at least five years immediately preceding the presentation of the petition.

(*b*) by the wife on the ground that her husband has since the celebration of the marriage been guilty of rape, sodomy or bestiality.

(2) It deals with clause (1) (*a*) (*ii*) of the Act and provides details concerning 'desertion'.

(3) It deals with clause (1)(*a*)(*iv*) of the section and gives required details to satisfy the ground of insanity.

(4) It also deals with clause (1)(*a*)(*iv*), further to clause (3) above.

Matrimonial Causes Act, 1965 is in 4 parts, i.e.,

Part I deals with Divorce, Nullity and other Matrimonial suits.

Part II deals with the Ancillary Relief.

Part III deals with Protection of Children.

Part IV deals with Miscellaneous and General Miscellaneous provisions.

Thus, this Act is comprehensive in nature. It is to be noted that except insanity, the law of divorce is based on the principle of matrimonial misconduct or popularly known as fault theory. Then there arose a general realisation that the ground of matrimonial misconduct is not enough. There can be other causes for the spouses to part asunder due to emotional or psychological behaviour. Thus, it was felt to probe further into the matter and to this effect a group was appointed by the Archbishop of Canterbury in January, 1964 and the report of the group was published in July, 1966.[18] In this report it was observed:

> Unsatisfactory as the law based on the matrimonial offence has proved in practice to be, it has yet to be shown that the substitution of some other basis would improve the situation. It is after all conceivable that the only alternative to the frying pan might turn out to be the fire in which case it would be safer to stick to the frying pan.[19]

So the group stuck to the frying pan as it was safer in their own estimation and recommended that breakdown of marriage should be the sole ground for divorce as it was by far the better alternative.

Meanwhile, the Law Commission which was also seized of the matter relating to matrimonial causes, also gave its report in November, 1966. Wherein the Law Commission endorsed the views

18. Putting asunder: *A Divorce Law for Contemporary Society — The Report of a Group* appointed by the Archibishop of Canterbury.

19. Para 46 of p. 33 of the Report (1966).

of the Archbishop's Group that the law based on the concept of fault was unsatisfactory.

The Law Commission observed:

> It does not achieve the maximum possible fairness to all concerned, for a spouse may be branded as guilty in law though not the more blameworthy in fact. The insistence on guilt and innocence tends to embitter relationships, with particularly damaging results to the children, rather than to promote future harmony. Its principles are widely regarded as hypocritical.[20]

The Law Commission did not subscribe to the concept of 'breakdown with inquest' as propounded by the Archbishop's Group but instead suggested that a good divorce law should be able to achieve two objectives:[21]

1. To buttress, rather than to undermine, the stability of marriage; and
2. when regrettably, a marriage has irretrievably broken down, to enable the empty shell to be destroyed with the maximum fairness and the minimum bitterness, distress and humiliation.

On the suggestion of the Law Commission the Divorce Reform Act was passed which got the Royal assent in October, 1969 and came into effect on January 1, 1971, wherein a single ground for divorce was substituted for the existing grounds based on specific matrimonial offences, namely the irretrievable breakdown of marriage. Accordingly, the whole of section 1 of the Matrimonial Causes Act, 1965, setting out the grounds of divorce is replaced by para 1 of the schedule of the 1969 Act.

Such breakdown had to be established by a petitioner satisfying the Court of one or more of the following facts.[22]

---

20. The Law Commission, *Reform of the Grounds of Divorce*; The field of choice para 28 at p. 16 (1966).
21. *Ibid.*, Para 15 at p. 10.
22. Divorce Reforms Act, 1969, section 2(*i*).

Section 2 (1)(*a*): That the respondent has committed adultery and the petitioner finds it intolerable to live with the respondent.

(*b*) that the respondent has behaved in such a way that the petitioner cannot reasonably be expected to live with the respondent.

(*c*) that the respondent has deserted the petitioner for a continuous period of at least two years immediately preceding the presentation of the petition.

(*d*) that the parties to the marriage have lived apart for a continuous period of at least two years immediately preceding the presentation of the petition and the respondent consents to a divorce being granted.

(*e*) the parties to the marriage have lived apart for a continuous period of at least five years immediately preceding the presentation of petition.

This substitution of a single ground for divorce — 'irretrievable breakdown' of marriage on the fact of it marks a notable change in the English Law of divorce, without, however, affecting the jurisdiction of the Court. Judges and practitioners will doubtless have to consider how far these facts which, during the Parliamentary Debates were styled 'guidelines', will come into play.[23]

These guidelines apart, the basic and the main question is still to be answered. 'Is the breakdown of marriage irretrievable'? So necessarily the Court had to keep in mind two things which are inherently present in the Act.

1. Balance of probabilities having regard to the evidence.

2. Possibility of reconciliation.

The various provisions of the Act, though appear simple apparently but latently appear to be very difficult to comply with. This is perhaps, which appears manifest, candid, clear and

---

23. Latey on Divorce (15th edn.).

comprehensive, the attempt to make divorce difficult and positively not easy, especially while pleading the matrimonial misconduct, as along with matrimonial misconduct, it is also to be shown as to how it is leading to the irretrievable breakdown of marriage.

For an example, in section 2(1) (*a*), two facts are to be proved:

1. The respondent has committed adultery.
2. It is intolerable to live with the respondent.

Not only that, it is a complex situation whether these two facts are independent in nature or linked with each other. In *Goodrich* v. *Goodrich*[24] it was held that the phrase 'has committed adultery and the phrase 'and the petitioner finds it intolerable to live with the respondent', were independent of each other. Between the two phrases the word 'and' is used. But in *Roper* v. *Roper*, Faulks J.,[25] took the stand that

> I think common sense tells you that where the finding that has got to be made is that the respondent has committed adultery and the petitioner finds it intolerable to live with the respondent, it means, 'and in consequence' of the adultery the petitioner finds it intolerable to live with the respondent.

Text writers such as Raydon,[26] Tolstoy,[27] Bromley,[28] and Passingham,[29] subscribe to the view taken in *Goodrich*'s case whereas Barton,[30] has advocated that there must be some link between adultery and intolerability. Rosenbaum,[31] says that to construe that there need be no link between adultery and

24. [1971] 2 AllER 1340.
25. (1971) 3 AllER 668.
26. Rayden on *Divorce* 205 (1972).
27. Tolstoy on *Divorce* 54 (7th edn., 1971).
28. Bromley, *Family Law* 209 (4th edn., 1971).
29. Passingham, *The Divorce Reform Act*, 1969, 86 LQR 348 (1970).
30. Barton, *Questions on the Divorce Reforms Act* 1969, 86 LQR 348 (1970).
31. Rosenbaum, *Divorce Reforms in England*. The decline of the Matrimonial offence, 12 J Fam L 365 at 370 (1972-73).

intolerability, is to betray the intention of the drafter of the Divorce Reform Act.

The legislative intention as manifest is:

1. That section 2(1)(*a*) and 2(1)(*b*) which speak of matrimonial misconduct, have been relegated to a very low position.
2. That section 2(1)(*c*) which is also a matrimonial misconduct has been qualified with the phrase 'continuous period of two years'. So it has to be read with section 3(5) of the Act. So here the case is of actual desertion (see para 37 at 16 in Passingham's the Divorce Reforms Act, 1969.
3. section 2(1)(*d*) speaks of mutual consent but 'living apart' for a continuous period of two years is a prerequisite. 'Living apart' is again a complex phrase as to whether it means physical separation or not.[32] Whether intention 'never to return' is to be reckoned or not. Or whether two years period is a mere formality.
4. Section 2(1)(*e*) poses again a complex situation that whether a 'continuous period of five years' is a blameless period or blemished period on the part of the petitioner because for centuries the hallmark of English Law of divorce had been that no one should be allowed to take advantage of his own wrong.
5. Then the ground of divorce has to be seen in the light of section 4 and section 5 of the Act which are the defences available. In *Banik* v. *Banik*,[33] though the case fell under section 2(1)(*e*), but the plea of the wife that she will not only have financial hardship and also being a Hindu she will be regarded as outcast and shall carry a social stigma. The Court agreed readily and set aside the *decree nisi* granted by the lower Court.

---

32. See *Santos* v. *Santos* [1972] 2 All ER 246. Where it is said that "living apart" did not mean physical separation.
33. [1973] AllER 45.

Even in *Richards* v. *Richards*[34] she filed a petition under section 2(1)(*b*) that her husband had become mentally ill, suffered from moodiness, taciturnity and insomnia and had behaved in such a way as to make her life intolerable. All was proved in evidence but still the Court did not grant decree of divorce as she failed to establish that the husband behaved in such a way that she could not reasonably be expected to live with him. If we analytically look to the complex sub-grounds along with safeguards provided, this Act had not made divorce easy but rather difficult.

If we go through the various judicial decisions, we find two things:

1. Firstly, this Act is not to make divorce easy, but it is an indirect vigorous attempt to save marriage. It has shown utmost respect for the canonical concept of marriage that it is indissoluble and it must be protected.
2. However, if the marriage is subjected to such strains of misconduct or otherwise unbearable stresses, it is better to let it dissolve so that the stigma of bitterness and the element of undesirability is buried once for all. It is again a negative approach to save the institution of marriage. So the whole stress is on the marriage and not on divorce.

In *Ash* v. *Ash*[35], Bagnall J., quoting the Law Commission's Reform of the grounds of divorce in section 2(1)(*b*) said:

> The objects of the 1969 legislation . . . are not, in my view simply to make divorce easier but . . . to buttress, rather than to undermine, the stability of marriage and when regrettably, a marriage has irretrievably broken down, to enable the empty shell to be destroyed with the maximum fairness, and the minimum bitterness, distress and humiliation.

In *Santos* v. *Santos*[36] it is said that it has sometimes been said that

---

34. [1972] 3 AllER 695.
35. [1972] Fam 135 at 140.
36. [1972] 2 WLR 889, 901 CA. See also *Huxford* v. *Huxford* [1972] 1 WLR 210, 213, 214, Hollings J. giving leave to a wife to file an answer alleging admitted adultery.

the object of the Act of 1969 is to make divorce easy, but that hardly seems correct when in some instances it has made it more difficult. . . . It is more appropriate to say that whilst in practice additional grounds for divorce are provided by the Act of 1969, yet it is designed to assist maintenance of marriages other than those reduced to a mere shell. Whilst sympathising . . . with those Judges who have to take the undefended list, it is still the case that the Legislature intended the procedure before them to involve Judicial Care as opposed to rubber stamping.

So in view of bars, defences, reconciliation, proof of breakdown, financial and other hardships, the Legislative intention is manifestly clear to make divorce 'a rare of rarest' concept and as such, such provisions are incorporated in the Act.

This being so, the said Act has been replaced by the Matrimonial Causes Act, 1973 which is simply a replica of the Divorce Reforms Act, 1969 and stress on the stability of marriage is paramount. The possibility of reconciliation should be explored as more conducive to the happiness of spouses and their children than the forensic prosecution of matrimonial litigation and regarding 'wrong', in order to construe it as such, regard must be had to the circumstances of those involved, including children and to the balance which must be maintained between upholding the sanctity of marriage and the desirability of ending marriages which have become empty shells.[37]

## Scottish Law of divorce

Comparatively, Scotland also got enacted The Divorce (Scotland) Act, 1976 which came into operation on January 1, 1977, making irretrievable breakdown of marriage the sole ground of divorce in Scotland but distinctive in nature than that of the Divorce Reform Act, 1969 of England (which was replaced by the Matrimonial Causes Act, 1973).

By section 1(1):

The Court of Session may grant a decree of divorce if, but

37. *Talbot* v. *Talbot*, *The Times*, Oct 19, 1971. Dunn J. has said, see also *Mathias* v. *Mathias*, *The Times*, May 3, 1972 CA.

only if, it is established in accordance with the following provisions of this Act that the marriage has broken down irretrievably.

Section 1(2):

irretrievable Breakdown of a marriage shall . . . be taken to be established in an action for divorce if the pursuer can prove at least one of the five facts laid down in the sub-section. The section 1(2) facts are that:

(*a*) Since the date of the marriage the defender has committed adultery; or

(*b*) Since the date of the marriage the defender has at any time behaved (whether or not as a result of mental abnormality and whether such behaviour has been active or passive), in such a way that the pursuer cannot reasonably be expected to cohabit with the defender; or

(*c*) The defender has wilfully and without reasonable cause deserted the pursuer, and during a continuous period of two years immediately succeeding the defender's desertion —

(*i*) there has been no cohabitation between the parties, and

(*ii*) the pursuer has not refused a genuine and reasonable offer by the defendant to adhere; or

(*d*) There has been no co-habitation between the parties at any time during a continuous period of two years after the date of the marriage and immediately preceding the bringing of the action and the defender consents to the granting of a decree of divorce; or

(*e*) There has been no co-habitation between the parties at any time during a continuous period of five years after the date of the marriage and immediately preceding the bringing of the action.

The Act propounds only one ground of divorce, i.e., irretrievable breakdown of marriage, but in essence it is founded on the acts of matrimonial misconduct and naturally the question arises as to whether it is a reform or a compromise or a step towards making divorce more difficult and thus an attempt to strengthen the ties of marriage. So we have to briefly look to the statutory interpretation coupled with judicial attitude.

Section 1(1) is to be read in three parts:

(i) If, but only if,

(ii) the marriage has broken down irretrievably,

(iii) due to any of the five facts stipulated in section 1(2).

So first of all the proof of a section 1(2) fact is necessary condition for a divorce. This proof may be inferred from the balance of probabilities but this is only the first stage towards granting of divorce. Section 1(2) also states that "irretrievable breakdown of a marriage shall be taken to be established in an action for divorce if one of the facts is made out". It looks apparently that the facts stated in section 1(2) are easier in nature and once made out, then there is no restrictive aspect is left behind to hinder the grant of divorce if it is to be read with "irretrievable breakdown of marriage shall be taken to be established".

But if we dive a little deeper, we find that section 1(2) is preliminary in nature. It is still under the growing shadow of the phrase 'If, but only if' stipulated in section 1(1) of the Act. The Legislative intention is very clear when it has used the word 'if' and then this 'if' is further qualified with 'but only if'. It clearly indicates that once any of the facts stated in section 1(2) is made out then it is to be considered as to whether the marriage has broken down irretrivably or any such possibility of saving the marriage is still in existence and if so it is to be explored. Then section 2(1) of the Act comes into operation. By section 2(1) of the Act, if at any time before granting a decree, it appears to the Court that there is a reasonable prospect of a reconciliation between the parties then the Court 'shall continue or further continue', the action for a period or periods during which attempts can be made at reconciliation. So section 1(1) is to first be read with section 1(2) and then with section 2(1) and this satisfies the phrase 'if but only if'.

Then we have to see again the phrase 'may grant a decree of divorce' used in section 1(1) of the Act. The word 'may' implies that the Court of Session has a general discretion to refuse a decree of divorce. In the earlier Legislation[38] and the specific provision in this Act, i.e., section 1(5) expressly states that the Court 'shall not be bound to grant decree' when irretrievable breakdown has been established by reason of section 1(2)(*e*) of the Act, if in the opinion of the Court the grant of decree would result in grave financial hardship to the defender. Again by section 8 of the Matrimonial Proceedings (Children) Act, 1958, the Court is under a duty not to grant a decree unless and until satisfactory arrangements have been made for the custody, maintenance and education of any children affected by the divorce. So the Divorce (Scotland) Act, 1976 in essence is on the pattern of the Matrimonial Causes Act, 1973 wherein the English Law recognises that a petitioner is no longer entitled to a divorce on proof of the respondent's matrimonial fault and that divorce should only be available when a marriage, in fact, has broken down irretrievably and the judges are constrained from allowing divorce to degenerate into a matter of rubebr stamping[39] as under English Law proof of a section 1(2) fact is necessary but not always sufficient to establish irretrievable breakdown of marriage.[40] So the Divorce (Scotland) Act, 1976 is neither a reform not a compromise but a step towards discouraging divorce, making it difficult but only with one escape route that where marriage, in fact, has become an empty shell. So in fact this Act is having a conclusive titling tendency towards stability of marriage which at all costs must be protected and preserved.

Even if we take individually the section 1(2) facts then we again reach the same goal that law has started thinking in terms of spiritual values of marriage tie, simultaneously discarding the matrimonial misconduct.

---

38. The Divorce (Scotland) Act, 1964.
39. *Santos* v. *Santos* [1972] 2 AllER 246, per Sachs LJ.
40. *Pheasant* v. *Pheasant* [1972] 1 All ER 587.

Section 1(2)(*a*) speaks of adultery. Spouse's adultery is not necessarily indicative of matrimonial breakdown. Section 1(2)(*a*) of the Matrimonial Causes Act, 1973 and the Divorce (Scotlant) Act, 1976 are the product of this thought.[41] The new statute leaves adultery with most of the features of the old matrimonial offence. Section 1(3) retains the traditional bars of 'lenocinium'[42] and condonation. So adultery is not such a misconduct which is not pardonable. Rather the proverb 'forgiveness is the best form of revenge' is applicable in this case too and the concept of condonation is legally recognised and thus resumption of marital relationship was necessary to establish condonation. So adultery is not such an act of misconduct which is not erasable. It can be removed from memory.[43]

Section 1(2)(*b*) speaks of behaviour. This Act differs with the Matrimonial Causes Act, 1973. Section 2(1)(*b*) of the Matrimonial Causes Act speaks: "that the respondent has behaved in such a way that the petitioner cannot reasonably be expected to live with the respondent". So basically it connotes the old grounds of cruelty and constructive desertion.[44] But whereas section 1(2)(*b*) of this Act has explained the behaviour as follows:

1. Behaviour caused by mental abnormality or not.
2. Passive as well as active behaviour.
3. That the pursuer cannot reasonably be expected to cohabit with the defendant as consequence to such behaviour.

This clause has encompassed every aspect of behaviour which can be detrimental to the marital tie. Be it by an abnormal mind or a sane mind. Be it passive or active in nature. 'Active' generally means violent in nature. But since the concept of behaviour has

41. J.M. Thompson, *Divorce Scottish Style — ICLO*, Vol. 26, p. 648.
42. Clive & Wilson, *Husband & Wife*. It means pursuer's active connivance in the defender's adultery.
43. *Annan* v. *Annan* 1948 SC 532 (Scotlant) wherein the Court held that a resumption of marital relationship was necessary to establish condonation.
44. *Spill* v. *Spill* [1972] I WLR, 793 (Cruelty), *Pheasant* v. *Pheasant* [1972] 2 WLR 353 (Desertion), *Jordan* v. *Jordan* — *The Times*, June, 9, 1972 (Not the same as old cruelty).

been taken in its totality, it has confounded this clause in itself and the whole burden has fallen on the legal shoulders of the Judge as to whether the Scottish Judges have to act independently or to follow the English cases in this regard.[45]

It is worth noting what Bagnall J. has said in *Ash* v. *Ash*:

> A violent petitioner can reasonably be expected to live with a violent respondent; a petitioner who is addicted to drink can reasonably be expected to live with a respondent similarly addicted; a taciturn and morose spouse can reasonably be expected to live with a taciturn and morose partner; a flirtatious husband can reasonably be expected to live with a wife who is equally susceptible to the attention of the other sex; and if each is equally bad, at any rate in similar respects, each can reasonably be expected to live with each other.

So to say this clause has cast a burden on the pursuer to come to the Court with a specific charge under section 1(2)(*b*) and not a charge of general nature and as such all defences applicable to such specific charge shall be available to the defendant and more so the pursuer has to show to the Court as to how it led to the irretrievable breakdown of marriage. So this section 1(2)(*b*) is entirely a new provision, incomprehensible in nature, most confusing and is restricted by all doctrines of defences.

Section 1(2)(*c*) has to be looked as follows:

(*i*) The defender has wilfully and without any reasonable cause deserted the pursuer;

(*ii*) During the period of two years (continuous) immediately succeeding the defendant's desertion there has been no cohabitation between the parties; and

(*iii*) The pursuer has not refused a genuine and reasonable offer by the defendant to adhere;

---

45. *Ash* v. *Ash* [1972] Fam 135, *Livingstore Stalland* v. *Livingstore Stallard* [1974] 2 AllER 766, *O'Neil* v. *O'Neil* [1975] 3 AllER 289, *Pheasant* v. *Pheasant* [1972] 1 AllER 587.

Previously, the pursuer had to prove that:

(*i*) The desertion is wilful and without any reasonable cause; and

(*ii*) That the defendant had persisted in the desertion for a period of not less than three years (the triennium).[46] So there was, however, a presumption that once the initial act of desertion was proved, the defender's intention to desert persisted throughout the triennium. However, this presumption was rebuttable and this caused hardship if, for example, the defender became insane during the triennium.[47] Later on this difficulty was removed.[48]

So the primary ingredient or the initial act of desertion must be proved as wilful and without any reasonable cause, which means factum of desertion and *animus deserendi*. Once this initial act of desertion has been established and it is shown to be wilful and without reasonable cause, the matter does not end there. The pursuer has also to show that, during the continuous period of two years immediately succeeding the defender's desertion, (i) there was no cohabitation between the parties and (ii) the pursuer has not refused a genuine and reasonable offer by the defender to adhere. The use of word 'and' is legally significant which exists in section 1(2)(*c*)(*i*) and 1(2)(*c*)(*ii*). Whether the word 'and' is to be read or interpreted conjunctively or to be construed disjunctively. The clear view emerges is that the pursuer must show to the Court that the two years period was continuous[49] and there was no cohabitation and he has also to show that no genuine and reasonable offer was made by the defendant to adhere.

Thus, this clause, though looks so simple, but is punctuated with many complexities to make divorce more difficult.

Section 1(2) (*d*): It is noteworthy that in this clause the phrase

---

46. Section 1(1)(*a*) of the Divorce (Scotland) Act, 1938.
47. *Mudie* v. *Mudie* 1956 SC 318 (Scotland).
48. Section 2 of the Divorce (Insanity and Desertion) Act, 1958. This Act was consequently repealed by section 12(2) of the Divorce (Scotland) Act, 1976.
49. See section 2(4) of the Divorce (Scotland) Act, 1976.

'desertion' is not used but instead the phrase 'no cohabitation' is used. This section is in two parts:

1. No cohabitation between the parties during a continuous period of two years after the date of marriage and immediately preceding the bringing of the action.

and

2. The defender consents to the granting of decree of divorce.

Cohabitation[50] means

> choice of matrimonial home — it is a husband's duty to provide his wife a home according to his circumstances. There is no absolute rule whereby either party is entitled to dictate to the other where the matrimonial home shall be; the matter is to be settled by agreement between the parties, by a process of give and take by reasonable accommodation.

However, if we go by section 13(2) of the Divorce (Scotland) Act, 1976 the parties shall be held to cohabit with one another only if they are 'in fact living together as man and wife'. The said provision, i.e., section 1(2)(*d*) can be interpreted in two ways:

1. There is no cohabitation even though the spouses are not physically separated, provided they are not living together as man and wife.

2. There is no cohabitation, provided they are physically separated.

So if we read section 1(2)(*d*) with section 13(2), then the parties are held to cohabit with one another 'only when they are in fact living together as husband and wife'. So it is clear that if the parties are physically separated, the parties are not living together and therefore they cannot be said to be cohabiting.

Even if a liberal view is to be taken, even then the next question will arise as to who is liable for this act of misconduct. If one spouse by his words and conduct compels the other spouse to leave the marital home, then it is the former who would be guilty of desertion

50. See *Halsbury's Laws of England*, 4th edn., Vol. 13, para 623.

though it is the latter who is physically separated from the other.[51] In fact, the party who intends bringing cohabitation to an end and whose conduct in reality causes its termination, commits the act of desertion.[52]

So the pursuer has to show to the Court of non-cohabitation due to the fault of the defendant which is inherently present in the clause. Section 1(2)(*d*) of the Act and the parallel provision 1(2)(*d*) of the Matrimonial Causes Act, 1973 are apparently on different footing so far as the concept of 'living part' is concerned.[53]

So this provision should not be construed as divorce by mutual consent. The pursuer has to prove to the satisfaction of the Court that during the said period prescribed under law, there was no cohabitation. Regarding consent, it does not mean that the situation of the irretrievable breakdown of marriage has convincingly reached. The Court now need not apply its mind to find out whether the marriage in fact has broken down due to the consent given by the defendant for the grant of decree of divorce but still the Court has to look to section 1(4) of the Divorce (Scotland) Act, 1976.

Provision is to be made by Act of Sederunt,[54] which will —

(*a*) ensure that the defender has been given such information as will enable him to understand both the consequences of his consenting to the decree and the steps which he must take to indicate his consent, and

(*b*) prescribe the manner in which the consent or its withdrawal is to be indicated. Consent given in the prescribed way will be sufficient evidence of the defender's consent to decree. By section 5(6) of the Act, provision is also to be made by Act of Sederunt to impose a duty on the pursuer relying on section 1(2)(*d*) or (*e*) fact to inform the defender of his right to apply for financial provision and education of any child of

51. *Lang* v. *Lang* [1955] AC 402.
52. *Bowron* v. *Bowron* [1925] P 192. See also *Pratt* v. *Pratt* [1939] AC 417.
53. *Fuller* v. *Fuller* [1975] 2 AllER 650.
54. Section 1(4) of the Divorce (Scotland) Act, 1976.

> the marriage. This is perhaps the lacuna in the said Act.

But whatever may be the case, even this provision is not so easy to get divorce. The Court can go into the nature of consent and likely hardship to be caused to the defender. The Court must be given the power to delay the grant of decree of divorce as it is there in section 10(2), (3) and (4) of the Matrimonial Causes Act, 1973. Even though it is not there, even then this clause espousing ground for divorce is not that easy. Looking to the various other legal measure to be discussed later, will show that the Act 1976 is neither a step for reform, nor a compromise but a step towards making divorce difficult as the stress now is on the stability of marriage and protection to women and children of the marriage

Section 1(2)(*e*):

> This section only speaks of 'no cohabitation' between the parties at any time during a continuous period of five years after the date of marriage and immediately preceding the bringing of the action.

This clause is true replica of section 2(1)(*e*) of Matrimonial Causes Act, 1973 but distinct in the sense that it has to be read with other clause of the Act of 1976 which are differently propounded. Whereas section 2(1)(*e*) of Matrimonial Causes Act, 1973 is to be read with section 5 and section 10(2), (3), (4) of the said Act, 1973, but here section 1(2)(*e*) is to be read with section 1(5) of the Divorce (Scotland) Act, 1976 where the defender is given the special protection in that the Court is not bound to grant decree notwithstanding that irretrievable breakdown has been established by reason of section 1(2)(*e*) if, in the Court's opinion, the decree would result in grave financial hardship to the defender.

This section appears to be superfluous but still it is incorporated by way of abundant caution that perhaps such remotest possibility if arises, then how to meet it. Five years separation is too long a period which clearly indicates a peak height of tolerance which is not possible and if possible then by that time the charm of marriage must have totally evaporated leaving behind an empty shell. Thus, this clause may give a mere satisfaction but is a futile exercise on imaginative basis.

However, the Divorce (Scotland) Act, 1976[55] has to be read with section 9 of the Conjugal Rights (Scotland) Act, 1861, section 1(1) of the Custody of Children (Scotland) Act, 1939, and section 7 of the Matrimonial Proceedings (Children) Act, 1958.

Divorce (Scotland) Act, 1976 is to be read with further legal measures adopted like the first Conciliation Service established in Scotland in 1983, the Family Law Act passed in 1985,[56] and the various judicial cases,[57] Law Reform (Parent and Child) Act, 1986. In general the cases litigated under the Family Law Act, 1985, appear to reflect the usual clarifying process which follows a new statute and their relatively small number suggests that the Act is working reasonably well. The eternal problem is that it is more expensive for two people to live apart than together and there is little that the law can do about it.[58]

Thus, in short there is a visible shift in the philosophy of law that its centre of gravity is shifted from divorce to stability of marriage, suppressed and embattled spouses and innocent but victimised children. It is a welcome sign that Europe thickly materialistic in concept and conviction is reeling back to the ecclesiastical canon that marriage is a sacred tie and is indissolube. Conceptions and perceptions are changing and even the day is not far off when the last barbarian concept of irretrievable breakdown of marriage is also wiped out and the concept of spiritual values and family prevails.

## Spanish divorce law

Most of the Spanish and Italian people belong to Catholic Church which considers marriage to be a union for life and does not allow any divorce. So a divorce law in Spain and Italy must necessarily dissolve the canonical marriage as well as the civil marriage. Earlier

---

55. Clive, The Divorce (Scotland) Act 1976 (Edinburg, 1976).
56. Elaine Sutherland, *Scotland, The Reform Process Continues*, 26 JFamL 179 (1987).
57. *Carroll* v. *Carroll* 1988 SCLR 104, *Phillip* v. *Phillip* 1988 SCLR 427, *Me Devitt* v. *MeDevitt* 1988 SCLR 206, *Petri* v. *Perti* 1988 SCLR 390.
58. Elaine Sutherland, *Scotland: Financial Provision*, The status of children and Child Protection J. Fam L. 588 Vol. 28.

the laws of Spain,[59] and Itly,[60] provided only for judicial separation without dissolution of the bond of matrimony in agreement with the Catholic doctrine of the indissolubility of marriage. The divorce law was thus enacted in both these countries against the determined objection of the Catholic Church.

Spain had its divorce law in 1932 which was the result of a politically left oriented government in the country and it took the traditionally conservative Spanish legal community completely by surprise.[61] It was a divorce law along the lines of divorce statutes in European countries and in the United States. So a divorce law enacted by the Law of March 2, 1932,[62] remained in force only during the republic and lapsed on its defeat in the Spanish Civil War in 1939. So full dissolution of marriage with the right to enter into a new marriage has not been permitted in Spain except during the brief period of the Republic in 1931-9.

However, after the death of General Franco in 1975, a new Spanish Constitution was enacted in 1978, and an Article 32(2) provides for divorce legislation to be enacted by the Cortes and thus after a strenuous legal and political hickling and hackling, the Spanish Divorce Law of 1981 was enacted as Law No. 30 of July 7, 1981 which modifies the provisions concerning marriage in the Civil Code and proceedings for annulment, judicial separation and the dissolution of marriage.[63]

Spain traditionally recognises two types of marriage, a religious marriage and a civil marriage,[64] and thus law of divorce has to deal with both types of marriage. The Divorce Law of Spain of 1981 has to be seen in all its perspectives to understand its nature and applicability.

---

59. Codigo Civil, Articles 104-107.
60. Codice Civile, Articles 49-158.
61. Joaquin Dualde in the preface to Manuel Casals Torres's *Divorcio Civil* (Barcelona).
62. Law of Divorce of March 2, 1932 published in correct form in the Gaceta de Madrid on March 11, 1932.
63. Boletin Official del Estado No. 172, July 20, 1981.
64. Codigo Civil, Article, 49.

According to Spanish Law, promise to marry does not give rise to an obligation to contract it or to perform it as agreed, but however, a breach of promise to marry imposes upon the promisor to compensate the other party for the expenditure incurred and the obligations contracted with a view to the promised marriage.[65] No action can be brought after a year has run from the day of refusal to marry.[66] The requirements[67] of marriage are covered by various articles in the Civil Code, covering prohibitions, consent and minority[68] and marriage.

The new Spanish Law gives parties the choice of entering into marriage in a civil ceremony before an officer of state or in a religious ceremony before a minister of religion.[69]

The present law places a marriage according to the rites of a legally recognised religion on a par with that according to the rites of the Catholic Church.[70] The celebration of marriage before a Judge or other officer is governed under various provisions.[71] Celebration of marriage in a religious form is also covered by various provisions of the Civil Code.[72]

As marriage produces legal effects as from its celebration, it requires registration in the civil registry for its full effect, as an unregistered marriage does not affect rights of third parties acquired in good faith.[73]

Codigo Civil[74] has a peculiar but very relevant provision with respect to the rights and duties of the spouses. The spouses are equal with respect to rights and duties. They have to respect and assist each other and act in the interests of the family. They have

65. Codigo Civil, Article 42.
66. *Ibid*., Article 43.
67. *Ibid*., Article 44 to 48.
68. Spaniards reach majority at 18 (Constitution, Article 12).
69. Codigo Civil, Article 49.
70. *Ibid*., Article 49.
71. *Ibid*., Article 51 to 58.
72. *Ibid*., Articles 59, 60.
73. *Ibid*., Article 61.
74. *Ibid*., Articles 66 to 71.

to live together, be faithful to each other and support each other. It is presumed that they live together unless proved otherwise. The spouses establish their common residence by agreement and in case of dispute the matter will be decided by the Court which will consider the interests of the family. Neither spouse may act for the other without an authorisation.

The annulment of marriage is covered under Articles 73 to 80 of Codigo Civil if it is in violation of the requirements and in particular Articles 46 and 47. There is also a provision to this effect in the Code of Civil Procedure.[75]

However, the dissolution of marriage is interconnected with judicial separation. So a detailed study of judicial separation is needed to appreciate the concept of dissolution of marriage.

Judicial separation may be decreed, irrespective of the form of celebration of marriage on the petition of both spouses or of one with the consent of the other beginning with second year of marriage. The petition must contain a proposed agreement between the spouses on matters listed in Articles 90 and 103[76] of the Civil Code in terms of Article 81(1) of Codigo Civil. Judicial separation may further be decreed on the petition of only one of the spouses when the other gives him a legal cause for separation.[77]

Article 82 speaks of grounds for judicial separation:

1. Desertion, adultery, injurious and vexatious conduct and any other serious or repeated breach of matrimonial duties. Adultery cannot be alleged if the spouses separated by mutual consent or by the act of the spouse who alleges it.
2. Any serious or repeated breach of duties towards children of the marriage or those of either spouse living in the family home.

---

75. Article 954 of the Code of Civil Procedure.
76. Articles 90 and 103 deal with matters like custody of children, rights of access, communication and staying with the parent having no custody, disposition of the family home, support of the children, distribution of matrimonial property, almony.
77. Codigo Civil 81(2).

3. Conviction followed by imprisonment exceeding six years.
4. Alcoholism, use of narcotics or mental derangement whenever the interest of the other spouse or of the family demands the suspension of cohabitation.
5. Effective and freely agreed living apart for six months. The agreement is treated as having been freely made when one spouse earnestly asks the other to make it and expressly appraises him of its purpose and the other does not contest it by any legal means or request any of the provisional orders referred to in Article 103 of the Civil Code within six months of the request.
6. Effective living apart for three years.
7. Any ground for the dissolution of marriage referred to in paragraphs 3, 4 and 5 of Article 86[78] of the Civil Code.

The decree of judicial separation authorises the spouse to live apart and withdraw the authority of one spouse to bind the property of the other in running the matrimonial household.[79] There is only one conclusion which can be drawn is that the Spanish Law considers judicial separation to be an independent step in solving matrimonial problems and treats it as precondition for divorce which in turn means that to get dissolution of marriage the spouses have to pass through the initial legal obstructions and as per Article 84, reconciliation terminates proceedings for judicial separation and annuls anything undertaken in this respect but the spouses should inform the Court where the proceedings are undertaken. Thus, it is a step to prevent divorce or delay it, for change of mind may take place.

Dissolution of marriage is covered under two Articles. It is dissolved by the death or the declaration of death of one of the spouses by divorce, irrespective of the form at the time of its celebration.[80] The grounds for dissolution by divorce are:

78. Article 86 speaks of grounds for dissolution of marriage.

79. Codigo Civil, Article 83.

80. *Ibid.*, Article, 85. Grounds for dissolution are covered under Article 86.

1. Effective and uninterrupted living apart for at least one year from the bringing of the petition for judicial separation by both spouses, or by one with the consent of the other, not earlier than the second year of the marriage.

2. Effective and uninterrupted living apart for at least one year from the bringing of the petition for judicial separation by the petitioner or from the counter petition of the other spouse in accordance with Article 82[81] of the Civil Code, as soon as the decision granting judicial separation takes effect in law or failing, a decision by the trial Court within that time.

3. Effective and uninterrupted living apart for at least two years, viz.:

   (a) Since the freely agreed actual separation of the spouses, or since the decree of judicial separation took effect in law, or since a spouse has been declared missing, on the petition of either spouse, or

   (b) When the spouse petitioning for dissolution alleges that, at the time of the actual separation of the spouses, the other gave him a cause for judicial separation.

4. Effective living apart for at least five years, on the petition of either spouse.

5. A legally effective conviction for an attempt on the life of the other spouse, his ascendants or descendants.

A petition brought by both spouses or by one with the consent of the other must contain a proposed agreement between the spouses on the matters listed in Articles 90 and 103 of the Civil Code.

The effective living apart[82] of the spouses is compatible with the maintenance or temporary re-establishment of cohabitation due to necessity on the part of one or both spouses, to reconciliation or to interests of children, if this is shown in the proceedings for judicial

81. Article 82 speaks of grounds for judicial separation.

82. Referred in Articles 82 and 86 of Codigo Civil.

separation or dissolution of marriage. An interruption of cohabition does not imply effective living apart if it is due to reasons of employment, professional activity or the like.[83]

A suit for dissolution of marriage lapses on the death of either spouse or in the case of reconciliation. A reconciliation effected after the petition for the dissolution of marriage has been filed must be expressly made. Reconciliation after divorce is ineffective but the divorced couple may remarry.[84]

Dissolution of marriage may be decreed only by a judgement which dissolves it and the dissolution becomes effective only when the judgement takes effect. It will not affect third parties in good faith until it is recorded in the civil register.[85]

If we analyse critically, we find the legislation imposes waiting periods of differing lengths as a precondition. It nearly always requires the proceedings for judicial separation to precede those for the dissolution of marriage. It, thus, imposes a hurdle of duplicate proceedings. The duplication involves time, effort and expense on the part of the parties. It is also a clogging of Court calenders and expense on the part of the Courts. The idea of duplicate proceedings and imposition of waiting period shows the legislative intention to make this difficult and to prevent hasty divorces. Only those parties will comply with who are dead determined whatever may be the circumstances. The objective is clear of keeping families together.

This Spanish Law of Divorce may be aptly called the Civil Marriage Law. The stress is more on the marriage than on divorce. This Act is basically meant to abolish the virtual monopoly of the Catholic Church over marriages and the choice is left to the parties to the marriage to have a civil marriage or religious marriage.

The divorce law is more complicated and does not grant divorce easily. However, Spain, reluctantly, had to bring some reforms in family law as this upsurge had already taken place in France,[86]

83. Codigo Civil, Article 87.

84. *Ibid.*, Article 88.

85. *Ibid.*, Article 89.

86. Law No. 75-617 of July 1975.

Germany[87] and Italy.[88] One indication is very clear that though much legislative thought has been bestowed on divorce, but no emphasis has been laid on it. Legal procedures and compliance thereto was made difficult and tiring to desist people from resorting to it as the stability of marriage, no society wants to shatter, but so-called reformers do clamour for easy divorce.[89]

## New Zealand divorce law

New Zealand Law, being originally derived from English law, is also built to a considerable extent on the offence theory but the influence of breakdown theory is clearly to be seen as well and additions to the structure made from time to time tended to increase that influence.

In 1920, Divorce and Matrimonial Causes (Amendment) Act, 1920 (New Zealand) was enacted. Section 4 of the said Act provided separation by agreement for three years or more was introduced as a ground for divorce. But in 1921 two major judicial pronouncements created a congenial situation in this regard.

In *Manson* v. *Manson* Sir John Salmond,[90] an eminent jurist and member of the New Zealand Supreme Court summed up the discretionary granting of the decree of divorce on the ground of separation thus:

> *Prima facie*, when husband and wife have been separated for three years, whether by a judicial decree or by mutual agreement, each of them is entitled to a dissolution of marriage which has for that period been a marriage in name only and not in substance, in law and not in fact. The policy underlying this legislation is that it is not conducive to the public interest that men and women should remain bound

---

87. The First Marriage and Family Reform Law of June 14, 1976.
88. Law No. 898 of December 1, 1970 and on the Dissolution of Marriage Law No. 151 of May 19, 1975.
89. George E. Gloss, The Spanish Divorce Law of 1981, *International and Comparative Law Quarterly*, Vol. 32, p. 667.
90. [1921] NZLR 955, 961.

> together in permanence by the bonds of a marriage, the duties of which have long ceased to be observed by either party and the purpose of which has irremediably failed. Such a condition of marriage in law which is no marriage in fact leads only to immorality and unhappiness and the Court has now been entrusted with a discretionary jurisdiction to put an end to it.
>
> The jurisdiction has been made discretionary in order to enable the Court to refuse a decree in those cases in which a dissolution of the marriage would for some special reason be contrary to the public interest. . . . The reasons for making a decree of dissolution and the results of such a decree when made, are in ordinary circumstances exactly the same whether it is made at the suit of the guilty party or of the innocent one.

And in another case *Lodder* v. *Lodder*, Sir John Salmond[91] said:

> The legislature must, I think, be taken to have intended that separation for three years is to be accepted by this Court as *prima facie* a good ground for divorce. When the matrimonial relation has for that period ceased to exist *de facto*, it should, unless there are special reasons to the contrary, cease to exist *de jure* also. In general it is not in the interests of the parties or in the interests of the public that a man and woman should remain bound together a husband and wife in law when for a lengthy period they have ceased to be such in fact. In the case of such a separation the essential purposes of marriage have been frustrated, and its further continuance is in general not merely useless but mischievous.

Thus, as a result of these judicial pronouncements, there came a Divorce and Matrimonial Causes Act, 1921-22 (New Zealand). By section 2 of the Act, the respondent was given the right to prevent the granting of a decree if he or she could show that the separation was due to the petitioner's fault.

---

91. [1921] NZLR 876-7.

By Divorce and Matrimonial Causes Act, 1928 (N.Z.), the Court is required to refuse a decree for divorce if it found that the petition had been persented or prosecuted in collusion with either of the respondent. Though it was a provision of the Matrimonial Causes Act, 1857 (U.K.), but remained the law of New Zealand where adultery[92] was the ground for the petition but in other cases[93] a finding of collusion gave the Court a discretion whether or not to grant a decree.

However, in 1953, came the Divorce and Matrimonial Causes Amendment Act, 1953. Section 7 of the said Act, a provision was made that divorce was possible where the parties had been living apart for at least seven years and were unlikely to be reconciled, but even then it was felt that public opinion was not ready for the idea that a so-called 'guilty' person should be able to procure a divorce against the wish of the other and the Legislature imported into the ground the same provision as attached to a petition based on a separate agreement.[94]

Then in Matrimonial Proceedings Act, 1963, by section 31, the provision governing collusion was changed into a discretionary bar only even in the case of a petition on the ground of adultery. It went further, however, and restricted the scope as well, by adding the words, 'with intent to cause a perversion of justice', to the relevant provisions. Though such provision was made but it was having a mere existence on the statute book and its position is like 'unwept, unhonoured and unsung' as reported cases reveal.

Section 29(4) and (5) provided a period of two months for continuation or resumption of cohabitation to be ignored for the purpose of condonation if it has been done with a view to effecting a reconciliation. But, whatever, the changes were brought, 'the doctrine of breakdown' was not tended to be forgotten.

Though the pattern of law in matrimonial field in New Zealand was more or less on the lines of the developments in English law,

---

92. Divorce and matrimonial Causes Act 1928, section 17.

93. *Ibid.*, 1928, section 15.

94. Patricia M. Webb, Breakdown versus fault — *International and Comparative Law Quarterly*, Vol. 14 (Jan. 1965).

but New Zealand, due to its peculiar situation at home, made or adopted changes, which appear to be their own but the law in New Zealand was clearly heading to achieve the concept of 'breakdown' theory.

Thus, Family Proceedings Act, 1980, No. 94 brought the contemplated change and by section 39 of the Act, 'irreconcilable breakdown' can only be established by two years separation. Thus, Marriage Breakdown is the sole ground for divorce in New Zealand.

It can be only said that the doctrine of breakdown is in reality the consequence of non-observance of matrimonial duties which are self-imposed but sanctified one and thus the spiritual values of marriage and family, glaringly come to the forefront, which are lacking.

## Australian law of divorce

In Australia, being federal in constitutional structure, since the first Victorian Act of 1861[95] each colony created its own laws based upon the English Law of 1857.[96] As time went on, each colony or state departed to some extent from the original model. In 1959, after some years of discussion and a valiant attempt at the introduction of a private divorce Bill by Mr. Percy Joseke, the Commonwealth, under the leadership of the then Attorney General Sir Garfield Barwick finally chose to exercise its constitutional power to legislate in the fields of marriage and divorce and thus came the Commonwealth Matrimonial Causes Act of 1959. Altogether some fourteen grounds of divorce were inserted.

Section 28 of the Act contains the grounds for divorce from (*a*) to (*n*).

(*a*) adultery.

(*b*) desertion, with the period of separation reduced from three years to two years.

---

95. An Act to amend the Law relating to Divorce and Matrimonial Causes Act, 1861, No. CXXV.

96. Matrimonial Causes Act, 1857.

(*c*) wilful and persistent refusal to consummate the marriage.

(*d*) habitual cruelty for one year became a ground by itself without the petitioner having to establish drunkenness.

(*e*), (*g*), (*h*), (*i*) the grounds are based on various forms of sexual offences, frequent convictions involving long-term of imprisonment, or attempts to murder the petitioner.

(*f*) habitual drunkenness or drug taking for a period of two years.

(*j*) failure to support.[97]

(*k*) failure to comply with a decree of restitution of conjugal rights.[98]

(*l*) unsoundness of mind and confinement in an institution, of the respondent.[99]

(*m*) that the parties had lived separately and apart for a continuous period of not less than five years.

(*n*) that the other party has been absent from petitioner for such time and in such circumstances as to provide reasonable grounds for presumption of death.

It is worth mentioning that of all the grounds the one which created worst controversy was separation (section 28(*m*)).[100] A typical comment was that of Mr. Arthur Calwell, then the Deputy Leader of the Federal Parliamentary Opposition who attacked it in these emphatic terms:

I refuse to help to raise the palsied arm of this Government,

---

97. New ground for Victoria taken from the previous legislation in South Australia.

98. New ground for Victoria taken from the previous legislation in New South Wales.

99. Taken from the earlier Victorian Act and new ground for New South Wales.

100. H.A. Finlay, Divorce Law Reform: The Australian Approach, *Journal of Family Law*, Vol. 10, 1970.

> as it seeks to bestow a benediction on promiscuity. I refuse to join the Attorney-General in giving some sort of smelly, secular sanctification to barnyard morality.[101]

The controversy on this ground for divorce was basically based on the legal hypothesis that every ground for divorce required a petitioner to establish the commission of some offence as recognised by matrimonial law, but in this case it was considered that it is a ground independent of guilt and that the 'guilty', after the term of five years separation, was entitled to divorce the 'innocent' party.

This section 28 is to be read with sections 9-17 and section 71. Sections 9-17 are the provisions designed to encourage reconciliation between spouses contemplating divorce. Sections 9-13 are concerned to bring about a settlement of the parties' differences and to preserve the marriage at an early stage. They provided for the recognition of marriage guidance organisations, and create machinery for their operation. Rules made under the Act contain provisions requiring solicitors to bring the reconciliation provisions to the notice of their clients and directing that an endorsement be made by the solicitor on all petitions, answers and some other pleadings certifying that he has done so and has also discussed with the client the possibility of reconciliation.[102]

Section 14 lays it down as the duty of the Court to give consideration 'from time to time' to the possibility of reconciliation in cases which have actually reached the stage of trial in Court but where there appears a reasonable prospect of the parties being reconciled. Sections 15 and 16 provide necessary safeguards to protect the parties from the result of incautious admissions made during conferences or discussions held with a view to reconciliation.[103]

Section 71 requires the Court to be satisfied that proper arrangements have been made for the children of broken marriage as are under 16 years old and unless a declaration is made to this

---

101. 25 Commonwealth Parliamentary Debates (H of R) 2697 (1959).

102. Statutory Rules 1960 No. 97 rule 15 as amended by Statutory Rules 1968, No. 29 rule 8.

103. E.H.E. Barber, *Divorce, the Changing Law — Divorce, Society and the Law*.

effect, or the Court finds special circumstances, no decree can be made absolute.

This section is to be read as supplement to section 37. Section 37(1) compels a refusal of a decree if the Court is satisfied that by reason of the conduct of the petitioner or for any other reason, it would be harsh and oppressive to the respondent or contrary to public interest to grant a decree.

Section 37(2) provides that where the Court is of the opinion that it is just and proper in the circumstnaces that the petitioner should make provision for respondent's maintenance, or settlement of property for her benefit, no decree may be granted until arrangements satisfactory to the Court are made by petitioner to provide such benefits for respondent.

Section 37(3), by this sub-section the Court is specifically given discretion to refuse a decree if the petitioner has committed adultery.

Section 37(4) provided that where petitions by both parties are before the Court, no decree may be pronounced on the separation gound if the Court is able to make a decree on any other ground such as adultery, desertion or such other ground as may be proved.

This Act is a gradual emergence of breakdown of marriage as the basis for divorce replacing the previously punitive solution based primarily on fault that the guilty be punished and the innocent be saved. It has loosened the view that marriages were ordained in heaven and whom God has put together man should not put asunder.

But still the concept is intact that the stability of marriage is paramount and it must be protected and preserved at any cost unless it is totally reduced to an empty shell. Not only that, provisions are made that the embattled wives and innocent but unfortunate children, must be economically protected. Of course, it is a very poor substitute for the malady through which they have to go through socially and psychologically. Perhaps the body be saved from starvation and neglect but what about the neglect and distress of mind. To cure one disease, if it is there, and as a consequence to cause another disease and then start curing it, is an exercise in futility. It is a remedy worst than a problem. Alas! divorce, thy victim is social ethos which are to be preserved for the strength of the society and state.

However, the matter has not ended here. The seeds of breakdown of marriage as sown under section 28(*m*) of the Commonwealth Matrimonial Causes Act, 1959, grew into a full-fledged plant and marriage breakdown is now the sole ground in Australia. So irretrievable breakdown of marriage is the only ground in Australia and this can only be established on proof of one year separation under section 48 of Family Law Act (Australia), 1975, No. 53.

It is now a case where surgery along with treatment by medicine has been considered equally important. To which side we are drifting away, only God knows. Our faith in God is still not shaken. We worship him but started feeling reluctant to obey His command that the marriages are destined in heaven but only celebrated on earth.

## Divorce law in Canada

Divorce Law in Canada has to be read in three stages, i.e.,

1. Before 1968.
2. Divorce Act, 1968.
3. Post Act, 1968 developments.

### BEFORE 1968

The matrimonial relief of divorce was very difficult to obtain in Canada. Although the British North American Act, 1867 had empowered the Dominion Parliament to enact laws concerning divorce, Parliament was slow to exercise this power. So the law of divorce in Canada was basically the Matrimonial Causes Act, 1857 of England which was followed by the Courts or pre-confederation provincial statutes applicable to each province and the grounds of divorce were different from Province to Province. So Canada's divorce laws remained unchanged for decades.

In eight provinces, they were based upon a literalist

interpretation of the Gospel according to St. Mathew[104] and divorces through the Courts were granted almost exclusively on the basis of adultery. In two Provinces, they are based upon a literalist interpretation of the Gospel of St. Mark[105] and no divorces were granted by the Courts, although a private Bill of divorce may be granted by Parliament at Ottawa. So the concept of matrimonial relief prior to 1968 was based solely on 'fault', more vigorously the fault was 'adultery'. There was a cry here and there to increase the grounds of divorce and even judicial pressure also mounted in favour of proliferation of grounds.[106] Many members of the Canadian Parliament tried to introduce private Bills for divorce reforms but all their efforts remained futile. However, finally, in March, 1966, a special joint committee of Houses of Parliament was appointed, on the recommendations made thereto, a Bill was introduced for reform of divorce laws in December 1967 and two broad features or objects were stressed upon:

1. To salvage marriage wherever possible.
2. To give a legal burial to marriages which have died.

On December 19, 1967 it was passed by the House of Commons and by the Senate in January, 1968 to become the Divorce Act, 1968.

DIVORCE ACT, 1968

By this Act, not only grounds of divorce were extented but also introduced an element of permanent breakdown of marriage. Thus, two theories of divorce were introduced, i.e., matrimonial fault and breakdown of marriage.

Section 3 of the Act stipulates :

That the respondent since the celebration of the marriage:

---

104. "And I say to you; whoever divorces his wife, except for unchastity, and Marries another, Commits adultery" (Mathew 19.9).

105. "And he said to them, whoever divorces his wife and marries another, commits adultery against her" (Mark 10: 11).

106. *Thomas* v. *Thomas* [1945] 2 WWR 379.

(*a*) had committed adultery;

(*b*) had been guilty of sodomy, bestiality or rape or had engaged in a homo-sexual act;

(*c*) had gone through a form of marriage with another person; or

(*d*) had treated the petitioner with physical or mental cruelty of such a kind as to render intolerable the continued cohabitation of the spouses.

Section 4 of the Act stipulated additional grounds for divorce:

(*a*) that the respondent —

(*i*) was imprisoned, pursuant to his conviction for one or more offences, for a period or an aggregate period of not less than three years during the five-year period immediately preceding the presentation of the petition; or

(*ii*) was imprisoned for a period of not less than two years immediately preceding the presentation of the petition pursuant to his conviction for an offence for which he was sentenced to death or to imprisonment for a term of ten years or more, against which conviction or sentence, all rights of the respondent to appeal to a Court having jurisdiction to hear such an appeal had been exhausted;

(*b*) that respondent had, for a period of not less than three years immediately preceding the presentation of the petition, been grossly addicted to alcohol, or a narcotic as defined in the Narcotic Control Act, and there was no reasonable expectation of the respondent's rehabilitation within a reasonably foreseeable period;

(*c*) that the petitioner, for a period of not less than three years immediately preceding the presentation of the petition, had no knowledge of or information as to the whereabouts of the respondent and, throughout that period, had been unable to locate the respondent;

(*d*) that the marriage has not been consummated and the respondent, for a period of not less than one year, had been unable by reason of illness or disability to consummate the marriage, or has refused to consummate it; or

(*e*) that the spouses had been living separate and apart —

(*i*) for any reason other than that described in sub-paragraph (*ii*), for a period of not less than three years, or

(*ii*) by reason of the petitioner's desertion of the respondent, for a period of not less than five years immediately preceding the presentation of the petition.

Section 4(2) stipulates that where the existence of any of the circumstances described as above had been established, a permanent breakdown of the marriage by reason of those circumstances should be deemed to have been established.

These provisions are to be read with the bars to such relief.

According to section 9(1)(*d*) where a decree of divorce was sought pursuant to the grounds set out in section 4 of the Act, it was the duty of the Court to refuse the decree if there was a reasonable expectation that cohabitation would occur or be resumed within a reasonable foreseeable period. The Court could also refuse the decree if there were children of the marriage and the granting of the decree would prejudicially affect the making of reasonable arrangements for their maintenance.

According to section 9(1)(*f*) the relief under section 4(1)(*e*)(*i*) and (*ii*) can be circumscribed and section 9(1)(*f*) provided that where a decree of divorce was sought by reasons of circumstances described in section 4(1)(*e*), it was the duty of the Court to refuse the decree if the granting of it would be unduly harsh or unjust to other spouse, or would prejudicially affect the making of reasonable arrangements for the maintenance of either spouse.

Section 9(1)(*e*) speaks of condonation or connivance. It stipulates that on a petition for divorce it shall be the duty of the Court where a decree is sought under section 3, to satisfy itself that there has been no condonation or connivance on the part of the petitioner, and to dismiss the petition if the petitioner has condoned or connived at the act or conduct complained of unless in the opinion of the Court, the public interest would be better served by the decree.

But the concept of divorce assumed unproportionate dimensions that after a decade or so it was estimated that one out of every three marriages now ends in divorce. The following statistics of the petitions filed in 1983 speaks volumes about divorce:

| | |
|---|---|
| Adultery | 27,592 |
| Physical cruelty | 13,756 |
| Mental cruelty | 20,348 |
| Others | 210 |
| Sub Total | 61,906 |
| Marriage breakdown by reason of: | |
| Addiction to alcohol | 1,204 |
| Separation for not less than three years | 26,553 |
| Desertion by petitioner not less than five years | 1,016 |
| Others | 335 |
| Sub Total | 29,108 |
| Total | 91,204[107] |

LATER DEVELOPMENTS

Then it was found that the Canadian Divorce Act, 1968 was no longer the best way to resolve marital conflict and all cross-sections of the society echoed. The Law Reform Commission, in 1976,

107. See S.P. Khetarpal — Divorce Law in Canada — Past and Present — *Islamic and Comparative Law Quarterly*, Vol.IX (1989); Statistics Canada (Health Division) Marriage and Divorce, vital statistics Vol (ii) Chart I (Catalogue 894-205, Annual, 1985).

completed a major study of family law in Canada and made various recommendations:

(*i*) (*a*) The fault principle should be eliminated, and 'marriage breakdown' established if either spouse asserts that the marriage has failed, should be adopted as the only basis for divorce.

(*b*) The principle of 'fault' should not be used in determining economic settlements between the spouses or the custody of children.

(*c*) The purpose of maintenance awards, when granted to meet needs created by the marriage, should be to enable a formerly dependent spouse to overcome economic disadvantages and become economically self-sufficient — maintenance should not be seen as a guarantee of security for life.

(*d*) Adversarial proceedings in divorce actions should be limited.

(*e*) The interests of children should be protected in the divorce process.

(*ii*) Matrimonial property:

Each spouse should have a right to an equal share in property acquired during the marriage.

(*iii*) Unified family Courts:

(*a*) Unified Courts should be established to deal with all family law matters, including divorce.

(*b*) Adversarial proceedings in these Courts should be limited.

(*c*) Counselling and mediation services should be provided by these Courts as an alternative to the formal trial, as a method of resolving family conflict.

This recommendation and variety of pressure from all fronts, made the Liberal Government of Canada to bring a Divorce Bill on

January 19, 1984[108] which was a complete revision of the Divorce Act, 1968. The features of the Bill are:

(*i*) it proposed to make one year separation the sole ground for divorce and although proceedings could be initiated prior to one year separation having run, no decree could be granted by a Court prior to the expiry of one year period. Fault grounds would be eliminated in favour of breakdown and the defences of condonation, connivance and collusion would be abolished;

(*ii*) the old two part *decree nisi* and decree absolute process would be replaced by a provision that the order of dissolution takes effect at the expiration of a 30-day appeal period if no notice of appeal with respect to 'marriage breakdown' has been filed, provision for the order of dissolution to take effect at an earlier date if the Court is of the opinion that it would be in the public interest to do so, and the parties waive the right to appeal or any appeal taken has been abandoned;

(*iii*) a duty would have been placed on both legal advisers and the Courts to promote reconciliation and mediation of support and custody issues;

(*iv*) in addition each province would be permitted to make new rules of Court to permit the granting of divorce without the need for a trial in the traditional sense;

(*v*) the Court would be able to order maintenance for limited periods of time for spouses and children. The courts would also have increased powers in relation to custody and access including allowing grandparents to access to their grand-children.

But this Bill was, however, lost when Parliament was prorogued and the Government changed before the introduction of this Bill C-10. The new conservative Government introduced a Bill C-47

---

108. Alastair Bisset, Johnson, The Divorce Bill (1983-4), *Annual Survey of Family Law* (Published by the International Society of Family Law).

on 1st May 1985. The Bill was assented to on February 13, 1986 and came into effect on June 1, 1986.

The sole ground[109] under the Divorce Act, 1985 for granting a divorce is that there has been a breakdown of parties' marriage. Breakdown of a marriage is established if:[110]

(a) the spouses have lived separate and apart for at least one year immediately preceding the determination of the divorce proceeding and were living separate and apart at the commencement of the proceedings; or

(b) the spouse against whom the divorce proceedings is brought has since the celebration of marriage,

  (i) committed adultery, or

  (ii) treated the other spouse with physical or mental cruelty of such a kind as to render intolerable the continued cohabitation of the spouses.

Along with this, provisions for reconciliation have been provided and the Act stipulates that except where the circumstances of the case are of such nature that it would clearly not be appropriate to do so, a barrister, solicitor, lawyer or advocate acting on behalf of a spouse in a divorce proceeding must:

(a) draw to the attention of the spouses those provisions of the Divorce Act that have as their object the reconciliation of spouses [section 9(1)(*a*)].

(b) discuss with his client the possibility of the client's reconciliation with his or her spouse.

(c) inform his client of the marriage counselling or guidance facilities known to him or her that might be able to assist the spouses to achieve a reconciliation [section 9(1)(*b*)]. The above requirement was also contained in section 7(*b*) of the former Act.

---

109. Section 8(1) of the Divorce Act, 1985.

110. Section 8(2) of the Divorce Act, 1985.

(d) As per section 9(2), lawyers are required to discuss with their clients the advisability of negotiation of custody and support matters and to inform them of mediation facilities that might be able to assist them in arriving at a negotiated settlement.

As per section 9(3), the lawyer or advocate who formally commences a divorce proceeding must endorse the petition with a certificate that he has complied with these requirements.

The main provisions of the Act designed to encourage reconciliation are those which:

(i) allow a 90 days[111] trial period of cohabitation for the purpose of reconciliation without giving rise to the bar of condonation, or without interrupting the period of separation.

(ii) reduce condonation[112] from an absolute to a discretionary bar.

(iii) give the Court power to adjourn[113] the hearing of the proceedings to afford the parties an opportunity of becoming reconciled.

(iv) give the Court power to appoint[114] a qualified or suitable person to assist the parties in becoming reconciled.

(v) marriage counsellors[115] nominated by the Court to help the spouses achieve a reconciliation cannot be compelled to disclose any communication made to them in their capacity as nominee of the Court.

(vi) that evidence of any admission[116] or communication made in the course of assisting the spouses to achieve a reconciliation is inadmissible in any legal proceedings.

---

111. Section 1(3), section 8(3)(*b*) of the Divorce Act, 1985.

112. Section 11(1)(*e*) of the Act, 1985.

113. Section 10(2) of the Act, 1985.

114. Section 10(2) of the Act, 1985.

115. Section 10(4) of the Act, 1985.

116. Section 10(5) of the Act, 1985.

Along with it section15 (spousal support, child support), section 16 (custody of and access to children), section 17 (corollary relief) are never final and variable according to changed circumstances, are the consequences of divorce.

According to this Divorce Act there are twin objectives, which are designed to be achieved:

(i) To buttress, rather than to undermine the stability of marriage and

(ii) to give a burial to the dead marriage with maximum fairness and minimum bitterness. More emphasis is laid on reconciliation which shows that the chief aim is to protect as far as possible, the stability of marriage. Breakdown of marriage has been taken as a last resort. Perhaps it is also taken to mean that to save the stability of marriage in general, some marriages, with reluctance, can be broken finally. The aim is laudable but impracticable because more stress should be laid on divorce to be made harder and harder so that it may have its natural death. The concept of marriage that it is god's grace should have to be made deeply rooted, then the concept of divorce will itself lose its all potentialities. Any so-called reforms in divorce law is an indication that stability of marriage is the essence and if stress is laid that marriage is sacrament, the problem of divorce and its attendant problems shall get solved and resolved very peacefully.

**Family law in Russia**

Prior to the Revolution of 1917, there was the ecclesiastical marriage law of the orthodox church. In the trail of the revolution came a system of radical secularism and individualism. Under the Czar hegemony, a religious ceremony was indispensable for the conclusion of marriage and for divorce, jurisdiction was vested in the religious bodies and grant of divorce was almost impossible for the reason that no ground other than adultery was considerable and the procedure was extremely expensive and long drawn out duration.

After the Revolution the conclusion and termination of marriage became strictly private matters. No ceremony of any kind and no intervention of any agency was required. Perhaps this shift was in accordance with the ideas which Engels had expressed in Marxism's Classical work on the family.[117]

Then again a different situation prevailed in Russia. Marriage was required to be concluded before an official of the state and to be officially recorded and no divorce is possible without the decree of a Court. The procedure followed is:

(i) In order to obtain divorce, an application is to be made to the people's Court.

(ii) The people's Court, thereupon, shall investigate the facts and to attempt a reconciliation of the parties.

(iii) If the parties do not reconcile and if there is insistence by both the parties or either of them, the matter is certified to a Higher Court.

(iv) Then there will be hearing of the matter in the Higher Court and in order to obtain hearing the petitioner had to pay a fee of considerable magnitude which is increased with every new divorce which he seeks to obtain.

(v) The statute does not list any grounds upon the proof of which the petitioner would be entitled to a divorce. So the matter rested exclusively with the sound discretion of the Court.

Thus, this change, i.e., the reintroduction of compulsory resort to the state is connected with the readmission of individual ownership in goods of immediate use and consumption as well as in savings and the re-establishment of a system of inheritance, testate or intestate of such assets of individual ownership and in order to determine a property owner's heirs, it is necessary to have authoritative evidence of his marital status. However, the change of attitude, more appears to be tilting towards emphasis upon

117. Der ursprung der Familie, des Privateigentums und des staats, 1884.

discipline and order which has come to permeate Soviet life.[118] The trend tilting towards discipline is manifest from various writings on the subject[119] like Harold J. Berman — *Justice In Russia* (1950), Vladimir Gsovski — *Soviet Civil Law: Private Rights and their Background under the Soviet Regime 152* (1948).

So the position in Russia is:

1. Soon after the revolution the soviet union introduced the consent theory of divorce.
2. Since 1944 the theory of irretrievable breakdown of marriage was adopted
3. Reconciliation between the parties is a prerequisite.
4. Discretion of the Court has the final say.

## Family law reform in Italy

Italy, as such, was a fragmented country, having many Italian states. In 1865, Austria was driven out. In 1870 the Pope lost his temporal power. The various Italian states were no more. Mazzini, Cavour and Garibaldi had brought out a new Italy, united but not fragmented, with its ancient capital Rome.[120]

The modern Civil Code for Italy was promulgated in 1866. Instead of six different systems of law and a host of special laws, there is now one law for the whole Italy. The Italian Civil Code is modelled on and embodies many of the rules of the Roman French Code Napolean.

To the Italian Law glamour is added by the jurists, moralists and legal philosophers to make it a truly and highly scientific in character. Besides, though the Papal power declined, the canon law retained its existence but as a subsidiary law, in particular to

118. Max Rheinstein, *Trends in Marriage and Divorce Law of Western Countries* — A paper presented at the fifteenth annual Groves Conference on Marriage and Divorce held on April 22, 1952 in Durham N.C.

119. John Hazard's, *Introduction to the Volume Entitled Soviet Legal Philosophy* (1951). Fuller, *A Study in the Development of Marxian Legal Theory* - 47. Mich. L.Rev 1157 (1949).

120. Sherman, *Roman Law in the Modern World*, 3rd edn., Vol.I (1937).

the law of marriage and divorce, known as Codex Juris Canonici, effective 1918.

Dissolution of marriage by divorce is now permitted by almost every modern system of law. The Italian Law still insists on judicial separation, though dissolution of marriage by divorce is allowed and thus it indicates the survival of Cannon Law.

Before taking up the family law of Italy, the view of various authorities is desired to be looked into. It was enunciated for the first time in F. Filomusi Guelfi's *Enciclopedia giuridica* published in 1873 which has been the first 'general theory of law' ever to appear in Italy, in the same year in which A Merkel expounded the programme of the new discipline. In this publication the Hegelian formulae of the family seen as a 'Universal ethical body', making up the reproductive cell of the state seems to be the thought deeply rooted in the legal culture of the Italian ruling class in the early twentieth century.[121] In Hegel's Phenomenology of mind he considers 'the essence of the divine law of family' as a 'negative essence' which appears to be the peculiar power of the community and the force of its self-preservation. Hegel thus acknowledged in the family 'the negative law' against the 'positive law' of the state Giorgiocian observed that the custom in family relation is not equivalent to an applied law; it may be many other things . . . it may be the custom of groups which differ from one another, and each case may still differ from that of the main group.[122]

So Hegelian concept of a family enclosed in the ethical body of the state was the backbone of the Italian judicial idealism of the twentieth century.

But the work of Antonio Cicu, *Family Law a General Theory* published in 1914 is the basis and the basis of the traditional framework of the theory of positive law as a set of norms sanctioned by state power pertaining to the theory of family law as his opinion was that family differs from 'private law bodies' and is closer to

121. Vittorio Frosini, *The Hegelian Ideals and the Metamorphosis of Family Law in Italy*.

122. Giorgiocian, *Introduction to the Commentario alla riforma del Liritto di famiglia* (1977), p. 25.

public law ones, because within the family, 'duty' is predominant over 'judicial' power. However, later on said that family law does not belong to public law. It is based on public interest.

The question of a new definition of family law, outlined by Cicu in 1914 was modified a few years later by Santi Romano in his essay 'Lordinamento giuridico' the first part of which was published in 1917. Cicu propounded that it is a social law whereas Santi Ramano called that family is a primitive and autonomous juridical system, an institution which should not be looked for in state rules since it dictates its own rules and does not receive them from outer sources. However, family is considered an 'active subject of duties'.

Though M. Hauriou's name is always mentioned along with that of Romano, but according to him, family is an institution as arising from an 'idea of work or undertaking, which is implemented and lasts, within a social environment'.[123] So whether it is Hegel or Cicu or Romano, there was a great emphasis on the concept of family though viewed from different angles. For Cicu family is having an 'internal structure' as well as 'external structure'. For Romano it is a permanent institution with a wide range of forms, a juridical system which generates perfect and complete juridical obligations and for Hegel the family is autonomous although it is 'nagative essence'.

The first reform of family law, which had been included in the Code of 1865 with clear Napoleonic influence, took place right after the First World War. Act No. 1776 of July, 1919 came into force which abrogated the institute of marital authorisation to meet the new social conditions.

There came a situation when the cases of adultery or concubinage tore apart the family and the social structure was crumbling down. Then the concept of state, church and family were considered as relevant to the natural order of the society and the family was considered the main character. Thus, by the Concordat between the Church and the State of February 11, 1929, family was given the status of great consideration by which is halted the

---

123. M. Hauriou, *Tecria dell'istituzione e della foundazione*, ed. by W. Cesarini Sforza (1967).

movement of the legal transformation of the family, which had begun in 1919 and crystallised the family structure within the framework of the Catholic inspired model.[124]

So in 1930 right after the Concordat, Guiseppe Capograssi wrote *Analisi deli'esperienza comune* (1975) edited by P.Piovani, Giuffre, Milano where he said that actually both marriage and family are considered, by the juridical system, as a real practice of sacrifice, the endless requirement for an individual to give up his desire for licentiousness and vagrancy as well as his repugnance to being held captive within the net of duties and responsibilities. But his words were unheeded at that time.

However, family did get a legal image and a report on family law was submitted to the first Italian Law Congress held in Rome in October, 1932. According to this report, the family is the fundamental nucleus of the national society and as such, its moral and material aspects should be reinforced, safeguarded and its most sublime expressions guaranteed.

The family must be revitalised and strengthened by the sound and intimate contact with the best and most stable currents of lineage; such currents start off from the most remote motives of history and head towards goals set by destiny.[125]

In 1936, G.B. Funaioli speaking about Civil Law in the University of Pisa said that tradition is the only and the Supreme Warrant confronting changes in law, when any sharp variation may be dangerous; especially within the family, a naturally static institution, more eternal than any other one, amidst the changing pace of social life and its systems. So there is a caution for the law-makers while dealing with the social changes in the perspective of the institution of the family.

Although the code had not yet been modified, in 1940 in Pisa the project for a 'Chapter of Law' was submitted at a Congress of Jurists. The project stated that 'the family is the fundamental nucleus of the national society. The unity, moral and economic stability of the fmaily are symptoms of the strength of the nation.

124. C. Cardia, *IP diritto di famiglia in Italia*, 1975.

125. G. Grisostomi, Marini — *Report on IL diritto di famiglia* (1932).

The state accepts the religious character of the establishment of the family structure; it makes up its patrimony; establishes the bodies of family power, controls their activity and; whenever they are lacking, it replaces them.

A shift in the trend had taken place in the second half of the century. There has been a process of interpretation of family law norms from the standpoint of private law. The essay written by Michele Giorgianni in 1956 is an evident example of it.[126] Lorenze Compagna wrote in 1966.

> The protection of the legitimate family is not seen by the present system, as the only acceptable form; therefore, nothing forbids us to accept situations other than that of the legitimate family, which represents, however, the qualification, the dignity and the protection of the family .... Legitimate family, natural family and adoptive family may thus co-exist.[127]

Another tendency towards change in the family structure took place on December 1, 1970 with the enforcement of the Act No. 898, on the dissolution of marriage. However, the Italian Act on the new family law, issued on May 19, 1975 marks a necessary stage. This Act records the basic changes which occurred within the family system, giving them the claims of legitimacy. Yet, each article of the law represents the fact of a different social reality. So a review of some of the Articles of the Italian Civil Code will throw a flood of light on the family system.

(i) Law of Italy provided only for judicial separation without dissolution of the bond of matrimony in agreement with the Catholic doctrine of the indissolubility of marriage. The divorce law thus enacted is against the determined objection of the Catholic Church.[128]

(ii) Marriage may be entered into in either form, religious

---

126. M. Giorgianni, *Problemi attuali di diritto familiare* (1956).

127. L. Compagna, *Famiglia Legittima e famiglia adottiva*, 1966.

128. Codice Civile, Articles 149-158.

marriage or civil marriage according to the wishes of the parties.[129]

(iii) The rights and duties of the spouses are euqal. They have to respect and assist each other and act in the interest of the family.[130]

(iv) There is a judicial separation by mutual consent of the spouses or at the petition of one or both spouses. Judicial separation on the petition of one or both spouses is based on the sole ground of insupportability.[131]

(v) Italian law does not require any term of living apart for a decree of judicial separation and it may be decreed at any time. Italian law makes judicial separation by mutual consent or on the ground of insupportability, a precondition for divorce.[132]

(vi) Italian Civil Code explains in detail the mistakes as to the personal qualities of the other spouse which affects the giving of consent.[133]

(vii) The waiting period in Italian law is five, six or seven years. Thus, Italian law is only a mild remedial statute.[134]

(viii) Law No. 151 of May 19, 1975 had reformed the law of December 1, 1970 to the extent to fulfil the better expectations of present-day society and an attempt at the secularisation of the canonical marriage.

Though, everywhere the efforts are there to come out of the stranglehold of the canonical law and there is an attempt towards secularisation of family law, but one thing is glaringly apparent that the religious touch connected with marriage is still there. It is

---

129. Codice Civile, Articles 82-4, 106.

130. *Ibid.*, Articles 143-148.

131. *Ibid.*, Article 150.

132. *Ibid.*, Articles 150-1 & Law No. 898 of December 1, 1970, section 3 (2)(*b*).

133. *Ibid.*, Articles 117-129.

134. Law No. 898 of December 1, 1970 on dissolution of marriage, Article 3(2)(*b*).

only that the doctrine of indissolubility has been given a go bye under certain circumstances to be determined judicially and the concept of stability of marriage is still intact. This is why the divorce has been taken as a necessary evil and not a desire of the society to be fulfilled.

**Law of divorce in Greece**

The new Act of Family Law, Act No. 1250/1982 was implemented on February 18, 1983. Until 1982 the religious marriage ceremony was the only way of creating a marriage recognised in Greece. Article 1367 of Family Law and Court decisions had made a religious ceremony a condition of the existence of marriage. This ceremony was also required for Greek nationals marrying outside Greece, though it was contrary to the constitutional provision of religious freedom.[135] Thus, a change occurred by which the Greek orthodox Church, as well as any other religion recognised in Greece is allowed to establish its own rules to be followed when marriages are created under their rituals. So also an institution of civil marriage as an alternative form of creating marriage, also came into picture outside Greece if such marriage has taken place and considered valid.

The new Greek Law on divorce made two basic reforms:

1. Irretrievable breakdown of marriage.
2. Divorce by mutual consent.

The irretrievable breakdown of marriage was objective in character. It tried to balance the tendency towards the establishment of the objective breakdown of the marriage and the tendency of maintaining element of fault. In other words, fault principle is the objective breakdown. Thus, fault became the latent factor in the cause of divorce or in the cause of breakdown. So breakdown of marriage is the object and fault is the cause. It may be, the fault of one or both of the spouses. But here 'cause' has been taken in wider concept than fault. It may include acts other than fault. So cause includes:

1. Principle of fault.

135. Greek Constitution, Article 13 (1975).

2. Other situations bringing in breakdown.

So adultery, bigamy, desertion, and an attempt on the life of the spouse constitute presumption of breakdown.[136] Now these are the situations which coincide with fault. They were previously the grounds for divorce prior to the new Act. Now they are the grounds presumed to be the cause of breakdown.

This new Act brought in the new concept of divorce by mutual consent. Though this concept was vogue in practice but excluded by law until the reform was brought in. The new legislation recognised it officially. Previously the divorce was de-dramatised, unless conflicts are avoided and the law is protected from falling into contempt and there were divorces by latent mutual consent.[137]

But for divorce by mutual consent, three conditions were a prerequisite:

1. The marriage must have lasted at least one year before the divorce action is brought.
2. The spouses' agreement to divorce must be declared twice before Court in two Court sessions with at least a six months period between them.
3. If the spouses have common minor children, they must submit to the Court a written agreement for the custody and the right of communication with them.

However, divorce by mutual consent is delayed for seven further months, at which point the decision becomes irrevocable.[138] This period of seven months is basically meant for the public prosecutor's right either to exercise an appeal or to waive or not to waive this right.

Thus, the new Act discloses many factors:

---

136. Civil Code Article, 1439 II.

137. George Koumantos and Christine Stambelu — Greece. "Digesting the New Family Law" — *Journal of Family Law*, Vol. 28 (1989-90).

138. See *Family Law* 1, Article 1441, Clause 3.1.4.3.7. See Also Civil Code, Article 1438.

1. The fault theory has been given a go-bye but the principle of fault was kept intact as a cause for breakdown.
2. Divorce by mutual consent was brought in to avoid the contempt to which law is sure to fall.
3. In reality, the trend, as in other countries, has shifted from the fault theory to the breakdown theory, which means that the stability of marriage must be preserved unless it gets reduced to a mere empty shell and the theory of divorce by mutual consent is to save the spouses from the trials and tribulations of the long drawn out legal procedure.

## Divorce in Jewish law

Marriage in Judaism is neither sacrament nor civil contract *per se*. It is not viewed as an 'outward sign of inward and divine grace, yet it is respected as a sacred institution'.[139] Though Judaism frowns on celibate life yet it does not regard marriage as a concession to mortal weakness. The Hebrew religion sees no conflict between man's duty to his family and man's duty to his God. In Judaism marriage is positively not looked from an angle of contract but from a socio-moral percepts. This is why we find the highest values of purity, sanctity and stability vested in Jewish family. So basically there are two concepts in marriage looked conclusively from the traditional, moral and religious concept such as procreation and co-habitation. Procreation, though contains an element of sex, but is not exclusively based on the foundation of sexuality and co-habitation is a perfect harmony based on unflinching love and affection. The first injunction in the *Bible* to man and woman is: 'Be fruitful and multiply'.[140] We find further that 'it is not good that the man should be alone; I will make a helpmate for him'.[141] These two biblical ordinances amply speak of procreation and cohabitation based on righteous conduct and smells fragrance of morality. Besides, various essential elements in a traditional Jewish wedding

---

139. Dr. Isreal T.Naamani, *Marriage and Divorce in Jewish Law — Journal of Family Law* Vol. I, p. 177.
140. Genesis, 1:27.
141. Genesis, 2:18.

ceremony, there is a marriage contract not to be confused with any materialistic contract, called 'Ketubah'. It stipulates the bride's rights and the groom's obligations. It is drawn up in Aramaic and is read at the marriage ceremonies by the *rabbi*. The document must bear the signatures of two competent witnesses. The most important sentences are:

> Be thou my wife according to the law of Moses and Israel, and I will work for thee, honour, support, and maintain thee in accordance with the custom of Jewish husbands who work for their wives, honour, support and maintain them in truth . . . the bridegroom has taken upon himself the responsibility for all the obligations of this ketubah, as is customary with other ketubot made for the daughters of Israel in accordance with the institution of the sages — may their memory be for a blessing.

This being the nature of marriage clothed in religious and moral fabric, how then divorce intervenes to shatter the marriage. Talmud proclaims poignantly:

> He who divorces the wife of his youth — even the temple altar sheds tears for him.[142]

Now let us scan the various grounds of divorce before making general comments on it. It is divided into five categories.

AT THE SUIT OF EITHER PARTY

1. *Physical incapacity to cohabit*: The Court could compel the incapable spouse to consent to a 'get'.[143]

2. *Refusal to cohabit*: The unwilling spouse could be compelled to divorce at suit of the other.[144]

3. *Apostasy*: If the wife became converted the husband could send her a 'get' without her consent, while if he became an

---

142. The biblical passage is 'Man shall cleave to his wife and they shall be as one flesh.

143. See Nedarim 91; Middah 12; E.H. 54, 7: 117, 71.

144. Ketubot 63.

apostate, the Jewish Court would even enlist the aid of Gentile authorities to compel him to give a bill of divorce.[145]

4. Ten[146] years of childless marriage upon the petition of either spouse. According to the Talmud the husband should be compelled by the Court to divorce a barren wife after ten years of marriage. But during the period of the Posekim, Courts ceased to enforce such compulsory divorce,[147] and R. Moses Isserles doubted that in his time (1520-72) either party could be compelled to divorce on this ground.[148]

5. Breaches[149] of observances of the 'Religion of Moses', by either spouse which caused the other to sin, were a ground at the suit of such other party.

AT THE SUIT OF HUSBAND ONLY

6. Indecent[150] and brazen conduct by the wife in breach of the 'Jewish religion', not to speak of immoral and promiscuous behaviour, was a ground for which she might forfeit all of her Ketubah, besides being compelled to accept a 'get'.

AT THE SUIT OF THE WIFE ONLY

7. *Loathsome disease*: She could demand a 'get' if her husband had contracted a disease like leprosy which made cohabitation disgusting, but not if he suffered physical infirmity, even though it be serious, like the loss of an arm, a leg or an eye, since such defects did not usually render cohabitation repulsive.[151]

---

145. TUR E.H. 134, Bet Joseph.
146. Ketubot 77b, Yevamot 64.
147. E.H. 1,3; 154, 6, 10.
148. TUR, ib., Darke Moshe.
149. M. Ketubot VII, 6, Ketubot 72; E.H. 115, 1; 154, 1 REMA.
150. M. Ketubot ib; Ketubot 72, E.H. 115, 4, 5.
151. Ketubot 77, M.T. Marriage XXV; E.H. 154, 118, 11 REMA.

8. *Malodorous occupation*: Occupations like tanning, etc., which made the husband's person disgusting.[152]

9. The husband's licentiousness.[153]

10. *Cruelty*: Harsh treatment like wife beating,[154] and even mental cruelty. Thus, unreasonable restrictions on her freedom of movement, like preventing her from attending weddings, funerals and similar social celebrations entitled her to a 'get'.

11. *Non-support*[155]: After the Court had been unsuccessful in finding and attaching any property of the husband to be applied to her support, or in compelling him to work to that end, the wife could demand a 'get'.

BY THE COURT AGAINST THE WISHES OF THE PARTIES

In cases where the 'Kiddushin' took effect, but the marriage was forbidden by law, the Court would compel the parties to divorce. Such were, for instance: Incestuous Unions of the second degree (Rabbinical incest), marriage with a 'mamzer',[156] marriage of a Jew with a non-Jew,[157] marriage of an adulteress with her paramour.[158]

BY MUTUAL CONSENT[159]

If both parties agree to divorce, it was to be granted. The Court was not required to investigate or seek proof of the wrongful conduct and to hold any of the spouse to be the 'offender'. The Court, however, is to look for:

1. That both parties should be acting with full knowledge and without fraud or duress.

---

152. M. Ketubot VII, 10.
153. E.H. 134, 1 REMA.
154. E.H. 154, 3 REMA.
155. Ketubot 77; E.H. 154, 3.
156. M. Yevamot VIII, 3.
157. Avodah Zarah 36b.
158. M. Yevamot II, 8.
159. George Horowitz, *The Spirit of Jewish Law*, (1963), p. 277.

2. That minor children, if any, be provided for.

3. That property rights of the parties, especially the wife be fairly and honestly adjudged.

4. That proper formalities be observed of the divorce, so that no doubt could be cast on the validity of divorce. The 'Get' is a bill of divorce, signed by two witnesses and is examined by the *rabbi* and it is sufficient that the 'get' be placed in the wife's possession or within her reach, provided she knew its import and contents.

The contents briefly are:

> I do release thee[160] and send thee away, and put thee aside, that thou mayest have permission and control over thyself, to go to be married to any man that thou mayest desire; and none shall hinder thee from this day forever more; and thou are permitted to any man, and this shall be unto thee from me a bill of dismissal, a document of release, and a letter of freedom, according to the law of Moses and Israel.

After the 'get' and going through the procedural formalities, and after satisfaction the Court shall issue a certificate of the nature:

> We,[161] the undersigned Court, having ascertained and clearly established, that the whole proceeding with respect to the aforementioned 'get' was done properly and in conformity with the ordinance of the sages, have torn the aforementioned get . . . "Behold, she is permitted to any man . . . " What transpired before us on such and such a date we have written and sealed here at such a place, and given this judicial record to her, such a one to serve her as proof.

As can be seen Jewish Law shows a frank acknowledgement that a marriage has failed or not successful and as marriage in Judaism is not sacrament but positively a religio-moral expression, the

---

160. M.T. Divorce IV, 12.

161. Asher Gulak, *Treasury of Shetars (in Hebrew) Jerusalem* 1926 No. 80, p. 77.

rabbinic authorities thought it not irrational to continue the bond where amicable and harmonious living is not possible. The sages of the Talmud gave a spiritual message that

> one who loves his wife more than he loves himself and honours his wife more than he honours himself, he can be sure that peace and harmony will reign in his house.[162]

Thus, the concept of love and affection in matrimonial home is the essence of marriage failing it will be a flower without fragrance.

The most important thing in divorce is 'unseemly thing' in the woman. Talmudic scholars interpreted it differently. One school of thought called it 'things of indecency' or sexual immorality. The other school of thought called it 'any case of incompatibility'. The above-said grounds of divorce speak of 'any case of incompatibility'. Thus, indirectly it leads to the clear conclusion that the harmony of the marital life cannot be allowed to shatter. Let not the dead body be exposed to stink, let it be given a decent burial.

But the grant of divorce is not that easy. The procedure is highly technical. Preparation of 'get' is fool proof. Rabbinic and orthodox law in matrimonial matters is still dominating and the passing of Women's Equal Rights Law in 1951 has made divorce difficult and the husband has to think twice before venturing. So in Judaism procreation and morals are the ornaments of the matrimonial home and if at all divorce is resorted to, it is to save the beauty of the matrimonial home and not influenced by a change in the outlook in the society.

## Divorce and Muslim law

Prior to Prophet Muhammad, divorce was frequently prevalent on the soil of Arabia. It was very easy process and no rule was to govern the divorce. The women were treated as chattel of the husband like other goods. Therefore, husband was to be the lord for the wife. She could be divorced at any time without assigning any reason. Arbitrarily and haphazardly, women could be divorced. Polygamy was everywhere welcomed by the Arabians, so that they can marry more than one wife and at any time they could divorce. Limit of

162. Yevamot 62b.

marriage and divorce was not controlled by any law or religion in Pre-Islamic Arabia.[163]

So the condition of women in Pre-Islamic Arabia was the worst. It is said that women were called 'devil's whip' and those among the new born girls who could escape the barbarous custom of female infanticide had to face throughout their lives all kinds of social indignities.[164] So there was a barbarous society and there was no notion of law. It was the period of 'Jahilliya' or the period of ignorance or dark period in the history of the Arabs as the tribes there being nomads, they were wandering from place to place. Their main business was to wage war, enjoy woman and wine. Thus, the society had no notion of womanhood.

Then came a change. Mohammed Sahib at the age of forty saw the celestial light by which he was enlightened with divine wisdom and was ordained by the Almighty to reform the sinful society and to refrain the people from committing derogatory practices and the divinely enlightened Holy Prophet, who was aghast with the pitiable condition of the women who were considered as mere chattels, worse than even animals, brought some revolutionary changes to ameliorate the condition of women to give them an honoured and exalted status in the society and such reforms of Holy Prophet marked a departure in the History of Eastern civilisation.[165] What Holy Prophet gave a divine message to the people who flocked around him and embraced his utterances and enshrined in their hearts is that Islam speaks of sex equality. It declares that all human beings are equal. Islam does not regard women in any way inferior to men. Men and women come from the same root. They are branches of the same tree.

The *Holy Korān* Says:[166]

O man kind-reverence
your Guardian-Lord

---

163. A.P. Nagore, *Mohammedan Law*.

164. Dr. Tahir Mahmood, *Womanhood in Islam*.

165. Ameer Ali, *Treatise on Mohammedan Law*, Vol.II, 472.

166. Lessons in Islam — Series V — *Marriage, Divorce and Sex in Islam*, pub. by S.H. Muhammad Ashraf, Kashnari Bazar, Lahore (Pakistan).

who created you
From a single person,
Created, of like nature,
His mate, and from them twain
Scattered (like seeds)
countless men and women — IV: 1

When Islam appeared in Arabia, it changed the condition and position of women. It stopped the practice of burying fremale children alive and declared that women should be treated with honour and respect. The *Holy Korān* declares[167] about women thus:

They are your garments (cover)
AND Ye are their garments.

In other words, as a garment gives warmth, protection and decency, so a husband and wife offer each other intimacy, comfort and protection from committing any acts considered undesirable by the society or religion. So Korānic teaching speaks of respect and dignity for woman as much as for man. The word garment can also be taken to mean that man's honour is defended and safeguarded by women and vice-versa. Even *Korān* has discarded the view held by those who consider woman as a sub-human creature and that it is a shame to have a female child. The *Holy Korān* clearly removes that misunderstanding that women in Islam have no right. It says:[168]

And women shall have rights
Similar to the rights
Against them according
To what is equitable

Islam believes in both rights and obligations. In a Muslim society a man has full responsibility for the maintenance of his family. It is not only a moral but also a legal obligation. Anything a wife earns is her own to dispose of, either to use it herself or to contribute it to the family budget if she wishes. She is responsible for the care of her home and welfare of the family. The best role that has been given to the woman is to keep the marital tie intact and strong for which the husband has been considered responsible for running

167. *Sura*, II : 187.

168. *Sura*, II : 228.

the affairs of the family and to assist him, she has to obey him even if his judgement is not correct except that his judgement does not go beyond the limits of Islam. This is the meaning of obedience in the context of marriage in Islam. So the loyalty of both to each other is the obedience of the Highest Law. This is how it is said in *Korān*:[169]

> Men are maintainers of women with the bounties which god has bestowed more abundantly on some of them than on others; and with what they may spend out of their possessions.

Regarding women, Prophet has said:[170]

> The best woman is she, who, when you see her you feel pleased and when you direct her she obeys. She protects your rights and keeps her chastity when you are absent.

*Korān* is the first source of Islamic Law which has given an exalted position to women along with duties for the happiness of the husband and physical and spiritual development of the children. Her endeavour is to make her family's life sweet and joyful and the home a place of security and peace. How much importance is given to woman can be perceived in the Arabic proverb: '*al-ummur madrasatun*' meaning, 'the mother is a school'. Duties of a woman should not be considered in the negative aspect as heaps of burden is cast on the shoulders and head of a woman. Out of obedience to duty shall flow the rights, that is the concept enshrined in Islam.

Even the next source of Law, i.e., 'Sunna' speaks in the same glorifying tone. Ibu Abbas[171] reports that the holy prophet said:

> If a daughter is born to a man and he brings her up affectionately, shows her no disrespect and treats her in the same manner as he treats his sons, the Lord will reward him with Paradise. — *Kanz-ul-Ummal*

---

169. *Sura*, IV : 34.
170. B. Aisha Lemu and Fatima Heeran, *Woman in Islam* (Delhi).
171. *Kanz-ul-Ummal*.

According to another report from Anas Bin Malik[172] the prophet said:

> Girls are a model of affection and sympathy and blessing to the family. If a person has one daughter, Allāh will screen him from the fire of hell owing to his daughter. If he has two daughters, *Allāh will make him* free of the duty of charity and *jihād*. — *Kanz-ul-ummal*

According to another saying:[173] The prophet has said:

> If a daughter is born to a person and he brings her up, gives her good education and trains her in the arts of life, I shall myself stand between him and the hell fire.

Another saying of the Prophet is:[174]

> A person who has a female slave with him and takes steps to give her sound eduction and trains her in arts and culture and then frees her and marries her, will be given a double reward.

Thus, the status of women in Islam is an honoured one and highly exalted. Not only that, from spiritual point of view women had status in no way inferior to men. The *Holy Korān* states categorically that men and women who practise the principles of Islam will receive equal reward. There are five pillars of Islam, i.e., Belief, Prayer, Fasting, Poor-due (Charity) and Pilgrimage. Each is as important for women as for men and there is no differentiation for their reward. A few of the verses of *Holy Korān* will illustrate this point:

> To men
> is alloted what they earn.
> AND to women what they earn.[175]

> If any do deeds
> of righteousness

172. *Kanz-ul-Ummal*. See also in this regard what Abu Huraira the Companion of Prophet says in the same tone.

173. Says Abdullah Ibu Masud.

174. Bukhari in *Kitab-un-Nikah*.

175. *Sura*, IV : 32.

Be they male or female
And have faith,
They will enter heaven,
And not the least injustice
will be done to them.[176]

Surely[177] for men who submit (to God) and for women who submit (to God), for believing men and believing women, for devout men and devout women, for truthful men and truthful women, for steadfast men and steadfast women, for humble men and humble women, for charitable men and charitable women, for men who fast and women who fast, for men who guard their chastity and women who guard, for men who remember god much and for women who remember — for them god has prepared forgiveness and a mighty reward.

Whosoever[178] performs good deeds, whether male or female and is a believer, we shall surely make him live a good life, and we will certainly reward them for the best of what they did.

The noblest[179] among you before God is the most heedful of you.

So if we go by the *Holy Korān* and Sunna, the preachings of Holy Prophet, we come to one and only one conclusion that in Islam the woman holds a very high position, as a child, a wife and a mother. Practices adoped by men, whereby they disregarded women, are contrary to the teachings of the Prophet and contrary to the divine law. The Holy Prophet laid great stress on marriage and family of which woman is the centre. She is the essence of the family which in turn is the foundation of society and the role of woman is positively understood as the greatest.

---

176. *Sura*, IV : 124.
177. *Sura*, XXXIII : 35.
178. *Sura*, XVI : 97.
179. *Sura*, XLIX : 13.

## MARRIAGE IN ISLAM

The structure of Islamic family rests on the following four pillars:[180]

1. Family life as a cradle of human society providing a secure, healthy and encouraging home for parents and growing children.
2. Family life as guardian of the natural erotic desires of men and women, leading this powerful urge into wholesome channels.
3. Family life as the very breeding place for human virtues like love, kindness, mercy.
4. Family life as the most secure refuge against inward and outward troubles.

So, in the light of such concept, Islam looks upon marriage as a sacred, social need and makes it a duty for every man and woman to get married unless he or she is physically unfit or has other important reasons for not marrying. The *Korān* advises the Muslim males to enter into marriage with good women whose moral conduct is good.

Except for these, all others
Are lawful, provided
Ye seek (them in marriage)
with gifts from your property
Desiring chastity not lust.[181]

This day are (all things)[182]
good and pure made lawful
unto you. The food
of the people of the Book
Is lawful unto you
And yours is lawful

180. B Aisha Lemu & Fatima Heeran, *Woman in Islam* — a paper read in The International Islamic Conference held in London from 3rd to 12th April, 1976.

181. *Sura*, IV : 24.

182. *Sura*, V : 6.

unto them
(Lawful unto you in marriage)
Are (not only) chaste women.
Who are believers, but
Chaste women among
The people of the Book
Revealed before you time,
When Ye given them
Their due dowers and desires
Chastity not lewdness.

Coupled with it some glimpses of Sunna[183] reveal the sacredness of marriage. Prophet says:

> It is necessary for you to marry, because marriage is a protection against the wickedness of the sight. If one of you can not marry them let him fast.
>
> Marriage is a sacred duty and whoever dislikes this way of life is not of me.
>
> When a man got married,[184] he has made his Islam half perfect. Then let him fear Allāh for the remaining half.

The reflections, that emanate from the above cited Korānic verses and the *hadith*, show that in Islam marriage is a sacred contract. It is a life-long contract provided the spouses remain within the bounds of Allāh. Kind treatment of wives and families is a part of the religion in Islam. The Prophet has said,

> From among the believers are those who have the kindest disposition and are kindest to their families, such are thoswe who show most perfect faith

and according to another

> *Hadith* the best among you are those who are kindest to their wives.[185]

---

183. Bhukhari.

184. Baihaqi.

185. B. Aisha Lemu and Fatima Heeran, *Women in Islam*.

Even the treatment expected from the husband whether or not he is on good terms with his wife, is clearly laid down in the *Korān* thus:

> Live with them in kidness;[186] even if you dislike them, perhaps you dislike something in which God has placed much good.

Thus, marriage in Islam, though called by many as pure and simple contract[187] which does not appear sound, is a solemn and sacred contract, Dr. Jung observes that Muslim marriage is like civil contract as well as devotional act. Sir Abdul Rahim said that the institution of marriage part-takes both the nature of *ibādat* or devotional acts and *muāmalāt* or dealings among men.

So much so that Mr. Justice Varghese Kalliath along with Mr. Justice Bhaskaran Nambiar in *Amina* v. *Hassan Koye*.[188] Considered the concept of marriage under three broad headings namely, Legal, Social and Religious. Juristically his Lordship observed that it may be contract as opposed to a sacrament, but it cannot be considered as a contract pure and simple to be governed exclusively by the provisions of the contract Act. Rules to be applied for interpreting a Muslim marriage are not exclusively confined and cabined within the four walls of the general statutes like Contract Act and Allied Acts. It is always to be understood and interpreted in the light of the personal laws of the parties and the ethic content and ethos of the institution of marriage, as popularly understood by the Muslims of the country.

Their Lordships further said that sacred *Korān* does not treat marriage as ordinary contract. There is well-known adage attributed to the holy Prophet that there is no monkery in Islam and this adage reveals the attitude of Prophet Mohammed towards celibacy very briefly but adequately. Marriage[189] in Islam is a solemn pact between a man and a woman though it takes the form of a contract and holy prophet did describe *nikāh* as his *sunnat* and every Muslim knows the sacred socio-religious significance of *sunnat* as recognised

186. *Sura*, IV : 19
187. See *Abdul Kadir* v. *Salima* [1886] 8 All 149 (FB) and AIR 1934 Cal 693.
188. 1985 CrLJ 1996. See also [1933] 55 ILR All 742.
189. Dr. Tahir Mahmood as cited in 1985 CrLJ, 1996.

by the Muslim religion. Though the great scholars[190] of Islam called marriage as an institution for the protection of society so that human beings may guard themselves from foulness and unchastity yet there is another extreme view[191] that Marriage among Muhammadans is not a sacrament but purely a civil contract. But it clearly appears that the definition given by Abdur Rahim is the most balanced one that marriage is both an *ibādat* and *muāmlāt*. These two words take in its ambit the concept of marriage in totality wherein the sacredness of marriage is inherently present. Sir Shah Mohd. Sulaiman C.J. in *Anis Begam* v. *Mohd Istafa*[192] observed that it may not be out of place to mention that Maulvi Samiullah collected some authorities showing that a marriage is not regarded as a mere civil contract but as a religious sacrament. A good deal of religious inspiration regarding marriage can be derived from what is stated in *Korān*.[193]

The concepts of *ijāb* and *qubūl* and *bulugh*[194] merely speak of consent and capacity and discretion which even are prescribed in Hindu Law. Such standards fixed by religion or law cannot be driven to the extreme that marriage is a contract and to be covered by the Contract Act. No doubt, indissolubility of marriage is provided but at what point of time and under what circumstances is a moot point to be pondered but in the light of the stability of marriage which Islam not only believed in but also ordained as per Korānic verses.

## DIVORCE IN ISLAM

Among the Arabs, the power of divorce at the disposal of the husband was unlimited and arbitrary. They recognised no rule of humanity or justice. The Prophet was aghast with this shameful state of affairs. With the enlightenment of the divine light, he set on a path to lead the uncultured and barbarous society to a religiously oriented civilised society and in reality all his reforms smell only spiritualism and for him woman is a foundation of the human society and in her

190. *See* Ameer Ali.
191. Justice Mahmood in *Kadir* v. *Salima* [1886] 8 All 149.
192. [1933] 55 ILR All 742.
193. *Sura*, IV : 1.
194. Offer, acceptance, majority.

protection lies the salvation of mankind and humanity. Thus, for the Holy Prohpet the object of marriage is that man and woman when tied together by *nikāh* shall live together in peace and happiness and raise a family for promoting the good of the society. But if husband and wife cannot live in peace and if they cannot co-operate in the affairs of home and the training of the children it is better the parties may separate. If they are still compelled to live together by law or the pressure of public opinion, not only will they remain unhappy, but the children will also suffer.

Therefore, Islam has given the right of divorce to both husband and wife. However, it has been emphasised that the right of divorce should be exercised only in exceptional cases when no other way is left open and all methods of making peace between husband and wife had failed. This approach shows that the true Islamic law in fact stood for what is known as the 'breakdown theory of divorce'.[195] Even Holy Prophet was not happy with it. All[196] his recorded sayings show that he looked upon the custom of divorce with extreme disapproval and considered its practice as calculated to undermine the foundations of the society. He[197] repeatedly declared that nothing pleased God more than emancipation of slaves and nothing displeased him more than divorce. He[198] unequivocally declared divorce to be the worst of all permitted things (*abghad-ul-muliāhat*).

The noble object of Holy Prophet, 'of all the things which have been permissible to men, divorce is the most hated by Allāh' and 'And their husbands have greater right to take them back in the period, if they wish for reconciliation' is reflected from Korānic verses and the *Hadith*.

And if you fear that they may not be able to keep[199] the limits of Allāh, then there is no sin for either of them, if the woman redeems herself with that.

195. Dr. Thir Mahood, *The Muslim Law of India*, 1980, p. 95.

196. Mir Mehrajuddin, Divorce under Islamic Law, *Cochin University Law Review*, p. 315.

197. Syed Ameer ali, Mohammedan Law, *Tagore Law Lectures*, 1929, pp. 7-9.

198. Dr. Tahir Mahmood, *The Muslim Law of India*, 1980, p. 95. See also Peer Mohammed Ebrahim, *Light, Knowledge, Truth, Family Life in Islam*, 1973, pp. 99-100.

199. *Sura*, II.229.

> If ye take a dislike to them,[200]
> It may be that ye dislike
> A thing, and God brings about,
> Through it a great deal.
>
> As for those from who[201]
> ye fear rebellion,
> admonish them and banish them
> to beds apart and then scourage them
> Then if they obey you
> seek not a way against them
> Lo! Allāh is ever high, Exalted, Great.
>
> And if ye fear a breach between them twain[202] (the man and wife), appoint an arbiter from his folk and an arbiter from her folk. If they desire amendment, Allāh will make them of one mind. Lo Allāh is ever knower, Aware.

Besides, there are some reports what holy Prophet has said:[203]

> Allāh does not like men and women who want to live for enjoying sexual pleasure and ask for divorce to seek pleasure.
>
> Allāh has cursed men and women who make use of divorce freely to enjoy sexual pleasure.
>
> The prophet of Allāh said, A woman who seeks divorce from her husband without any excess or injustice on his part will be cursed by Allāh and his angels.

So the Prophet pronounced *talāka* to be a most detestable thing before the Almighty God of all permitted things. If *talāka* is given without any reasons, it is stupidity and ingratitude to God.[204]

---

200. *Sura*, IV.19.
201. *Sura*, IV.34.
202. *Sura*, IV.35.
203. As said by Abu Dawud.
204. Ameer Ali, *Treatise on Mohammedan Law*, Vol.2, 5th edn., p. 472.

To quote Ammer Ali:[205]

> The law gives to the man primarily the power of dissolving the marriage if the wife, by her indocility or her bad character, renders the married life unhappy; but in the absence of serious reasons no Muslim can justify a divorce either in the eyes of religion or the law. If he abandons his wife or puts her away from simple caprice, he draws upon himself the divine anger, for 'the curse of God', said the Prophet, rests on him who repudiates his wife capriciously.

Even if we look to the various forms of divorce like *ahsāna*, it is a procedure which is and can be called a course prescribed for conciliation. It is an opportunity of *locus penitentiae*. Dr. Tahir Mahmood has referred[206] to the great Indian scholar of Islamic Law, Maulana Ashraf Ali Thanvi thus:

> A person pronounces a revocable Talaq. He then reconciles and resume cohabitation. Two or four years later, under provocation, he once gain pronounces a revocable Talaq. On recovering provocation, he again resume cohabitation. Now two Talaqs are over. Hereafter, whenever he pronounces a Talaq, it will be counted as a third Talaq which will dissolve the marriage forthwith and should a remarriage be desired by the parties, necessitates 'Halala'.

There is another form of *talāka* called *talāka-ul-bidāt*,[207] which came into being during the second century of Islam when Ommayyad monarchs endeavoured to find an escape from the strictness of law of divorce and found a loophole to effect their purpose. The neologic procedure of divorce is the one that contravenes the provisions of the *sunnat*.[208] In this form three pronouncements are made in a single *tuhr* either in one sentence or three sentences. The Holy

---

205. Ameer Ali refers to Ibrahim Halebi — author of Multeka.

206. Dr. Tahir Mahmood, *The Muslim Law of India*, 1980.

207. Firasat Ali and Furqan Ali, *Divorce in Mohammedan Law: The Law of Triple Divorce*, 1983.

208. Peer Mohammed Ebrahim, *Light, Knowledge, Truth*, Five Schools of Islamic Fiqa, Vol. 3, (1976) p. 87.

Prophet has very severely denounced this practice.[209]

Very recently, the judgement of the Lucknow Bench of the High Court of Allahabad delivered by Mr. Justice Harinath Tilhari on the concept of triple *talāka* that any customary or codified law if it perpetuated against the dignity of women and ran counter to the fundamental duty of the citizen, could not be deemed to be operative in a case of conflict between the constitutional provisions and the customary or codified law. In that case the constitution would prevail. He held that giving divorce at one sitting by uttering *talāka* thrice was illegal and unconstitutional.

This judgement created a stir as expected from the acute fundamentalists and the sober thinking Muslims like Asghar Ali Engineer in his Article[210] 'Talaq and Male Ego' has said that abolition of triple *talāka* will set a healthy trend. It would be wise for the Muslim Personal Law Board to take an early initiative in the matter and draft a law.

Dr. Tahir Mohamood reacting to the attitude adopted by the Muslim fundamentalists warned that whatever else one may say on the subject, a plea the Muslim Law is not justiciable at all in a Civil Court because it is foreign law, could have serious repercussions. The Indian Legal System recognised Muslim Law as part of the *lex loci* and it was as much a part of the law in this country as the Hindu Marriage Act.[211]

Thus in short, the Holy Prophet spoke of two things:

1. Reconciliation is a must which be preached both in theory and practice.

2. If reconciliation fails as marriage ceased to be a source of love and happiness, it is better to part.

Thus, as compared to the Pre-Islamic Arabia, divorce lost its arbitrariness and has become a scarce commodity resorted to only

---

209. Abdul Ala Maududi, *The Meaning of the Quran*, 1972, pp. 159-60. See also Maulana Sager Ahmad Rahmani, *Talaq Ki Istamal ka Tariqa*, 1981, pp. 27-9 (Urdu).

210. *The Hindu*, Madras 28-04-1994.

211. *Ibid.*, Madras 29-04-1994.

if marriage has reached a point of 'irretrievable breakdown'. Divorce is not an escape route in Islam. It is a route provided but its use is made 'seldom'.

This being the case, it is worthwhile to look around the position in various Muslim countries as to how the concept of divorce is being viewed as most of the Muslim countries have modified their family law, whereas in India the concept of immutability of Muslim Law is being put forth as any change in Muslim law is an intervention in the religion which is forbidden under the Indian Constitution.

Egypt has been the focus of attention of the outside world. Until 1920 the Muslim Personal Law followed exclusively the dominant views of the Hanafi Fiqh. It was the Law No. 25 of 1920 which for the first time introduced some changes in the existing legal provisions like Alimony to be treated as *aldain-al-qawi* (strong debt). So from time to time change in family law like Law No. 56 of 1923, Law No. 26 of 1929, Law No. 78 of 1931. However, by the end of 1953, desirable changes were made in 'the law of family rights'.

Even in Syria,[213] there was Ottoman Rule till 1918 and Ottoman Family Law was applied to Syria and remained in force till 1953 long after the termination of Ottoman Rule. The Ottoman Rule introduced the principle of *Talfiq* in the sphere of Muslim Personal Law which meant that Hanifi doctrines alone were not adequate to meet the needs of time and that the Legislature was free to adopt the views of the other schools of law after giving due consideration to the existing social and economic practices. In 1953, Syria by Law No. 59 introduced some modifications in Family Law such as *vilāyat*, *vasīyat* and inheritance. Article 17 laid down that the judge may not accord permission to the husband of a wife to contract another marriage in case it is proved that he is unable to support two wives. So it put restrictions on polygamy in round about manner.

Jordan also followed the Ottoman Family Law. Until 1951 when Jordanian Law No. 92 was promulgated which contained many of the provisions of the Ottoman Family Law. The Jordanian Law

---

212. See Mr. Fazur Rahman, *Contemporary Trends in Muslim Personal Law*, A paper read in Seminar held in 1968 at Aligarh under Islamic Research Centre.

213. *Ibid.*

introduces an innovation while it lays down that a Judge would not permit a marriage being contracted in case the difference between the parties exceeds twenty years, unless he has the express consent of the party younger in age and that no duress or compulsion has been exercised. Jordanian Law permits a wife to seek divorce in the cases where the husband declines to support her or when the husband is afflicted with defects. In such cases a Judge will appoint two arbiters and then may issue a decree of separation on the ground of *Khula*.

Iraq[214] Law of personal status was promulgated in 1959 which did not contain even an iota of Islamic teachings. It outrightly prohibited polygamous marriages. However, in 1963 the traditional Islamic Law was restored. But in Iraq views of five schools of *Fiqh* are applied.

The most revolutionary move was made by Tunisia.[215] Polygamy has been completely prohibited in Tunisia under section 18 of Tunisian Law of Personal Status. The husband who takes more than one wife is liable to imprisonment. Regarding marriage it has adopted Hanbali doctrine. Divorce is permitted strictly in accordance with *Korān*, the Sunna, the practice of the companions or the option of the jurists. Divorce cannot be effective if not supported by *Korān* or Sunna tradition.

Algeria followed suit by issuing an Ordinance in 1959 making all divorces subject to Judicial Adjudication.[216]

Pakistan is our next door neighbour and majority of Muslims migrated from the present Indian side. Muslim Family Law Ordinance of 1961 stipulates that Arbitration Council will give its consent only when it is satisfied that the proposed marriage is necessary and just. Similarly, repudiation of marriage will not be effective without the permission of the Court.

In the true spirit of Islam and *Holy Korān* a number of Muslim countries have developed a tilting tendency towards the stability and sanctity of marriage. Even an enforcement of Shariah (Religious

214. *Contemporary Trends in Muslin Personal Law.*

215. *Ibid.*

216. Rafiq Zakaria, *Status of Women in Islam*, Muslim India No. 8 (August 1983).

Law) Ordinance promulgated by Late President Zia on June 15, 1988 and even the revised Ordinance did not change or affect the Family Law Ordinance of 1961. By this Ordinance the minimum age of the girl for marriage was raised to 16 years, imposed administrative control on bigamy and unilateral divorce.[217]

It is seen that the concept of triple *talāka*, a creation of the society, is only holding ground in India.

If it is on the basis of religion it is a crime. It is against the tenets of *Korān* and Sunna. Even Muslim opinion is veering round to the point that *talāka* is an act of cruelty and its use should be restricted to the situations which may be extraordinary in nature and irreconcilable in spite of best efforts.

In *A. Yusuf Rowtham* v. *Sowramma*[218] it is said that Prophet viewed marriage as a permanent union and divorce as a last resort. Since infallibility is not an attribute of the judiciary, the view has been ventured by Muslim jurists that the Indo-Anglican judicial exposition of the Islamic Law of Divorce has not exactly been just to the holy Prophet or the holy book. Marginal distortions are inevitable when the Judicial Committee in Downing street has to interpret Manu and Mohammed of India and Arabia. The soul of a culture and law is largely the formalised and enforceable expression of a community's cultural norms, cannot be fully understood by alien minds. The view that the Muslim husband enjoys an arbitrary, unilateral power to inflict instant divorce does not accord with Islamic injunctions.

Even Khalid J. in *Hannefa* v. *Pothummal*[219] has said that the husband, how he does it, or in what manner he does it, is a piece of monstrosity and it has pricked the judicial conscience.

So even the concept of divorce in Muslim Law, though permitted, is still not respected but despised and its permissiveness is allowed with heavy heart to meet really critical situations betraying solution.

---

217. See Tahir Mahmood, *Pakistan — Family Law and the Protection of Women — Journal of Family Law*, 1989-90, p. 578.

218. AIR 1971 Ker 261.

219. 1972 KLT 512.